In the second half of this volume, the school trip arc begins!
Everyone's feelings are deepening, and things are shifting,
on the inside and the outside.
Where will it go? Find out in volume 17!

Naoshi Komi

Second time!

NAOSHI KOMI was born in Kochi Prefecture, Japan, on March 28, 1986. His first serialized work in *Weekly Shonen Jump* was the series *Double Arts*. His current series, *Nisekoi*, is serialized in *Weekly Shonen Jump*.

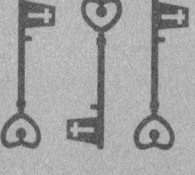

NISEKOI:
False Love
VOLUME 17
SHONEN JUMP Manga Edition

Story and Art by
NAOSHI KOMI

Translation ⟋ Camellia Nieh
Touch-Up Art & Lettering ⟋ Stephen Dutro
Design ⟋ Fawn Lau
Shonen Jump Series Editor ⟋ John Bae
Graphic Novel Editor ⟋ Amy Yu

NISEKOI © 2011 by Naoshi Komi
All rights reserved.
First published in Japan in 2011
by SHUEISHA Inc., Tokyo.
English translation rights arranged
by SHUEISHA Inc.

Printed in the U.S.A.

Published by VIZ Media, LLC
P.O. Box 77010
San Francisco, CA 94107

10 9 8 7 6 5 4 3 2 1
First printing, September 2016

www.shonenjump.com   www.viz.com

NISEKOI

False Love

vol. 17: Mistress

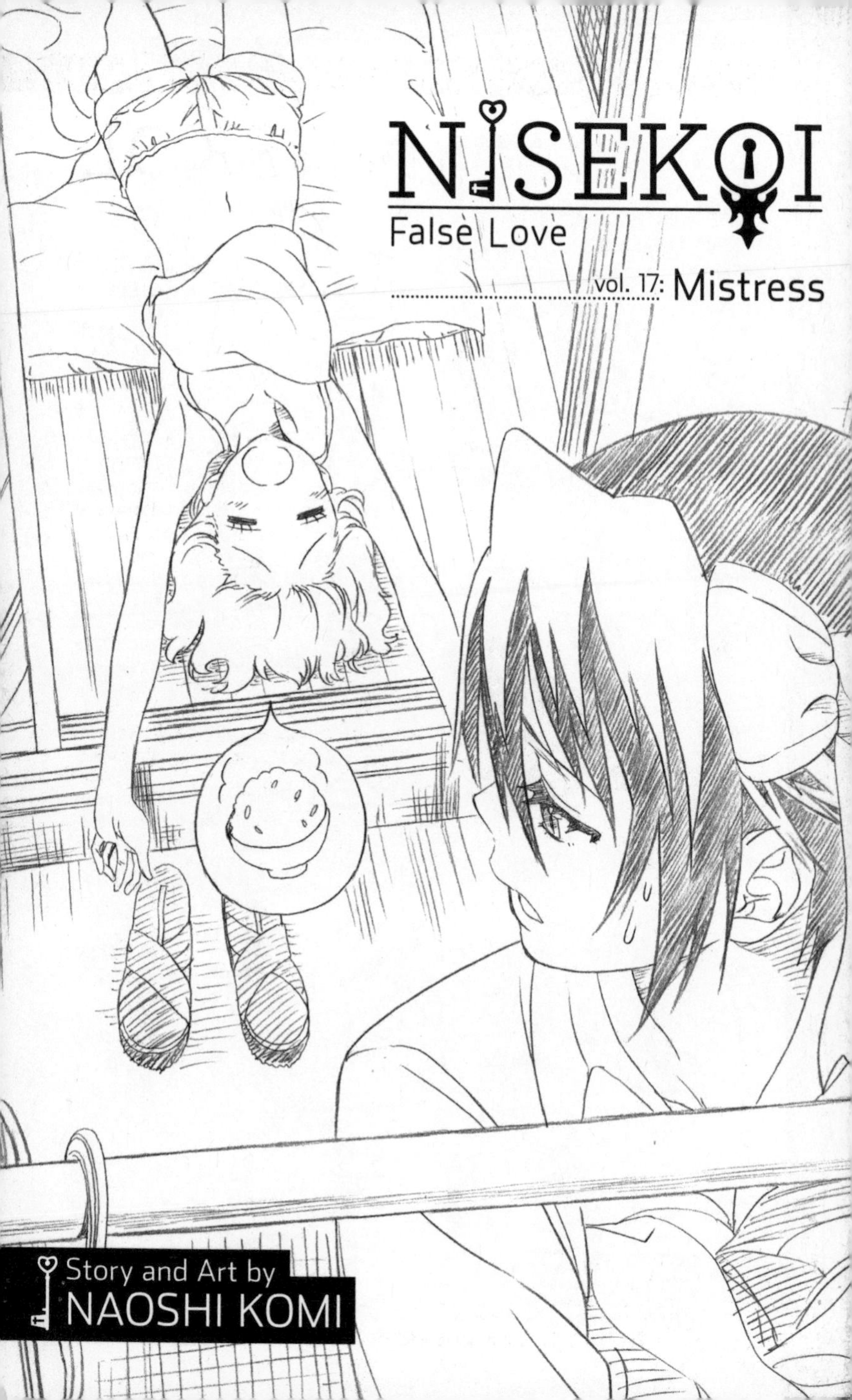

Story and Art by
NAOSHI KOMI

CHITOGE KIRISAKI

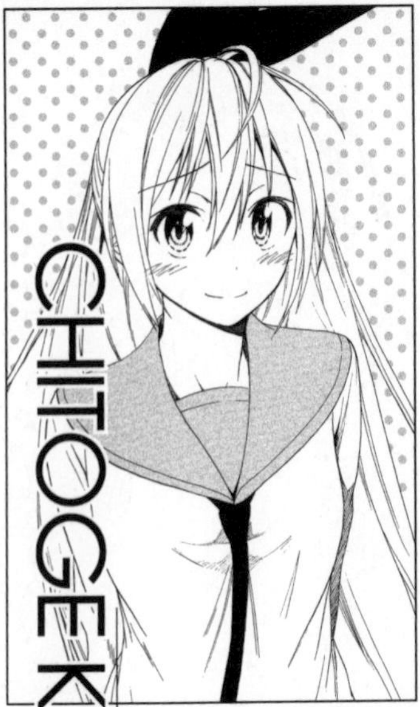

A half-Japanese bombshell with stellar athletic abilities. Short-tempered and violent. Comes from a family of gangsters.

RAKU ICHIJO

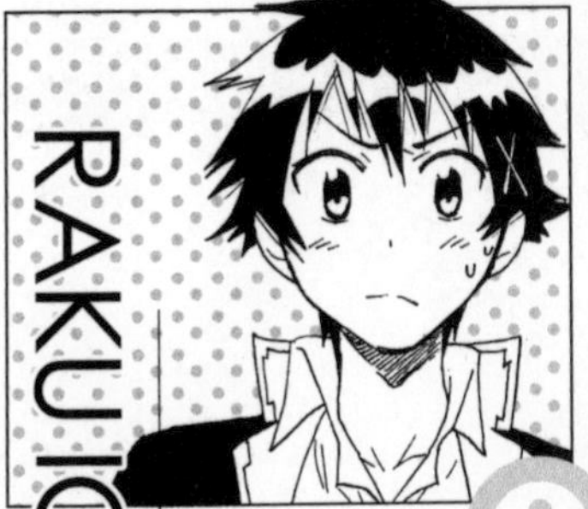

A normal teen whose family happens to be yakuza. Cherishes a pendant given to him by a girl he met ten years ago.

KOSAKI ONODERA

A girl Raku has a crush on. Beautiful and sweet, Kosaki has no shortage of admirers. She's a terrible cook but makes food that *looks* amazing.

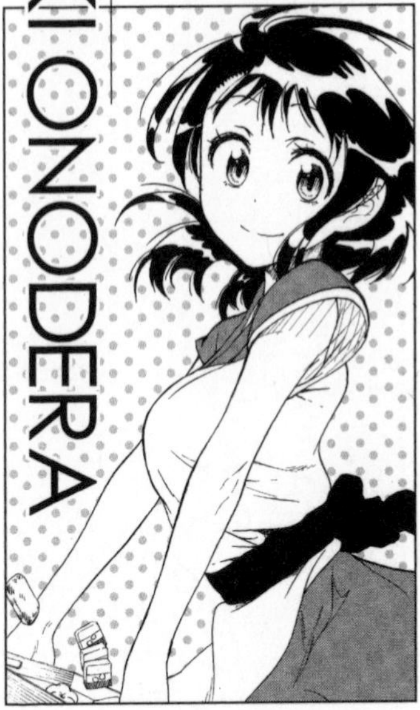

SHU MAIKO

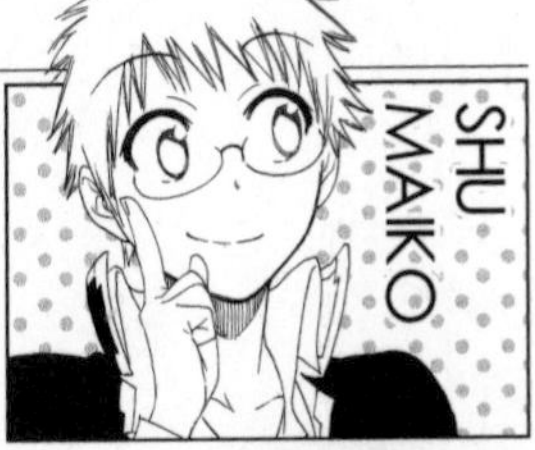

Raku's best friend is outgoing and girl-crazy.

RURI MIYAMOTO

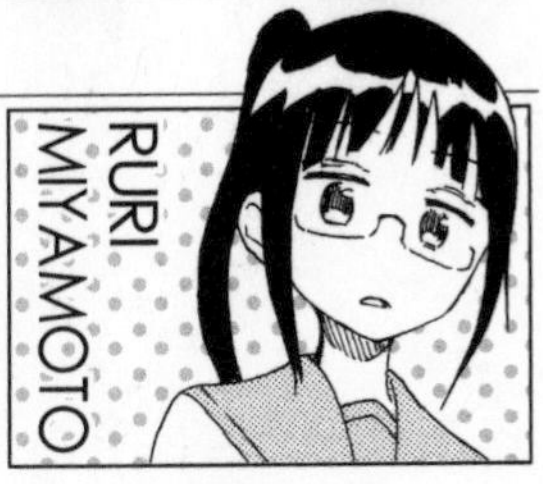

Kosaki's best gal pal. Comes off as aloof, but is actually a devoted and highly intuitive friend.

MARIKA TACHIBANA

Daughter of the chief of police, Marika is Raku's fiancée, according to an agreement made by their fathers—an agreement Marika takes very seriously! Also has a key and remembers making a promise with Raku ten years ago.

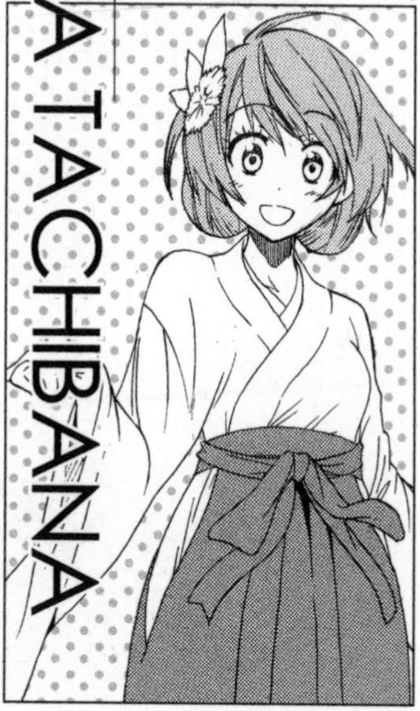

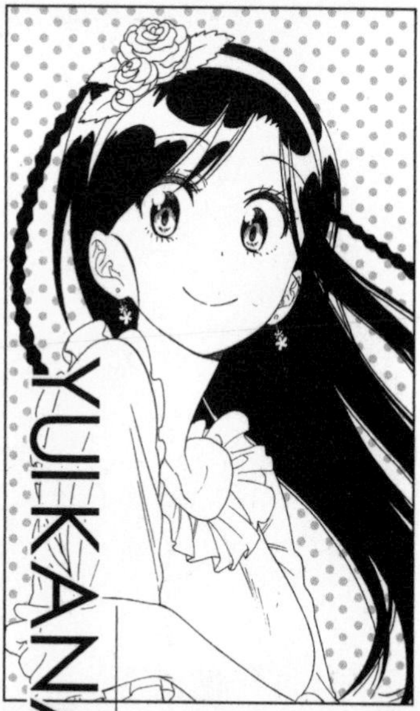

YUI KANAKURA

A childhood friend of Raku's, Yui is the head of a Chinese mafia gang and the homeroom teacher of Raku's class at his school. She is currently staying at Raku's house and also has a special key linked to some kind of promise...

CHARACTERS & STORY

Ten years ago, Raku Ichijo made a promise with a girl he loved that they would get married when they met again...and he still treasures the pendant she gave him to seal their pledge.

Thanks to his family's circumstances, Raku has to pretend he's dating Chitoge Kirisaki, the daughter of a rival gangster. Despite their constant spats, Raku and Chitoge manage to fool everyone. Chitoge has a token from her first love ten years ago—an old key. Meanwhile, Raku's crush, Kosaki, also has a key, as does Marika, the girl Raku's father has arranged for him to marry. Now, Raku's childhood friend Yui has been hired as their homeroom teacher. It turns out that she, too, has a key connected to a special promise. Raku's love life gets crazier and crazier!

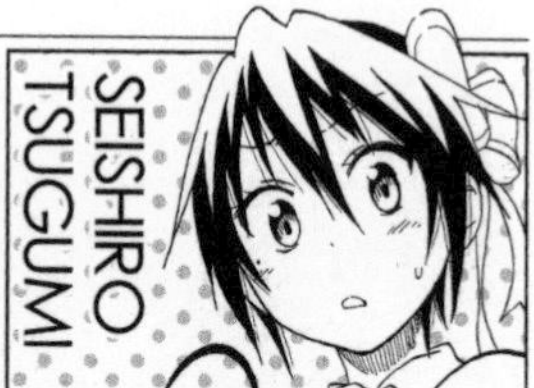

SEISHIRO TSUGUMI

Trained as an assassin in order to protect Chitoge, Tsugumi is often mistaken for a boy.

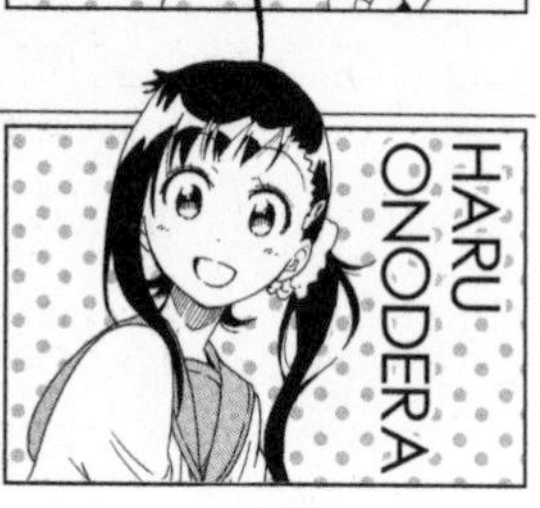

HARU ONODERA

Kosaki's adoring younger sister. Has a low opinion of Raku.

NISEKOI
False Love

vol. 17: Mistress

TABLE OF CONTENTS

chapter 144: Sleepover 7

chapter 145: Sports 27

chapter 146: Perfect 47

chapter 147: Big Sis Yui 67

chapter 148: Successor 87

chapter 149: Mistress 109

chapter 150: Groups 129

chapter 151: Trouble 151

chapter 152: Sound Asleep 171

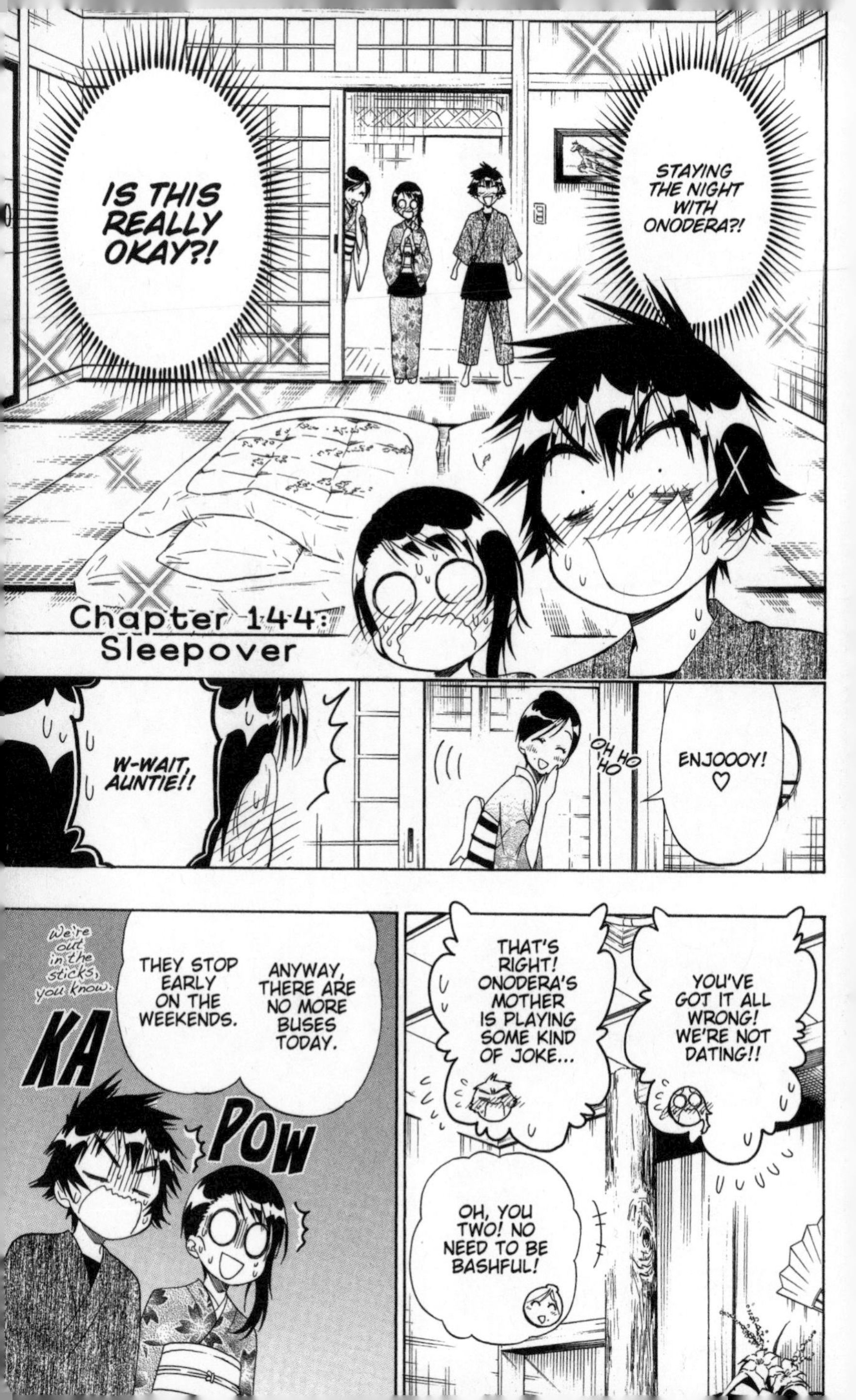
STAYING THE NIGHT WITH ONODERA?!
IS THIS REALLY OKAY?!
Chapter 144: Sleepover
ENJOOOY! ♡
OH HO HO
W-WAIT, AUNTIE!!
YOU'VE GOT IT ALL WRONG! WE'RE NOT DATING!!
THAT'S RIGHT! ONODERA'S MOTHER IS PLAYING SOME KIND OF JOKE...
OH, YOU TWO! NO NEED TO BE BASHFUL!
ANYWAY, THERE ARE NO MORE BUSES TODAY.
THEY STOP EARLY ON THE WEEKENDS.
We're out in the sticks, you know.
KA
POW

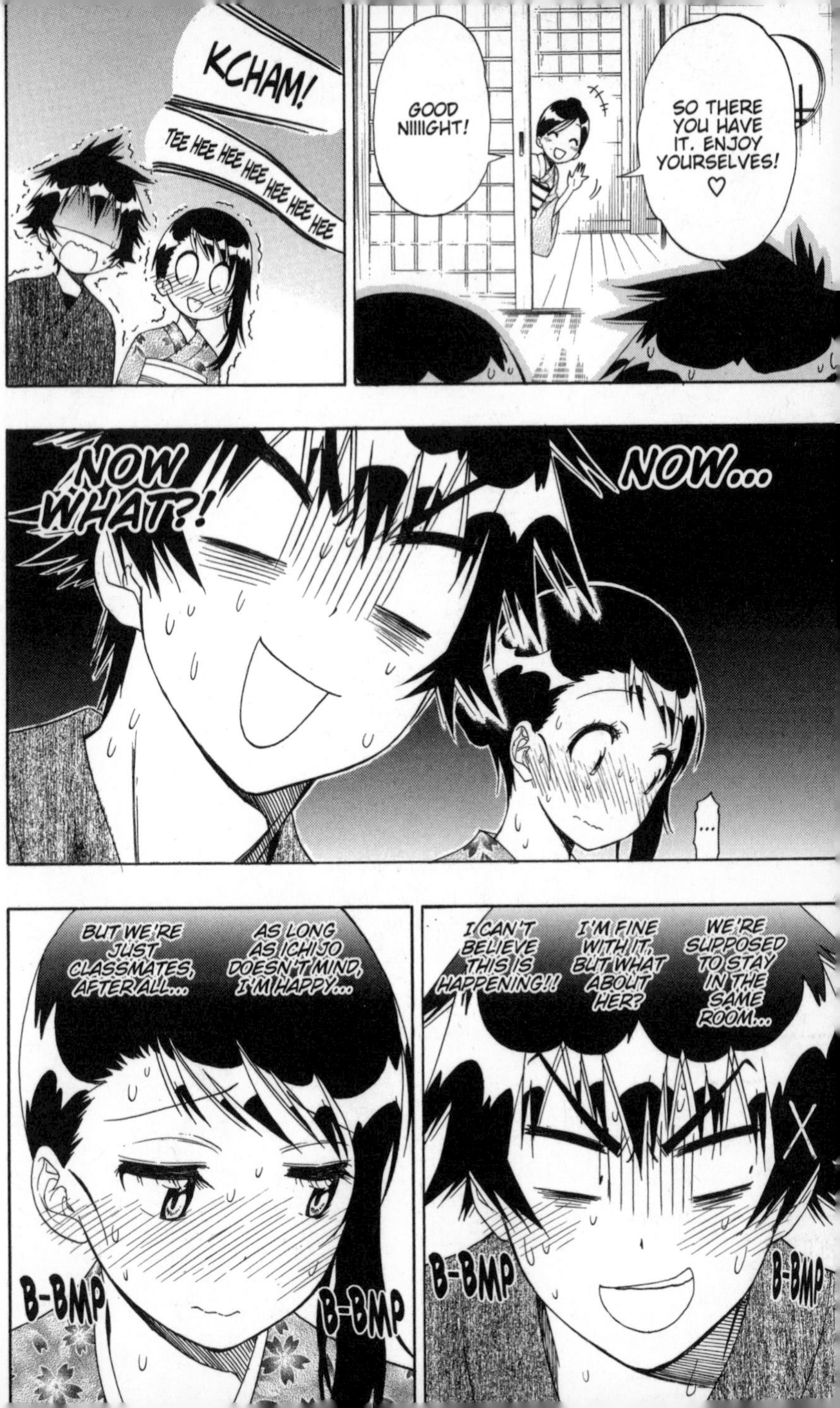
SO THERE YOU HAVE IT. ENJOY YOURSELVES! ♡
GOOD NIIIIGHT!
KCHAM!
TEE HEE HEE HEE HEE HEE HEE
NOW...
NOW WHAT?!
...
I CAN'T BELIEVE THIS IS HAPPENING!!
I'M FINE WITH IT, BUT WHAT ABOUT HER?
WE'RE SUPPOSED TO STAY IN THE SAME ROOM...
B-BMP
B-BMP
AS LONG AS ICHIJO DOESN'T MIND, I'M HAPPY...
BUT WE'RE JUST CLASSMATES, AFTER ALL...
B-BMP
B-BMP

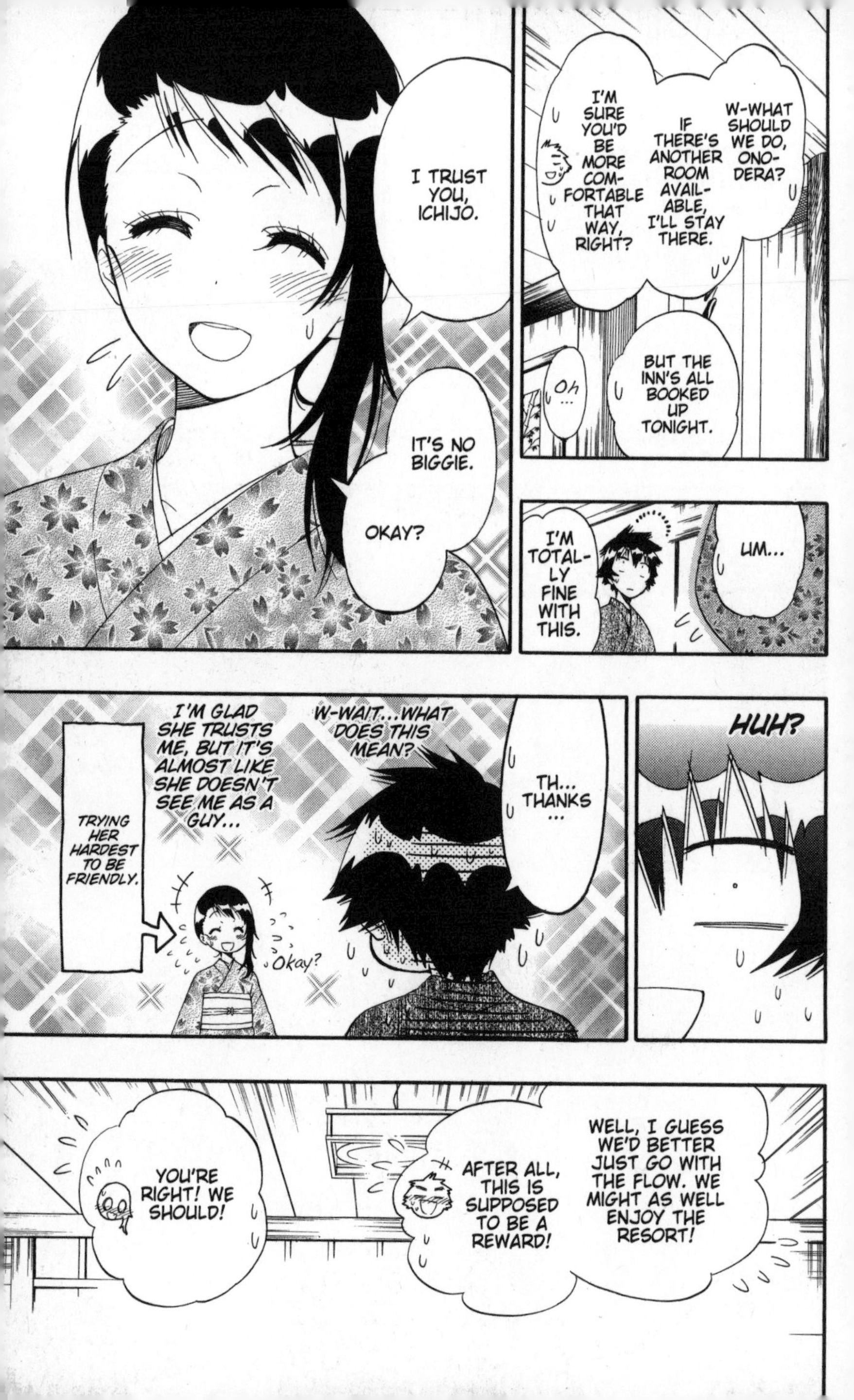
W-WHAT SHOULD WE DO, ONO-DERA?
IF THERE'S ANOTHER ROOM AVAIL-ABLE, I'LL STAY THERE.
I'M SURE YOU'D BE MORE COM-FORTABLE THAT WAY, RIGHT?
BUT THE INN'S ALL BOOKED UP TONIGHT.
Oh...
UM...
I'M TOTAL-LY FINE WITH THIS.
I TRUST YOU, ICHIJO.
IT'S NO BIGGIE.
OKAY?
HUH?
TH... THANKS...
W-WAIT...WHAT DOES THIS MEAN?
I'M GLAD SHE TRUSTS ME, BUT IT'S ALMOST LIKE SHE DOESN'T SEE ME AS A GUY...
TRYING HER HARDEST TO BE FRIENDLY.
Okay?
WELL, I GUESS WE'D BETTER JUST GO WITH THE FLOW. WE MIGHT AS WELL ENJOY THE RESORT!
AFTER ALL, THIS IS SUPPOSED TO BE A REWARD!
YOU'RE RIGHT! WE SHOULD!

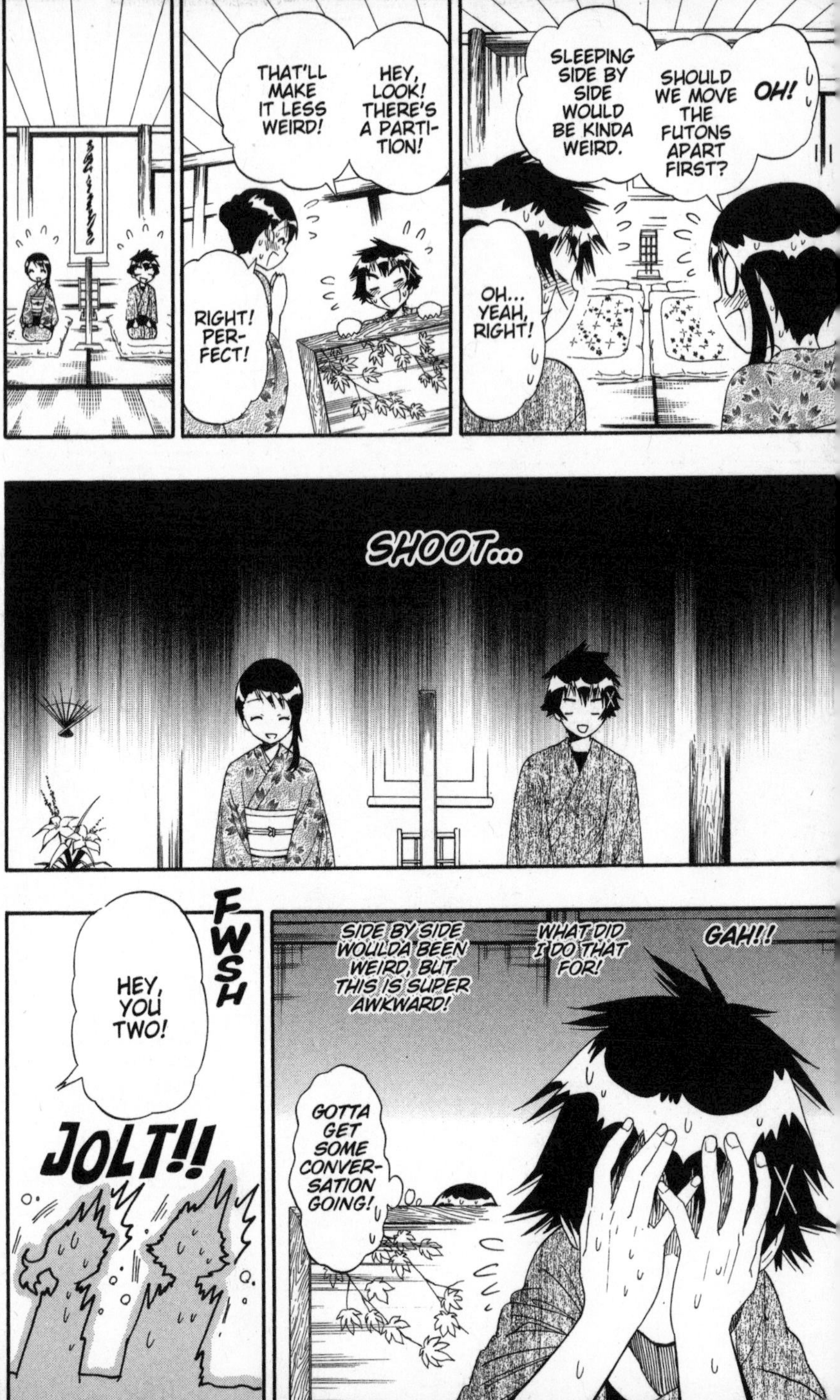
OH!
SHOULD WE MOVE THE FUTONS APART FIRST?
SLEEPING SIDE BY SIDE WOULD BE KINDA WEIRD.
OH... YEAH, RIGHT!
HEY, LOOK! THERE'S A PARTITION!
THAT'LL MAKE IT LESS WEIRD!
RIGHT! PERFECT!
SHOOT...
GAH!!
WHAT DID I DO THAT FOR!
SIDE BY SIDE WOULDA BEEN WEIRD, BUT THIS IS SUPER AWKWARD!
GOTTA GET SOME CONVERSATION GOING!
FWSH
HEY, YOU TWO!
JOLT!!

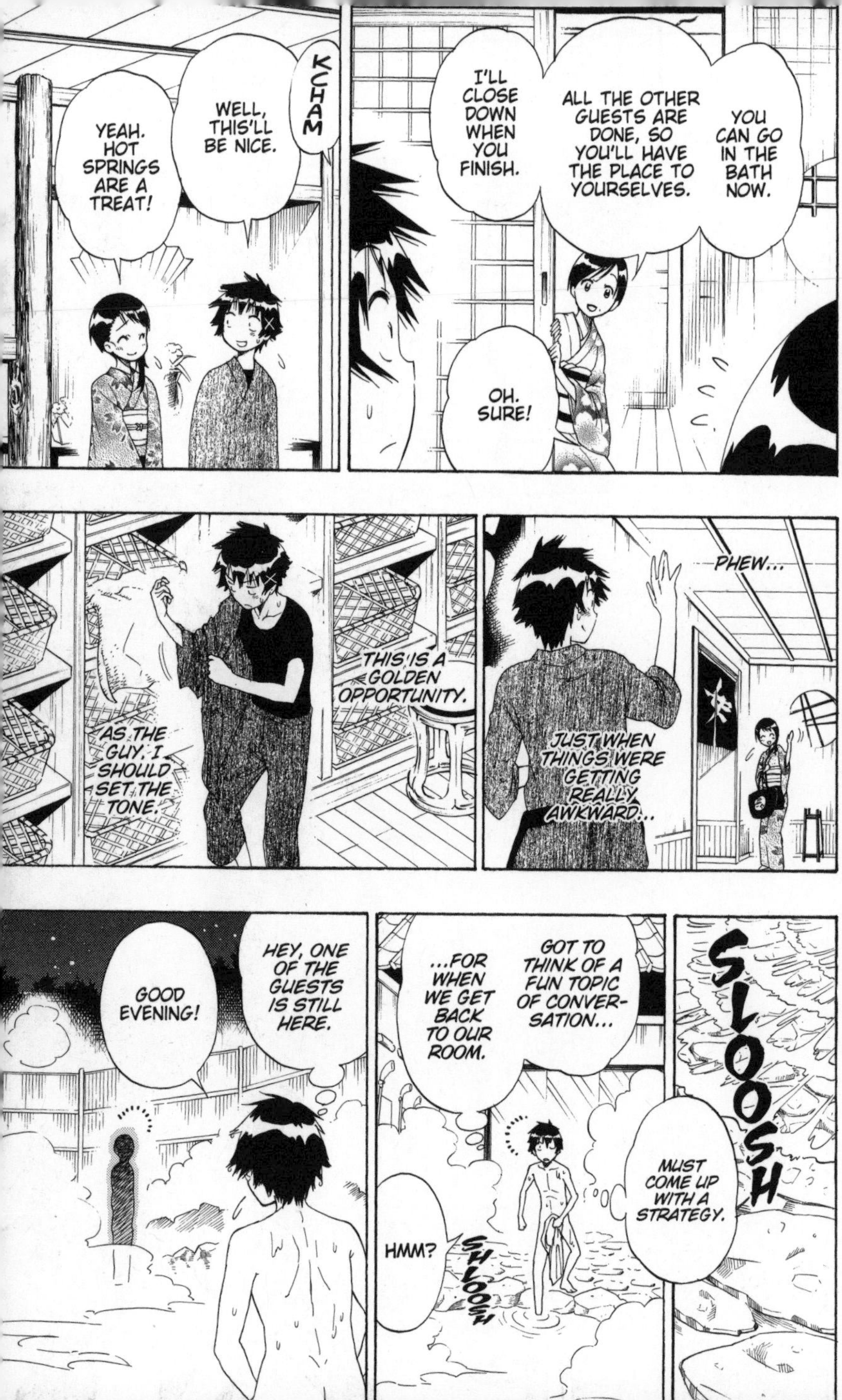
YOU CAN GO IN THE BATH NOW.
ALL THE OTHER GUESTS ARE DONE, SO YOU'LL HAVE THE PLACE TO YOURSELVES.
I'LL CLOSE DOWN WHEN YOU FINISH.
OH. SURE!
KCHAM
WELL, THIS'LL BE NICE.
YEAH. HOT SPRINGS ARE A TREAT!
PHEW...
JUST WHEN THINGS WERE GETTING REALLY AWKWARD...
THIS IS A GOLDEN OPPORTUNITY.
AS THE GUY, I SHOULD SET THE TONE.
SLOOSH
MUST COME UP WITH A STRATEGY.
GOT TO THINK OF A FUN TOPIC OF CONVER-SATION...
...FOR WHEN WE GET BACK TO OUR ROOM.
SHLOOSH
HMM?
HEY, ONE OF THE GUESTS IS STILL HERE.
GOOD EVENING!

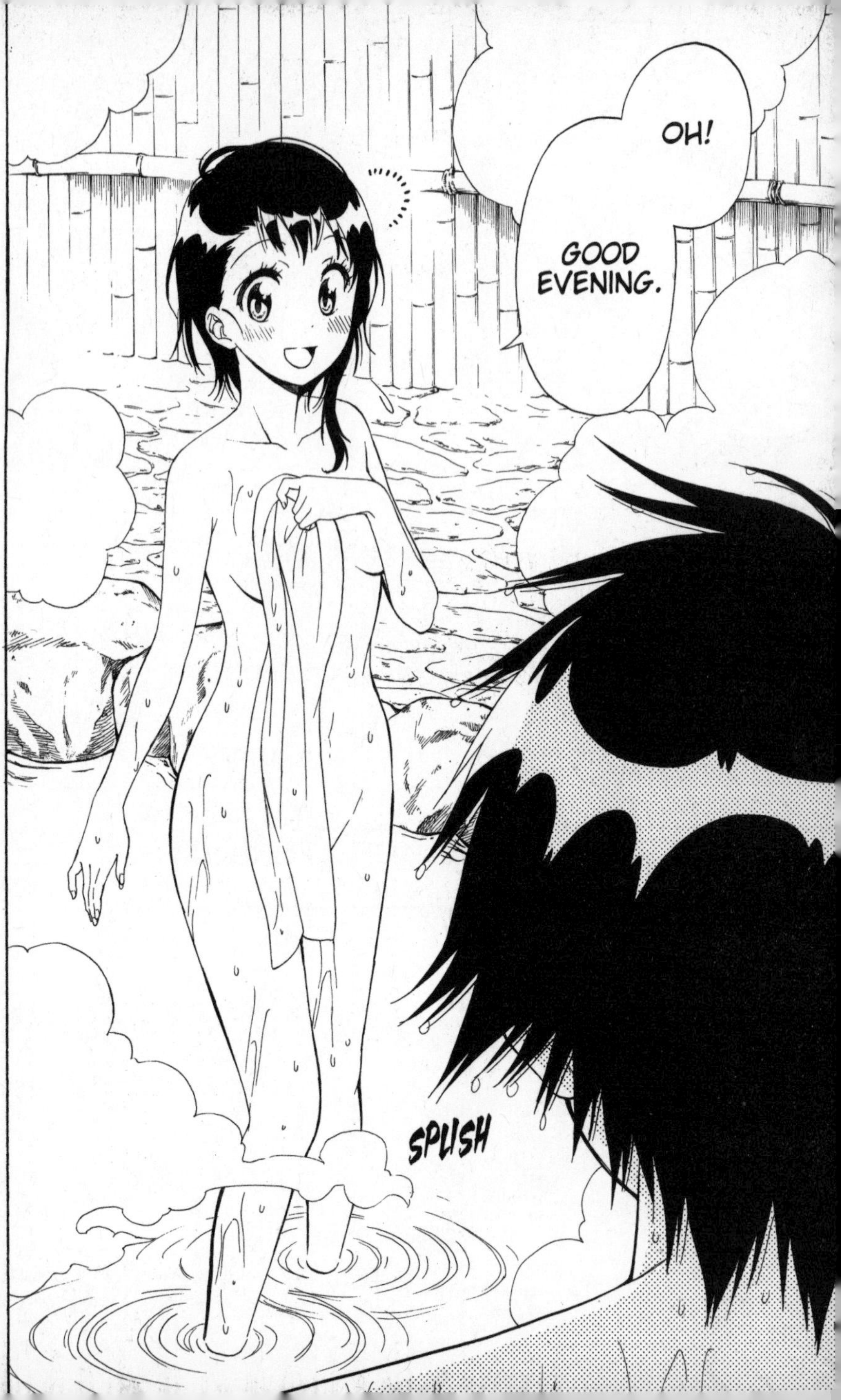
OH!
GOOD EVENING.
SPLISH

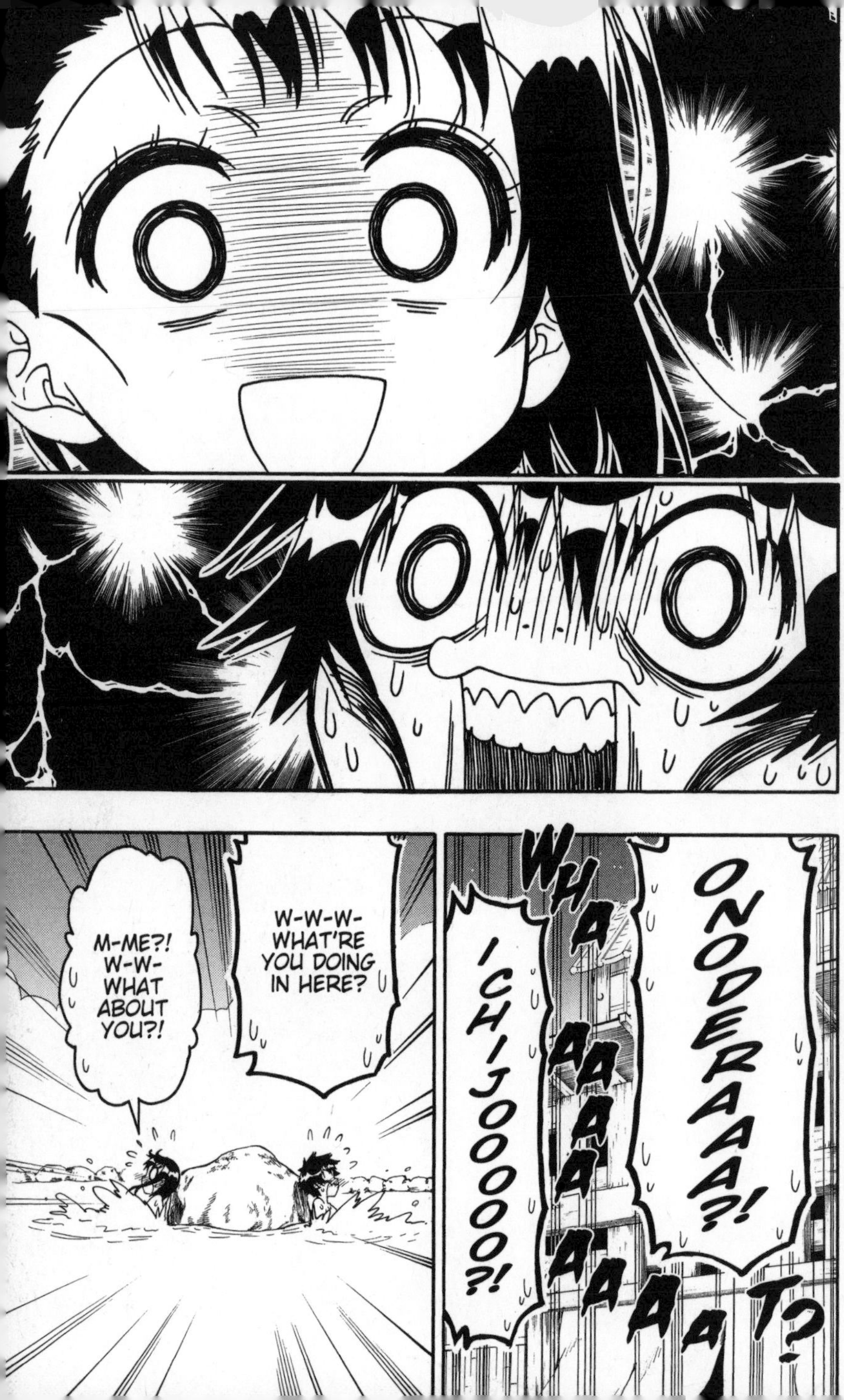
ONODERAAAA?!
WHAAAAAAAAAAT?
ICHIJOOOOOO?!
W-W-W-WHAT'RE YOU DOING IN HERE?
M-ME?! W-W-WHAT ABOUT YOU?!

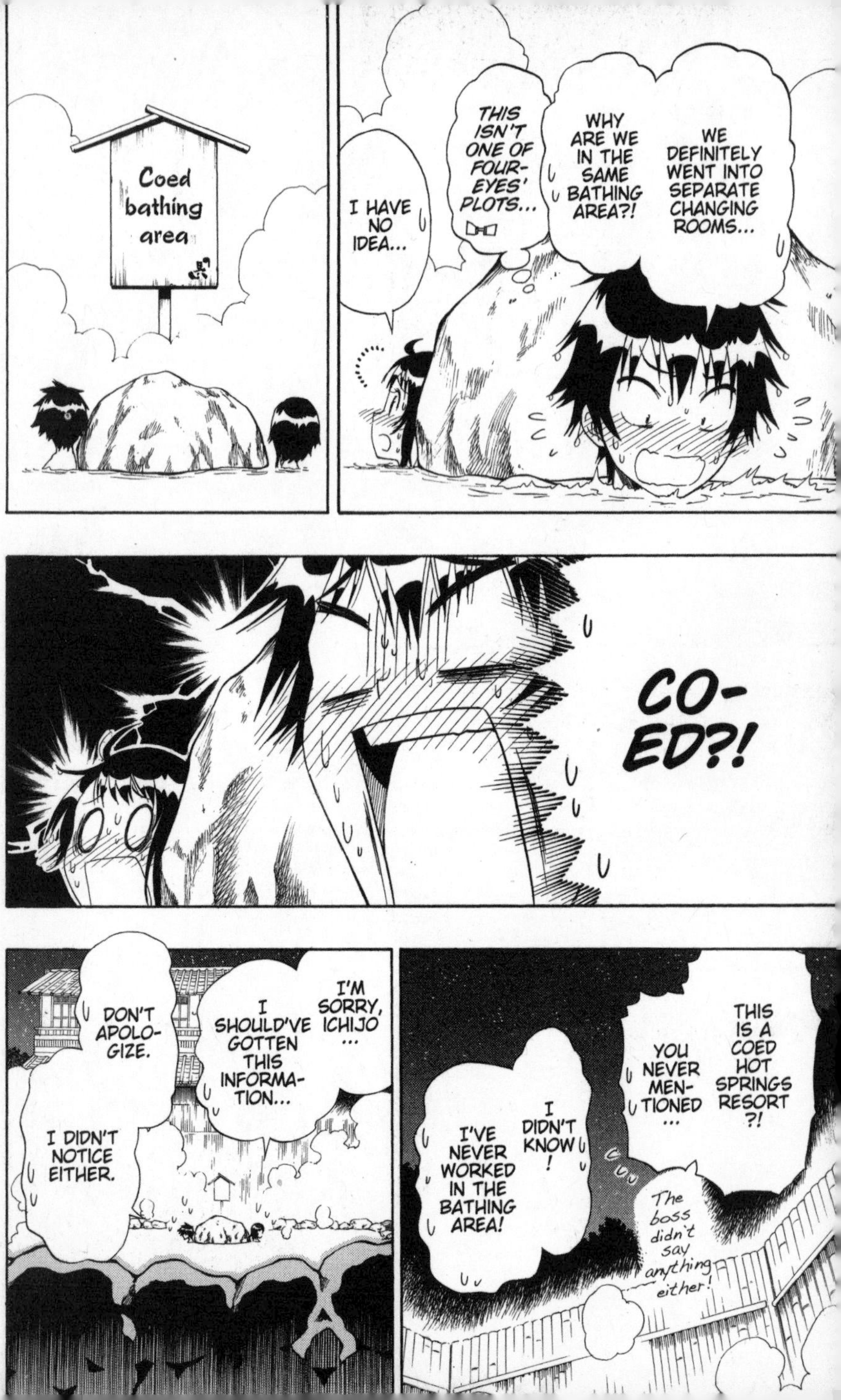
WE DEFINITELY WENT INTO SEPARATE CHANGING ROOMS...
WHY ARE WE IN THE SAME BATHING AREA?!
THIS ISN'T ONE OF FOUR-EYES' PLOTS...
I HAVE NO IDEA...
Coed bathing area
CO-ED?!
THIS IS A COED HOT SPRINGS RESORT ?!
YOU NEVER MEN-TIONED ...
I DIDN'T KNOW !
I'VE NEVER WORKED IN THE BATHING AREA!
The boss didn't say anything either!
I'M SORRY, ICHIJO ...
I SHOULD'VE GOTTEN THIS INFORMA-TION...
DON'T APOLO-GIZE.
I DIDN'T NOTICE EITHER.

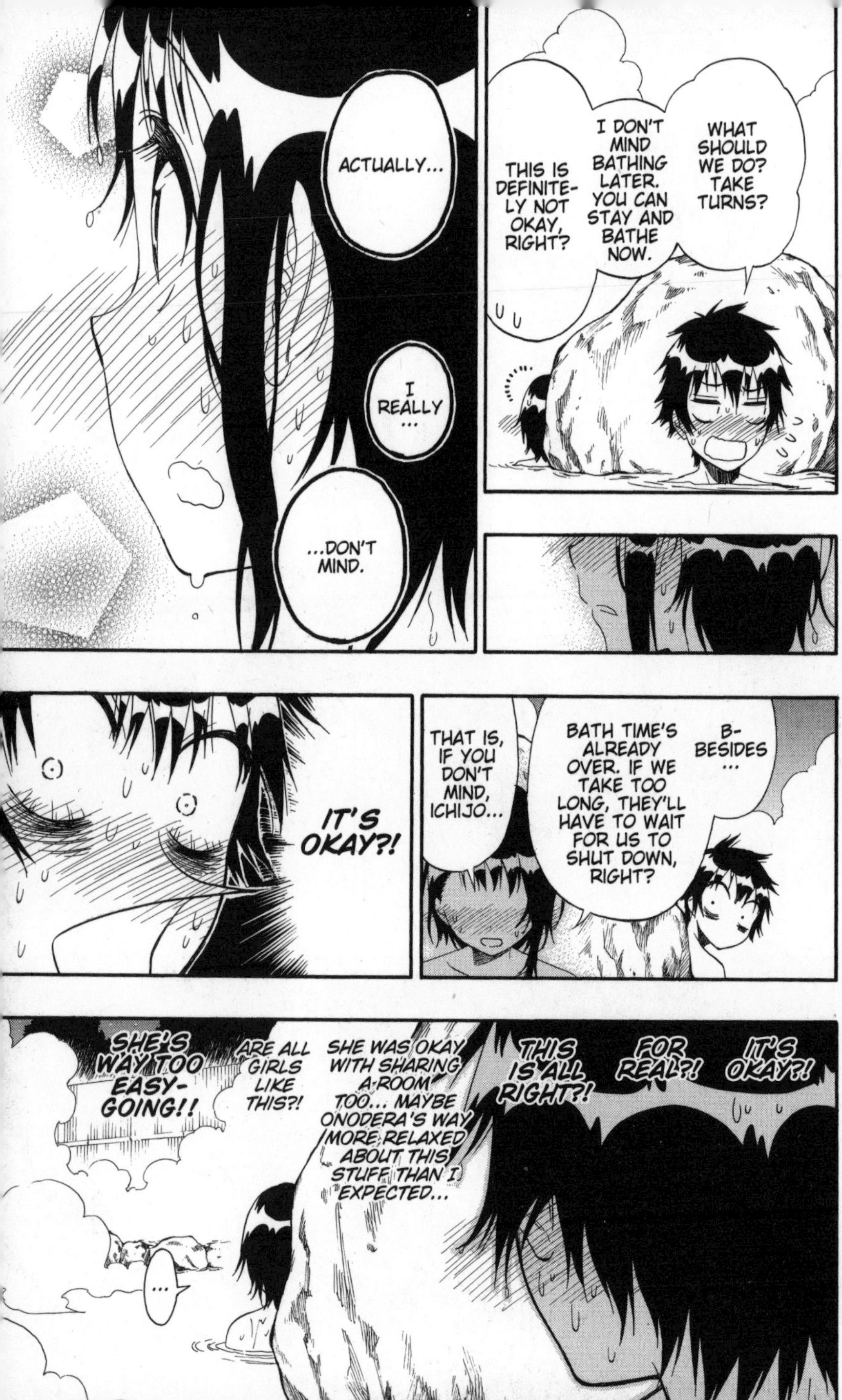
WHAT SHOULD WE DO? TAKE TURNS?
I DON'T MIND BATHING LATER. YOU CAN STAY AND BATHE NOW.
THIS IS DEFINITE-LY NOT OKAY, RIGHT?
ACTUALLY...
I REALLY...
...DON'T MIND.
B-BESIDES...
BATH TIME'S ALREADY OVER. IF WE TAKE TOO LONG, THEY'LL HAVE TO WAIT FOR US TO SHUT DOWN, RIGHT?
THAT IS, IF YOU DON'T MIND, ICHIJO...
IT'S OKAY?!
IT'S OKAY?!
FOR REAL?!
THIS IS ALL RIGHT?!
SHE WAS OKAY WITH SHARING A-ROOM TOO... MAYBE ONODERA'S WAY MORE RELAXED ABOUT THIS STUFF THAN I EXPECTED...
ARE ALL GIRLS LIKE THIS?!
SHE'S WAY TOO EASY-GOING!!
...

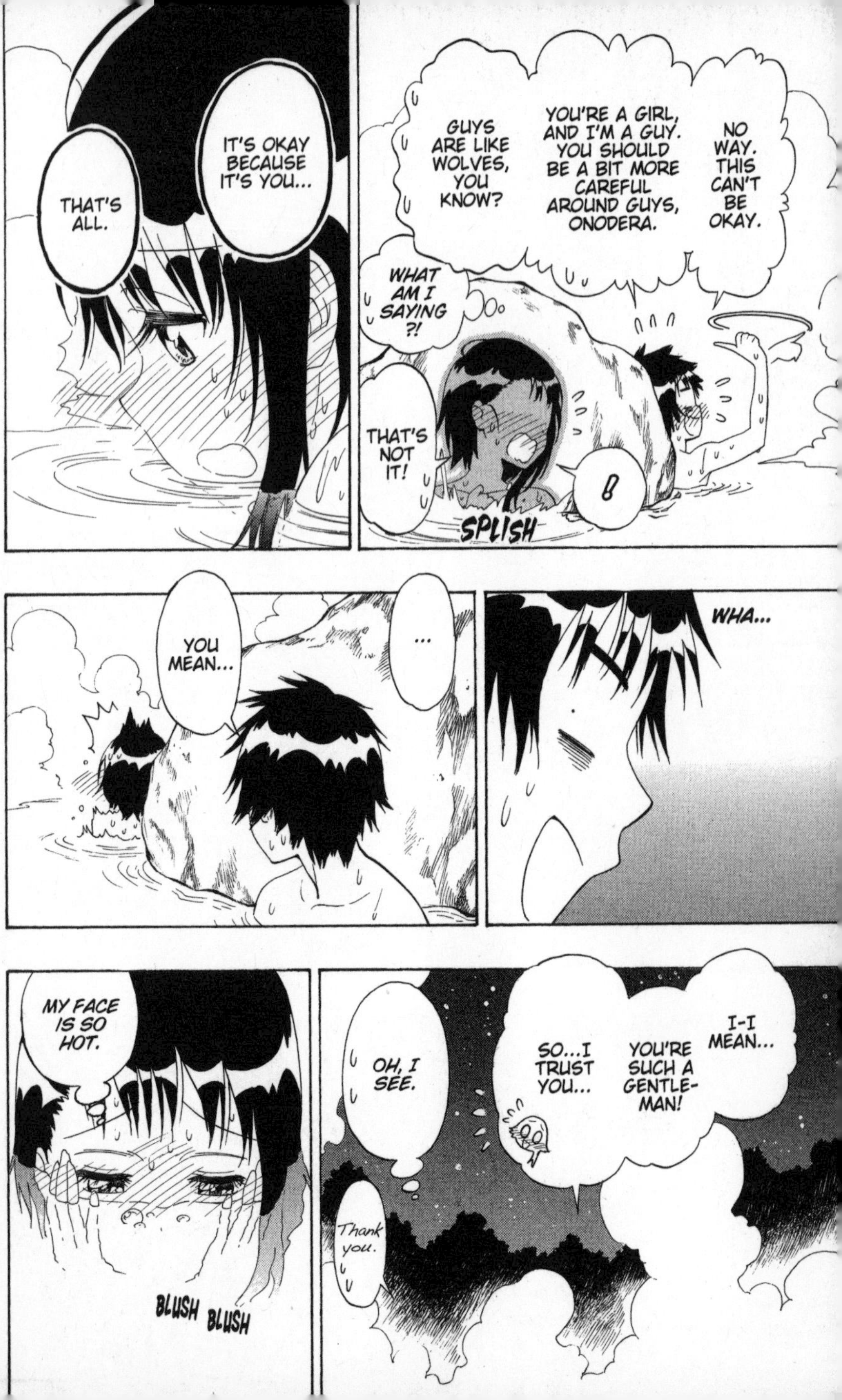
NO WAY. THIS CAN'T BE OKAY.
YOU'RE A GIRL, AND I'M A GUY. YOU SHOULD BE A BIT MORE CAREFUL AROUND GUYS, ONODERA.
GUYS ARE LIKE WOLVES, YOU KNOW?
WHAT AM I SAYING?!
!
SPLISH
THAT'S NOT IT!
IT'S OKAY BECAUSE IT'S YOU...
THAT'S ALL.
WHA...
...
YOU MEAN...
I-I MEAN...
YOU'RE SUCH A GENTLE-MAN!
SO...I TRUST YOU...
OH, I SEE.
Thank you.
MY FACE IS SO HOT.
BLUSH BLUSH

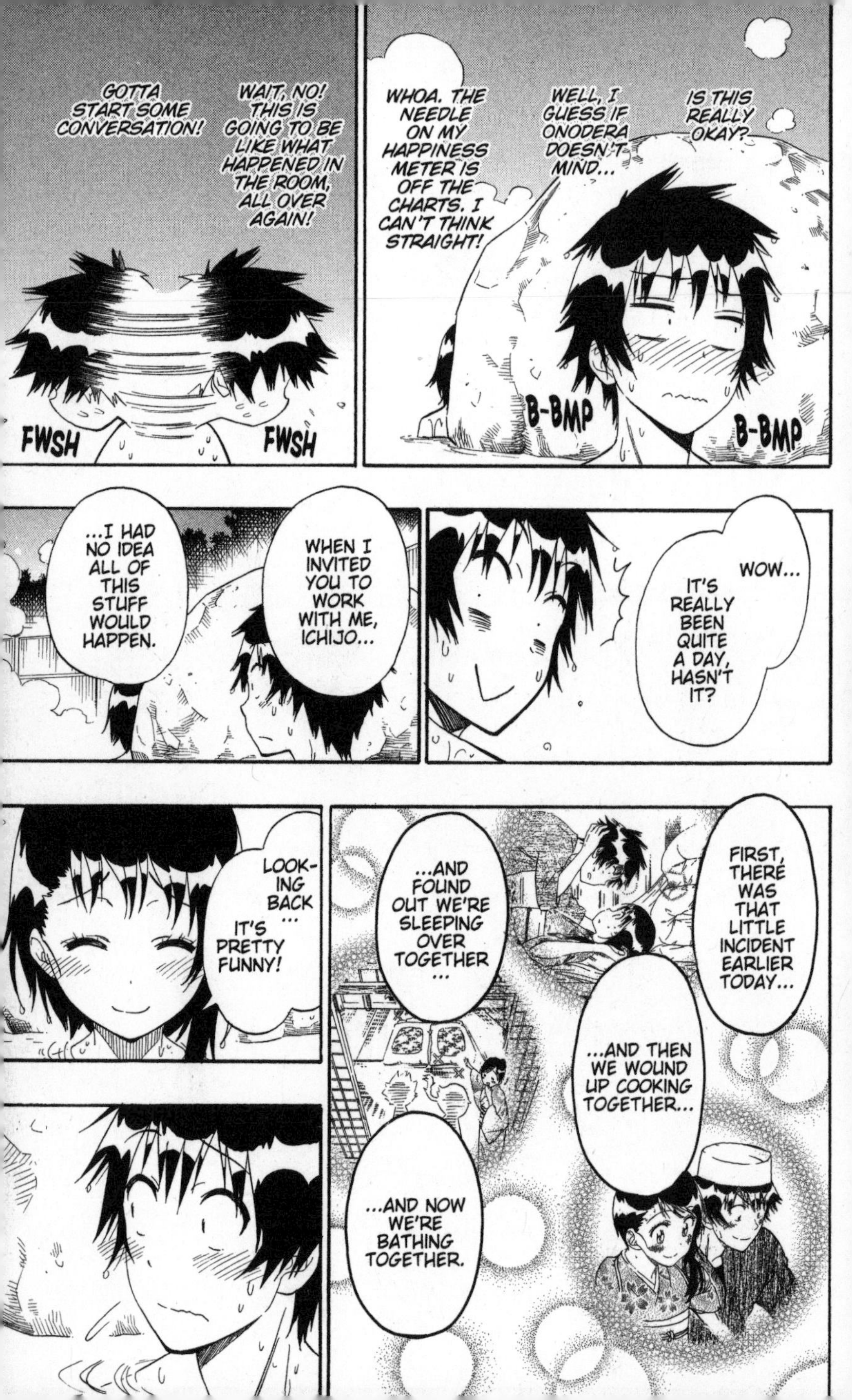
IS THIS REALLY OKAY?
WELL, I GUESS IF ONODERA DOESN'T MIND...
WHOA. THE NEEDLE ON MY HAPPINESS METER IS OFF THE CHARTS. I CAN'T THINK STRAIGHT!
B-BMP
B-BMP
WAIT, NO! THIS IS GOING TO BE LIKE WHAT HAPPENED IN THE ROOM, ALL OVER AGAIN!
GOTTA START SOME CONVERSATION!
FWSH
FWSH
WOW...
IT'S REALLY BEEN QUITE A DAY, HASN'T IT?
WHEN I INVITED YOU TO WORK WITH ME, ICHIJO...
...I HAD NO IDEA ALL OF THIS STUFF WOULD HAPPEN.
FIRST, THERE WAS THAT LITTLE INCIDENT EARLIER TODAY...
...AND THEN WE WOUND UP COOKING TOGETHER...
...AND FOUND OUT WE'RE SLEEPING OVER TOGETHER...
...AND NOW WE'RE BATHING TOGETHER.
LOOKING BACK...
IT'S PRETTY FUNNY!

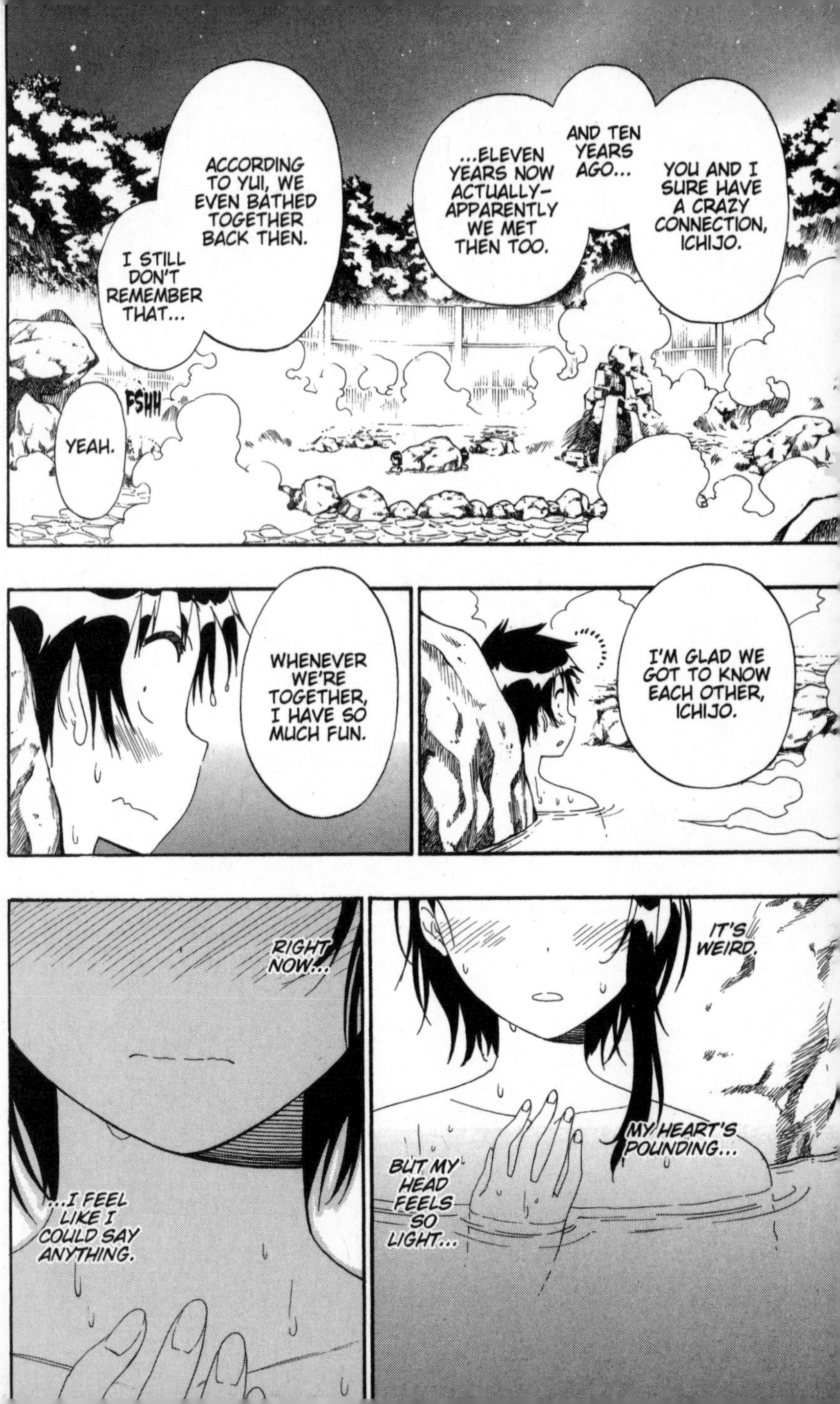
YOU AND I SURE HAVE A CRAZY CONNECTION, ICHIJO.
AND TEN YEARS AGO...
...ELEVEN YEARS NOW ACTUALLY—APPARENTLY WE MET THEN TOO.
ACCORDING TO YUI, WE EVEN BATHED TOGETHER BACK THEN.
I STILL DON'T REMEMBER THAT...
FSHH
YEAH.
I'M GLAD WE GOT TO KNOW EACH OTHER, ICHIJO.
WHENEVER WE'RE TOGETHER, I HAVE SO MUCH FUN.
IT'S WEIRD.
MY HEART'S POUNDING...
BUT MY HEAD FEELS SO LIGHT...
RIGHT NOW...
...I FEEL LIKE I COULD SAY ANYTHING.

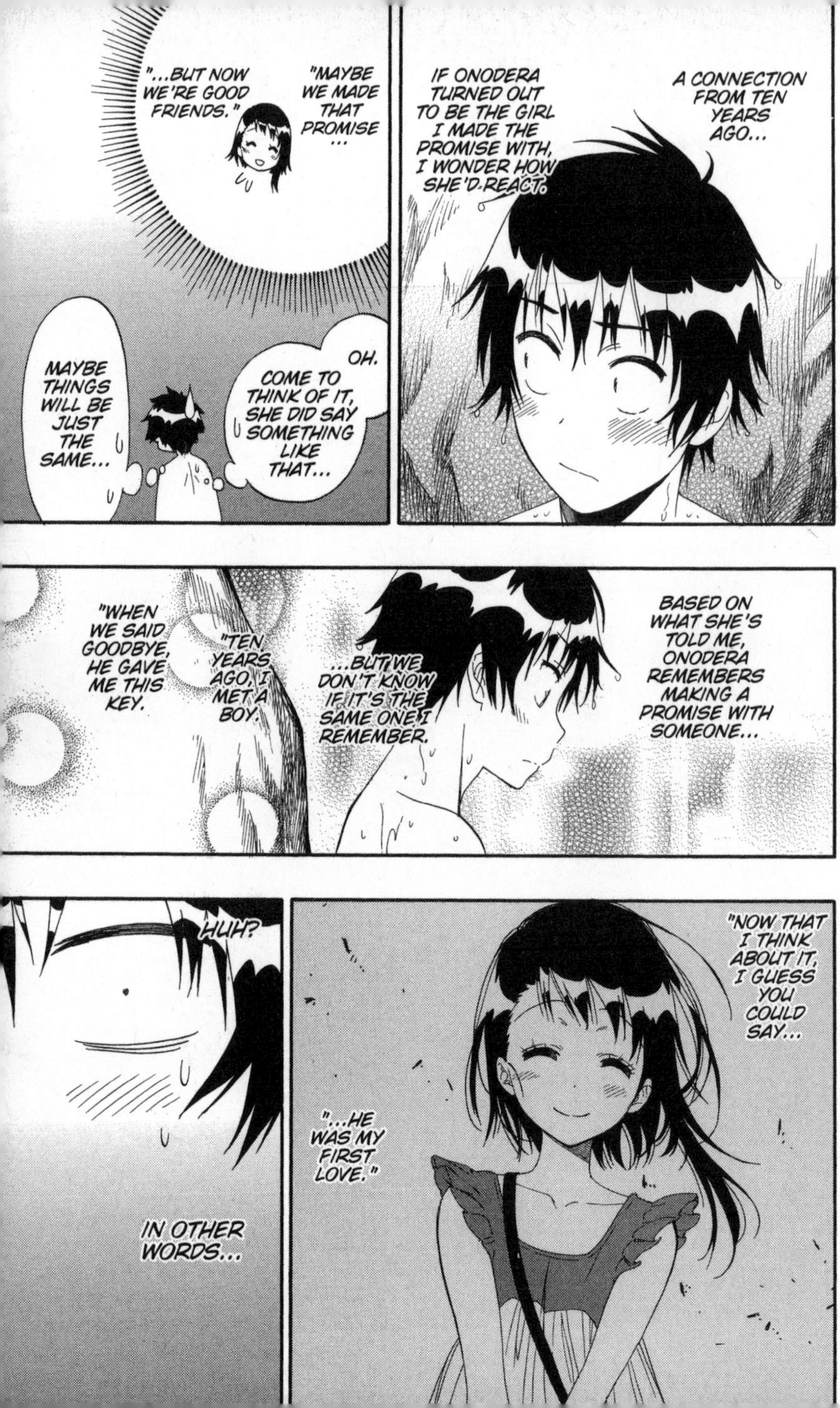
A CONNECTION FROM TEN YEARS AGO...
IF ONODERA TURNED OUT TO BE THE GIRL I MADE THE PROMISE WITH, I WONDER HOW SHE'D REACT.
"MAYBE WE MADE THAT PROMISE ...
"...BUT NOW WE'RE GOOD FRIENDS."
OH.
COME TO THINK OF IT, SHE DID SAY SOMETHING LIKE THAT...
MAYBE THINGS WILL BE JUST THE SAME...
BASED ON WHAT SHE'S TOLD ME, ONODERA REMEMBERS MAKING A PROMISE WITH SOMEONE...
...BUT WE DON'T KNOW IF IT'S THE SAME ONE I REMEMBER.
"TEN YEARS AGO, I MET A BOY.
"WHEN WE SAID GOODBYE, HE GAVE ME THIS KEY.
"NOW THAT I THINK ABOUT IT, I GUESS YOU COULD SAY...
"...HE WAS MY FIRST LOVE."
HUH?
IN OTHER WORDS...

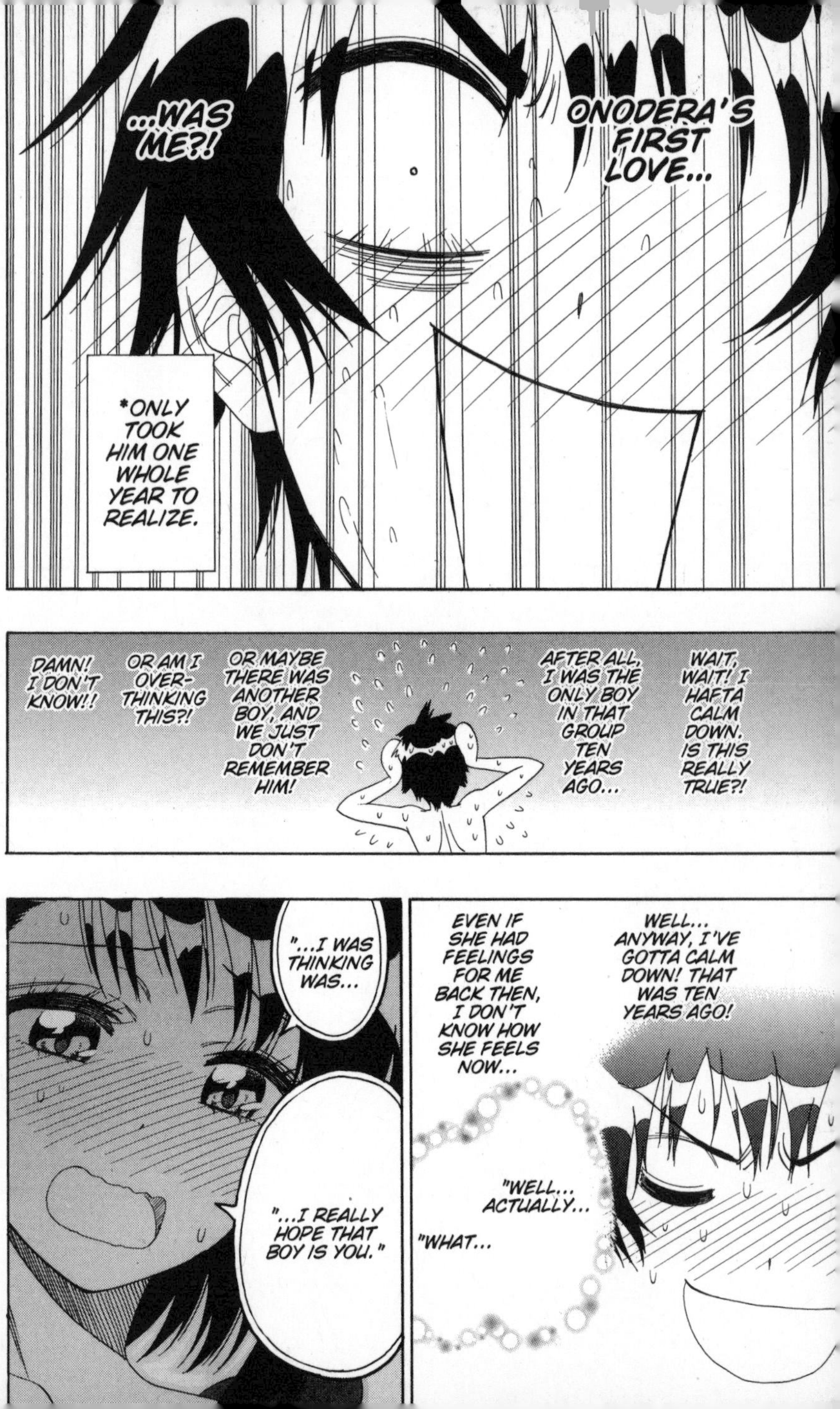
ONODERA'S FIRST LOVE...
...WAS ME?!
*ONLY TOOK HIM ONE WHOLE YEAR TO REALIZE.
WAIT, WAIT! I HAFTA CALM DOWN. IS THIS REALLY TRUE?!
AFTER ALL, I WAS THE ONLY BOY IN THAT GROUP TEN YEARS AGO...
OR MAYBE THERE WAS ANOTHER BOY, AND WE JUST DON'T REMEMBER HIM!
OR AM I OVER-THINKING THIS?!
DAMN! I DON'T KNOW!!
WELL... ANYWAY, I'VE GOTTA CALM DOWN! THAT WAS TEN YEARS AGO!
EVEN IF SHE HAD FEELINGS FOR ME BACK THEN, I DON'T KNOW HOW SHE FEELS NOW...
"WELL... ACTUALLY...
"WHAT...
"...I WAS THINKING WAS...
"...I REALLY HOPE THAT BOY IS YOU."

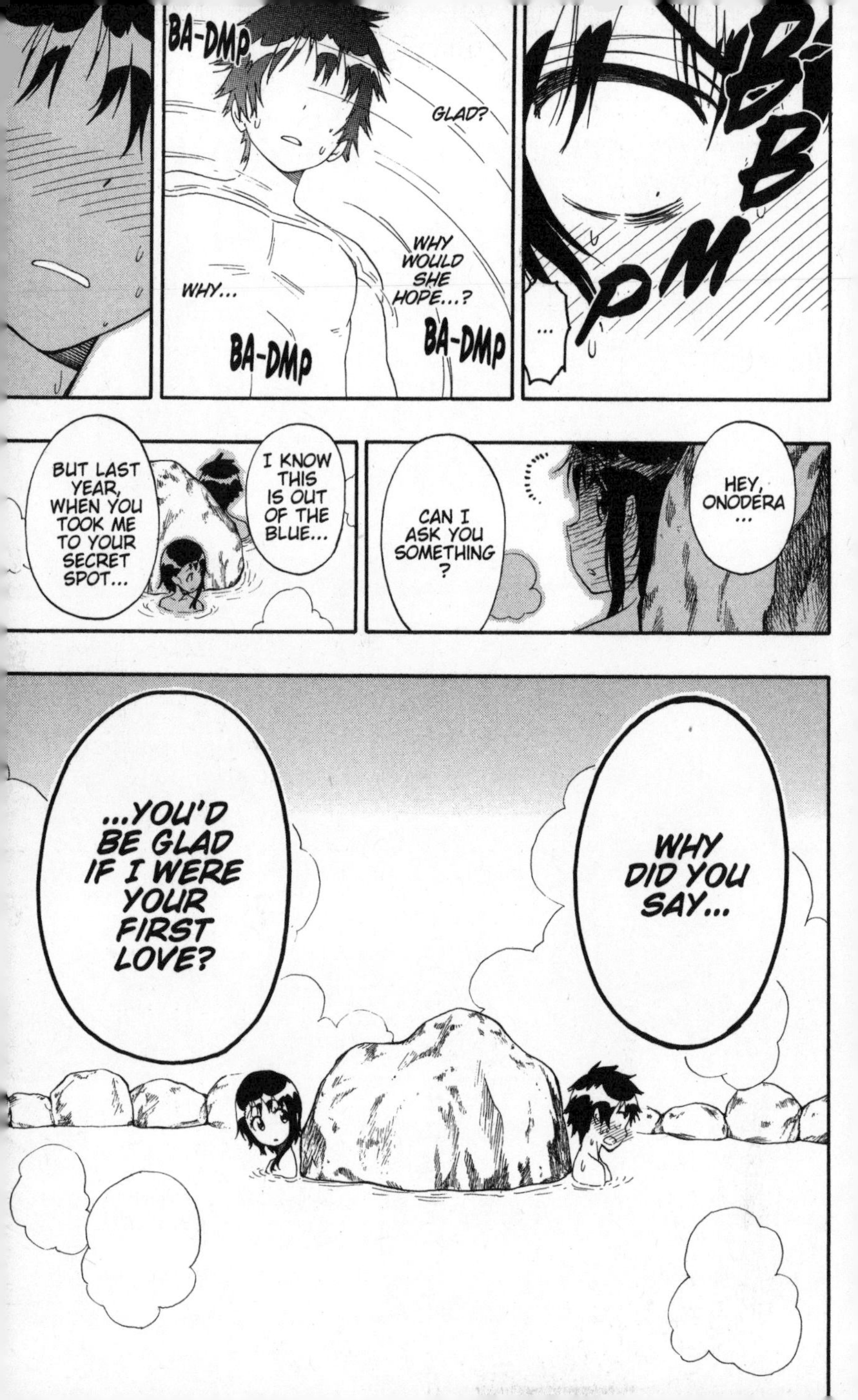
BBPM
...
GLAD?
WHY WOULD SHE HOPE...?
BA-DMP
WHY...
BA-DMP
BA-DMP
HEY, ONODERA...
CAN I ASK YOU SOMETHING?
I KNOW THIS IS OUT OF THE BLUE...
BUT LAST YEAR, WHEN YOU TOOK ME TO YOUR SECRET SPOT...
WHY DID YOU SAY...
...YOU'D BE GLAD IF I WERE YOUR FIRST LOVE?

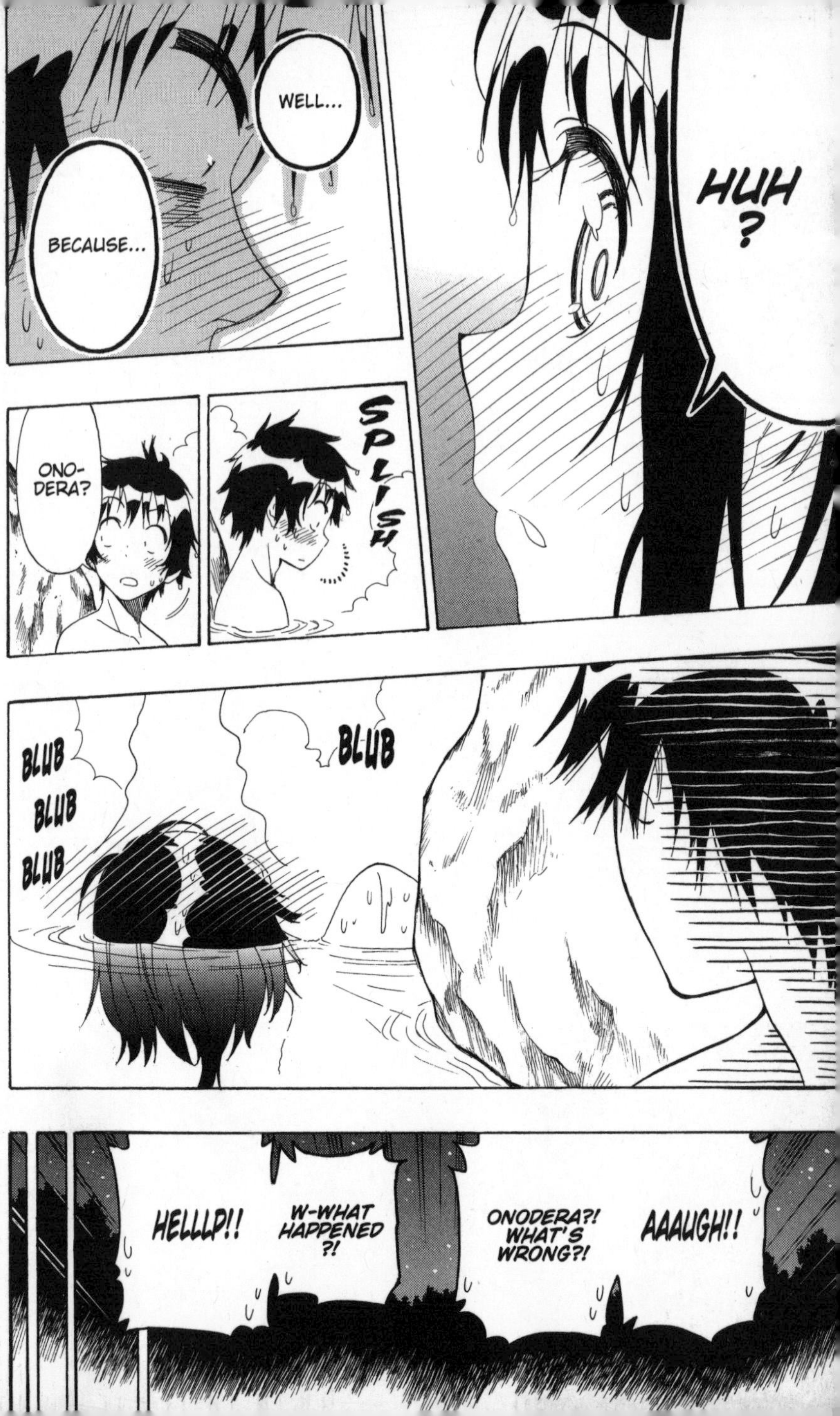
HUH?
WELL...
BECAUSE...
SPLISH
ONO-DERA?
BLUB
BLUB
BLUB
BLUB
AAAUGH!!
ONODERA?! WHAT'S WRONG?!
W-WHAT HAPPENED?!
HELLLP!!

OH, FOR PETE'S SAKE! I CAN'T BELIEVE YOU GOT OVERHEATED AND PASSED OUT IN THE BATH, KOSAKI!
I'M SO GLAD YOU'RE ALL RIGHT!
I was surprised!
I'M SO SORRY!
ICHIJO, I'M SORRY...
...I MADE YOU WORRY.
NO... I...
...
DID YOU...
...SEE?
N-N-N-NO!!
I JUST HELD YOU UP SO YOU COULD BREATHE. THE BOSS TOOK CARE OF YOU AFTER THAT!!
It's true!
Hellllp! Hellllp!
ZONK
WELL, ANYWAY, WE SHOULD GET TO BED NOW.
YOU MUST BE TIRED TOO, ONODERA.
YES.
Good night!
Good night!
IN THE END...
...I NEVER GOT AN ANSWER TO MY QUESTION.
...
...

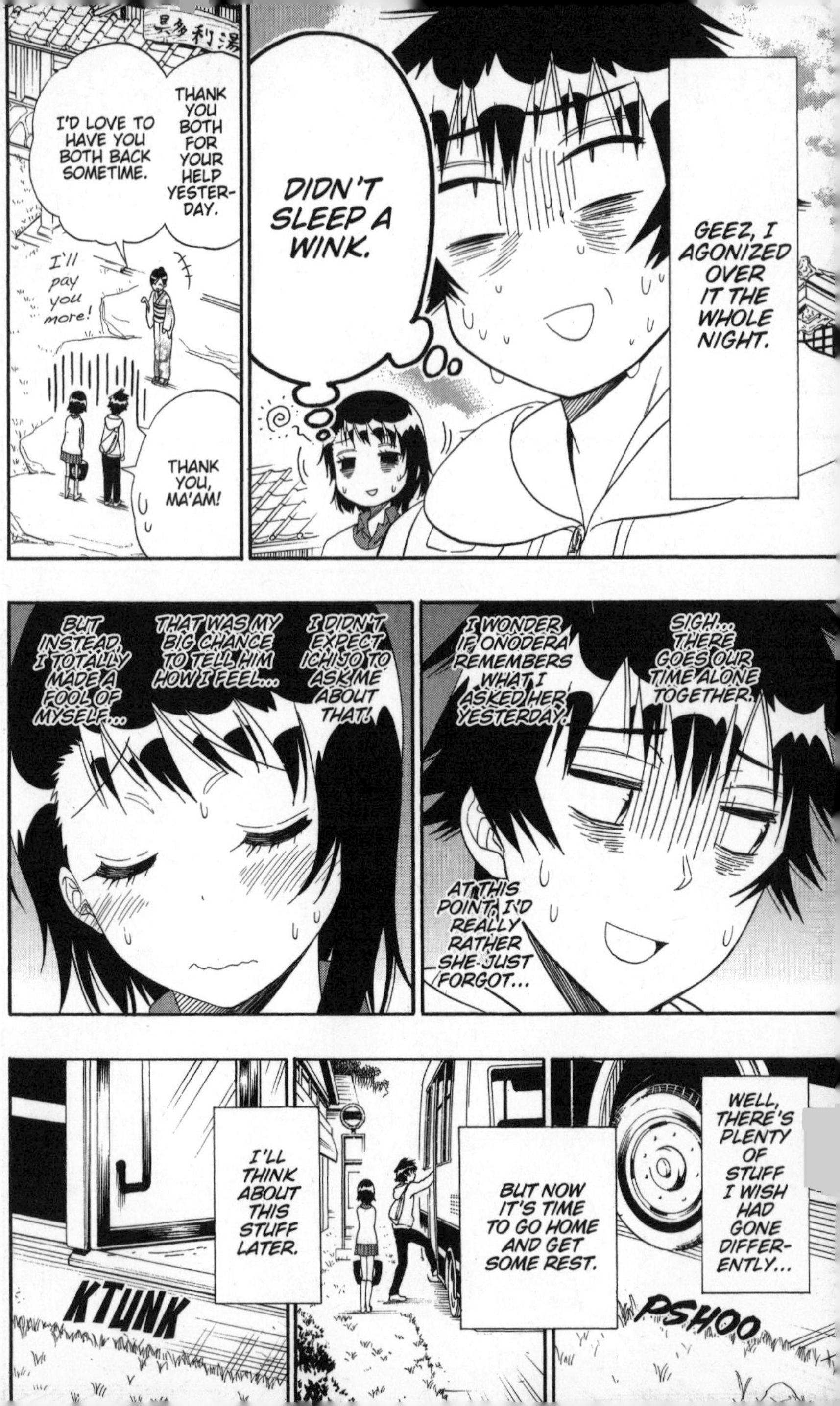
GEEZ, I AGONIZED OVER IT THE WHOLE NIGHT.
DIDN'T SLEEP A WINK.
THANK YOU BOTH FOR YOUR HELP YESTER-DAY.
I'D LOVE TO HAVE YOU BOTH BACK SOMETIME.
I'll pay you more!
THANK YOU, MA'AM!
SIGH... THERE GOES OUR TIME ALONE TOGETHER.
I WONDER IF ONODERA REMEMBERS WHAT I ASKED HER YESTERDAY.
AT THIS POINT, I'D REALLY RATHER SHE JUST FORGOT...
I DIDN'T EXPECT ICHIJO TO ASK ME ABOUT THAT!
THAT WAS MY BIG CHANCE TO TELL HIM HOW I FEEL...
BUT INSTEAD, I TOTALLY MADE A FOOL OF MYSELF...
WELL, THERE'S PLENTY OF STUFF I WISH HAD GONE DIFFER-ENTLY...
PSHOO
BUT NOW IT'S TIME TO GO HOME AND GET SOME REST.
I'LL THINK ABOUT THIS STUFF LATER.
KTUNK

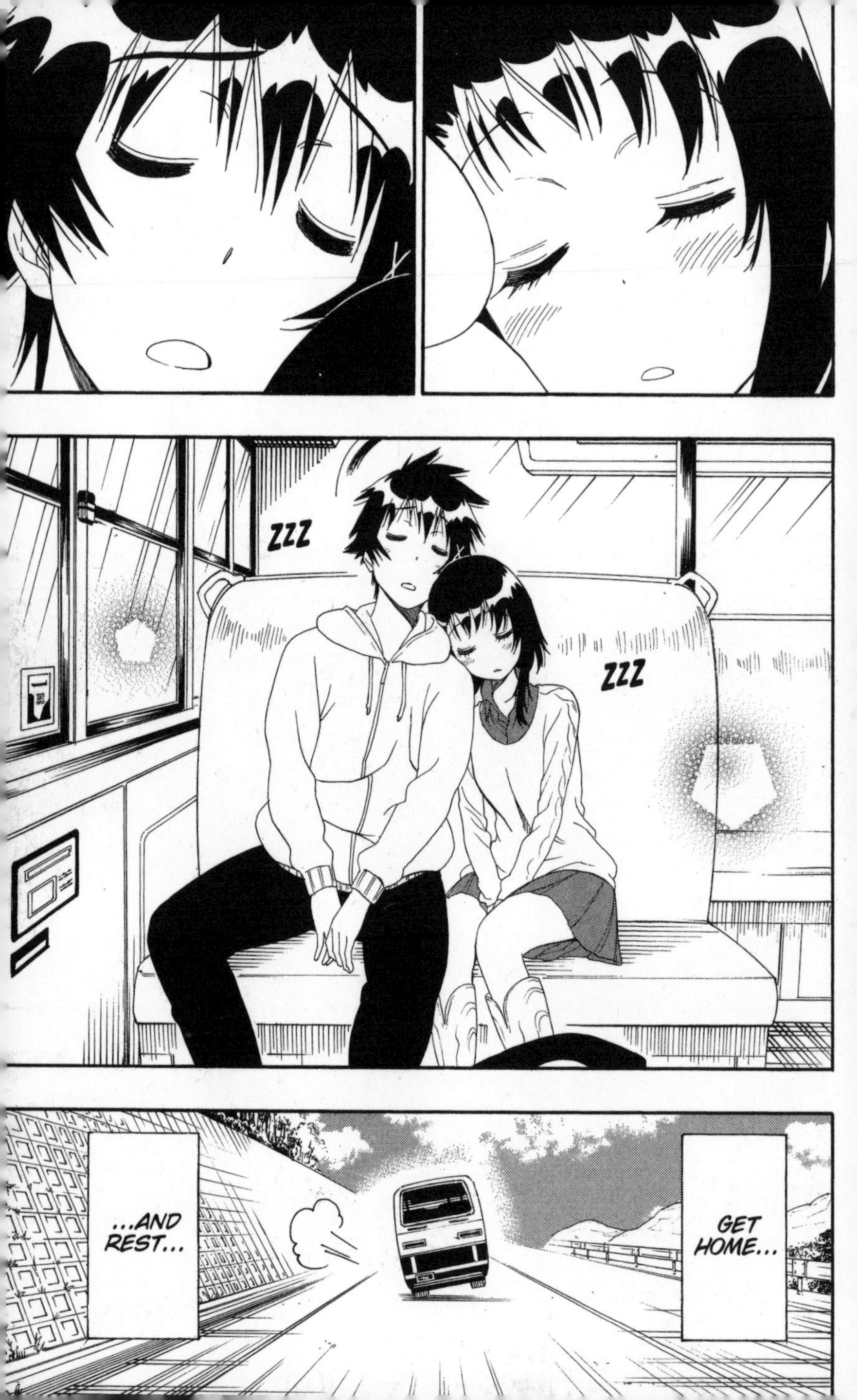
ZZZ
ZZZ
GET HOME...
...AND REST...

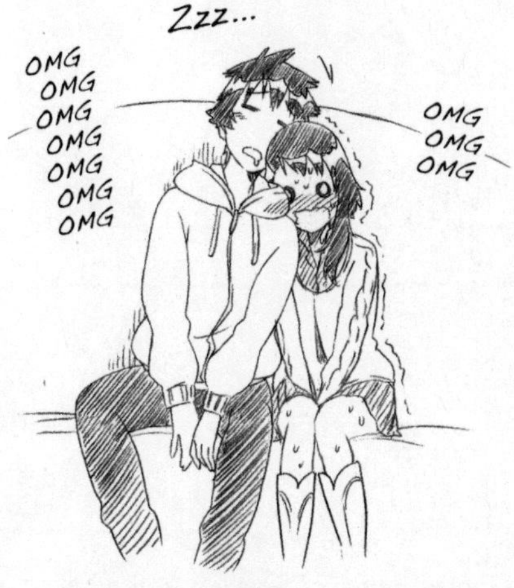
Zzz...
OMG
OMG
OMG
OMG
OMG
OMG
OMG
OMG
OMG
OMG

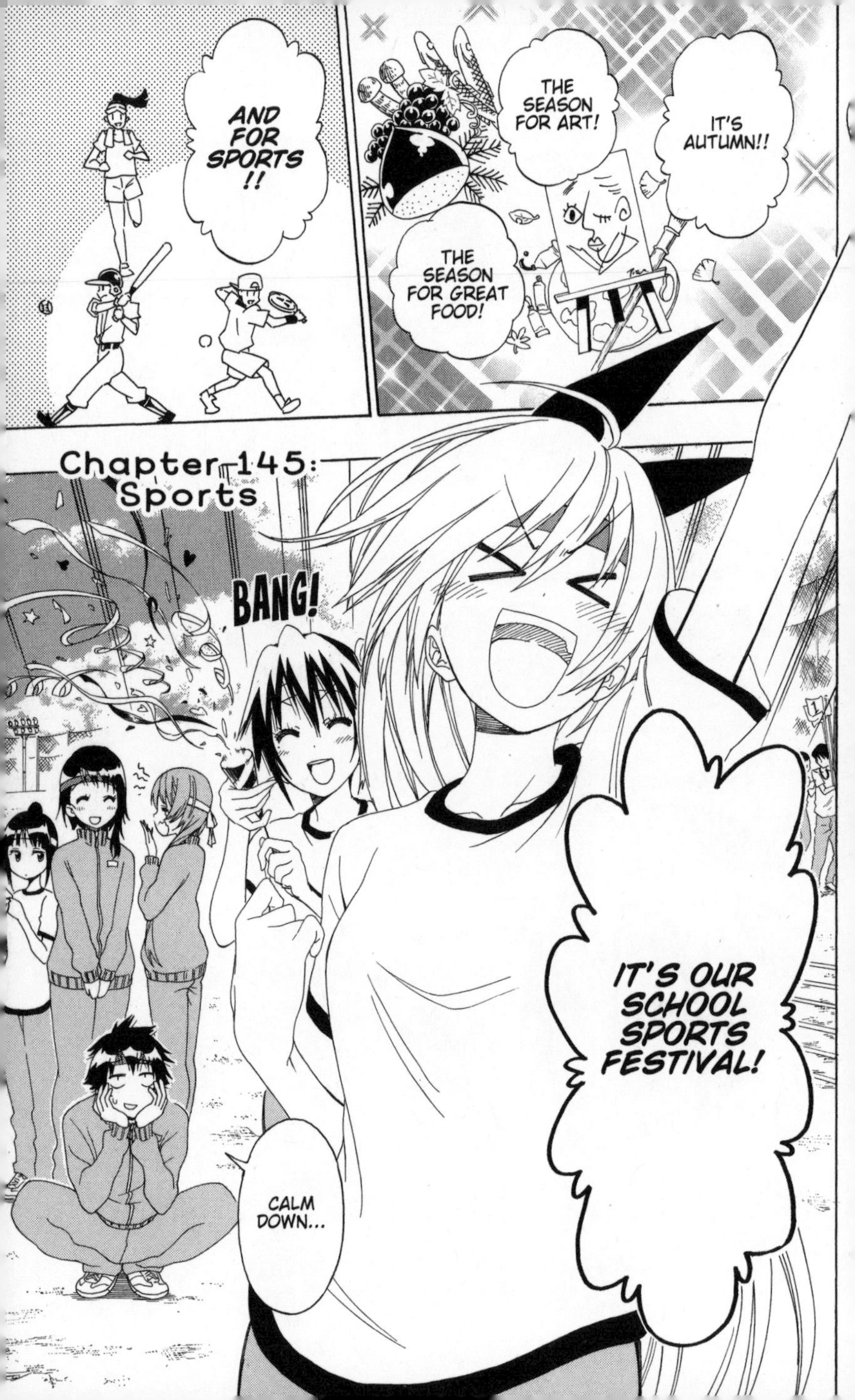
IT'S AUTUMN!!
THE SEASON FOR ART!
THE SEASON FOR GREAT FOOD!
AND FOR SPORTS !!
Chapter 145: Sports
BANG!
IT'S OUR SCHOOL SPORTS FESTIVAL!
CALM DOWN...

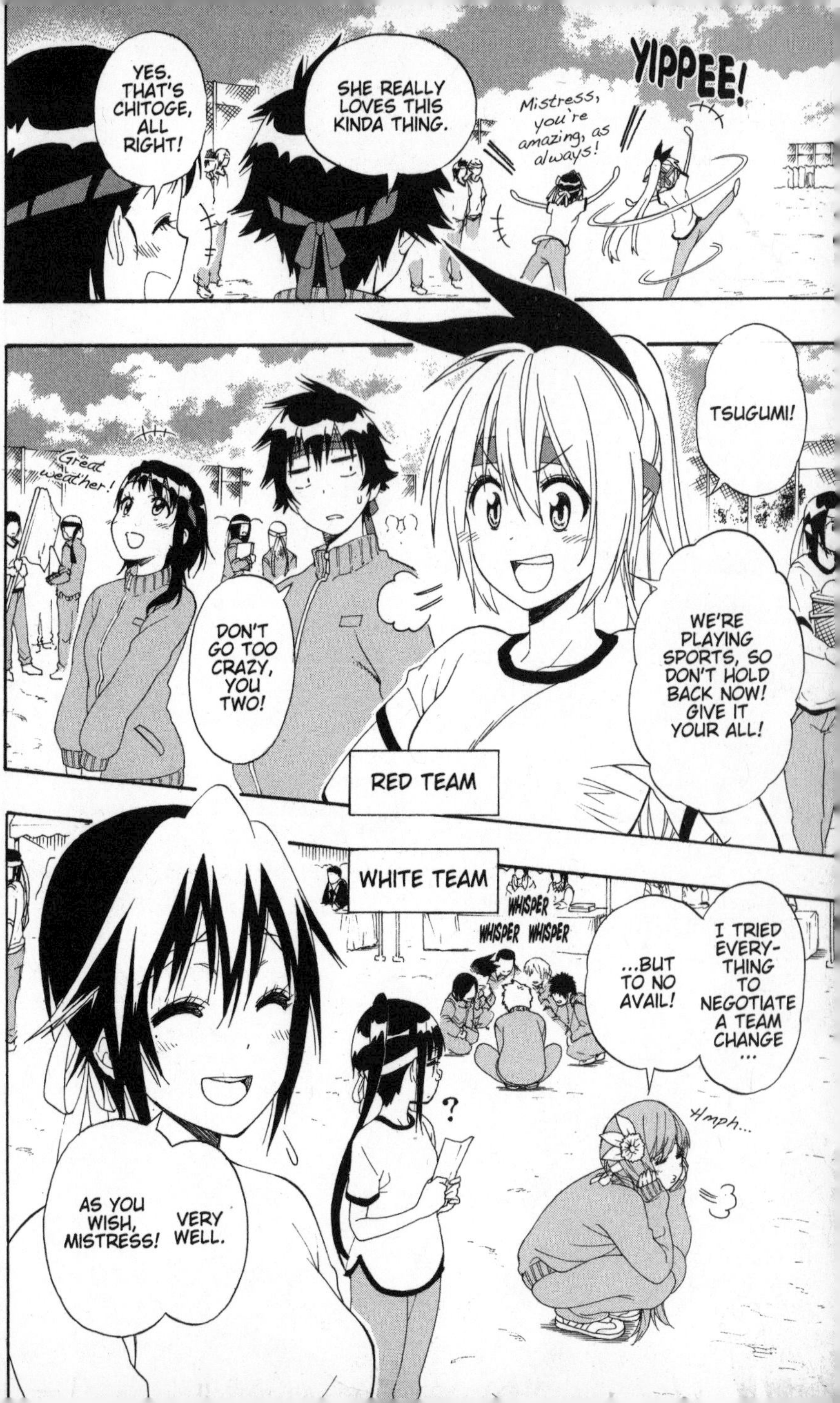
YIPPEE!
Mistress, you're amazing, as always!
SHE REALLY LOVES THIS KINDA THING.
YES. THAT'S CHITOGE, ALL RIGHT!
TSUGUMI!
WE'RE PLAYING SPORTS, SO DON'T HOLD BACK NOW! GIVE IT YOUR ALL!
DON'T GO TOO CRAZY, YOU TWO!
Great weather!
RED TEAM
WHITE TEAM
I TRIED EVERY-THING TO NEGOTIATE A TEAM CHANGE...
...BUT TO NO AVAIL!
WHISPER
WHISPER WHISPER
Hmph...
?
VERY WELL.
AS YOU WISH, MISTRESS!

GOOD LUCK, MISTRESS!
YOUNG MASTER! WE'RE CHEERING FOR YA!
UGH.
I TOLD THEM NOT TO COME...
GO! GO!
YOUNG MASTER!
GO!
MISTRESS!
Fight
BEE HIVE
WELL...
AT LEAST WE'RE USED TO IT.
Just try to tune it out.
WHISPER WHISPER
?
WHAT'RE YOU UP TO, SHU?
HEYA, RAKU!
JUST A FINAL POW-WOW ABOUT TODAY'S PLAN...
I'M ON THE EXECUTIVE COMMIT-TEE.
YOU'RE MEETING NOW?
The festival's starting...
TEE HEE HEE HEE HEE HEE HEE...
HEH...
GLEAM!
RAKU...
I SURE HOPE YOU'RE LOOKING FORWARD TO TODAY'S SPORTS FESTIVAL.
MWA HA HA HA HA HA HA HA
HA HA HA
KNOCK IT OFF. YOU'RE SCARING ME.
What're you plotting?!

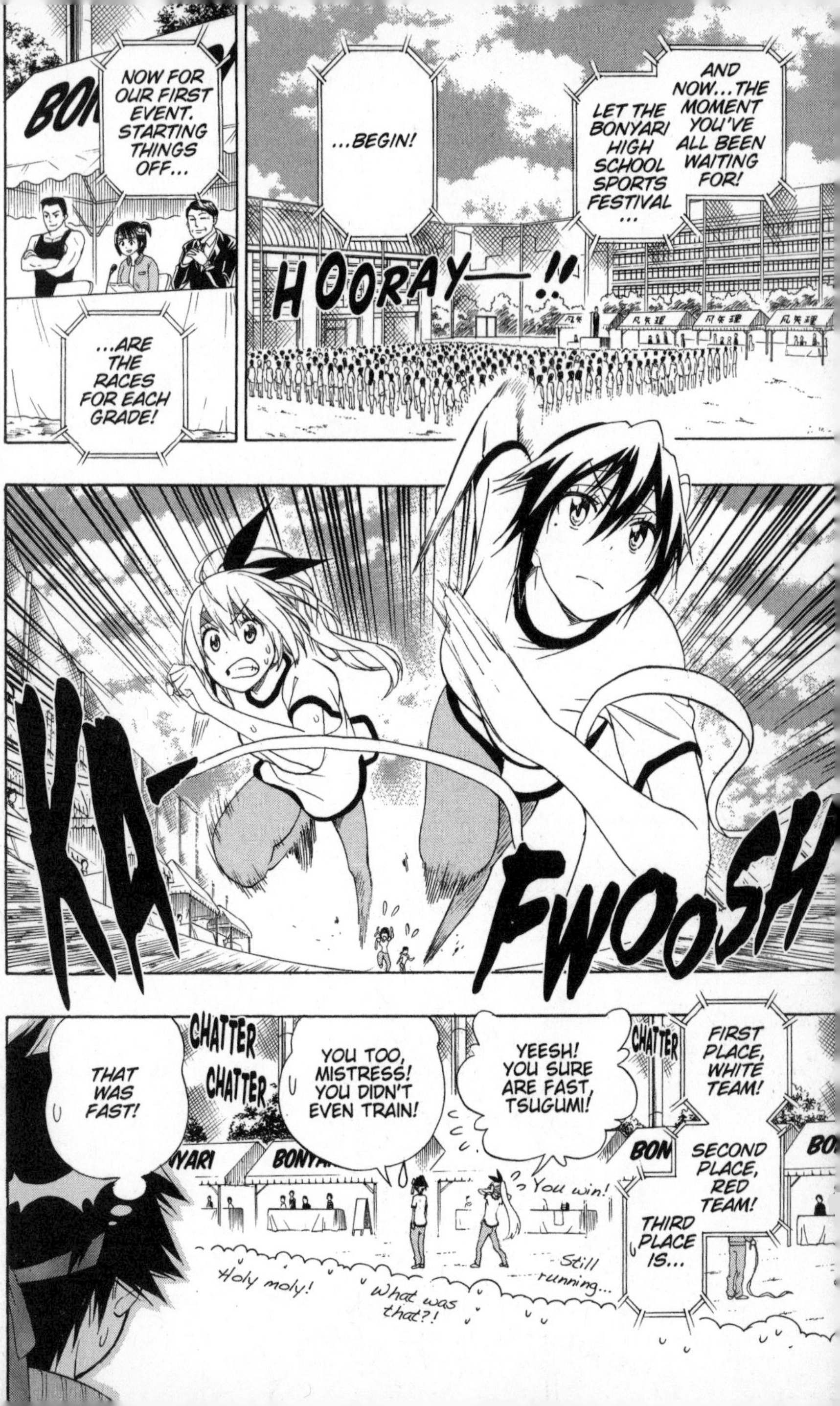
AND NOW...THE MOMENT YOU'VE ALL BEEN WAITING FOR!
LET THE BONYARI HIGH SCHOOL SPORTS FESTIVAL ...
...BEGIN!
HOORAY—!!
NOW FOR OUR FIRST EVENT. STARTING THINGS OFF...
...ARE THE RACES FOR EACH GRADE!
FWOOSH
KA
FIRST PLACE, WHITE TEAM!
SECOND PLACE, RED TEAM!
THIRD PLACE IS...
CHATTER
YEESH! YOU SURE ARE FAST, TSUGUMI!
You win!
Still running...
YOU TOO, MISTRESS! YOU DIDN'T EVEN TRAIN!
CHATTER CHATTER
What was that?!
THAT WAS FAST!
Holy moly!

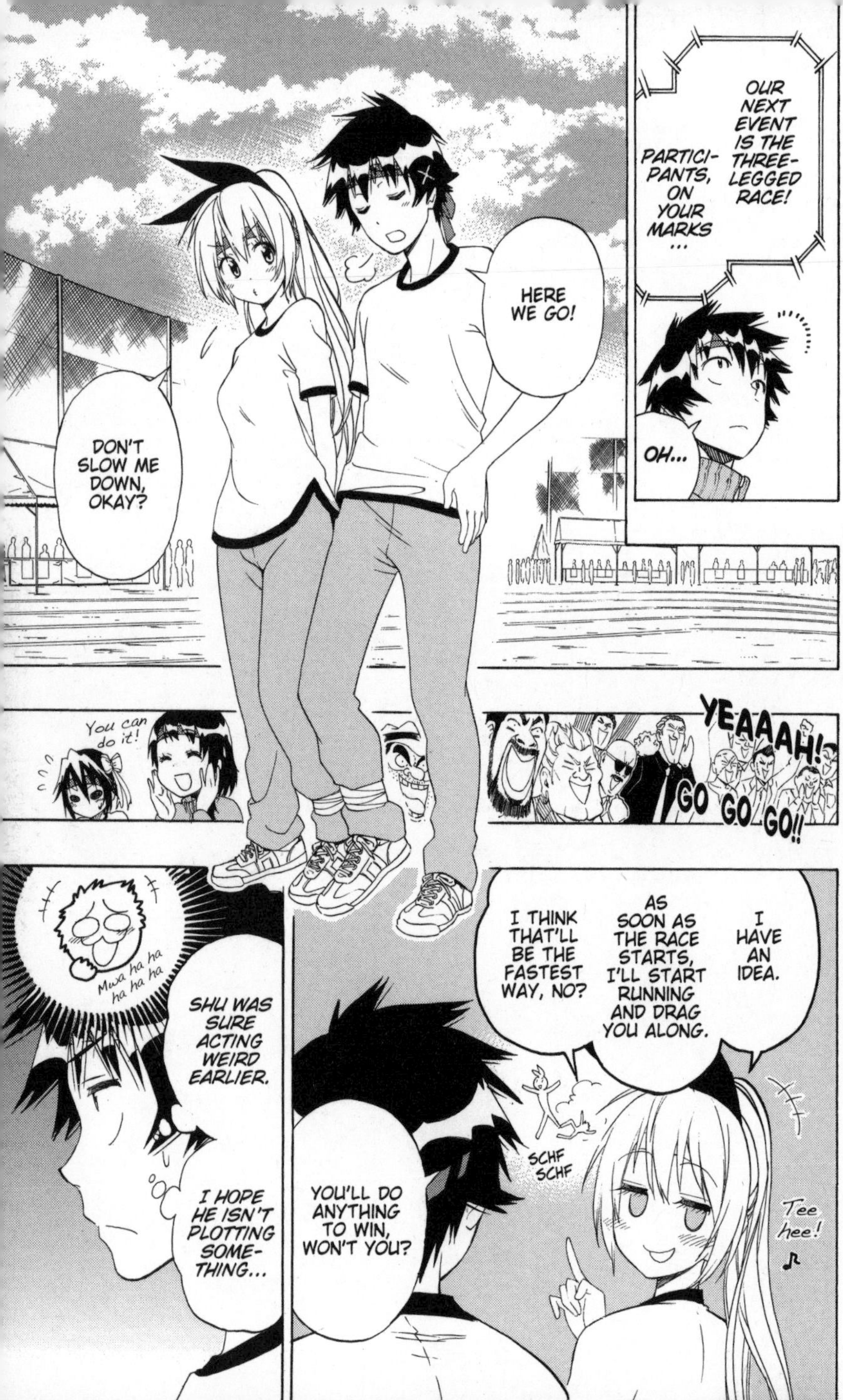
OUR NEXT EVENT IS THE THREE-LEGGED RACE!
PARTICI-PANTS, ON YOUR MARKS ...
OH...
HERE WE GO!
DON'T SLOW ME DOWN, OKAY?
YEAAAAH!
GO GO GO!!
You can do it!
I HAVE AN IDEA.
AS SOON AS THE RACE STARTS, I'LL START RUNNING AND DRAG YOU ALONG.
I THINK THAT'LL BE THE FASTEST WAY, NO?
Tee hee! ♪
SCHF SCHF
YOU'LL DO ANYTHING TO WIN, WON'T YOU?
Mwa ha ha ha ha ha
SHU WAS SURE ACTING WEIRD EARLIER.
I HOPE HE ISN'T PLOTTING SOME-THING...

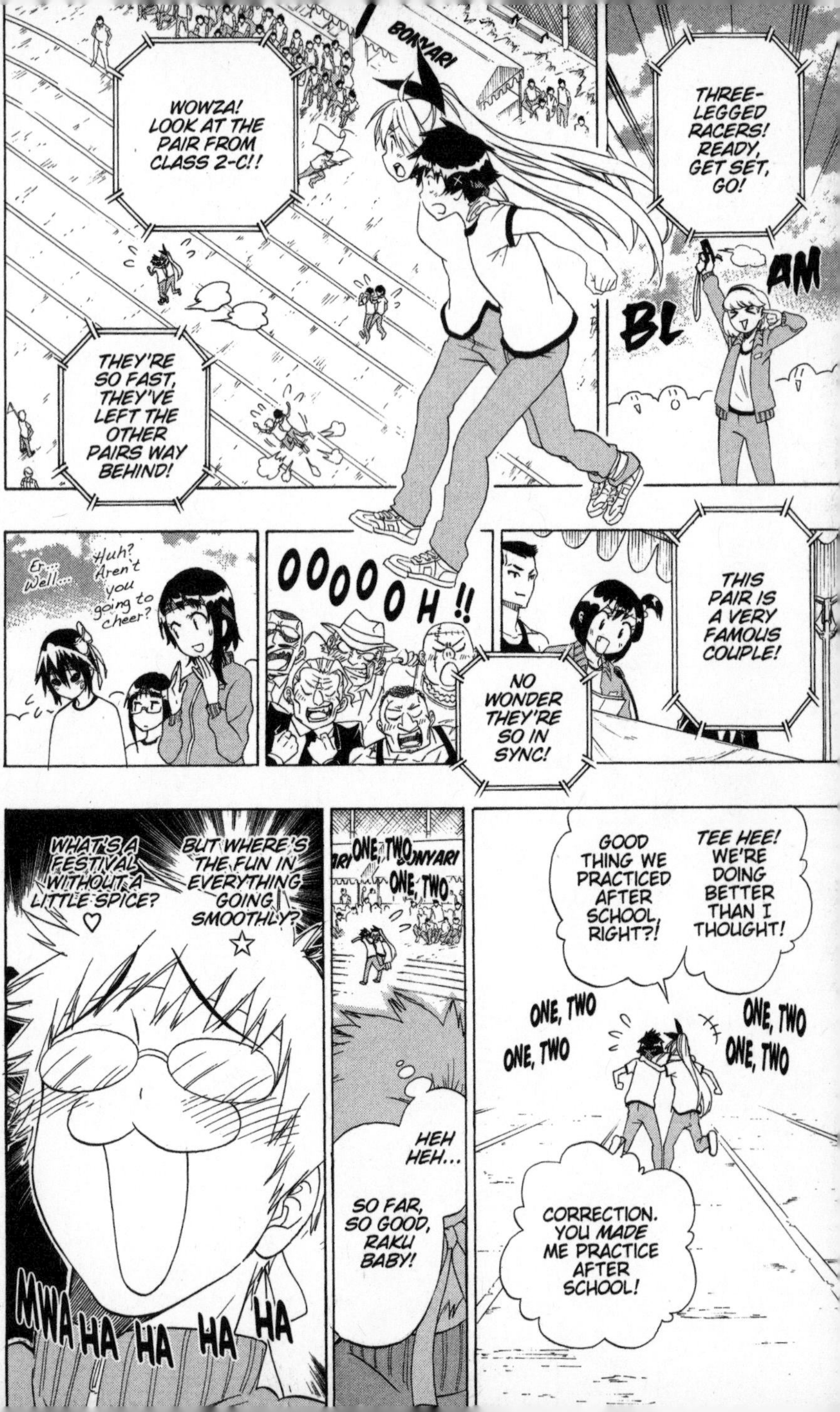
THREE-LEGGED RACERS! READY, GET SET, GO!
BLAM
WOWZA! LOOK AT THE PAIR FROM CLASS 2-C!!
BONYARI
THEY'RE SO FAST, THEY'VE LEFT THE OTHER PAIRS WAY BEHIND!
THIS PAIR IS A VERY FAMOUS COUPLE!
NO WONDER THEY'RE SO IN SYNC!
OOOOOOH!!
Huh? Aren't you going to cheer?
Er... Well...
TEE HEE! WE'RE DOING BETTER THAN I THOUGHT!
GOOD THING WE PRACTICED AFTER SCHOOL, RIGHT?!
ONE, TWO
ONE, TWO
ONE, TWO
ONE, TWO
CORRECTION. YOU MADE ME PRACTICE AFTER SCHOOL!
ONE, TWO
ONE, TWO
BONYARI
HEH HEH...
SO FAR, SO GOOD, RAKU BABY!
BUT WHERE'S THE FUN IN EVERYTHING GOING SMOOTHLY?
WHAT'S A FESTIVAL WITHOUT A LITTLE SPICE?
MWA HA HA HA HA

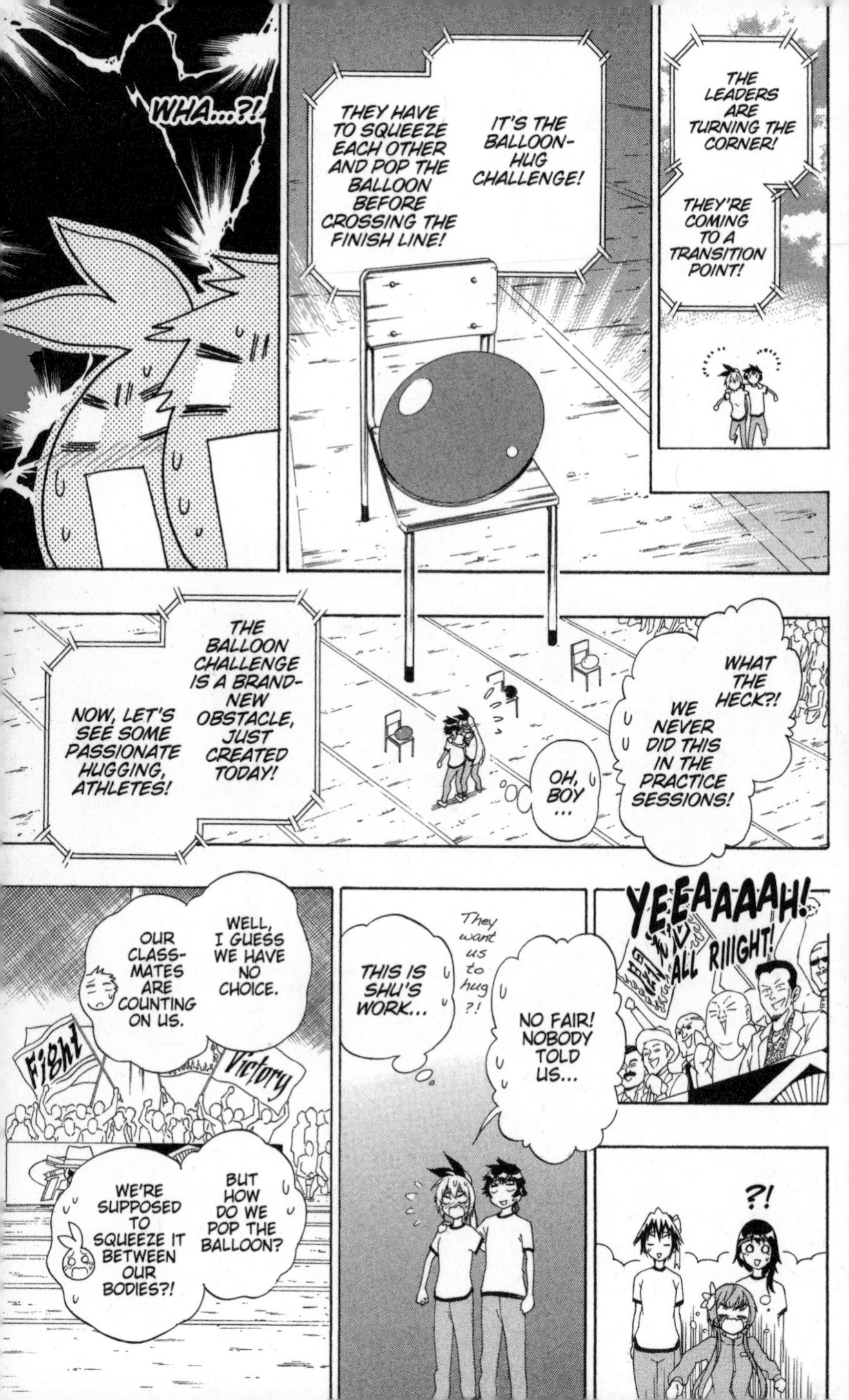
THE LEADERS ARE TURNING THE CORNER!
THEY'RE COMING TO A TRANSITION POINT!
IT'S THE BALLOON-HUG CHALLENGE!
THEY HAVE TO SQUEEZE EACH OTHER AND POP THE BALLOON BEFORE CROSSING THE FINISH LINE!
WHA...?!
WHAT THE HECK?!
WE NEVER DID THIS IN THE PRACTICE SESSIONS!
OH, BOY...
THE BALLOON CHALLENGE IS A BRAND-NEW OBSTACLE, JUST CREATED TODAY!
NOW, LET'S SEE SOME PASSIONATE HUGGING, ATHLETES!
YEEAAAAH!
ALL RIIIGHT!
?!
NO FAIR! NOBODY TOLD US...
They want us to hug ?!
THIS IS SHU'S WORK...
WELL, I GUESS WE HAVE NO CHOICE.
OUR CLASSMATES ARE COUNTING ON US.
Fight
Victory
BUT HOW DO WE POP THE BALLOON?
WE'RE SUPPOSED TO SQUEEZE IT BETWEEN OUR BODIES?!

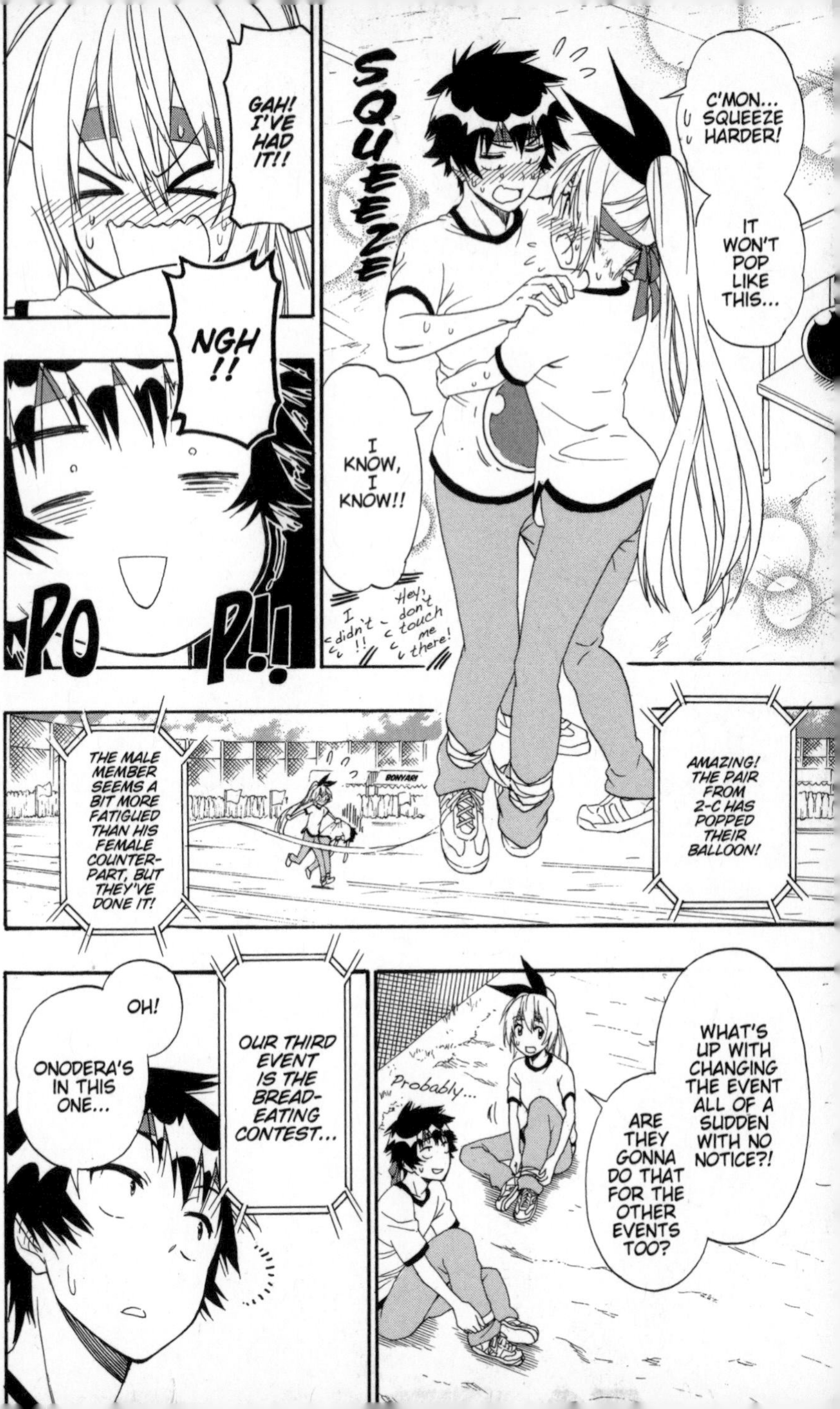
C'MON... SQUEEZE HARDER!
IT WON'T POP LIKE THIS...
SQUEEZE
I KNOW, I KNOW!!
Hey, don't touch me there!
I didn't!!
GAH! I'VE HAD IT!!
NGH!!
POP!!
AMAZING! THE PAIR FROM 2-C HAS POPPED THEIR BALLOON!
BONYARI
THE MALE MEMBER SEEMS A BIT MORE FATIGUED THAN HIS FEMALE COUNTER-PART, BUT THEY'VE DONE IT!
WHAT'S UP WITH CHANGING THE EVENT ALL OF A SUDDEN WITH NO NOTICE?!
ARE THEY GONNA DO THAT FOR THE OTHER EVENTS TOO?
Probably...
OUR THIRD EVENT IS THE BREAD-EATING CONTEST...
OH!
ONODERA'S IN THIS ONE...

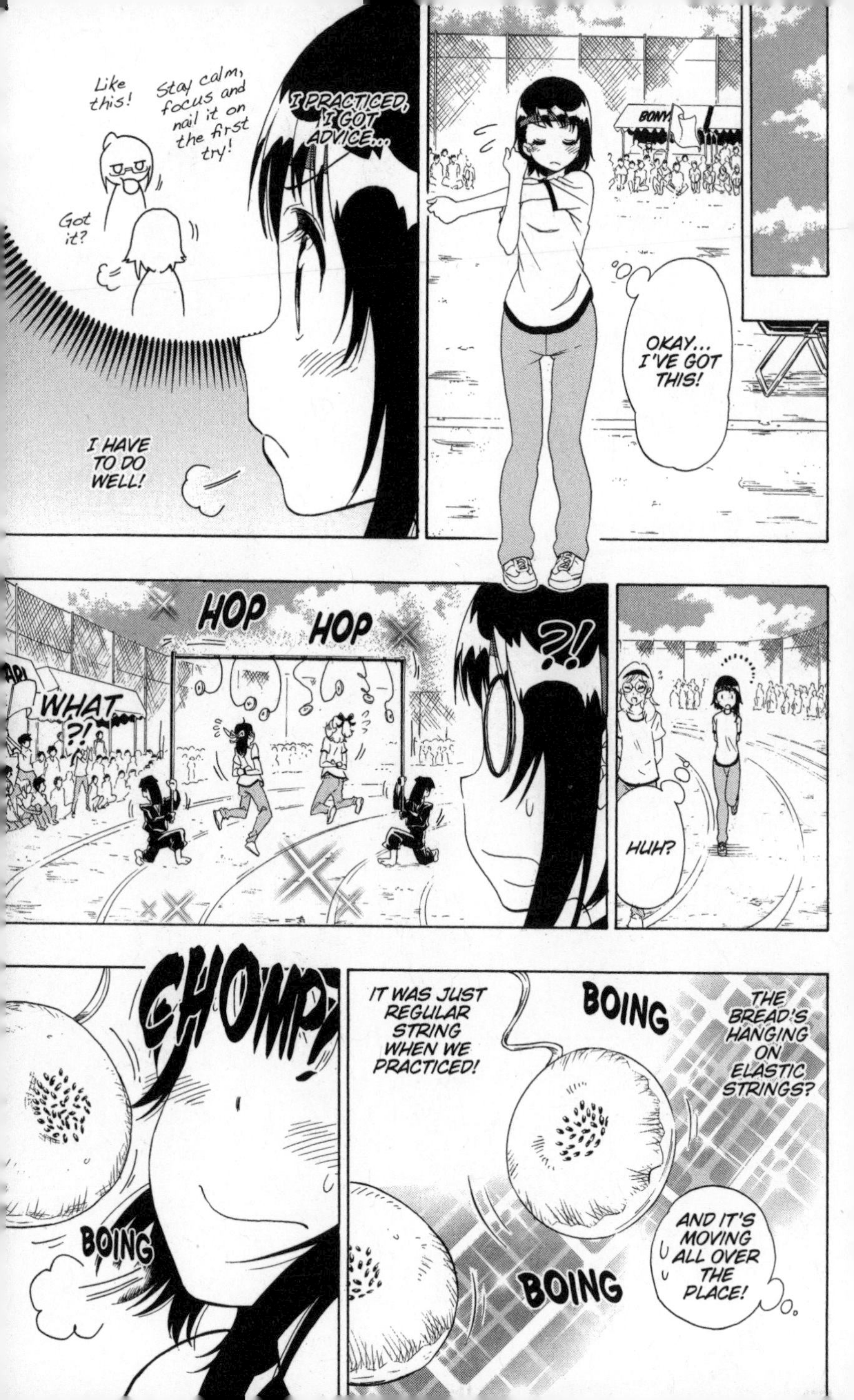
OKAY... I'VE GOT THIS!
BONY
I PRACTICED, I GOT ADVICE...
Stay calm, focus and nail it on the first try!
Like this!
Got it?
I HAVE TO DO WELL!
HUH?
?!
HOP
HOP
WHAT ?!
THE BREAD'S HANGING ON ELASTIC STRINGS?
BOING
IT WAS JUST REGULAR STRING WHEN WE PRACTICED!
AND IT'S MOVING ALL OVER THE PLACE!
BOING
CHOMP!
BOING

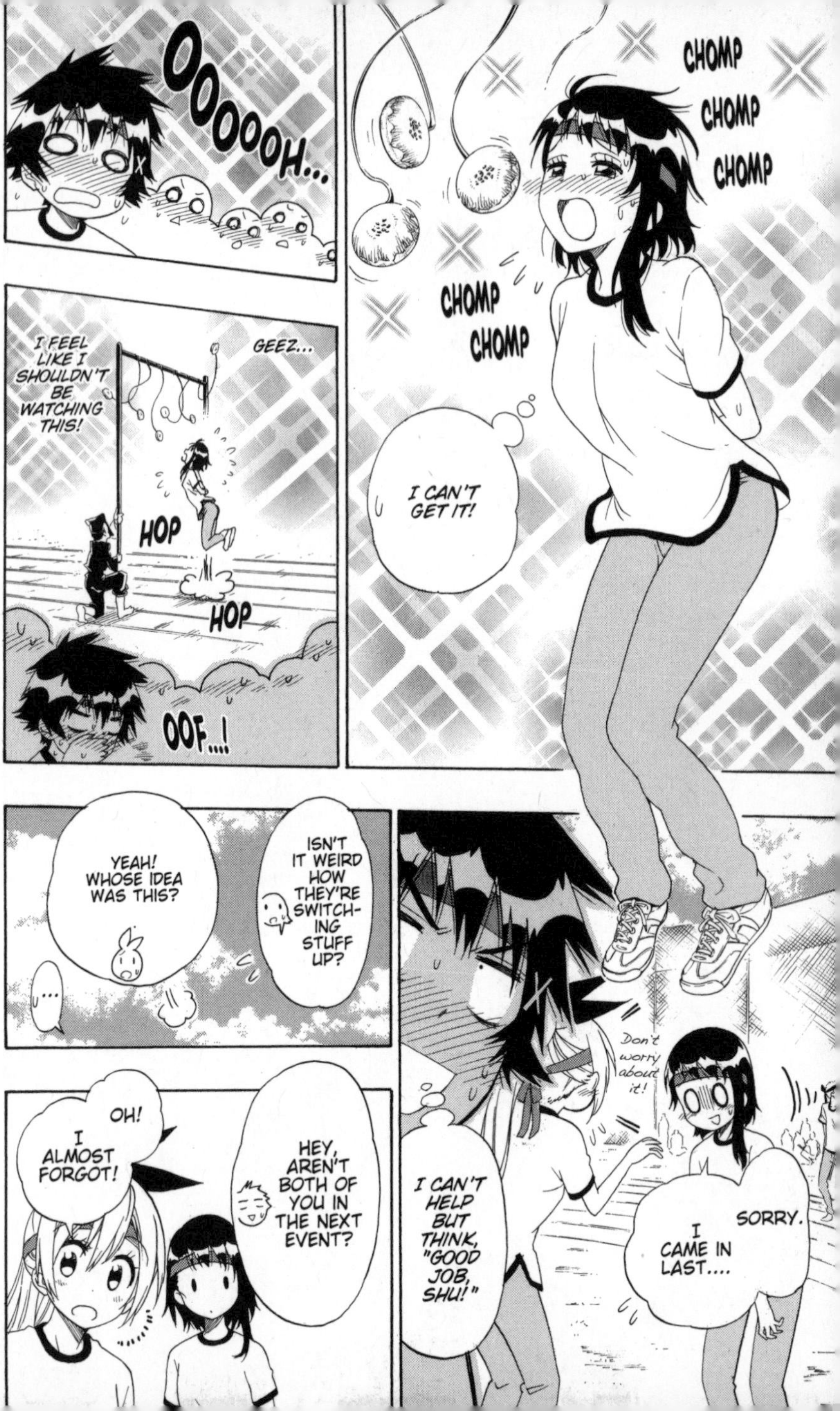
CHOMP
CHOMP
CHOMP
CHOMP
CHOMP
I CAN'T GET IT!
OOOOOOH...
I FEEL LIKE I SHOULDN'T BE WATCHING THIS!
GEEZ...
HOP
HOP
OOF...!
SORRY.
I CAME IN LAST....
Don't worry about it!
I CAN'T HELP BUT THINK, "GOOD JOB, SHU!"
ISN'T IT WEIRD HOW THEY'RE SWITCH-ING STUFF UP?
YEAH! WHOSE IDEA WAS THIS?
...
HEY, AREN'T BOTH OF YOU IN THE NEXT EVENT?
OH!
I ALMOST FORGOT!

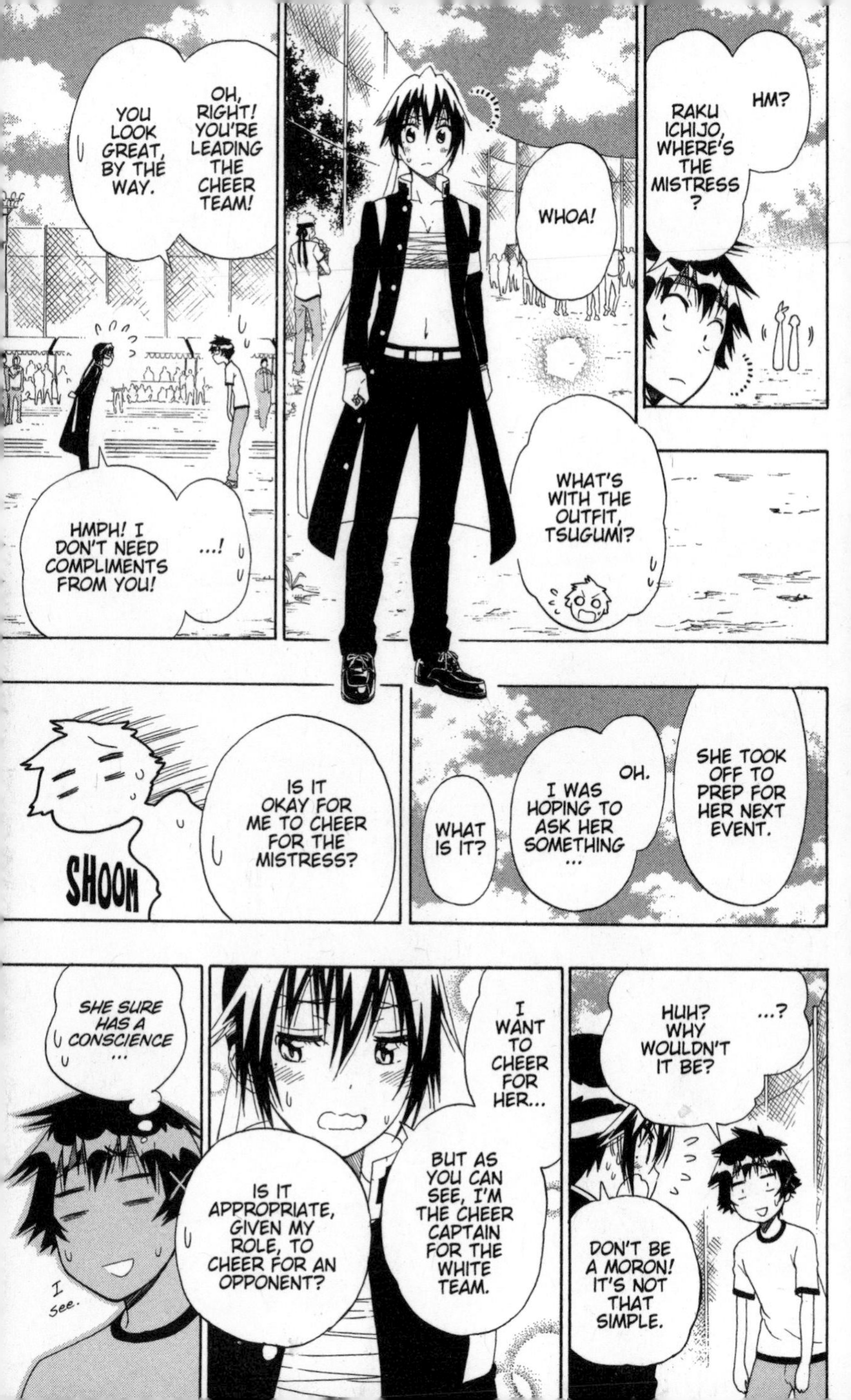
HM?
RAKU ICHIJO, WHERE'S THE MISTRESS?
WHOA!
WHAT'S WITH THE OUTFIT, TSUGUMI?
OH, RIGHT! YOU'RE LEADING THE CHEER TEAM!
YOU LOOK GREAT, BY THE WAY.
...!
HMPH! I DON'T NEED COMPLIMENTS FROM YOU!
SHE TOOK OFF TO PREP FOR HER NEXT EVENT.
OH. I WAS HOPING TO ASK HER SOMETHING...
WHAT IS IT?
IS IT OKAY FOR ME TO CHEER FOR THE MISTRESS?
SHOOM
...?
HUH? WHY WOULDN'T IT BE?
DON'T BE A MORON! IT'S NOT THAT SIMPLE.
I WANT TO CHEER FOR HER...
BUT AS YOU CAN SEE, I'M THE CHEER CAPTAIN FOR THE WHITE TEAM.
IS IT APPROPRIATE, GIVEN MY ROLE, TO CHEER FOR AN OPPONENT?
SHE SURE HAS A CONSCIENCE...
I see.

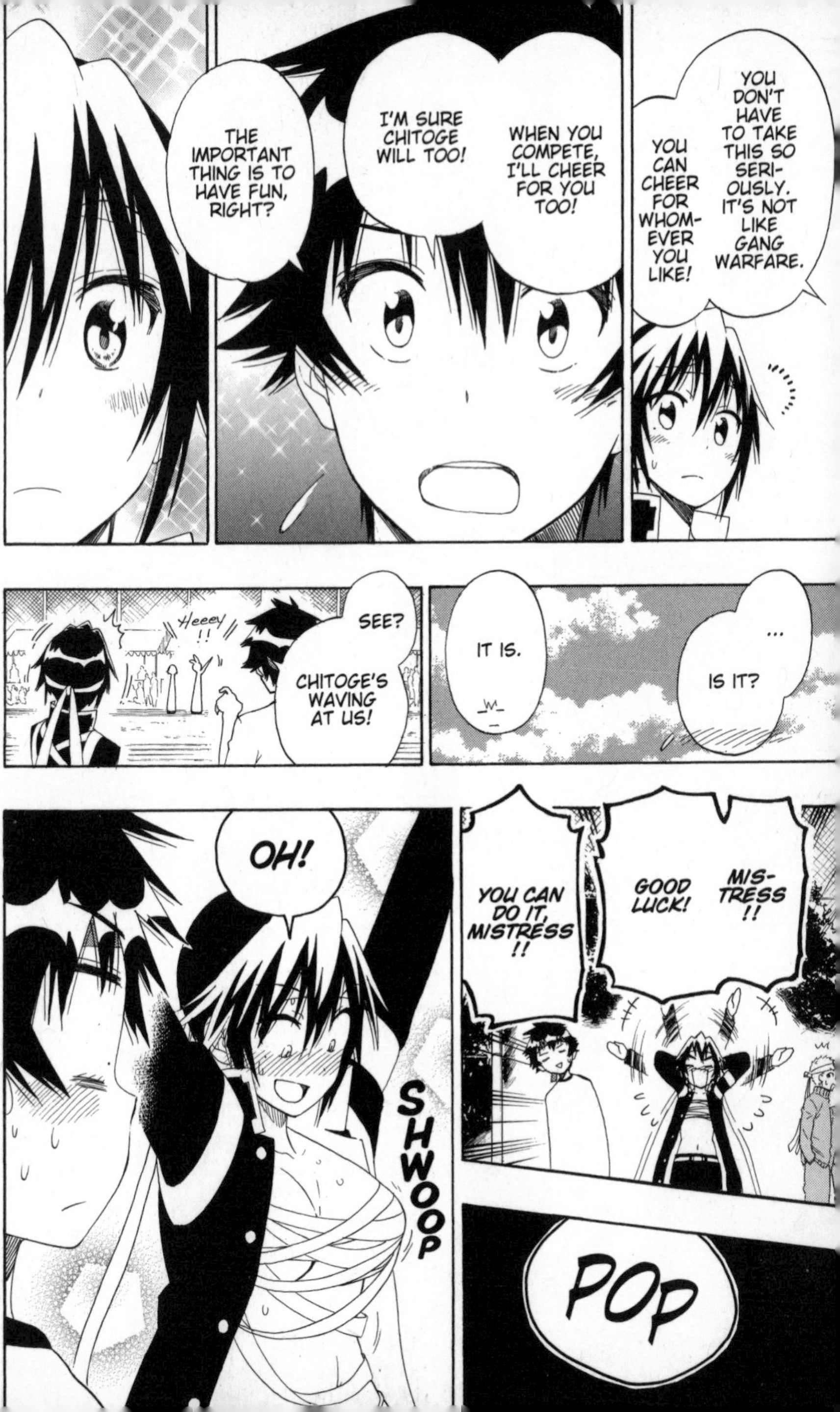
YOU DON'T HAVE TO TAKE THIS SO SERI-OUSLY. IT'S NOT LIKE GANG WARFARE.
YOU CAN CHEER FOR WHOM-EVER YOU LIKE!
I'M SURE CHITOGE WILL TOO!
WHEN YOU COMPETE, I'LL CHEER FOR YOU TOO!
THE IMPORTANT THING IS TO HAVE FUN, RIGHT?
...
IS IT?
IT IS.
SEE?
CHITOGE'S WAVING AT US!
Heeey !!
MIS-TRESS !!
GOOD LUCK!
YOU CAN DO IT, MISTRESS !!
POP
OH!
SHWOOP

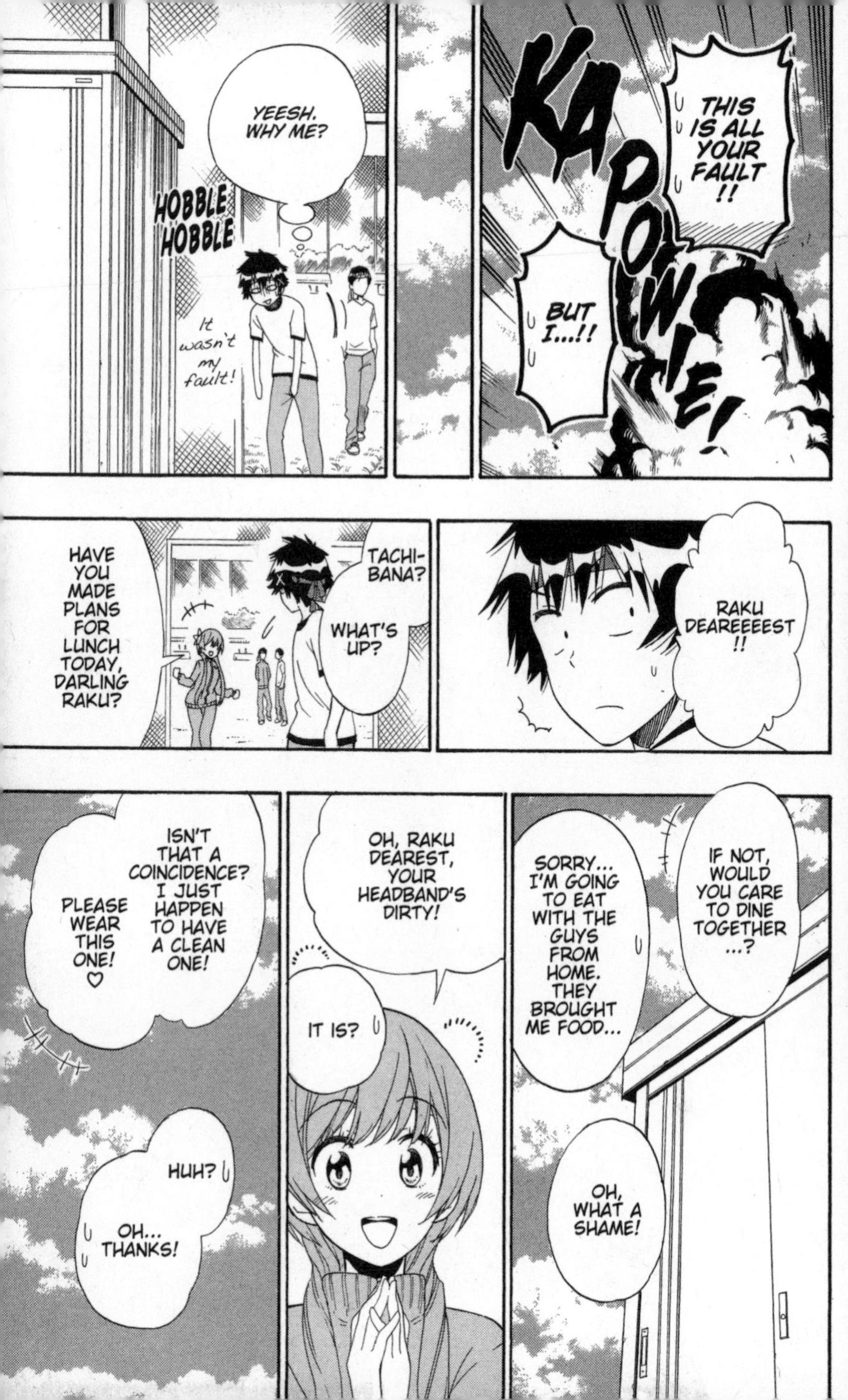
THIS IS ALL YOUR FAULT!!
KAPOWIE!
BUT I...!!
YEESH. WHY ME?
HOBBLE HOBBLE
It wasn't my fault!
RAKU DEAREEEEEST!!
TACHI-BANA?
WHAT'S UP?
HAVE YOU MADE PLANS FOR LUNCH TODAY, DARLING RAKU?
IF NOT, WOULD YOU CARE TO DINE TOGETHER...?
SORRY... I'M GOING TO EAT WITH THE GUYS FROM HOME. THEY BROUGHT ME FOOD...
OH, WHAT A SHAME!
OH, RAKU DEAREST, YOUR HEADBAND'S DIRTY!
IT IS?
ISN'T THAT A COINCIDENCE? I JUST HAPPEN TO HAVE A CLEAN ONE!
PLEASE WEAR THIS ONE! ♡
HUH?
OH... THANKS!

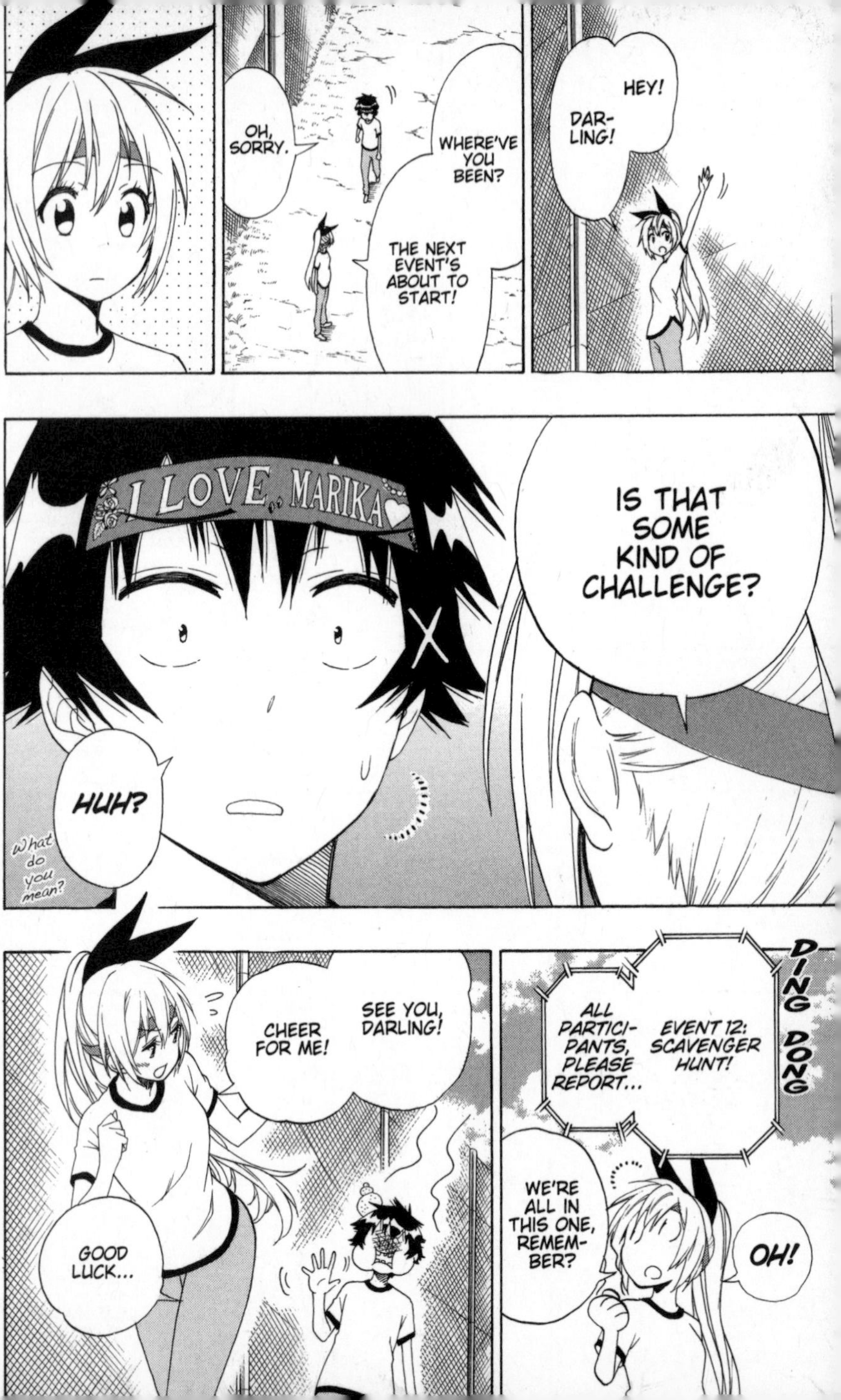
HEY!
DAR-LING!
WHERE'VE YOU BEEN?
THE NEXT EVENT'S ABOUT TO START!
OH, SORRY.
IS THAT SOME KIND OF CHALLENGE?
I LOVE MARIKA
HUH?
What do you mean?
DING DONG
EVENT 12: SCAVENGER HUNT!
ALL PARTICI-PANTS, PLEASE REPORT...
OH!
WE'RE ALL IN THIS ONE, REMEM-BER?
SEE YOU, DARLING!
CHEER FOR ME!
GOOD LUCK...

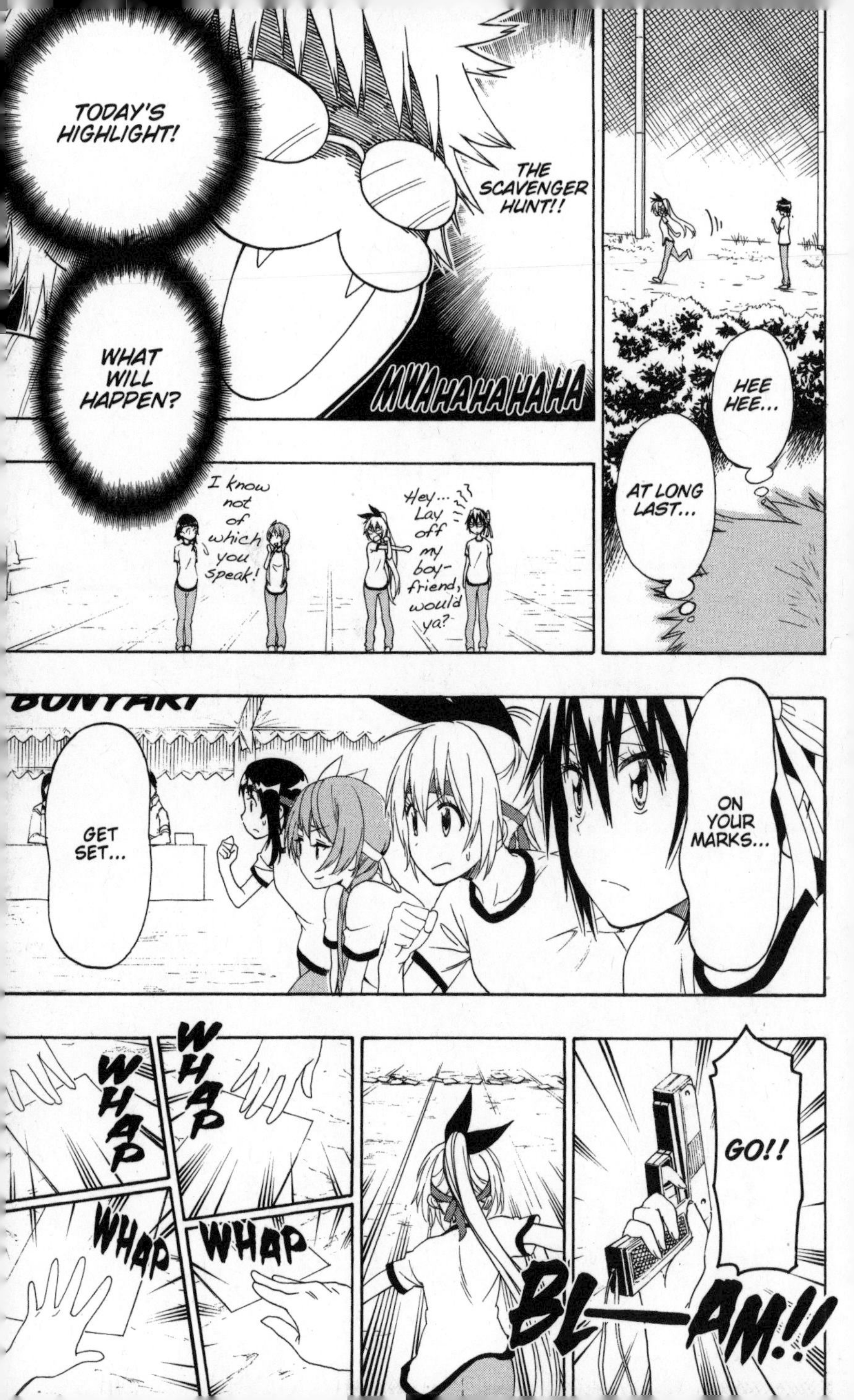
HEE HEE...
AT LONG LAST...
THE SCAVENGER HUNT!!
TODAY'S HIGHLIGHT!
WHAT WILL HAPPEN?
MWAHAHAHAHA
Hey... Lay off my boy-friend, would ya?
I know not of which you speak!
ON YOUR MARKS...
BUNTAKI
GET SET...
GO!!
BL—AM!!
WHAP
WHAP
WHAP
WHAP

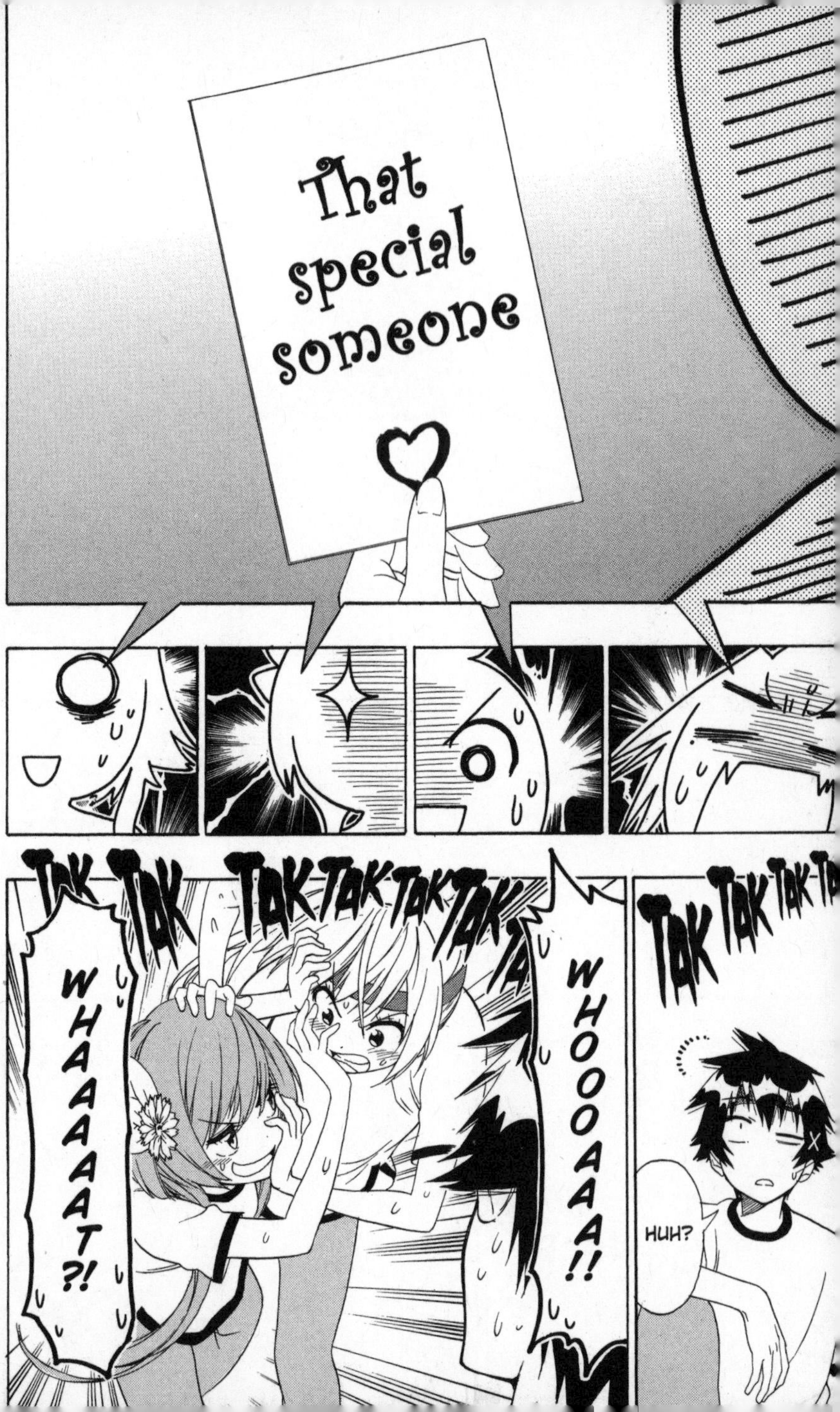
That special someone
TOK TOK TOK TOK
HUH?
TOK TOK TOK TOK TOK
WHOOOAAAA!!
WHAAAAAAT?!
TOK TOK

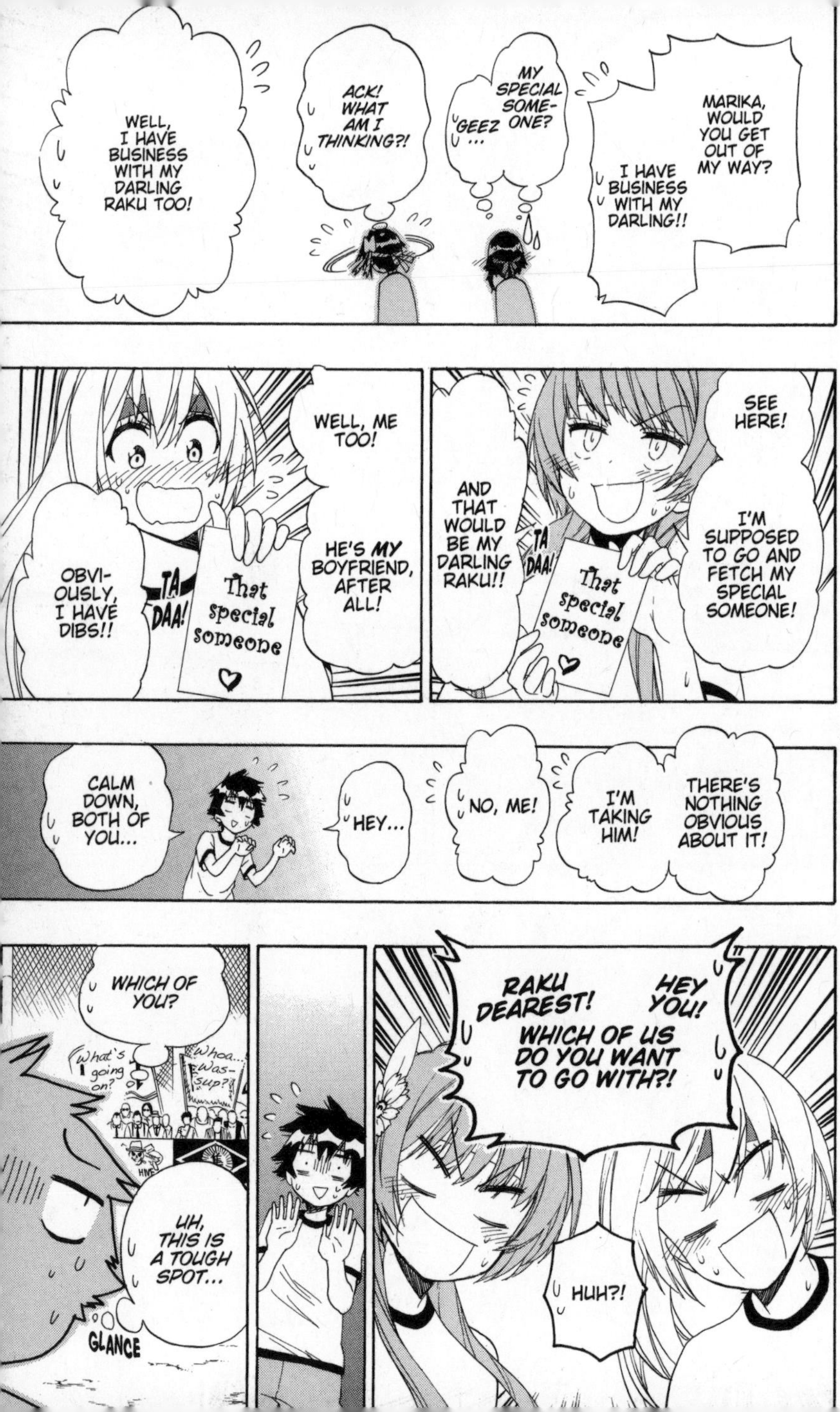
MARIKA, WOULD YOU GET OUT OF MY WAY?
I HAVE BUSINESS WITH MY DARLING!!
MY SPECIAL SOME-ONE?
GEEZ ...
ACK! WHAT AM I THINKING?!
WELL, I HAVE BUSINESS WITH MY DARLING RAKU TOO!
SEE HERE!
I'M SUPPOSED TO GO AND FETCH MY SPECIAL SOMEONE!
TA DAA!
That special someone
AND THAT WOULD BE MY DARLING RAKU!!
WELL, ME TOO!
HE'S MY BOYFRIEND, AFTER ALL!
TA DAA!
That special someone
OBVI-OUSLY, I HAVE DIBS!!
THERE'S NOTHING OBVIOUS ABOUT IT!
I'M TAKING HIM!
NO, ME!
HEY...
CALM DOWN, BOTH OF YOU...
HEY YOU!
RAKU DEAREST!
WHICH OF US DO YOU WANT TO GO WITH?!
HUH?!
WHICH OF YOU?
What's going on?
Whoa... Was-sup?
UH, THIS IS A TOUGH SPOT...
GLANCE

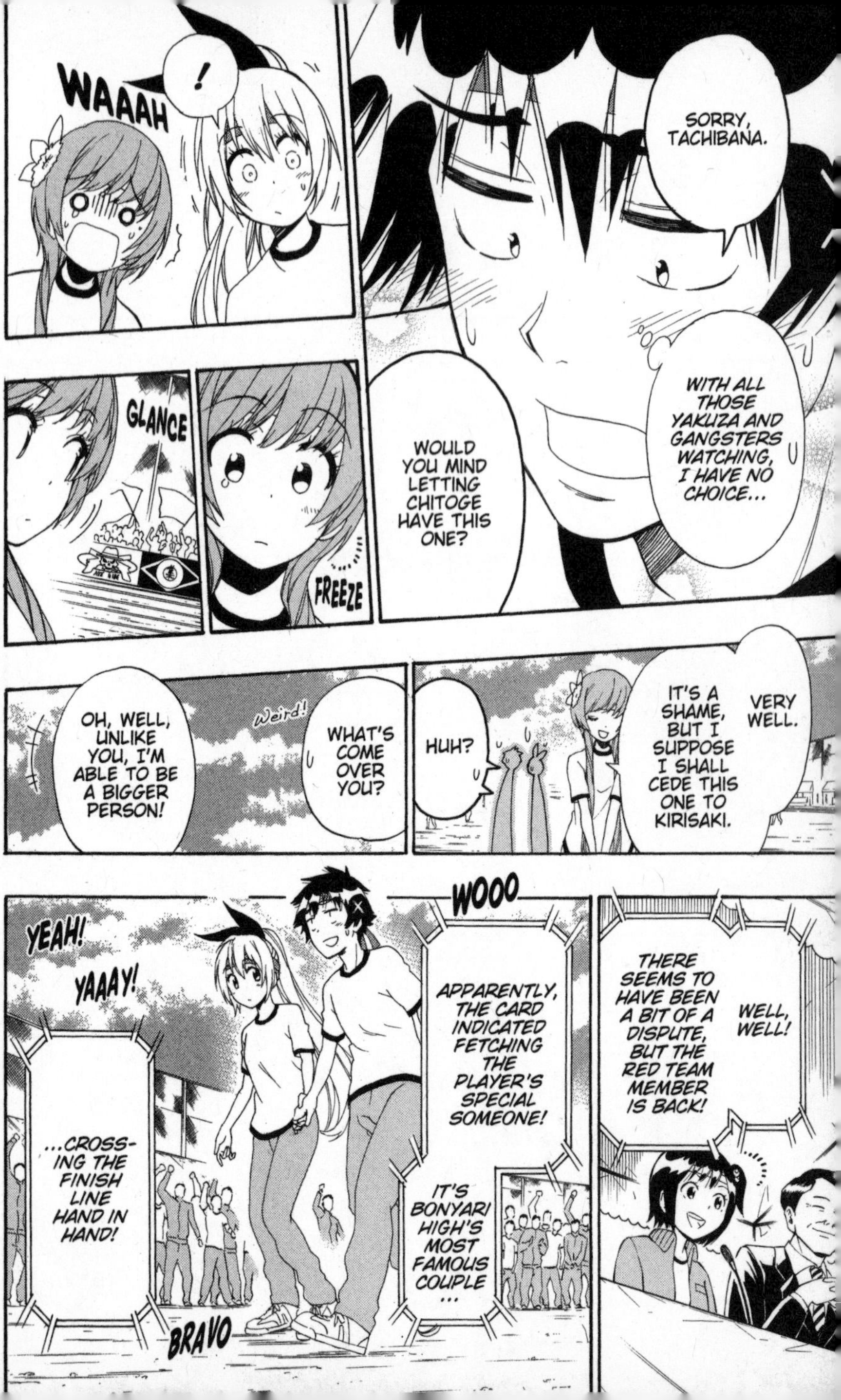
SORRY, TACHIBANA.
WITH ALL THOSE YAKUZA AND GANGSTERS WATCHING, I HAVE NO CHOICE...
WOULD YOU MIND LETTING CHITOGE HAVE THIS ONE?
!
WAAAH
FREEZE
GLANCE
VERY WELL.
IT'S A SHAME, BUT I SUPPOSE I SHALL CEDE THIS ONE TO KIRISAKI.
HUH?
WHAT'S COME OVER YOU?
Weird!
OH, WELL, UNLIKE YOU, I'M ABLE TO BE A BIGGER PERSON!
WELL, WELL!
THERE SEEMS TO HAVE BEEN A BIT OF A DISPUTE, BUT THE RED TEAM MEMBER IS BACK!
WOOO
APPARENTLY, THE CARD INDICATED FETCHING THE PLAYER'S SPECIAL SOMEONE!
IT'S BONYARI HIGH'S MOST FAMOUS COUPLE...
YEAH!
YAAAY!
...CROSSING THE FINISH LINE HAND IN HAND!
BRAVO

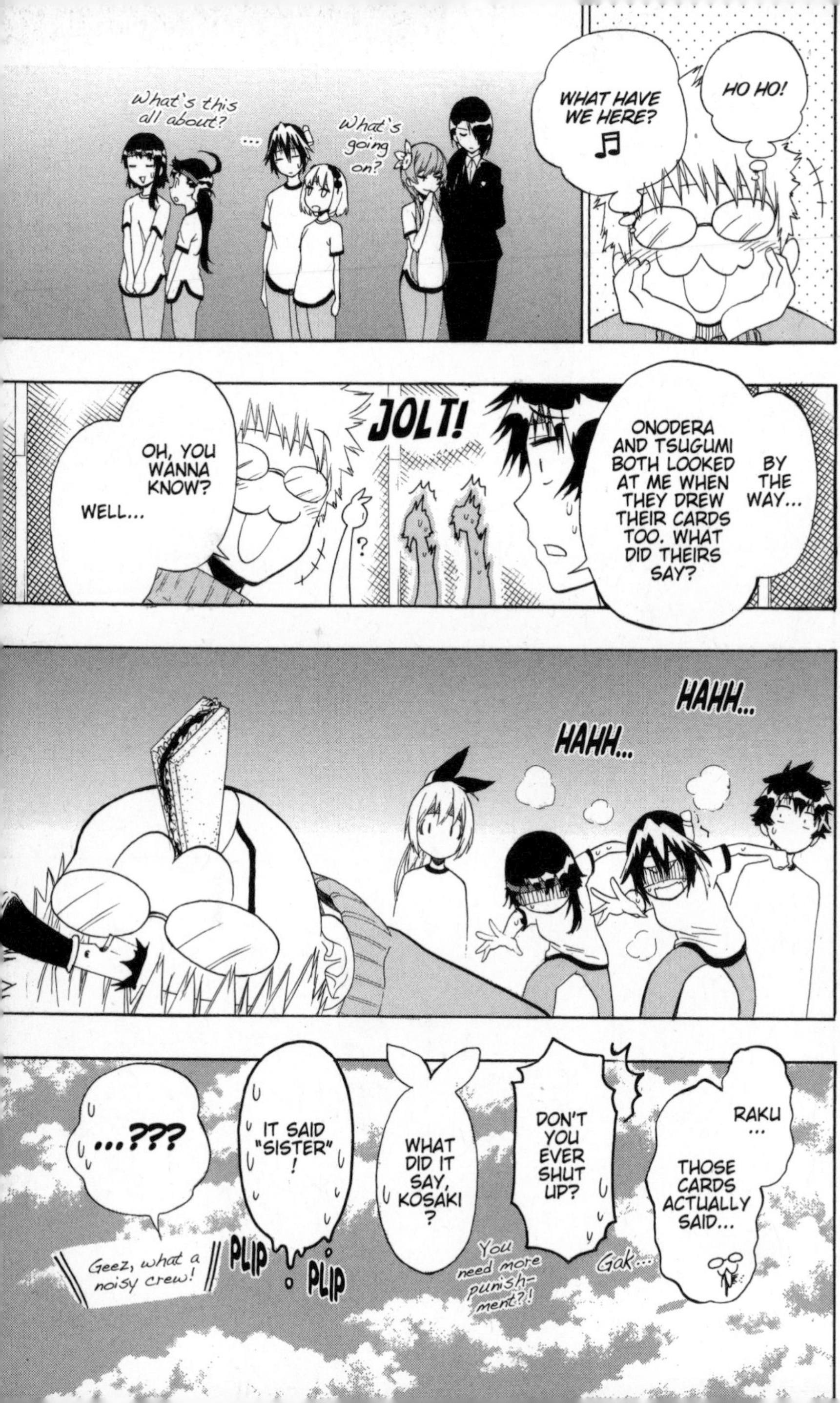
HO HO!
WHAT HAVE WE HERE? ♫
What's going on?
...
What's this all about?
BY THE WAY...
ONODERA AND TSUGUMI BOTH LOOKED AT ME WHEN THEY DREW THEIR CARDS TOO. WHAT DID THEIRS SAY?
JOLT!
?
OH, YOU WANNA KNOW?
WELL...
HAHH...
HAHH...
RAKU...
THOSE CARDS ACTUALLY SAID...
Gak...
DON'T YOU EVER SHUT UP?
You need more punish-ment?!
WHAT DID IT SAY, KOSAKI?
IT SAID "SISTER"!
PLIP
PLIP
...???
Geez, what a noisy crew!

DRIP DRIP...
BLRGG!!
W... What is this?!
It's bitter!! And spicy...?! And our...
WAAAH!!
Shu?!
You okay?!
KA-SPLUT!!
Shu's damage breakdown
9.5 : 0.5
(Onodera) (Tsugumi)

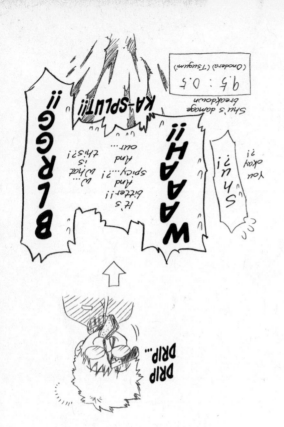

Chapter 146: Perfect

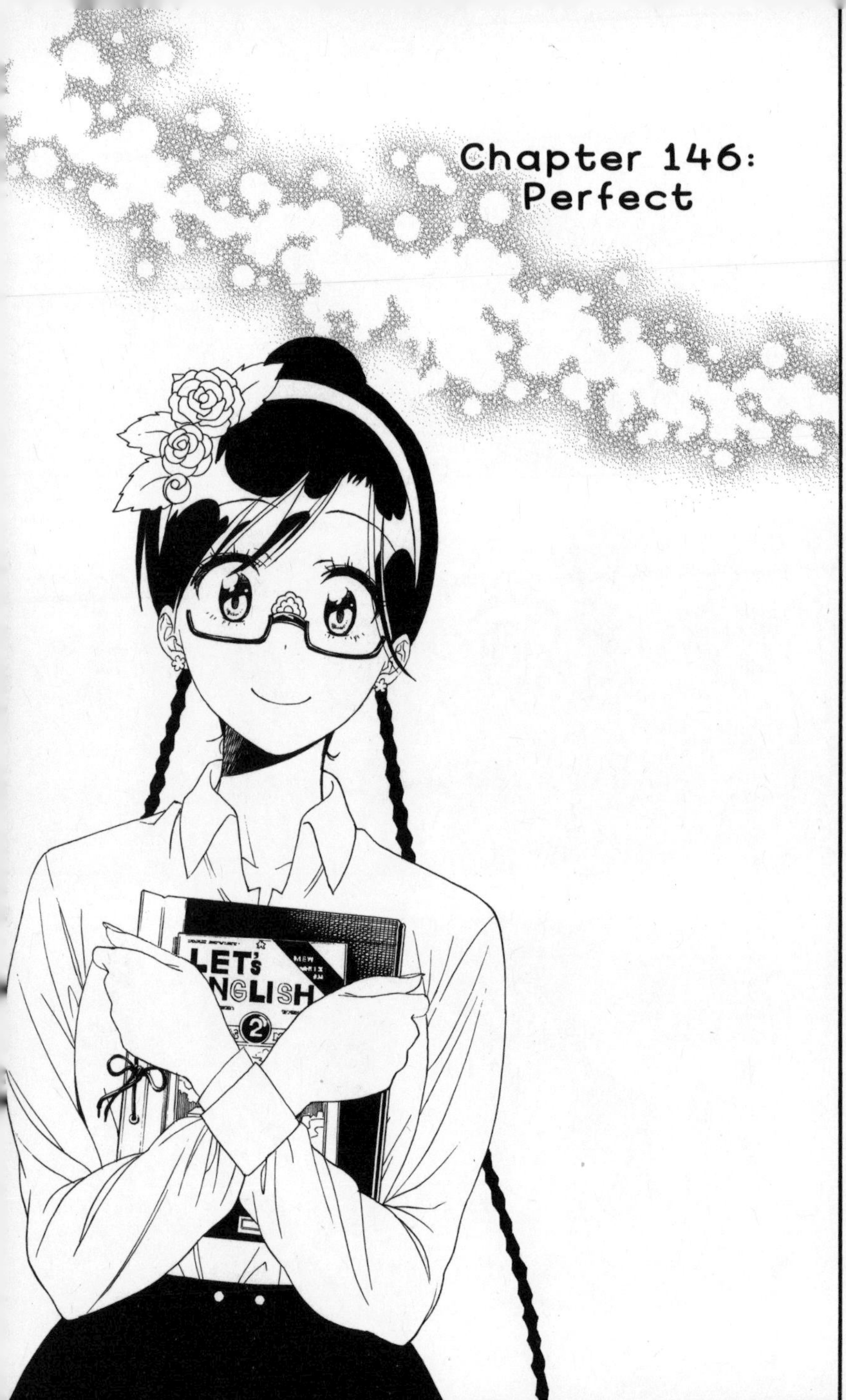
LET's
NGLISH
2

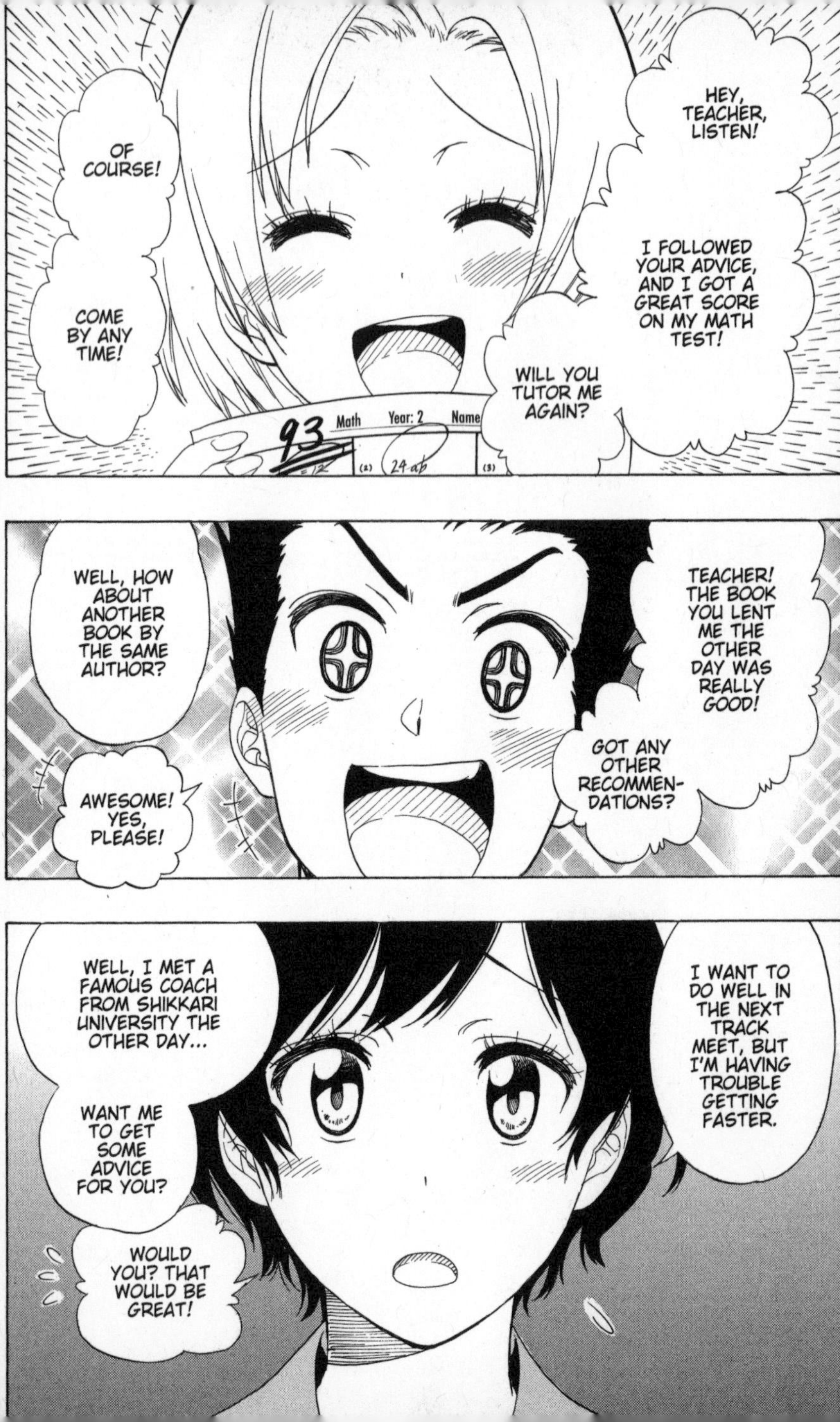
HEY, TEACHER, LISTEN!
I FOLLOWED YOUR ADVICE, AND I GOT A GREAT SCORE ON MY MATH TEST!
WILL YOU TUTOR ME AGAIN?
93 Math Year: 2 Name
OF COURSE!
COME BY ANY TIME!
TEACHER! THE BOOK YOU LENT ME THE OTHER DAY WAS REALLY GOOD!
GOT ANY OTHER RECOMMEN-DATIONS?
WELL, HOW ABOUT ANOTHER BOOK BY THE SAME AUTHOR?
AWESOME! YES, PLEASE!
I WANT TO DO WELL IN THE NEXT TRACK MEET, BUT I'M HAVING TROUBLE GETTING FASTER.
WELL, I MET A FAMOUS COACH FROM SHIKKARI UNIVERSITY THE OTHER DAY...
WANT ME TO GET SOME ADVICE FOR YOU?
WOULD YOU? THAT WOULD BE GREAT!

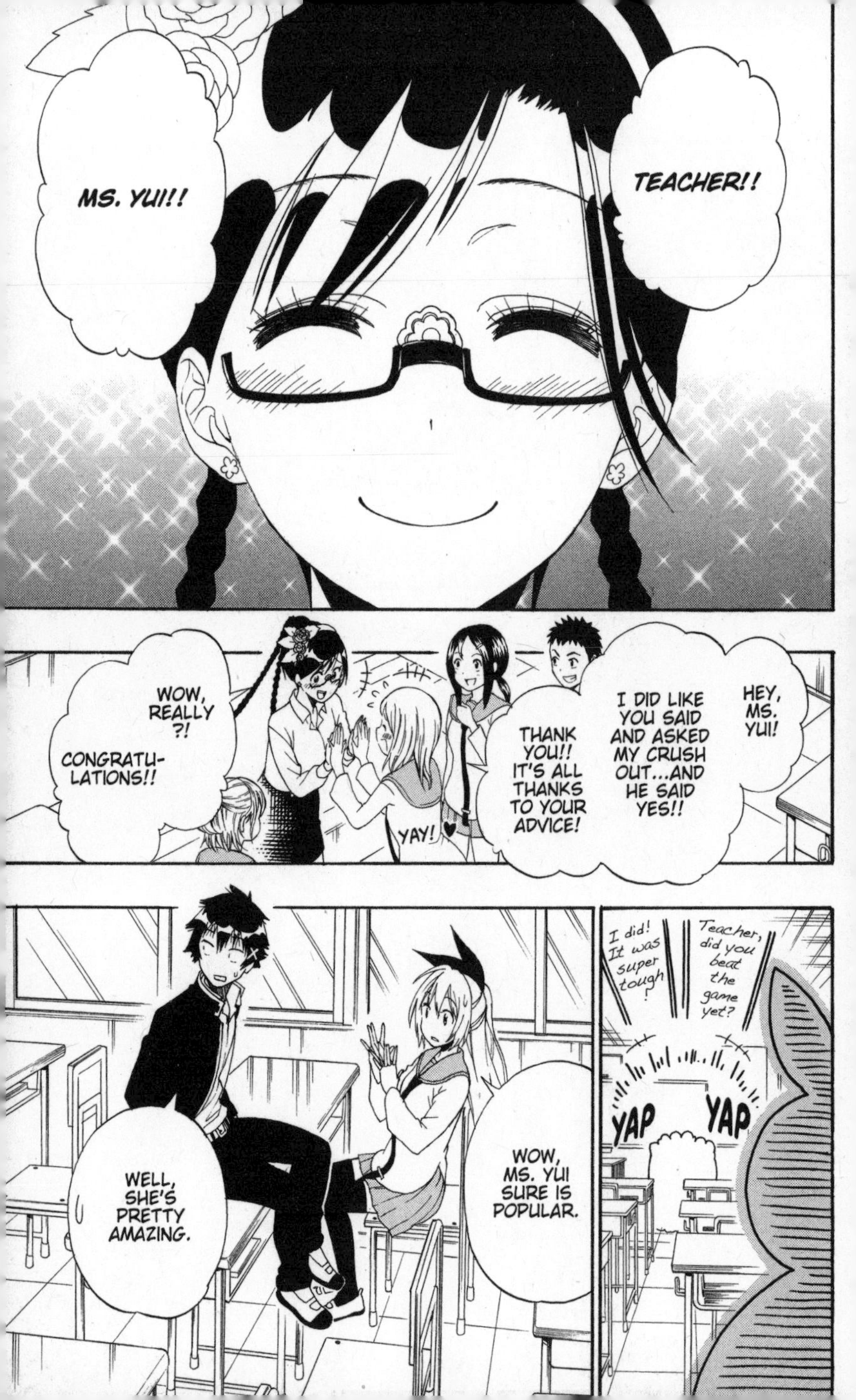
TEACHER!!
MS. YUI!!
HEY, MS. YUI!
I DID LIKE YOU SAID AND ASKED MY CRUSH OUT...AND HE SAID YES!!
THANK YOU!! IT'S ALL THANKS TO YOUR ADVICE!
YAY!
WOW, REALLY ?!
CONGRATU-LATIONS!!
Teacher, did you beat the game yet?
I did! It was super tough!
YAP YAP
WOW, MS. YUI SURE IS POPULAR.
WELL, SHE'S PRETTY AMAZING.

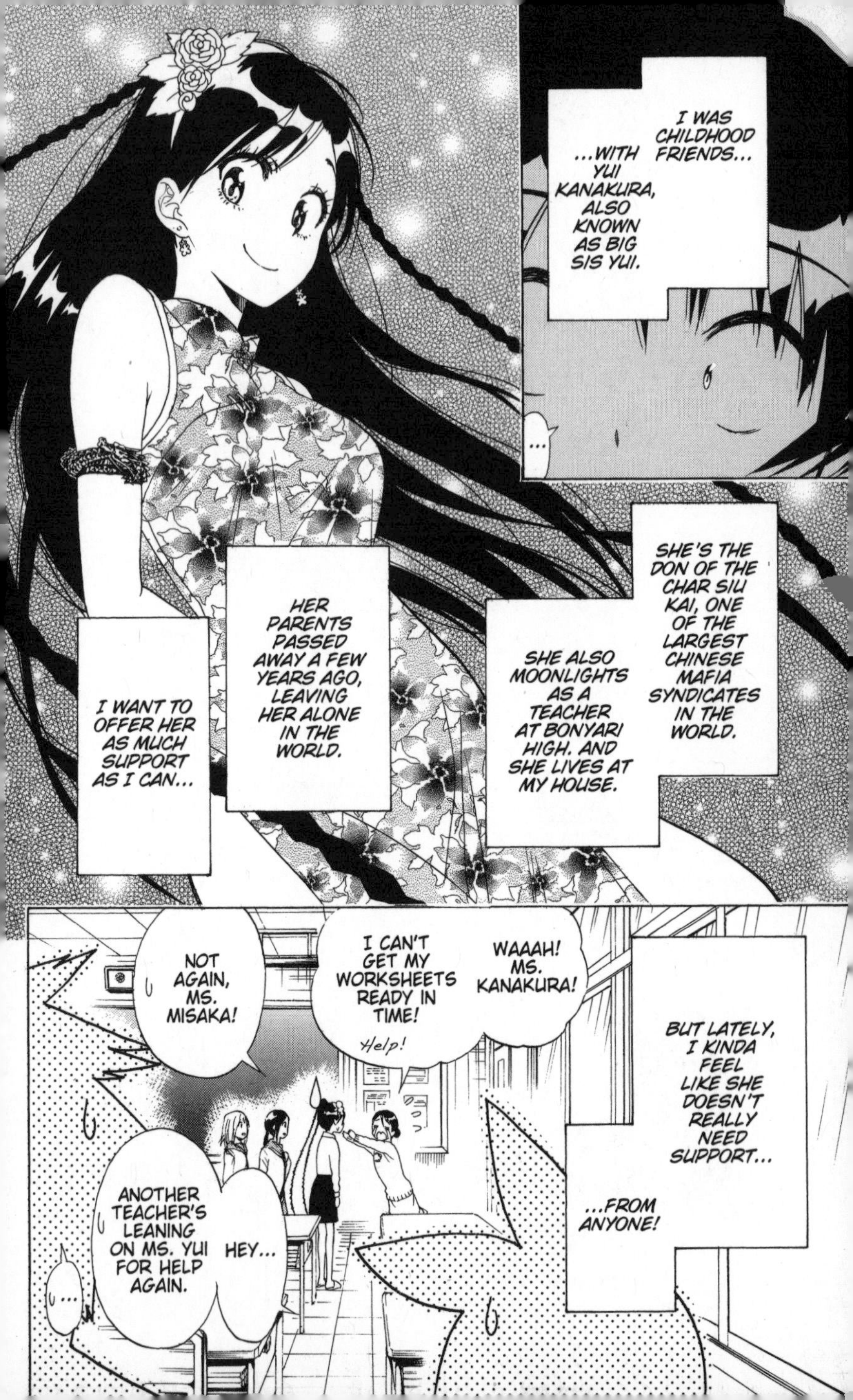
I WAS CHILDHOOD FRIENDS...
...WITH YUI KANAKURA, ALSO KNOWN AS BIG SIS YUI.
...
SHE'S THE DON OF THE CHAR SIU KAI, ONE OF THE LARGEST CHINESE MAFIA SYNDICATES IN THE WORLD.
SHE ALSO MOONLIGHTS AS A TEACHER AT BONYARI HIGH. AND SHE LIVES AT MY HOUSE.
HER PARENTS PASSED AWAY A FEW YEARS AGO, LEAVING HER ALONE IN THE WORLD.
I WANT TO OFFER HER AS MUCH SUPPORT AS I CAN...
BUT LATELY, I KINDA FEEL LIKE SHE DOESN'T REALLY NEED SUPPORT...
...FROM ANYONE!
WAAAH! MS. KANAKURA!
I CAN'T GET MY WORKSHEETS READY IN TIME!
Help!
NOT AGAIN, MS. MISAKA!
HEY...
ANOTHER TEACHER'S LEANING ON MS. YUI FOR HELP AGAIN.
...

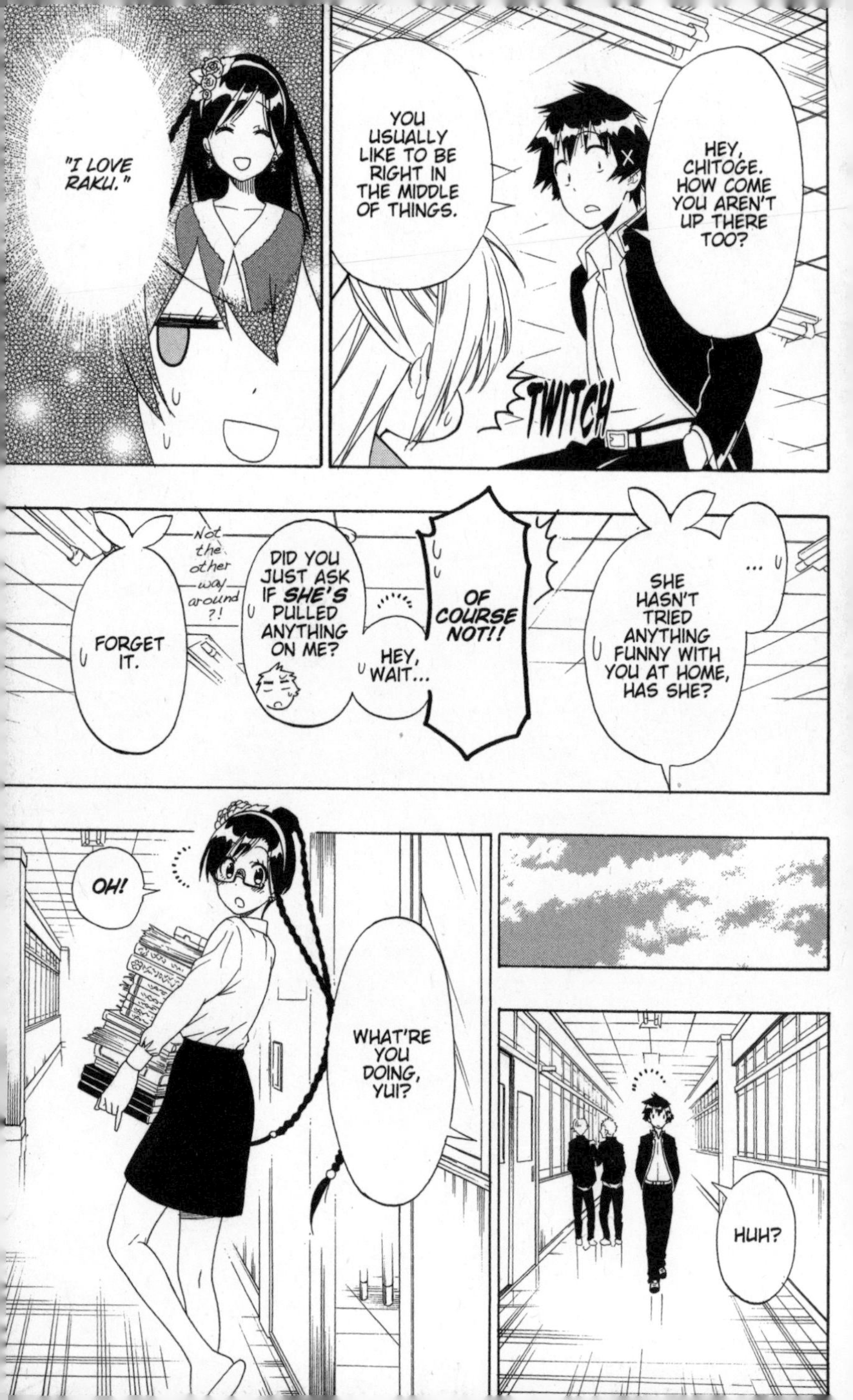
HEY, CHITOGE. HOW COME YOU AREN'T UP THERE TOO?
TWITCH
YOU USUALLY LIKE TO BE RIGHT IN THE MIDDLE OF THINGS.
"I LOVE RAKU."
...
SHE HASN'T TRIED ANYTHING FUNNY WITH YOU AT HOME, HAS SHE?
OF COURSE NOT!!
HEY, WAIT...
DID YOU JUST ASK IF SHE'S PULLED ANYTHING ON ME?
Not the other way around?!
FORGET IT.
HUH?
WHAT'RE YOU DOING, YUI?
OH!

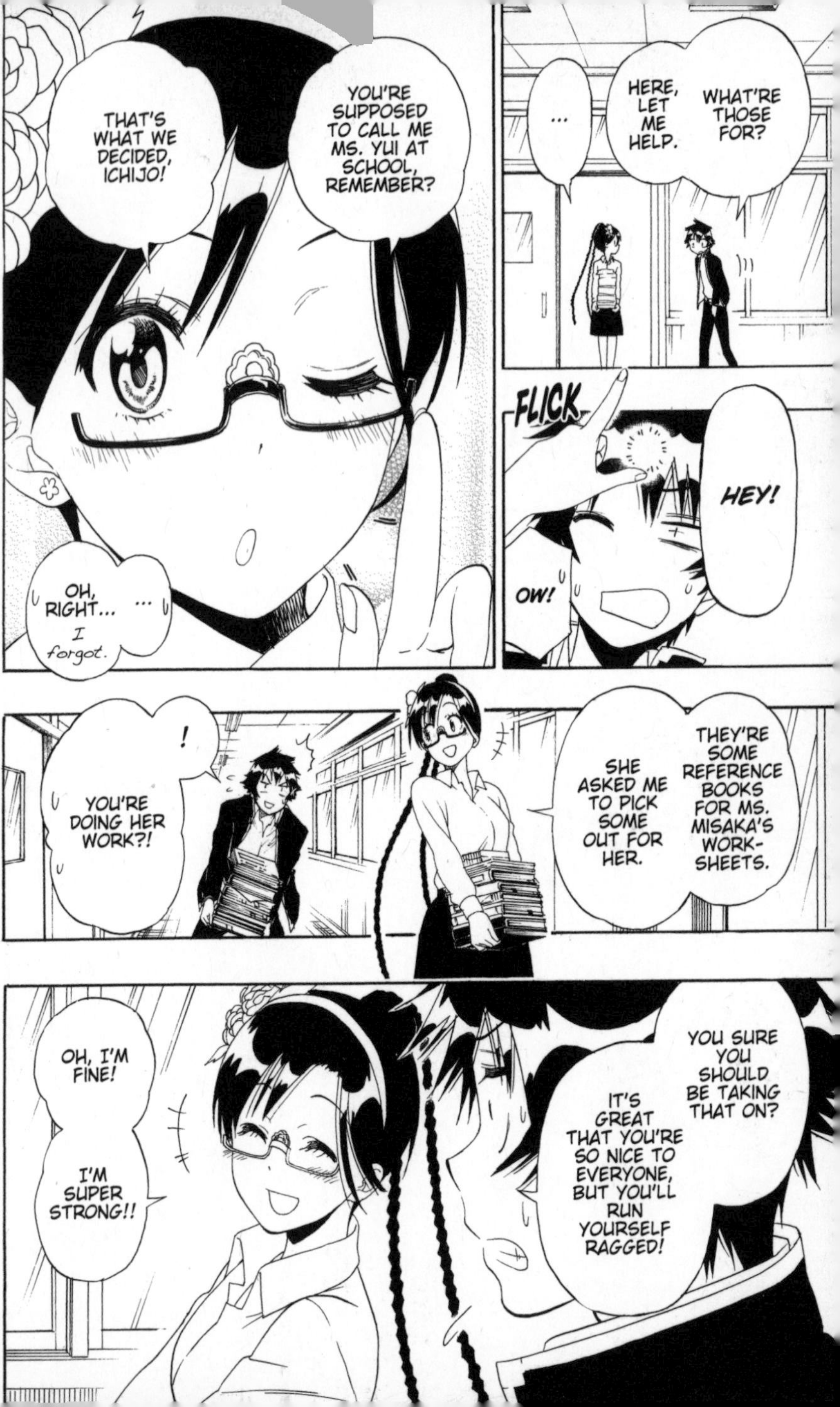
WHAT'RE THOSE FOR?
HERE, LET ME HELP.
...
FLICK
HEY!
OW!
YOU'RE SUPPOSED TO CALL ME MS. YUI AT SCHOOL, REMEMBER?
THAT'S WHAT WE DECIDED, ICHIJO!
OH, RIGHT... I forgot.
...
THEY'RE SOME REFERENCE BOOKS FOR MS. MISAKA'S WORK-SHEETS.
SHE ASKED ME TO PICK SOME OUT FOR HER.
!
YOU'RE DOING HER WORK?!
YOU SURE YOU SHOULD BE TAKING THAT ON?
IT'S GREAT THAT YOU'RE SO NICE TO EVERYONE, BUT YOU'LL RUN YOURSELF RAGGED!
OH, I'M FINE!
I'M SUPER STRONG!!

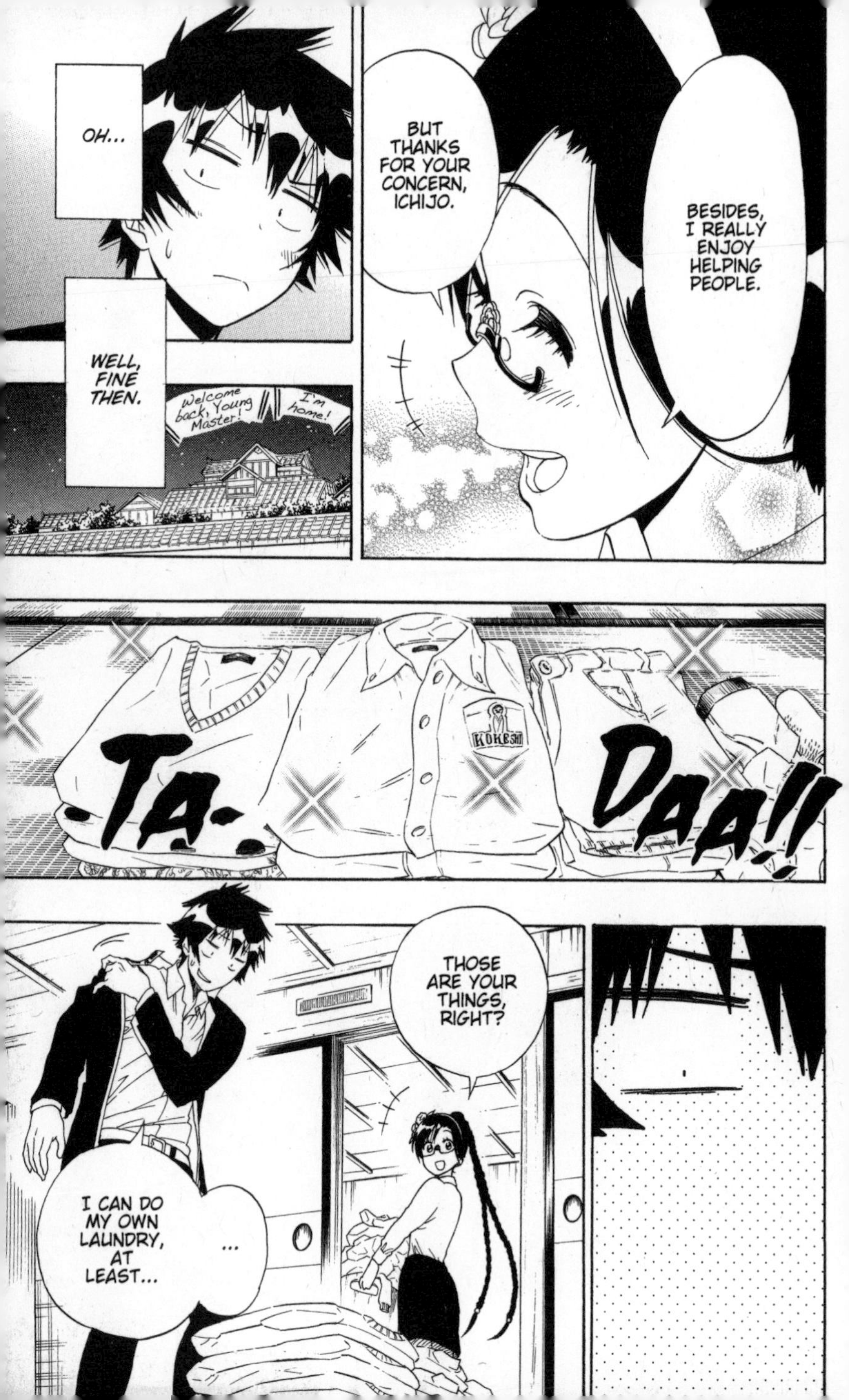
BESIDES, I REALLY ENJOY HELPING PEOPLE.
BUT THANKS FOR YOUR CONCERN, ICHIJO.
OH...
WELL, FINE THEN.
I'm home!
Welcome back, Young Master!
TA-
KOKESHI
DAA!!
...
THOSE ARE YOUR THINGS, RIGHT?
I CAN DO MY OWN LAUNDRY, AT LEAST...

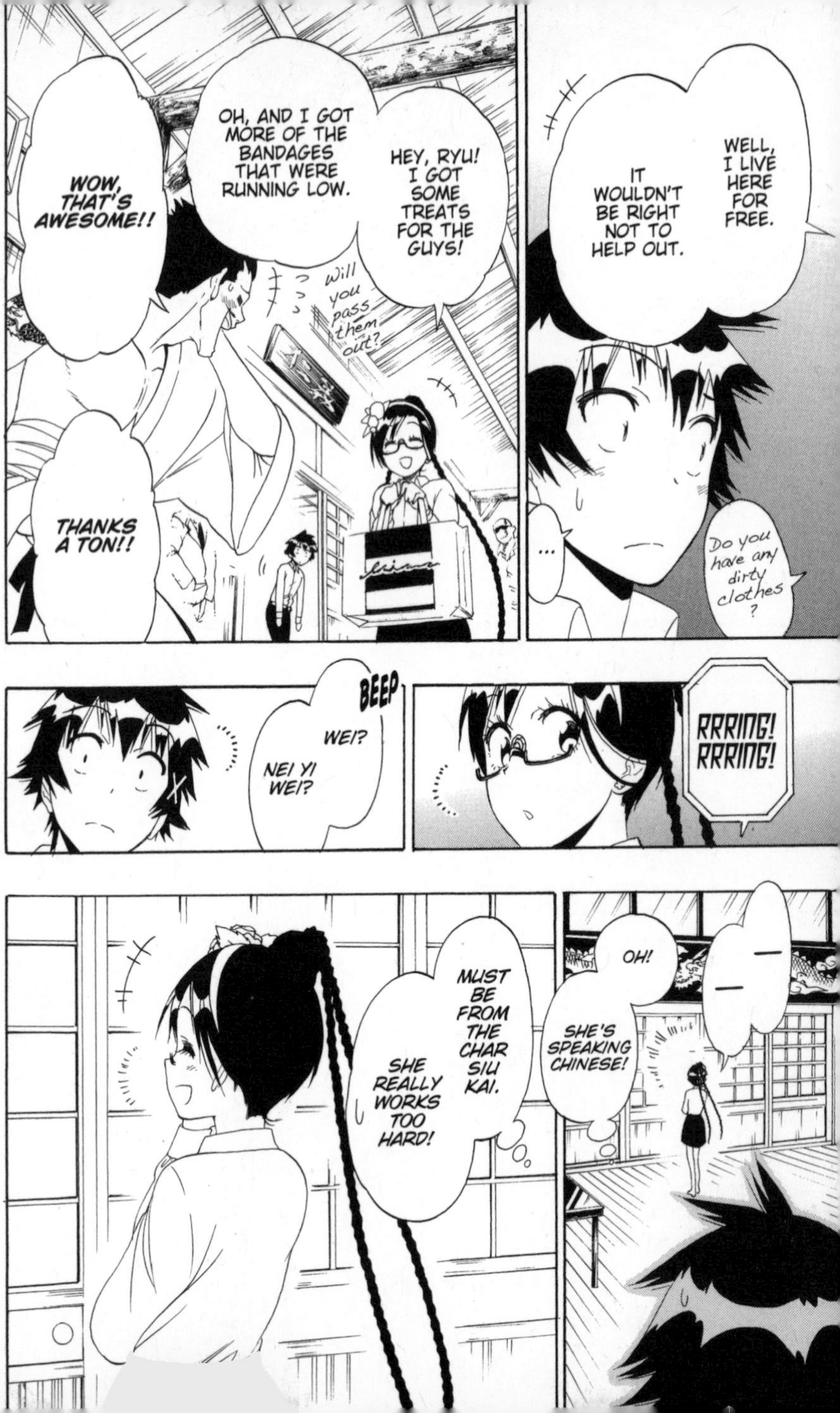
WELL, I LIVE HERE FOR FREE.
IT WOULDN'T BE RIGHT NOT TO HELP OUT.
Do you have any dirty clothes?
...
HEY, RYU! I GOT SOME TREATS FOR THE GUYS!
Will you pass them out?
OH, AND I GOT MORE OF THE BANDAGES THAT WERE RUNNING LOW.
WOW, THAT'S AWESOME!!
THANKS A TON!!
RRRING! RRRING!
BEEP
WEI?
NEI YI WEI?
OH!
SHE'S SPEAKING CHINESE!
—
MUST BE FROM THE CHAR SIU KAI.
SHE REALLY WORKS TOO HARD!

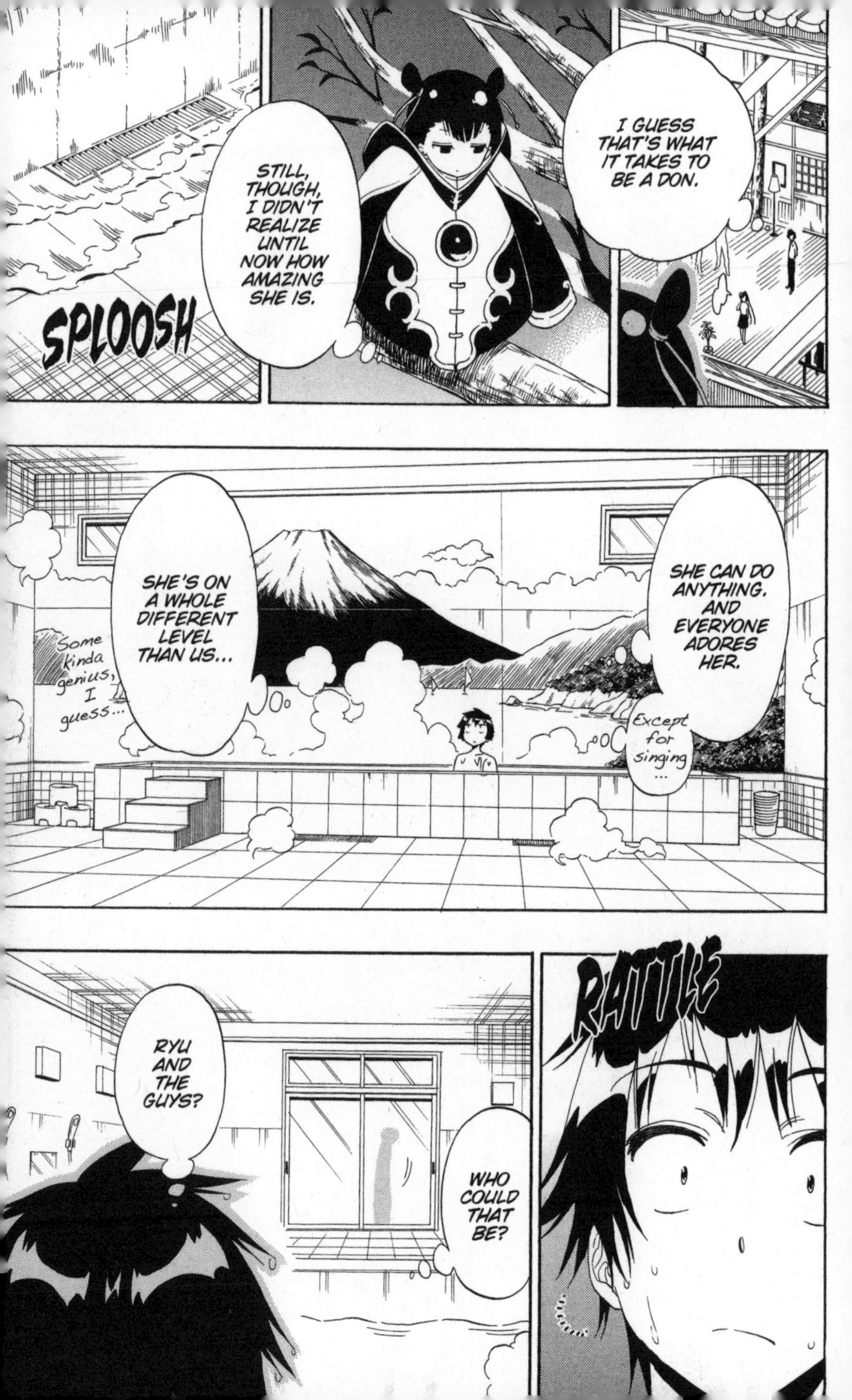
I GUESS THAT'S WHAT IT TAKES TO BE A DON.
STILL, THOUGH, I DIDN'T REALIZE UNTIL NOW HOW AMAZING SHE IS.
SPLOOSH
SHE CAN DO ANYTHING. AND EVERYONE ADORES HER.
Except for singing...
SHE'S ON A WHOLE DIFFERENT LEVEL THAN US...
Some kinda genius, I guess...
RATTLE
WHO COULD THAT BE?
RYU AND THE GUYS?

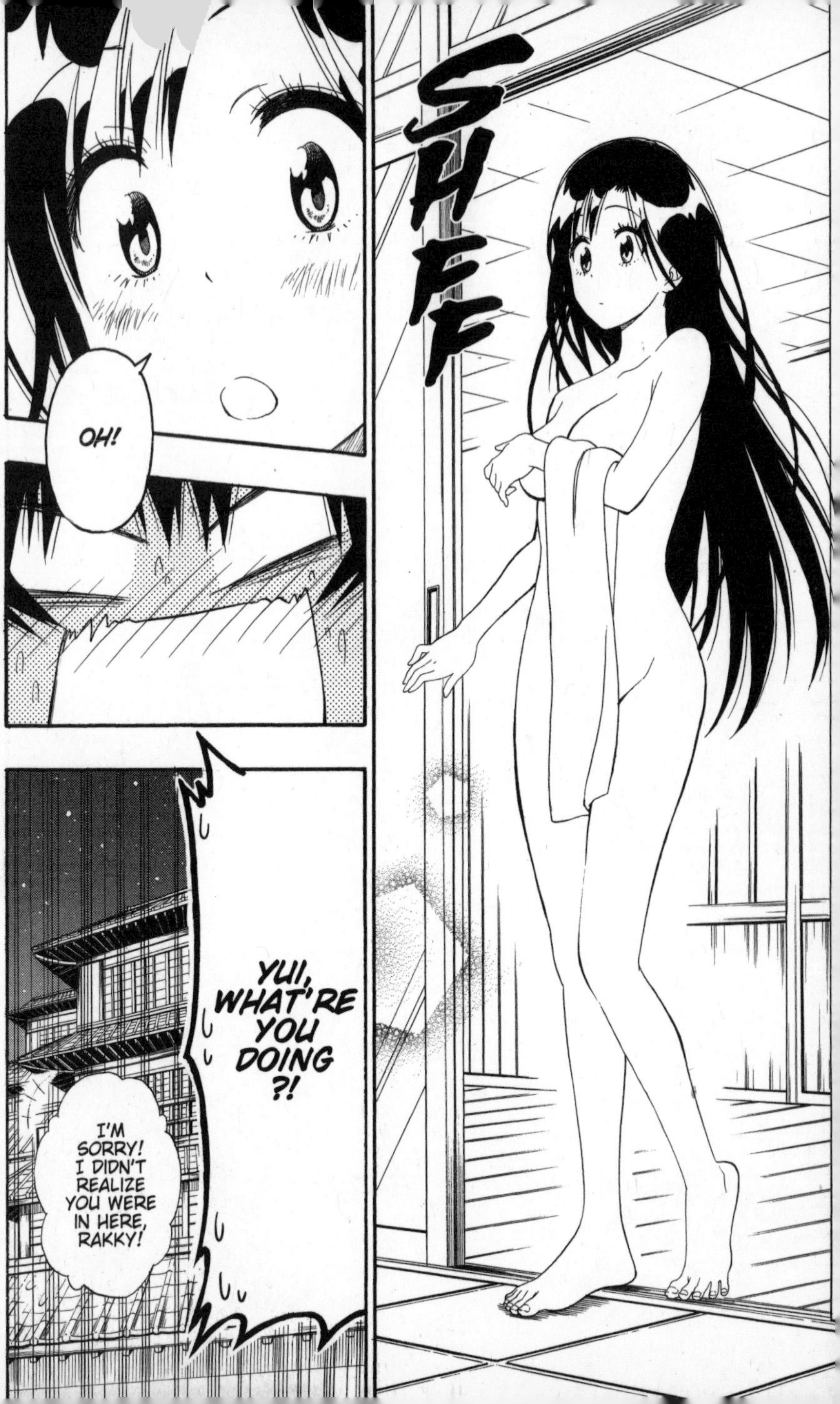
SHFF
OH!
YUI, WHAT'RE YOU DOING ?!
I'M SORRY! I DIDN'T REALIZE YOU WERE IN HERE, RAKKY!

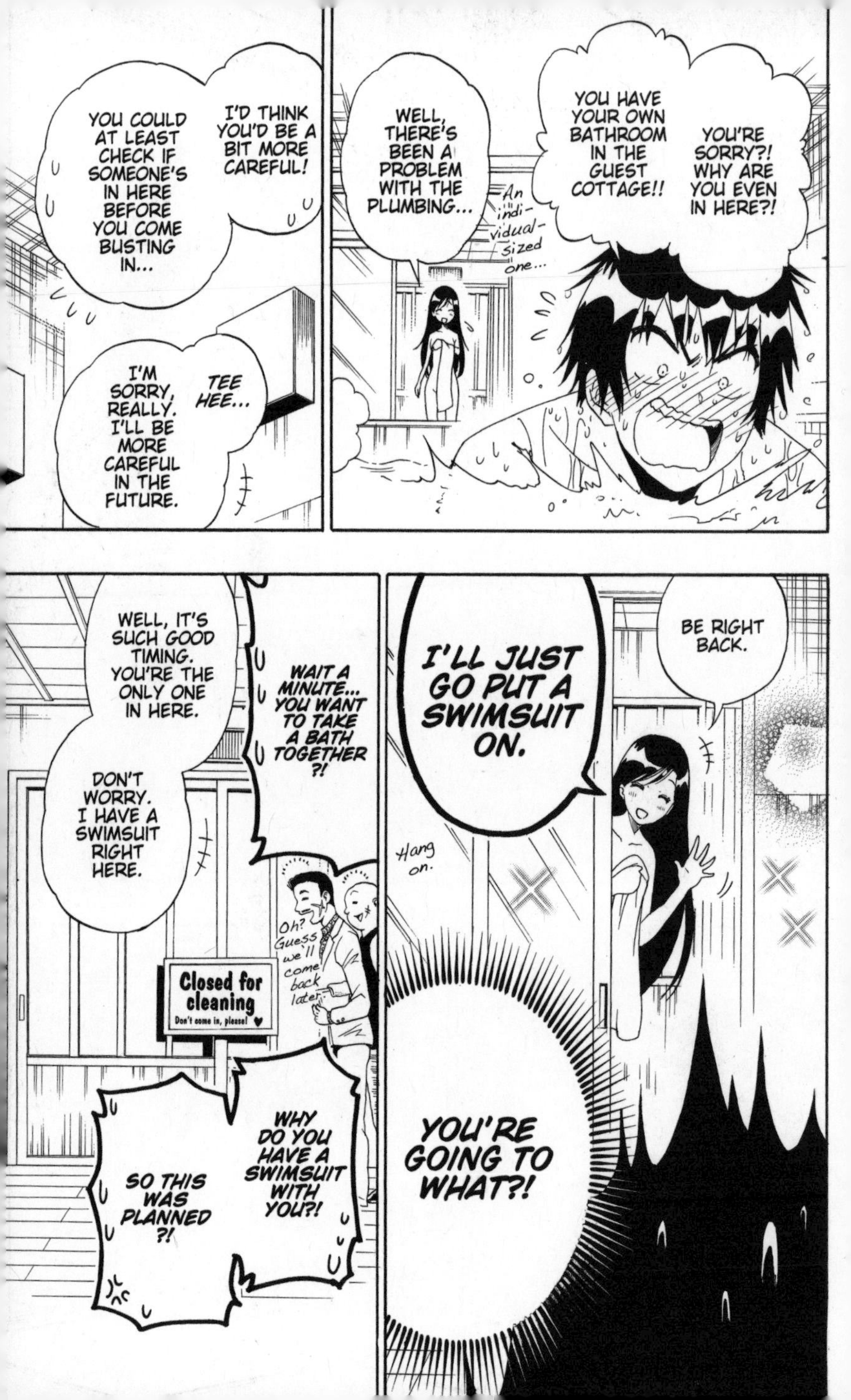
YOU HAVE YOUR OWN BATHROOM IN THE GUEST COTTAGE!!
YOU'RE SORRY?! WHY ARE YOU EVEN IN HERE?!
WELL, THERE'S BEEN A PROBLEM WITH THE PLUMBING...
An indi-vidual-sized one...
I'D THINK YOU'D BE A BIT MORE CAREFUL!
YOU COULD AT LEAST CHECK IF SOMEONE'S IN HERE BEFORE YOU COME BUSTING IN...
TEE HEE...
I'M SORRY, REALLY. I'LL BE MORE CAREFUL IN THE FUTURE.
BE RIGHT BACK.
I'LL JUST GO PUT A SWIMSUIT ON.
Hang on.
YOU'RE GOING TO WHAT?!
WAIT A MINUTE... YOU WANT TO TAKE A BATH TOGETHER?!
WELL, IT'S SUCH GOOD TIMING. YOU'RE THE ONLY ONE IN HERE.
DON'T WORRY. I HAVE A SWIMSUIT RIGHT HERE.
Oh? Guess we'll come back later.
Closed for cleaning
Don't come in, please!
WHY DO YOU HAVE A SWIMSUIT WITH YOU?!
SO THIS WAS PLANNED?!

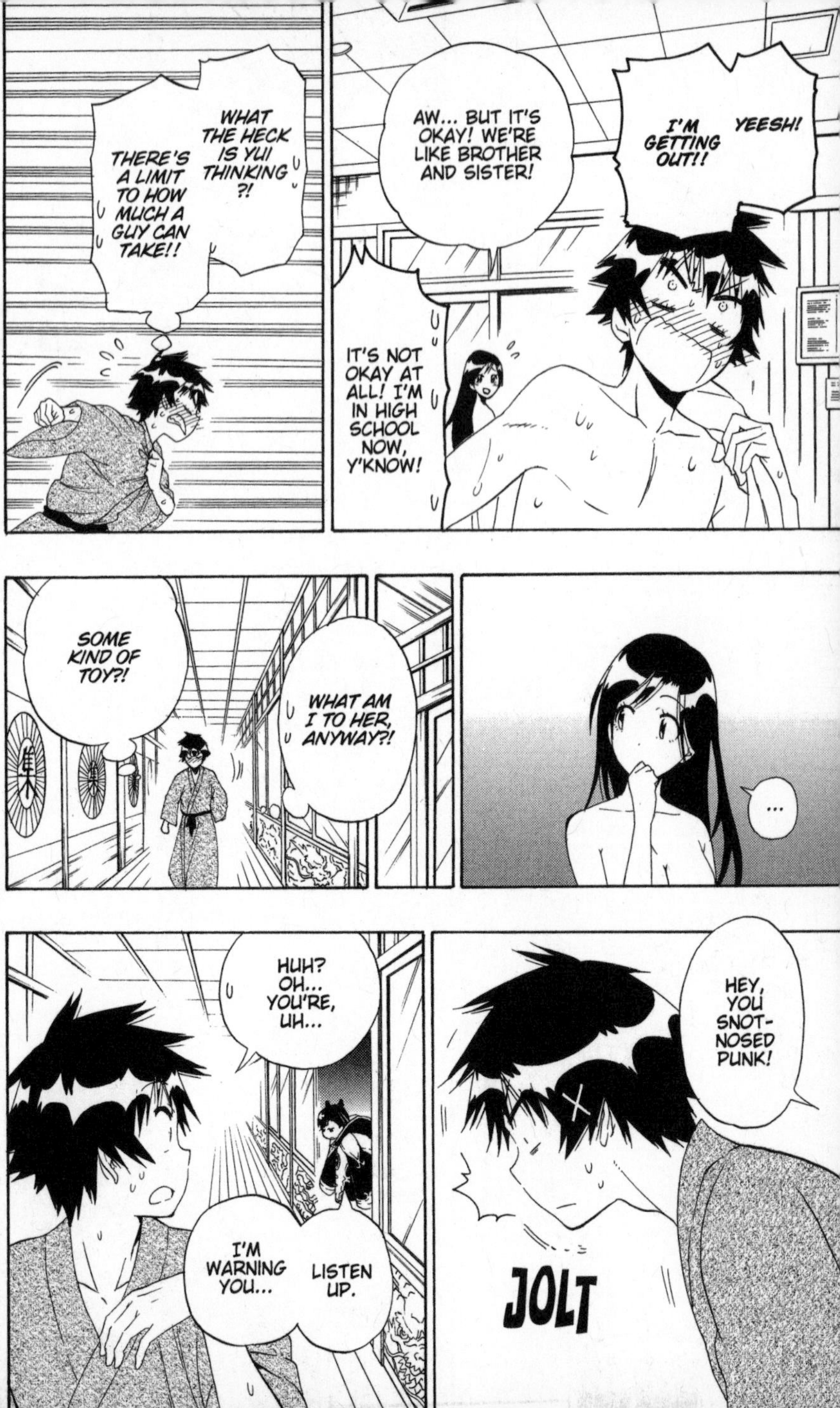
I'M GETTING OUT!!
YEESH!
AW... BUT IT'S OKAY! WE'RE LIKE BROTHER AND SISTER!
IT'S NOT OKAY AT ALL! I'M IN HIGH SCHOOL NOW, Y'KNOW!
WHAT THE HECK IS YUI THINKING?!
THERE'S A LIMIT TO HOW MUCH A GUY CAN TAKE!!
...
WHAT AM I TO HER, ANYWAY?!
SOME KIND OF TOY?!
HEY, YOU SNOT-NOSED PUNK!
JOLT
HUH? OH... YOU'RE, UH...
LISTEN UP.
I'M WARNING YOU...

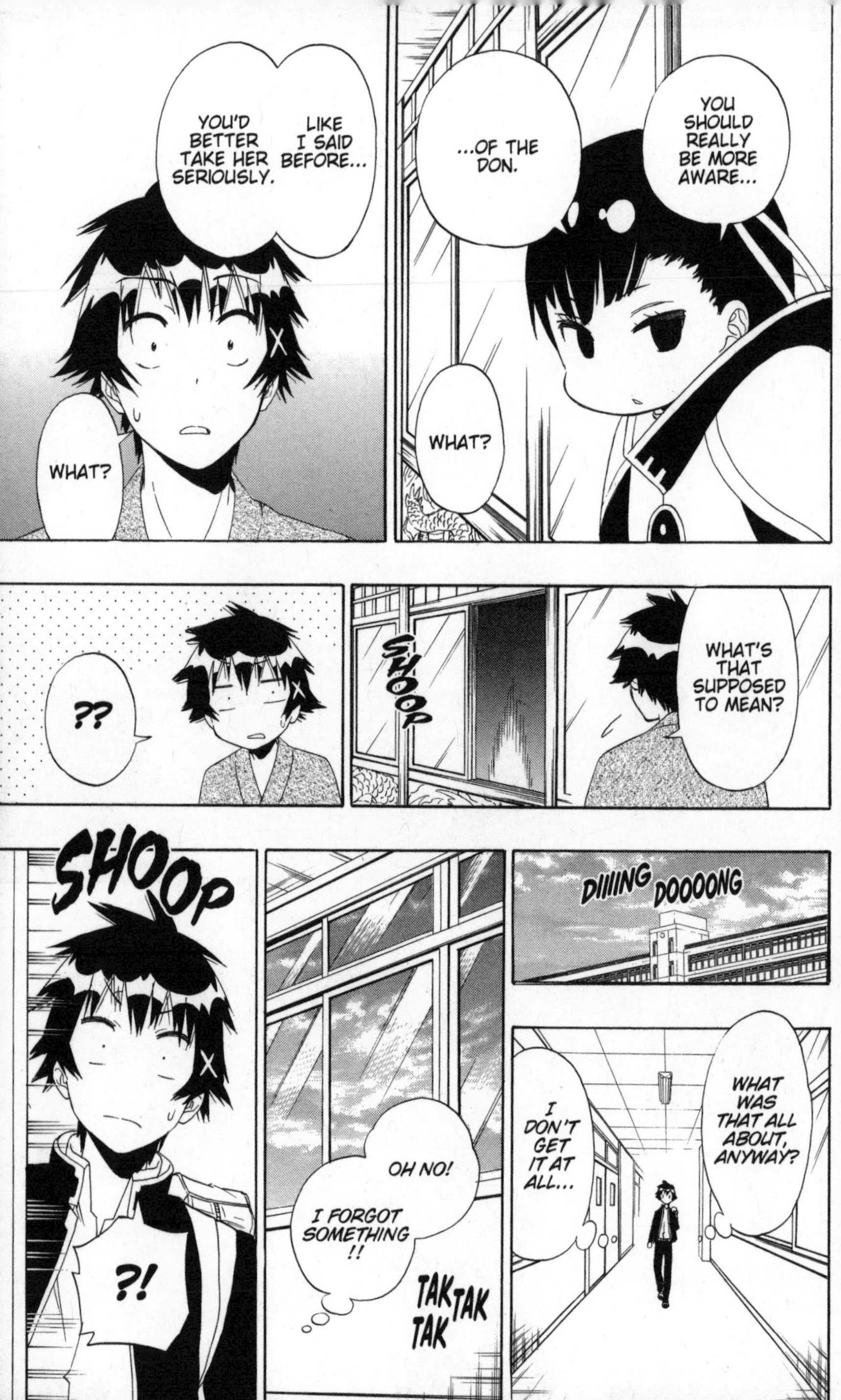
YOU SHOULD REALLY BE MORE AWARE...
...OF THE DON.
WHAT?
LIKE I SAID BEFORE...
YOU'D BETTER TAKE HER SERIOUSLY.
WHAT?
WHAT'S THAT SUPPOSED TO MEAN?
SHOOP
??
DIIIING DOOOONG
WHAT WAS THAT ALL ABOUT, ANYWAY?
I DON'T GET IT AT ALL...
OH NO!
I FORGOT SOMETHING !!
TAK TAK TAK
SHOOP
?!

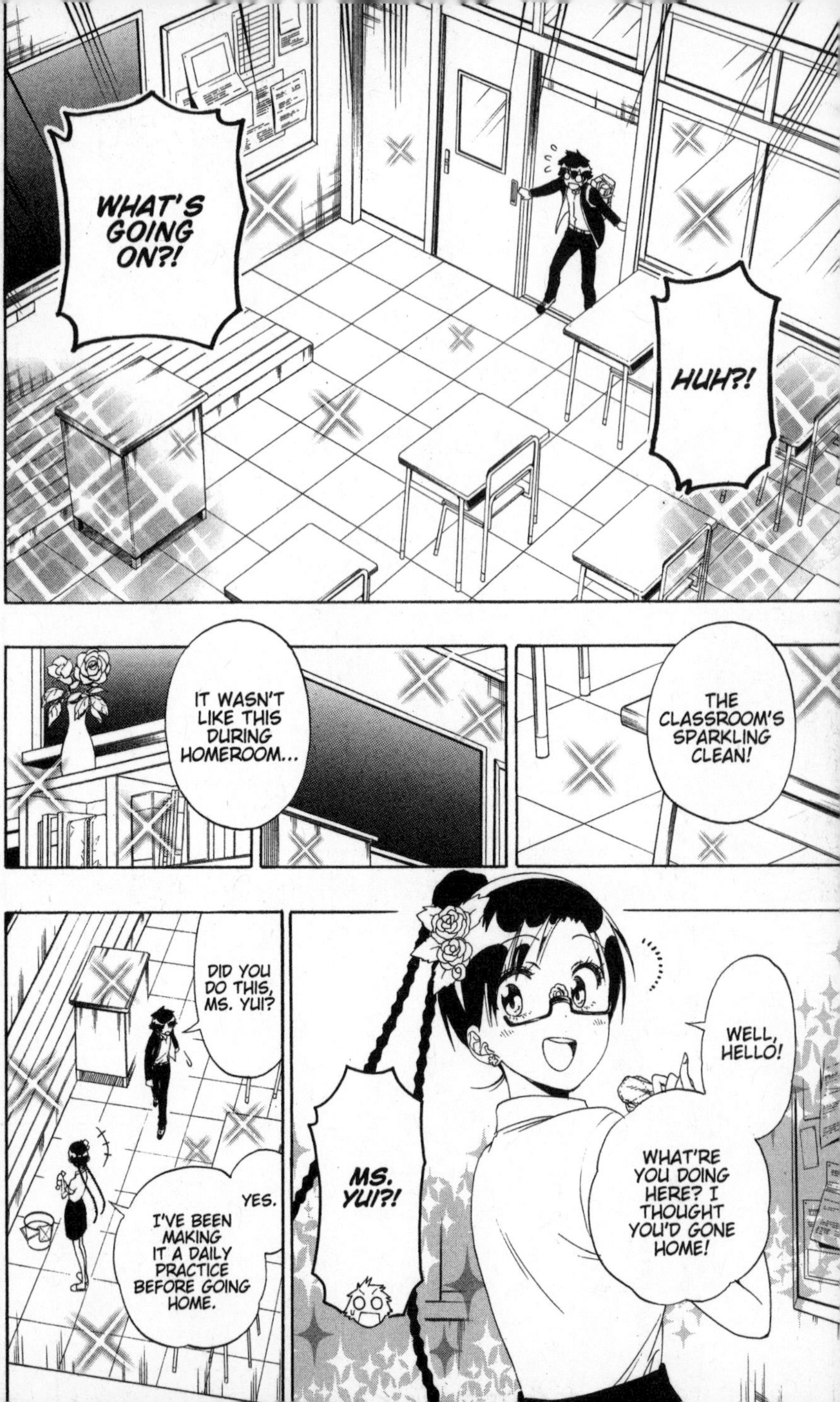
HUH?!
WHAT'S GOING ON?!
THE CLASSROOM'S SPARKLING CLEAN!
IT WASN'T LIKE THIS DURING HOMEROOM...
WELL, HELLO!
WHAT'RE YOU DOING HERE? I THOUGHT YOU'D GONE HOME!
MS. YUI?!
DID YOU DO THIS, MS. YUI?
YES.
I'VE BEEN MAKING IT A DAILY PRACTICE BEFORE GOING HOME.

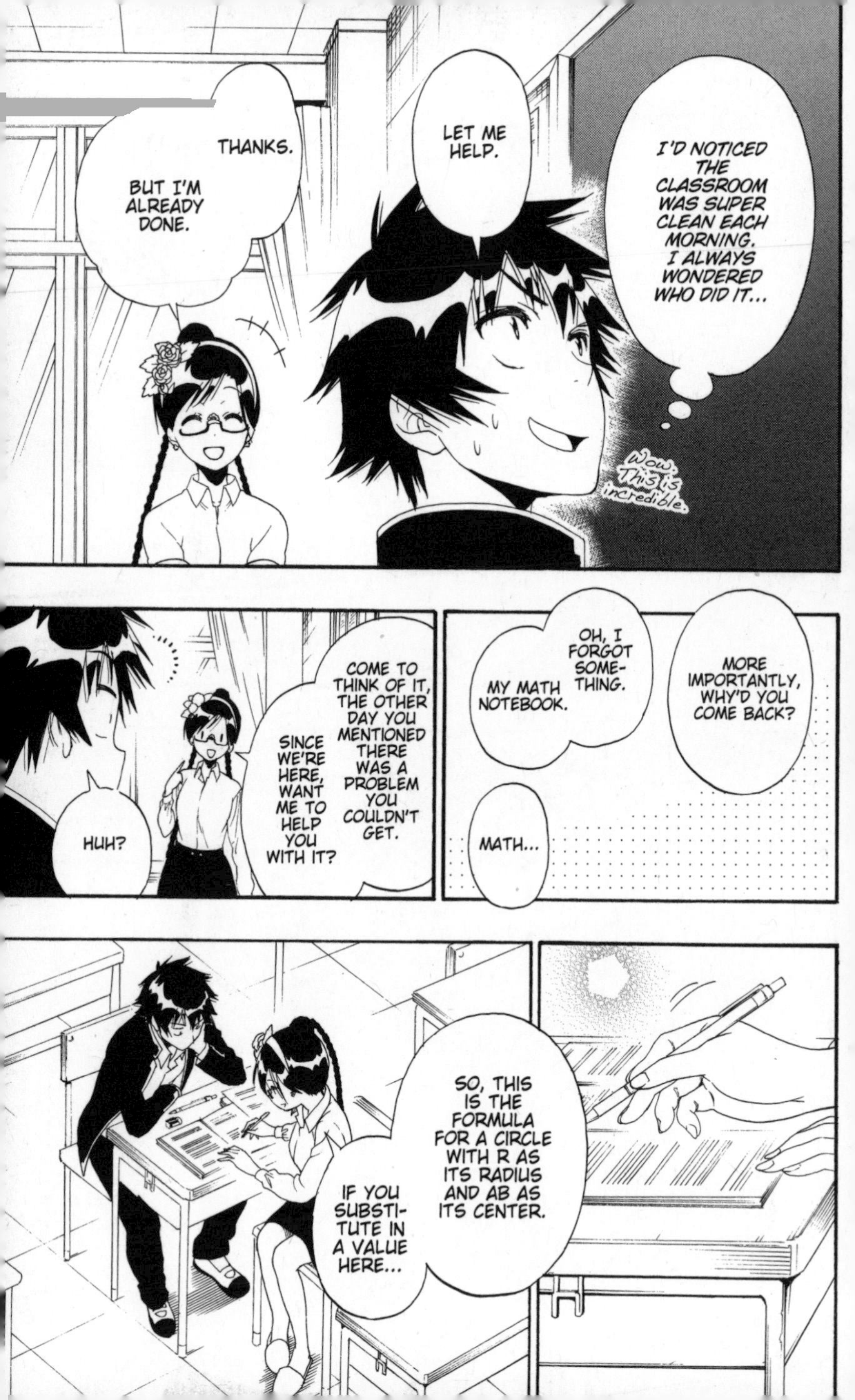
I'D NOTICED THE CLASSROOM WAS SUPER CLEAN EACH MORNING. I ALWAYS WONDERED WHO DID IT...
LET ME HELP.
THANKS.
BUT I'M ALREADY DONE.
Wow. This is incredible.
MORE IMPORTANTLY, WHY'D YOU COME BACK?
OH, I FORGOT SOME-THING.
MY MATH NOTEBOOK.
MATH...
COME TO THINK OF IT, THE OTHER DAY YOU MENTIONED THERE WAS A PROBLEM YOU COULDN'T GET.
SINCE WE'RE HERE, WANT ME TO HELP YOU WITH IT?
HUH?
SO, THIS IS THE FORMULA FOR A CIRCLE WITH R AS ITS RADIUS AND AB AS ITS CENTER.
IF YOU SUBSTI-TUTE IN A VALUE HERE...

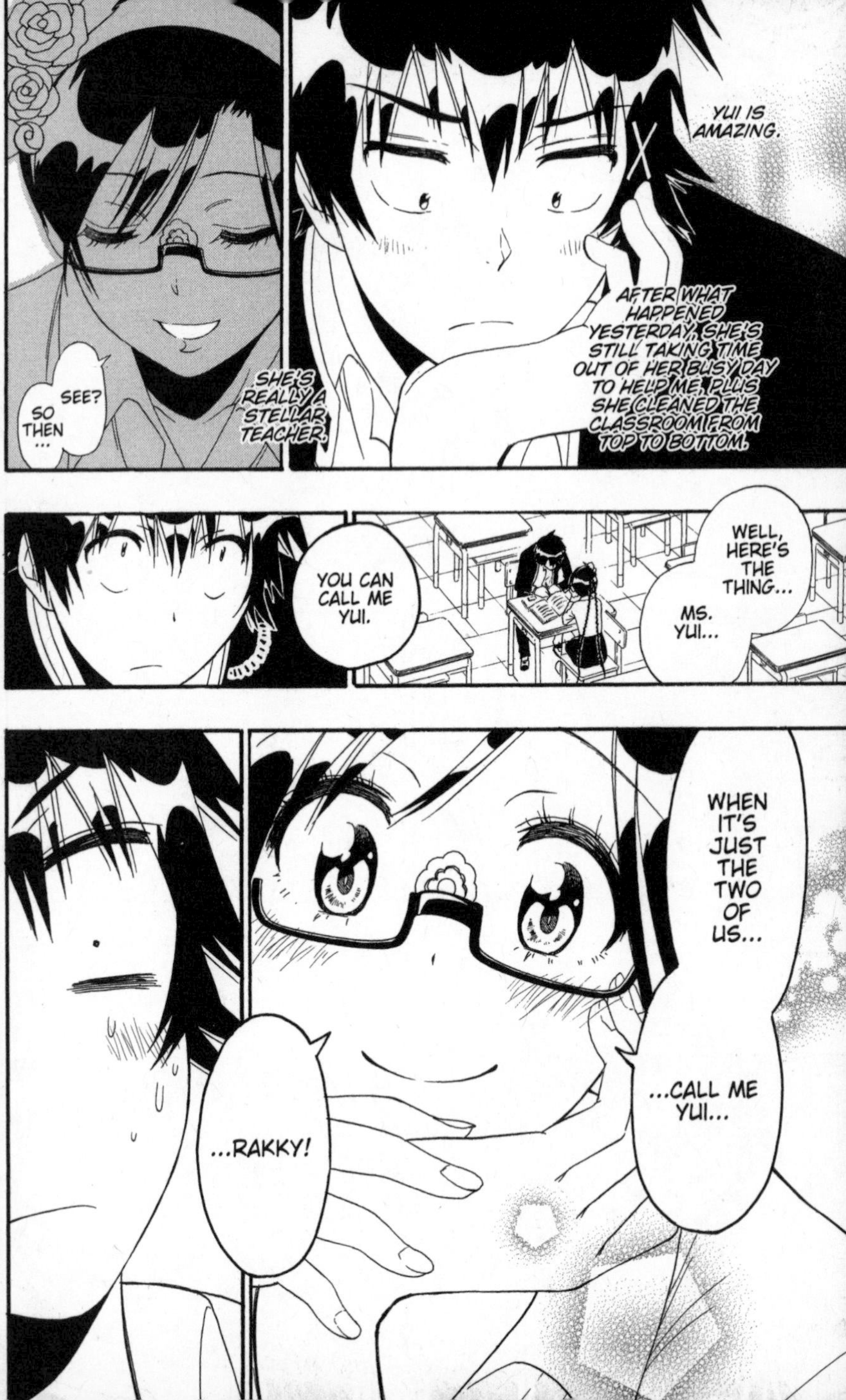
YUI IS AMAZING.
AFTER WHAT HAPPENED YESTERDAY, SHE'S STILL TAKING TIME OUT OF HER BUSY DAY TO HELP ME, PLUS SHE CLEANED THE CLASSROOM FROM TOP TO BOTTOM.
SHE'S REALLY A STELLAR TEACHER.
SEE? SO THEN ...
WELL, HERE'S THE THING...
MS. YUI...
YOU CAN CALL ME YUI.
WHEN IT'S JUST THE TWO OF US...
...CALL ME YUI...
...RAKKY!

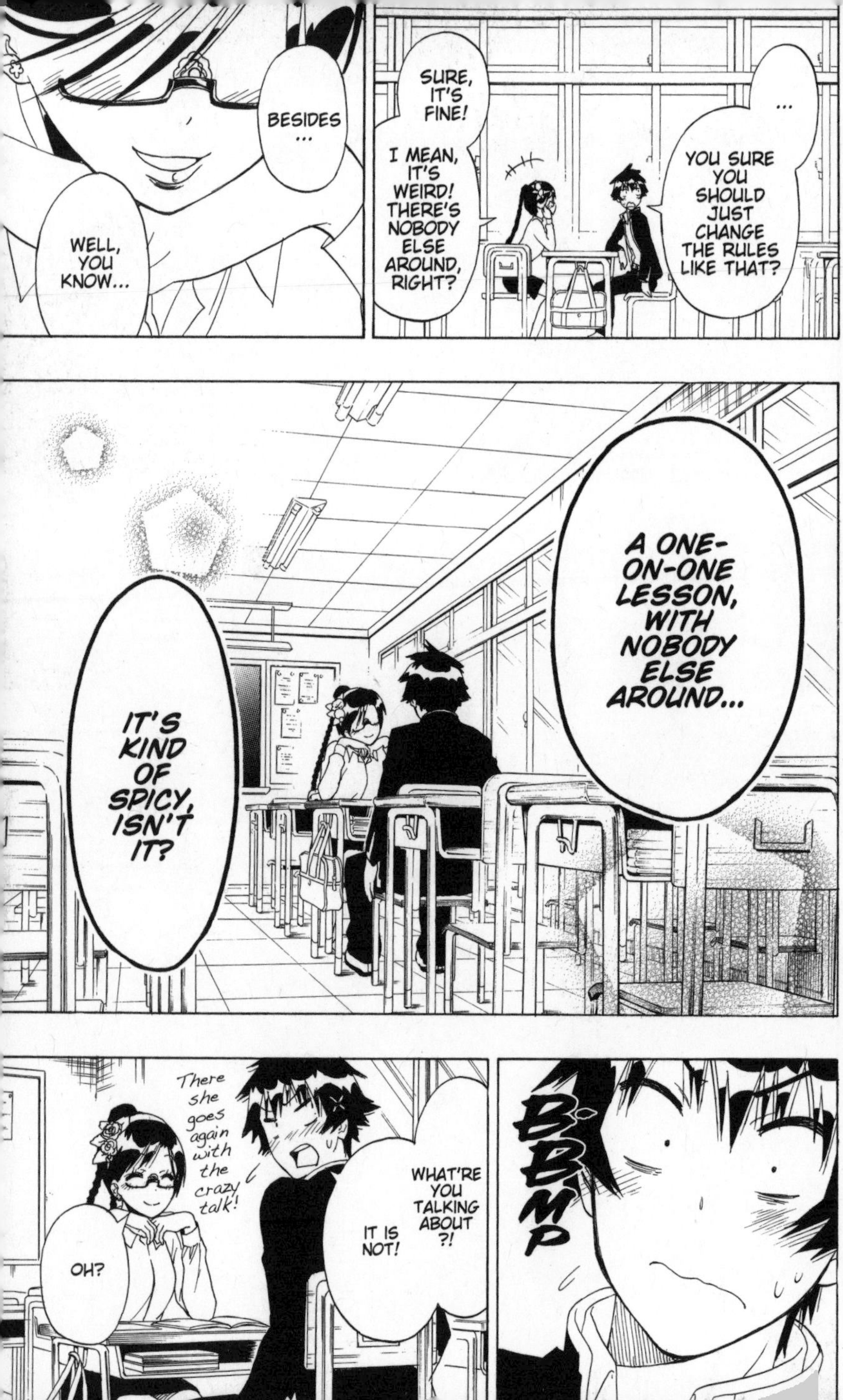
...
YOU SURE YOU SHOULD JUST CHANGE THE RULES LIKE THAT?
SURE, IT'S FINE!
I MEAN, IT'S WEIRD! THERE'S NOBODY ELSE AROUND, RIGHT?
BESIDES...
WELL, YOU KNOW...
A ONE-ON-ONE LESSON, WITH NOBODY ELSE AROUND...
IT'S KIND OF SPICY, ISN'T IT?
B'DMP
WHAT'RE YOU TALKING ABOUT?!
IT IS NOT!
There she goes again with the crazy talk!
OH?

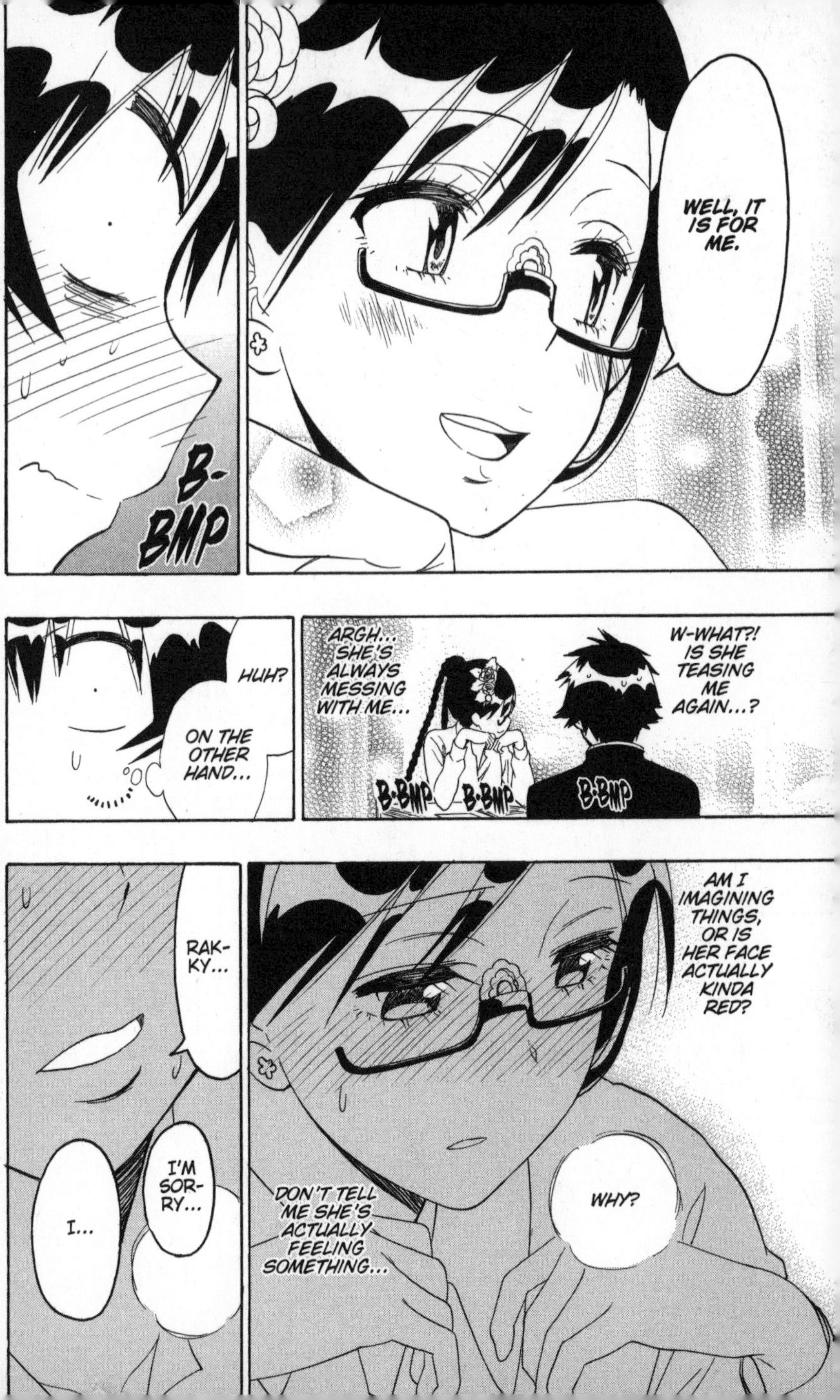
WELL, IT IS FOR ME.
B-BMP
W-WHAT?! IS SHE TEASING ME AGAIN...?
ARGH... SHE'S ALWAYS MESSING WITH ME...
B-BMP
B-BMP
B-BMP
HUH?
ON THE OTHER HAND...
AM I IMAGINING THINGS, OR IS HER FACE ACTUALLY KINDA RED?
WHY?
DON'T TELL ME SHE'S ACTUALLY FEELING SOMETHING...
RAKKY...
I'M SORRY...
I...

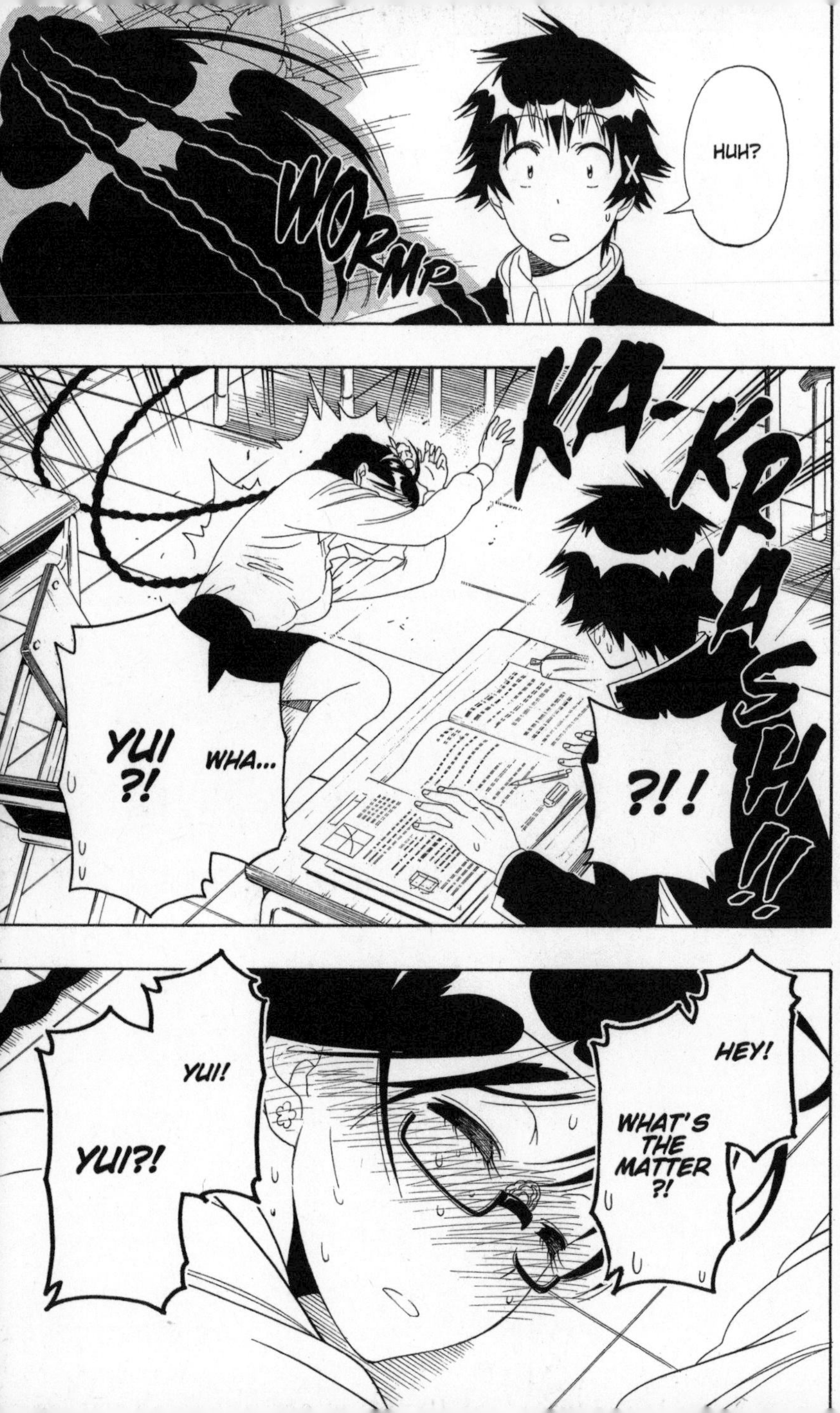
HUH?
WORMP
KA-KRASH!!
?!!
WHA...
YUI?!
HEY!
WHAT'S THE MATTER?!
YUI!
YUI?!

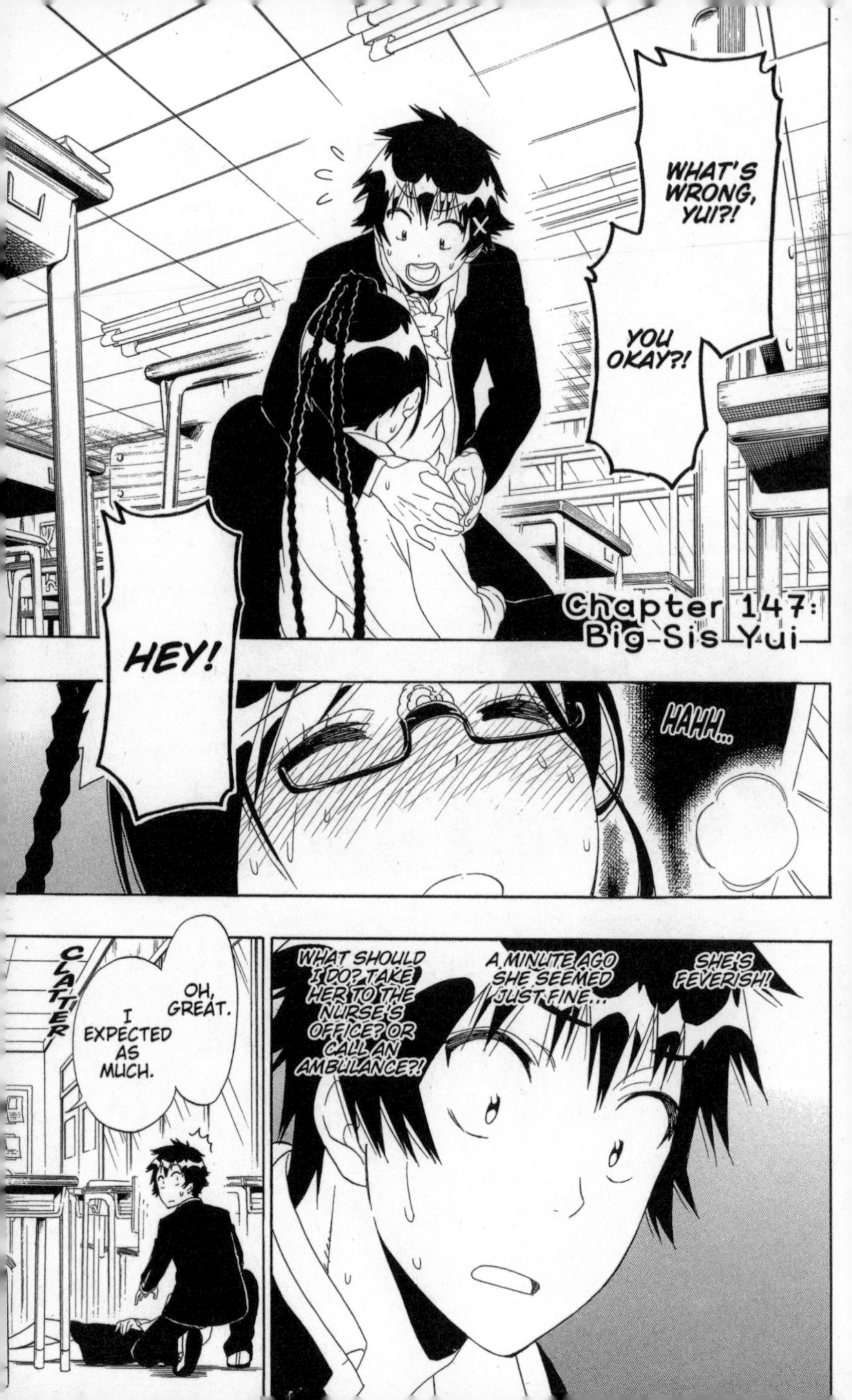
WHAT'S WRONG, YUI?!
YOU OKAY?!
HEY!
Chapter 147: Big-Sis Yui
HAHH...
SHE'S FEVERISH!
A MINUTE AGO SHE SEEMED JUST FINE...
WHAT SHOULD I DO? TAKE HER TO THE NURSE'S OFFICE? OR CALL AN AMBULANCE?!
CLATTER
OH, GREAT. I EXPECTED AS MUCH.

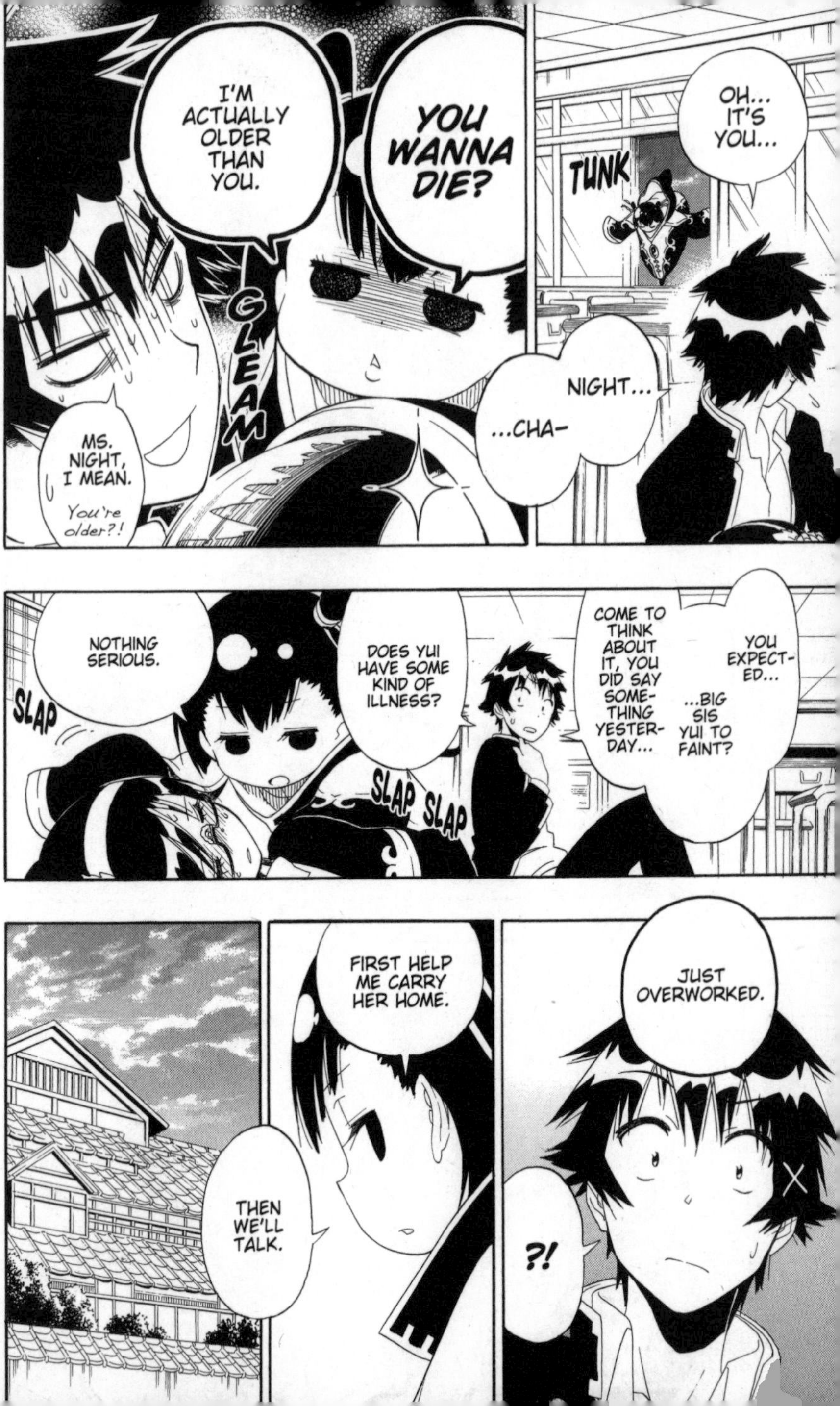
OH... IT'S YOU...
TUNK
NIGHT...
...CHA-
I'M ACTUALLY OLDER THAN YOU.
YOU WANNA DIE?
GLEAM
MS. NIGHT, I MEAN.
You're older?!
COME TO THINK ABOUT IT, YOU DID SAY SOME-THING YESTER-DAY...
YOU EXPECT-ED...
...BIG SIS YUI TO FAINT?
DOES YUI HAVE SOME KIND OF ILLNESS?
SLAP SLAP
NOTHING SERIOUS.
SLAP
JUST OVERWORKED.
?!
FIRST HELP ME CARRY HER HOME.
THEN WE'LL TALK.

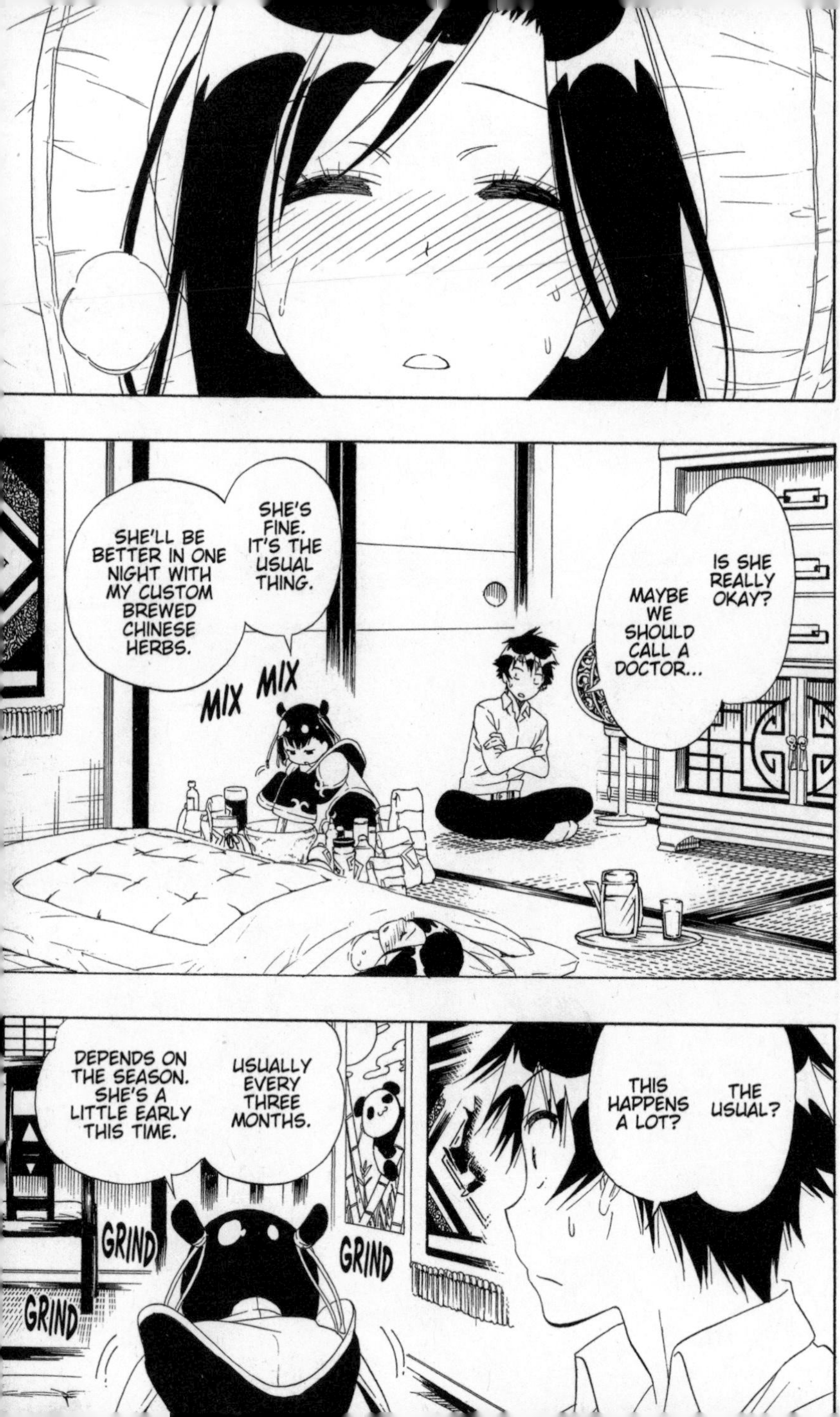
IS SHE REALLY OKAY?
MAYBE WE SHOULD CALL A DOCTOR...
SHE'S FINE. IT'S THE USUAL THING.
SHE'LL BE BETTER IN ONE NIGHT WITH MY CUSTOM BREWED CHINESE HERBS.
MIX MIX
THE USUAL?
THIS HAPPENS A LOT?
USUALLY EVERY THREE MONTHS.
DEPENDS ON THE SEASON. SHE'S A LITTLE EARLY THIS TIME.
GRIND
GRIND
GRIND

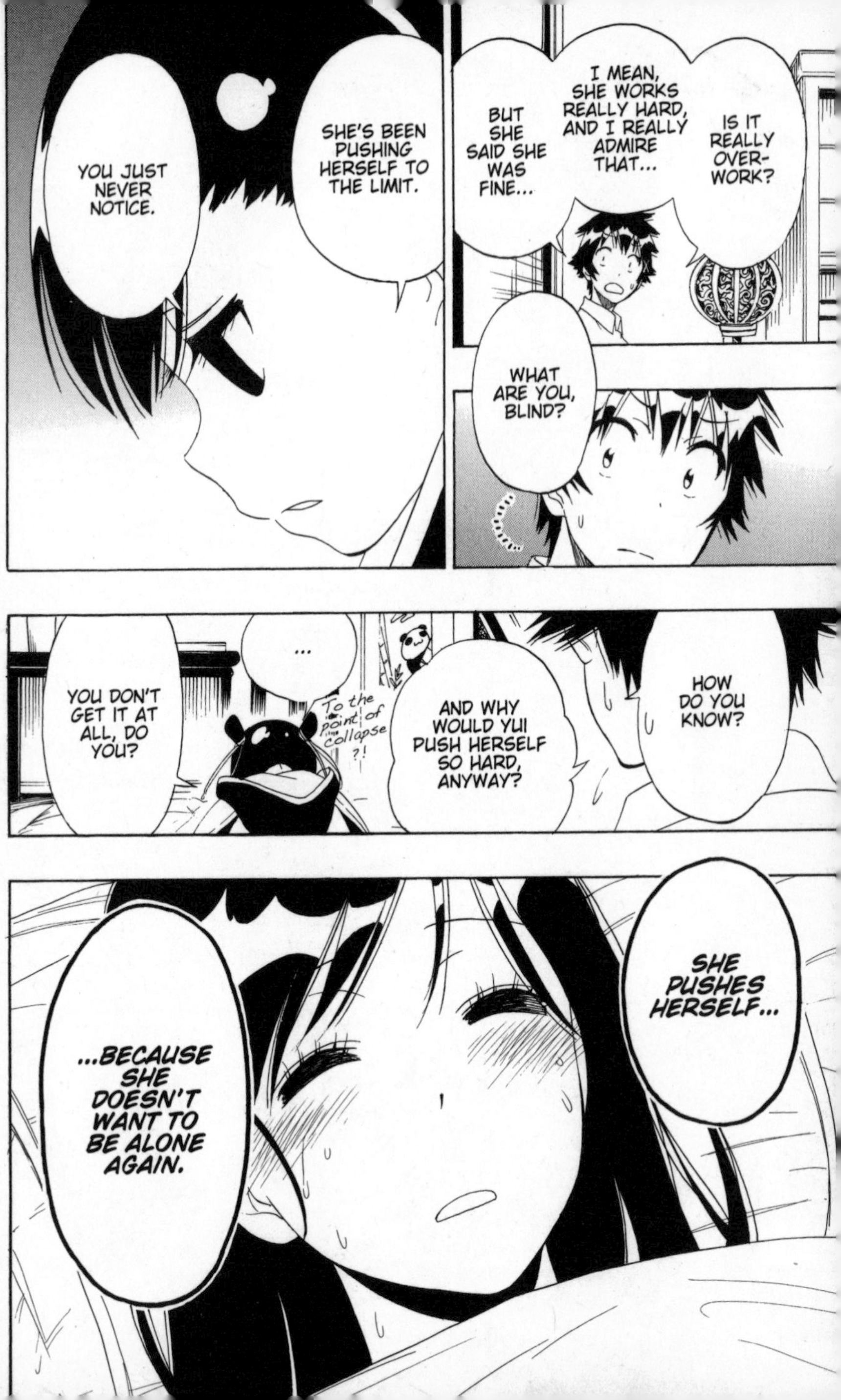
IS IT REALLY OVER-WORK?
I MEAN, SHE WORKS REALLY HARD, AND I REALLY ADMIRE THAT...
BUT SHE SAID SHE WAS FINE...
WHAT ARE YOU, BLIND?
SHE'S BEEN PUSHING HERSELF TO THE LIMIT.
YOU JUST NEVER NOTICE.
HOW DO YOU KNOW?
AND WHY WOULD YUI PUSH HERSELF SO HARD, ANYWAY?
To the point of collapse ?!
...
YOU DON'T GET IT AT ALL, DO YOU?
SHE PUSHES HERSELF...
...BECAUSE SHE DOESN'T WANT TO BE ALONE AGAIN.

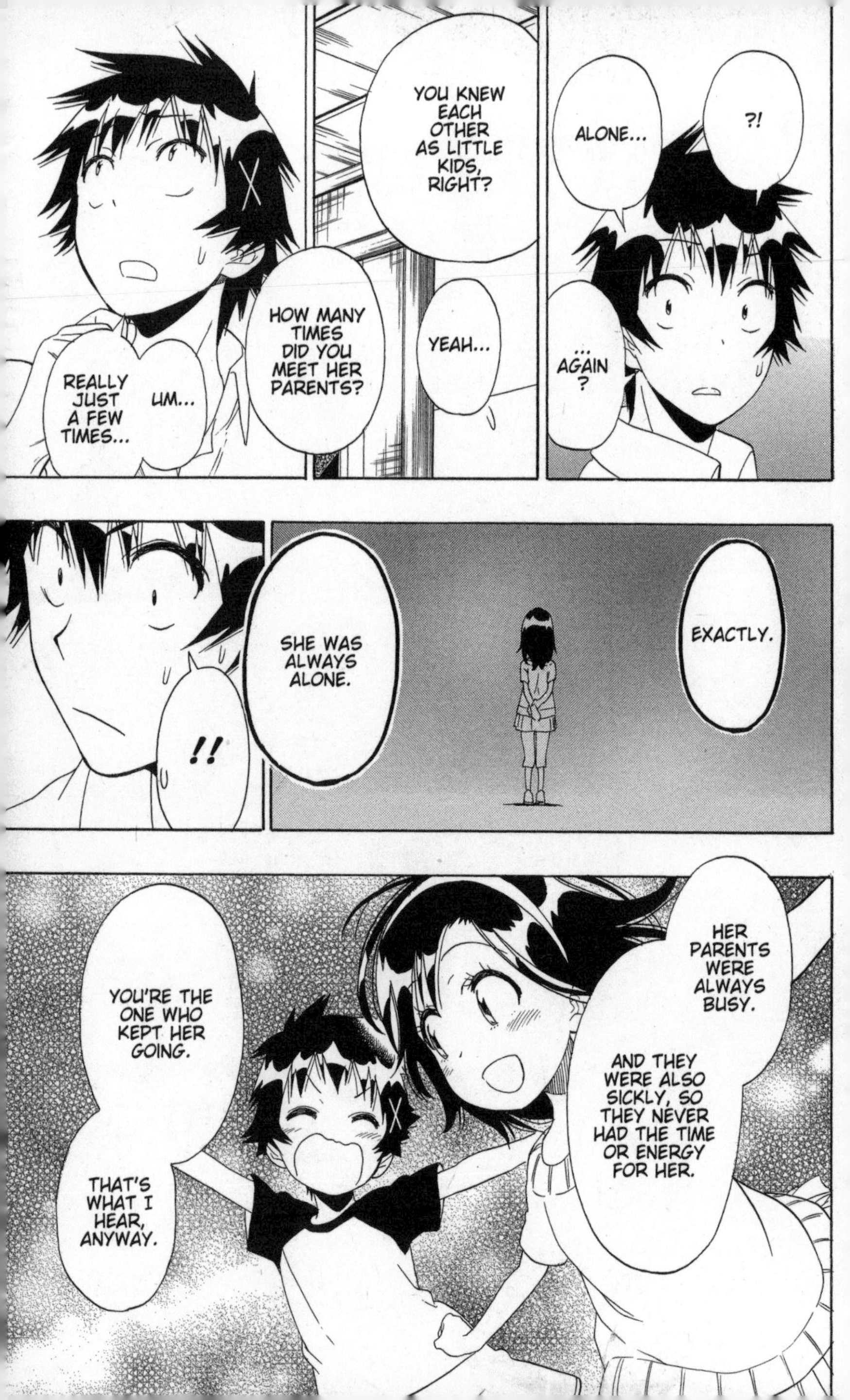
?!
ALONE...
...AGAIN?
YOU KNEW EACH OTHER AS LITTLE KIDS, RIGHT?
YEAH...
HOW MANY TIMES DID YOU MEET HER PARENTS?
UM...
REALLY JUST A FEW TIMES...
EXACTLY.
SHE WAS ALWAYS ALONE.
!!
HER PARENTS WERE ALWAYS BUSY.
AND THEY WERE ALSO SICKLY, SO THEY NEVER HAD THE TIME OR ENERGY FOR HER.
YOU'RE THE ONE WHO KEPT HER GOING.
THAT'S WHAT I HEAR, ANYWAY.

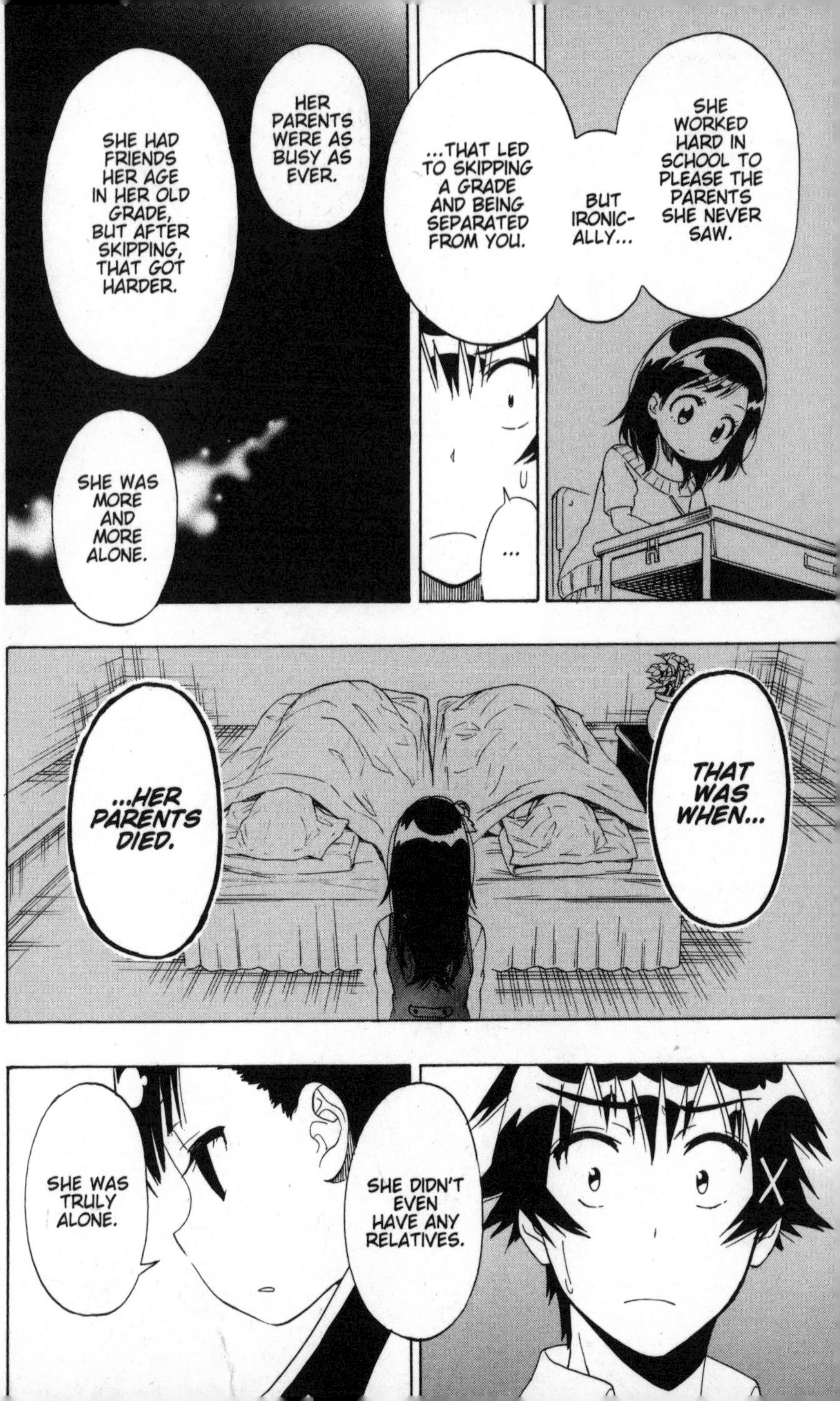
SHE WORKED HARD IN SCHOOL TO PLEASE THE PARENTS SHE NEVER SAW.
BUT IRONIC-ALLY...
...THAT LED TO SKIPPING A GRADE AND BEING SEPARATED FROM YOU.
...
HER PARENTS WERE AS BUSY AS EVER.
SHE HAD FRIENDS HER AGE IN HER OLD GRADE, BUT AFTER SKIPPING, THAT GOT HARDER.
SHE WAS MORE AND MORE ALONE.
THAT WAS WHEN...
...HER PARENTS DIED.
SHE DIDN'T EVEN HAVE ANY RELATIVES.
SHE WAS TRULY ALONE.

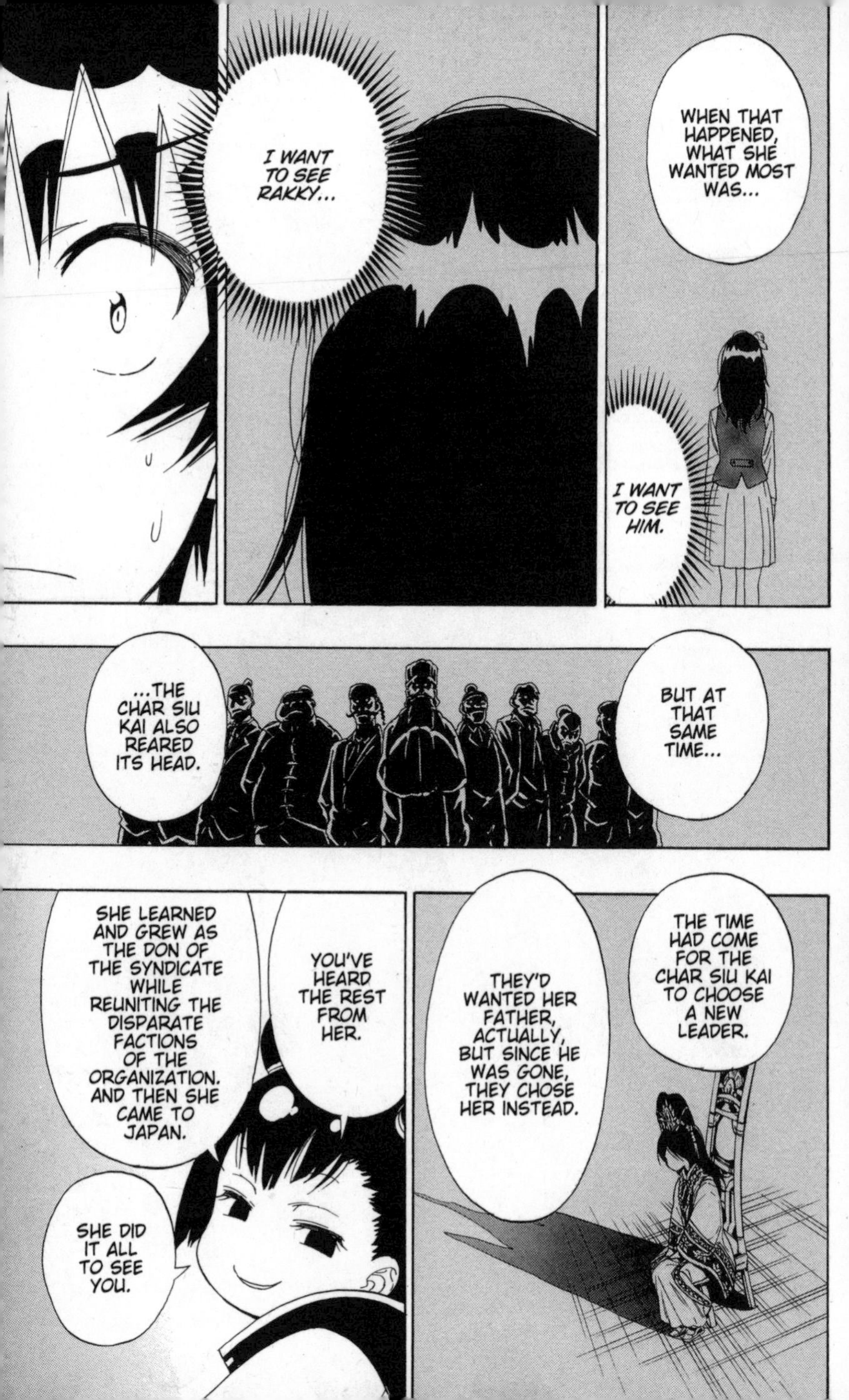
WHEN THAT HAPPENED, WHAT SHE WANTED MOST WAS...
I WANT TO SEE HIM.
I WANT TO SEE RAKKY...
BUT AT THAT SAME TIME...
...THE CHAR SIU KAI ALSO REARED ITS HEAD.
THE TIME HAD COME FOR THE CHAR SIU KAI TO CHOOSE A NEW LEADER.
THEY'D WANTED HER FATHER, ACTUALLY, BUT SINCE HE WAS GONE, THEY CHOSE HER INSTEAD.
YOU'VE HEARD THE REST FROM HER.
SHE LEARNED AND GREW AS THE DON OF THE SYNDICATE WHILE REUNITING THE DISPARATE FACTIONS OF THE ORGANIZATION. AND THEN SHE CAME TO JAPAN.
SHE DID IT ALL TO SEE YOU.

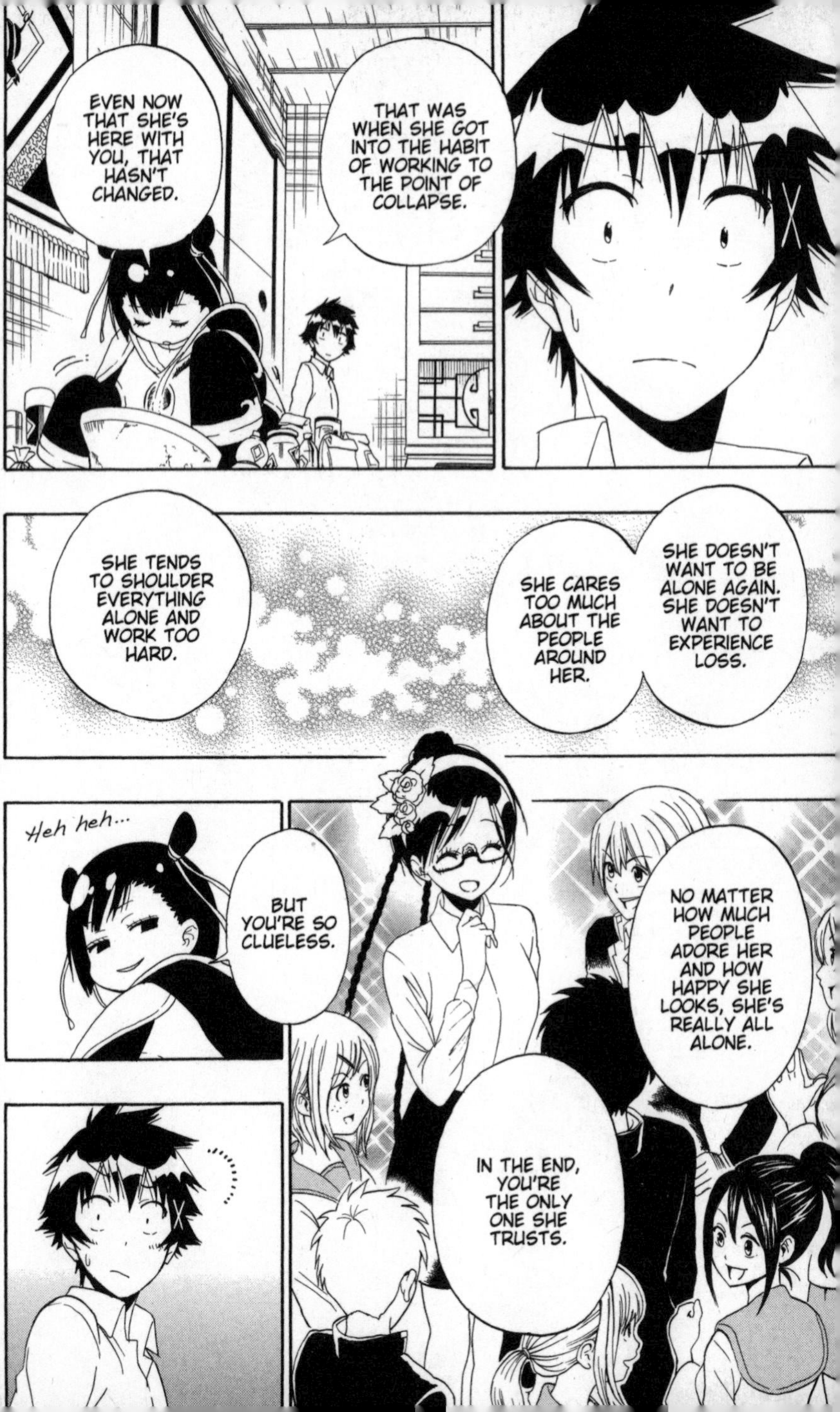
THAT WAS WHEN SHE GOT INTO THE HABIT OF WORKING TO THE POINT OF COLLAPSE.
EVEN NOW THAT SHE'S HERE WITH YOU, THAT HASN'T CHANGED.
SHE DOESN'T WANT TO BE ALONE AGAIN. SHE DOESN'T WANT TO EXPERIENCE LOSS.
SHE CARES TOO MUCH ABOUT THE PEOPLE AROUND HER.
SHE TENDS TO SHOULDER EVERYTHING ALONE AND WORK TOO HARD.
NO MATTER HOW MUCH PEOPLE ADORE HER AND HOW HAPPY SHE LOOKS, SHE'S REALLY ALL ALONE.
IN THE END, YOU'RE THE ONLY ONE SHE TRUSTS.
Heh heh...
BUT YOU'RE SO CLUELESS.
......

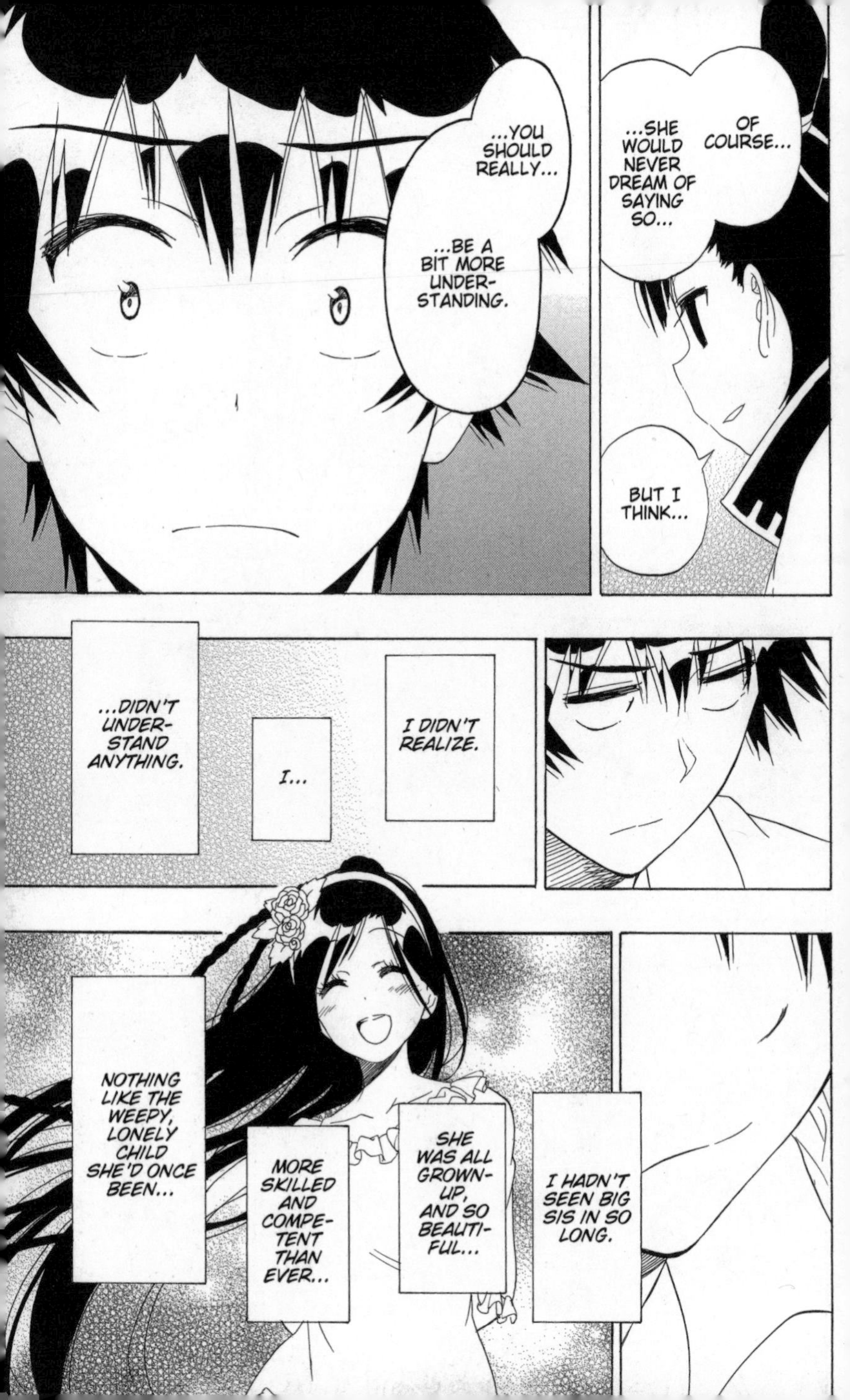
OF COURSE...
...SHE WOULD NEVER DREAM OF SAYING SO...
BUT I THINK...
...YOU SHOULD REALLY...
...BE A BIT MORE UNDER-STANDING.
I DIDN'T REALIZE.
I...
...DIDN'T UNDER-STAND ANYTHING.
I HADN'T SEEN BIG SIS IN SO LONG.
SHE WAS ALL GROWN-UP, AND SO BEAUTI-FUL...
MORE SKILLED AND COMPE-TENT THAN EVER...
NOTHING LIKE THE WEEPY, LONELY CHILD SHE'D ONCE BEEN...

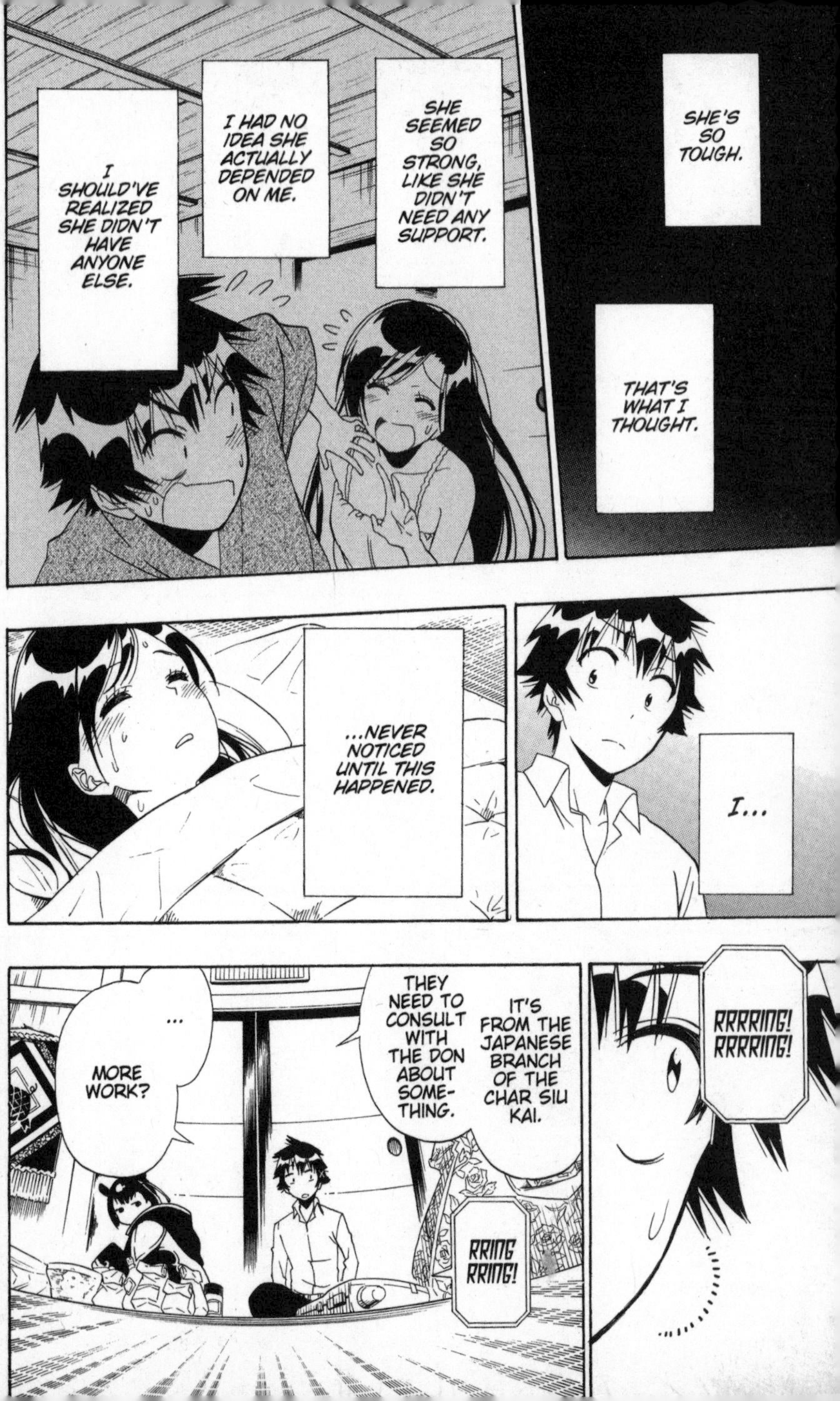
SHE'S SO TOUGH.
THAT'S WHAT I THOUGHT.
SHE SEEMED SO STRONG, LIKE SHE DIDN'T NEED ANY SUPPORT.
I HAD NO IDEA SHE ACTUALLY DEPENDED ON ME.
I SHOULD'VE REALIZED SHE DIDN'T HAVE ANYONE ELSE.
I...
...NEVER NOTICED UNTIL THIS HAPPENED.
RRRRING! RRRRING!
RRING RRING!
IT'S FROM THE JAPANESE BRANCH OF THE CHAR SIU KAI.
THEY NEED TO CONSULT WITH THE DON ABOUT SOME-THING.
...
MORE WORK?

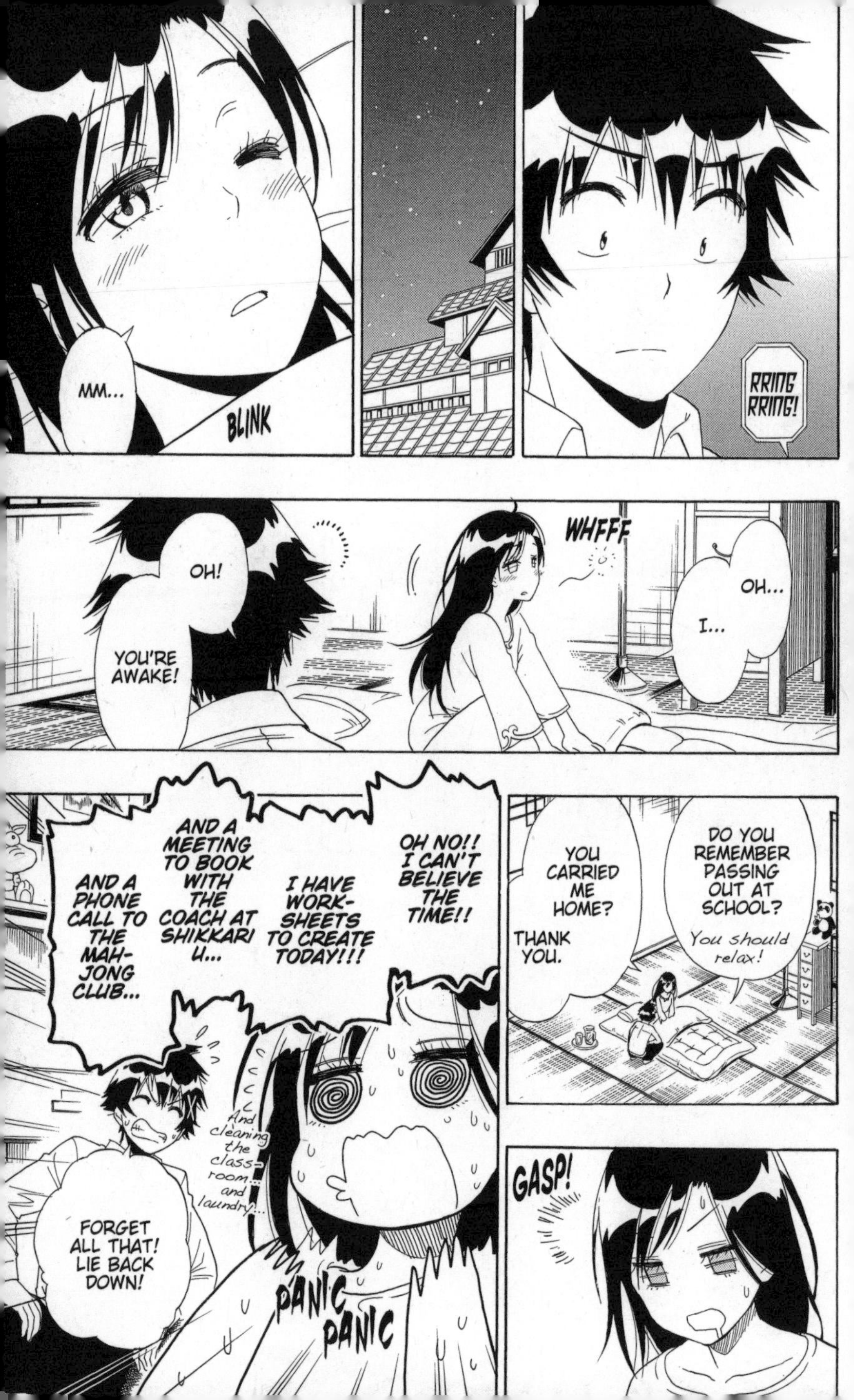
RRING RRING!
MM...
BLINK
OH... I...
WHFFF
OH!
YOU'RE AWAKE!
DO YOU REMEMBER PASSING OUT AT SCHOOL?
You should relax!
YOU CARRIED ME HOME?
THANK YOU.
GASP!
OH NO!! I CAN'T BELIEVE THE TIME!!
I HAVE WORK-SHEETS TO CREATE TODAY!!!
AND A MEETING TO BOOK WITH THE COACH AT SHIKKARI U...
AND A PHONE CALL TO THE MAH-JONG CLUB...
And cleaning the class-room... and laundry...
PANIC PANIC
FORGET ALL THAT! LIE BACK DOWN!

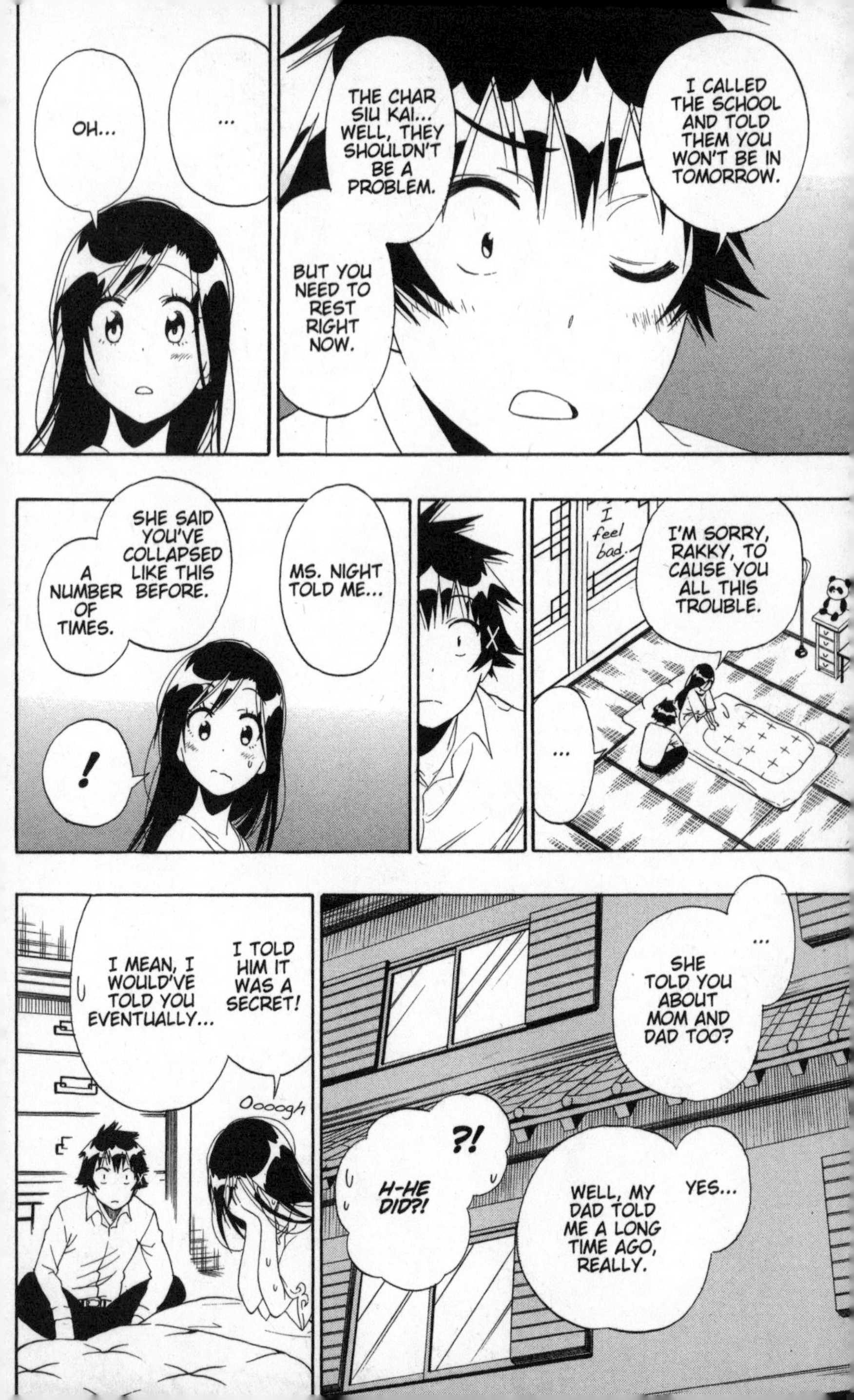
I CALLED THE SCHOOL AND TOLD THEM YOU WON'T BE IN TOMORROW.
THE CHAR SIU KAI... WELL, THEY SHOULDN'T BE A PROBLEM.
BUT YOU NEED TO REST RIGHT NOW.
...
OH...
I'M SORRY, RAKKY, TO CAUSE YOU ALL THIS TROUBLE.
I feel bad...
...
MS. NIGHT TOLD ME...
SHE SAID YOU'VE COLLAPSED LIKE THIS BEFORE.
A NUMBER OF TIMES.
!
...
SHE TOLD YOU ABOUT MOM AND DAD TOO?
YES...
WELL, MY DAD TOLD ME A LONG TIME AGO, REALLY.
?!
H-HE DID?!
I TOLD HIM IT WAS A SECRET!
I MEAN, I WOULD'VE TOLD YOU EVENTUALLY...
Oooogh

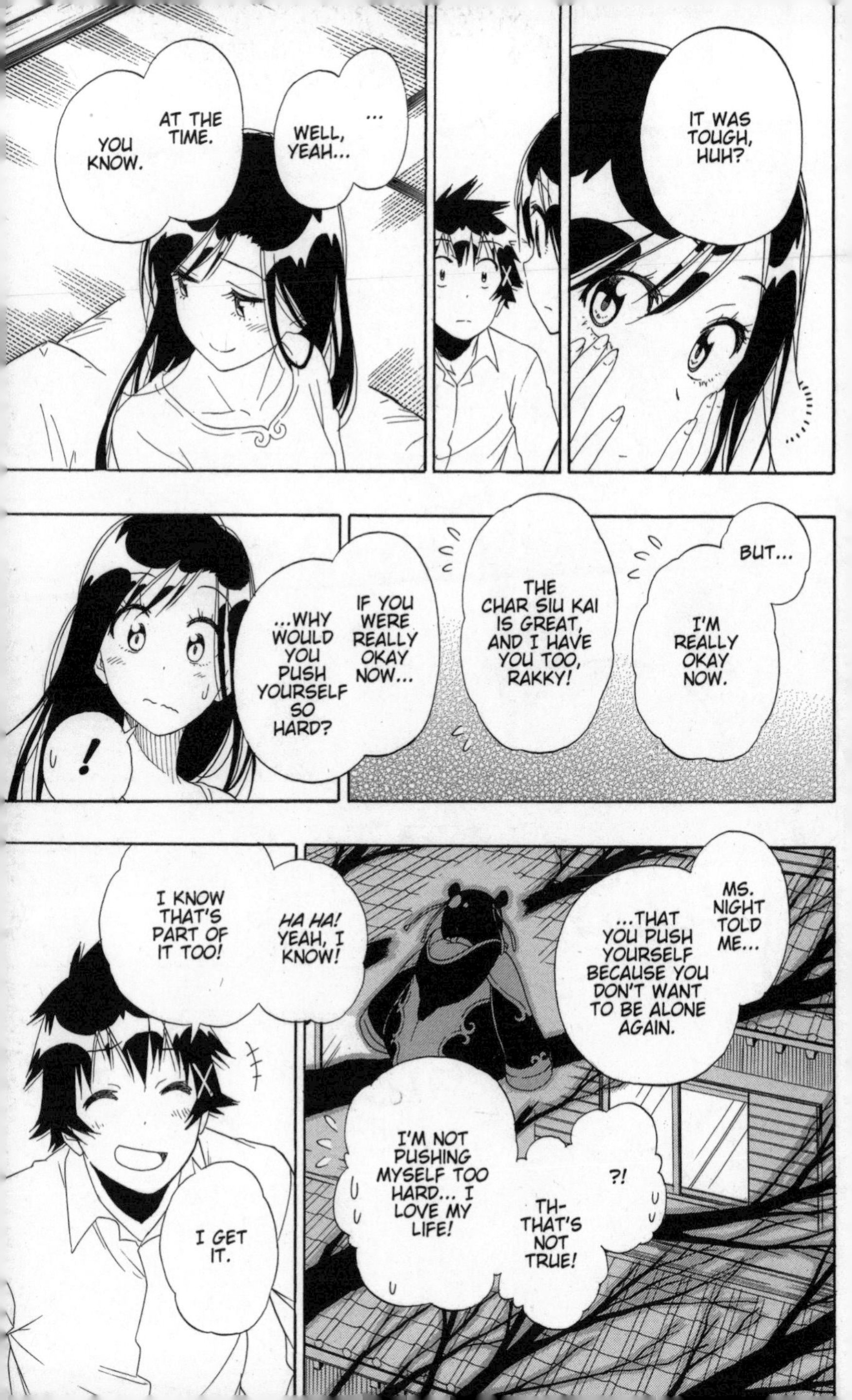
IT WAS TOUGH, HUH?
...
WELL, YEAH...
AT THE TIME.
YOU KNOW.
BUT...
I'M REALLY OKAY NOW.
THE CHAR SIU KAI IS GREAT, AND I HAVE YOU TOO, RAKKY!
IF YOU WERE REALLY OKAY NOW...
...WHY WOULD YOU PUSH YOURSELF SO HARD?
!
MS. NIGHT TOLD ME...
...THAT YOU PUSH YOURSELF BECAUSE YOU DON'T WANT TO BE ALONE AGAIN.
?!
TH- THAT'S NOT TRUE!
I'M NOT PUSHING MYSELF TOO HARD... I LOVE MY LIFE!
I KNOW THAT'S PART OF IT TOO!
HA HA! YEAH, I KNOW!
I GET IT.

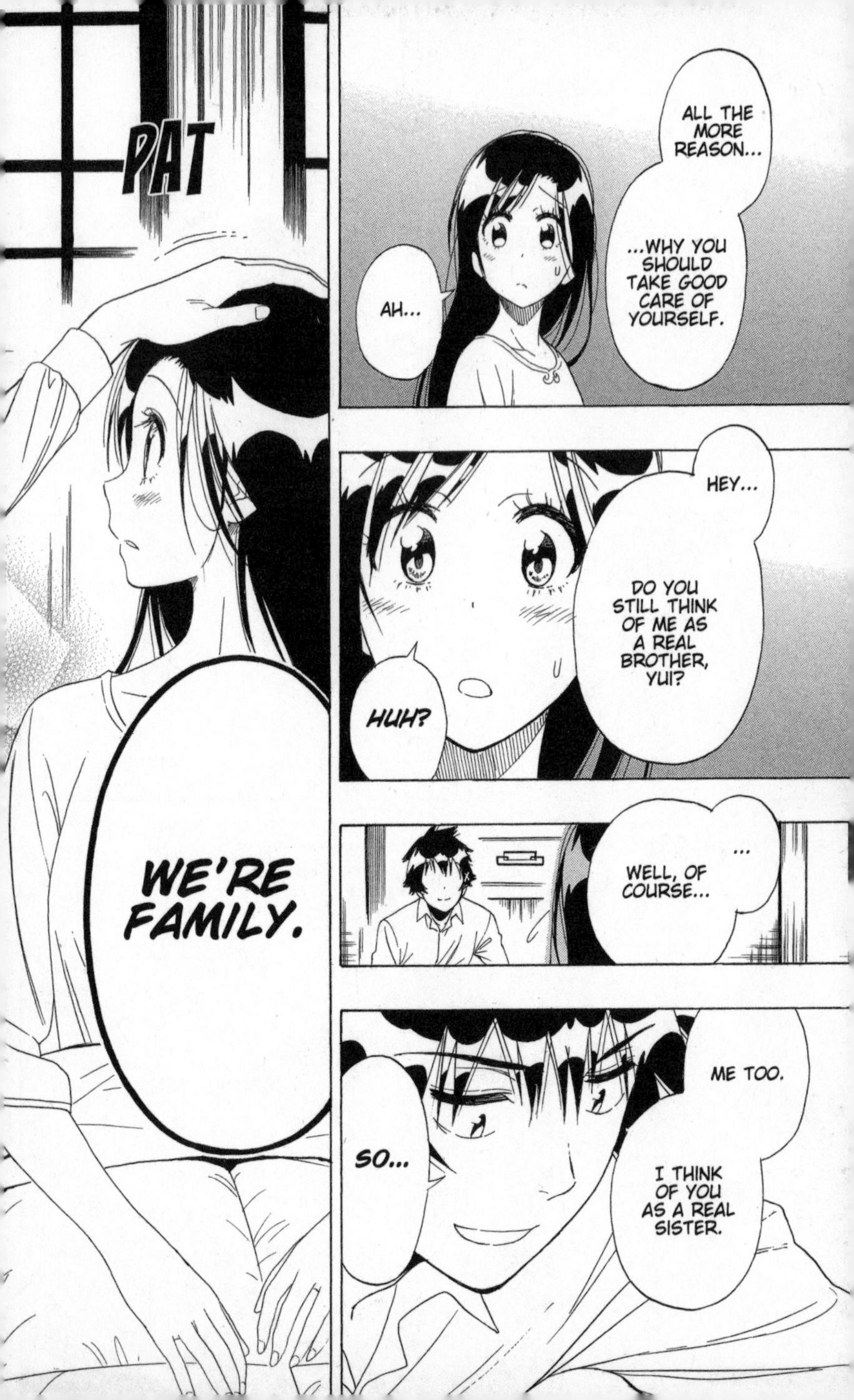
ALL THE MORE REASON...
...WHY YOU SHOULD TAKE GOOD CARE OF YOURSELF.
AH...
HEY...
DO YOU STILL THINK OF ME AS A REAL BROTHER, YUI?
HUH?
...
WELL, OF COURSE...
ME TOO.
I THINK OF YOU AS A REAL SISTER.
SO...
PAT
WE'RE FAMILY.

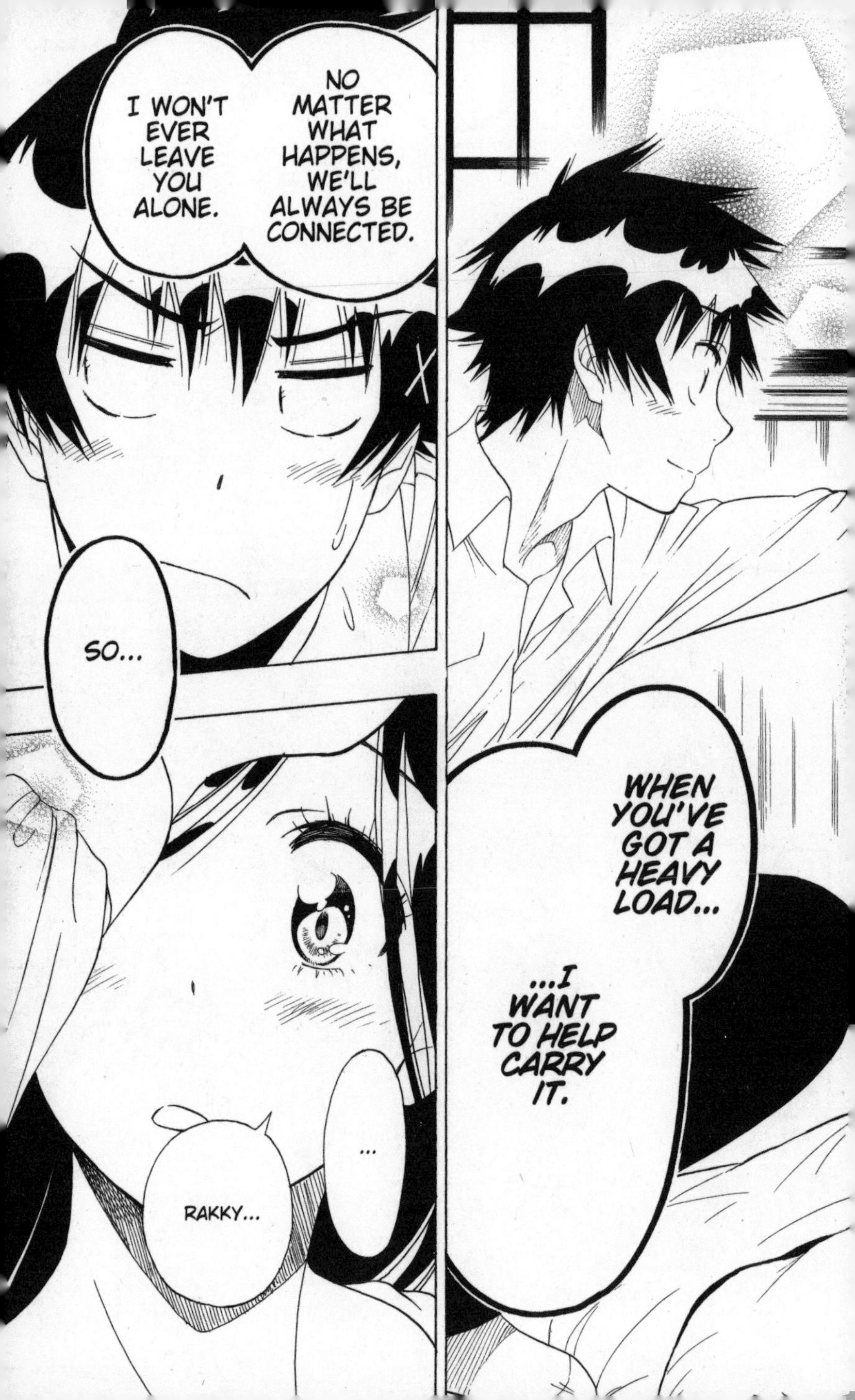
WHEN YOU'VE GOT A HEAVY LOAD...
...I WANT TO HELP CARRY IT.
NO MATTER WHAT HAPPENS, WE'LL ALWAYS BE CONNECTED.
I WON'T EVER LEAVE YOU ALONE.
SO...
...
RAKKY...

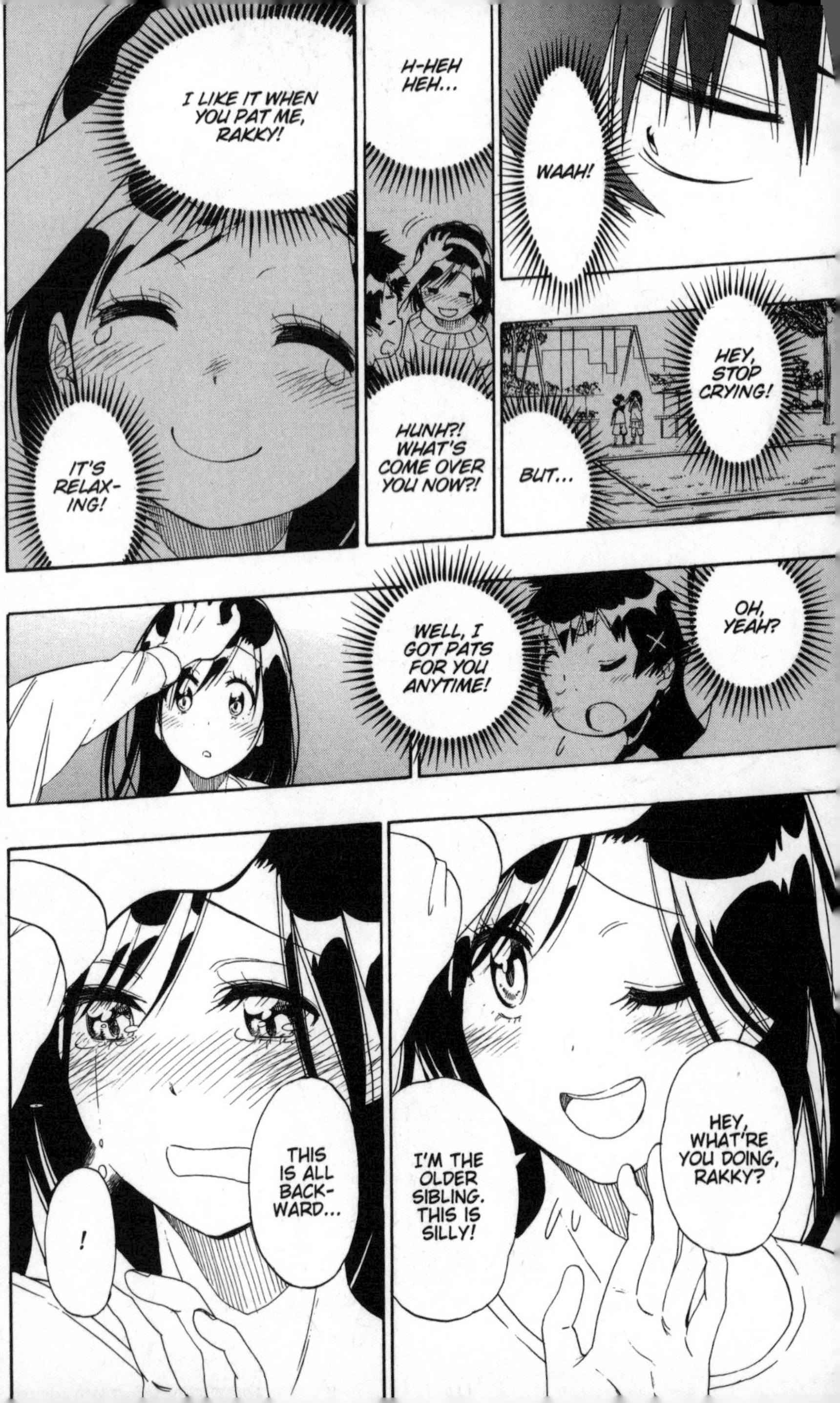
WAAH!
HEY, STOP CRYING!
BUT...
H-HEH HEH...
HUNH?! WHAT'S COME OVER YOU NOW?!
I LIKE IT WHEN YOU PAT ME, RAKKY!
IT'S RELAX-ING!
OH, YEAH?
WELL, I GOT PATS FOR YOU ANYTIME!
HEY, WHAT'RE YOU DOING, RAKKY?
I'M THE OLDER SIBLING. THIS IS SILLY!
THIS IS ALL BACK-WARD...
!

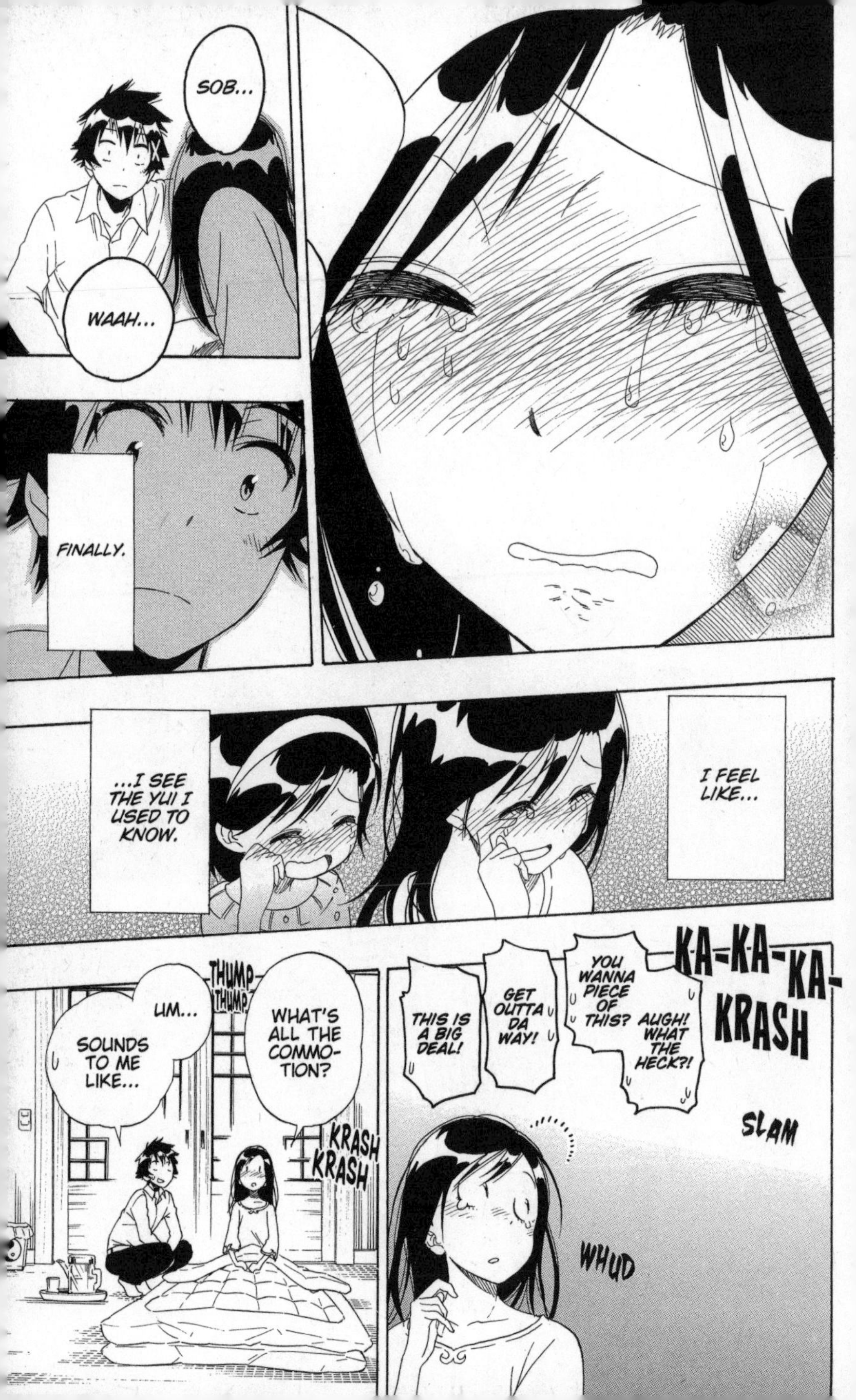
WAAH...
SOB...
FINALLY.
I FEEL LIKE...
...I SEE THE YUI I USED TO KNOW.
KA-KA-KA-KRASH
YOU WANNA PIECE OF THIS? AUGH! WHAT THE HECK?!
GET OUTTA DA WAY!
THIS IS A BIG DEAL!
SLAM
WHUD
THUMP THUMP
WHAT'S ALL THE COMMOTION?
KRASH KRASH
UM... SOUNDS TO ME LIKE...

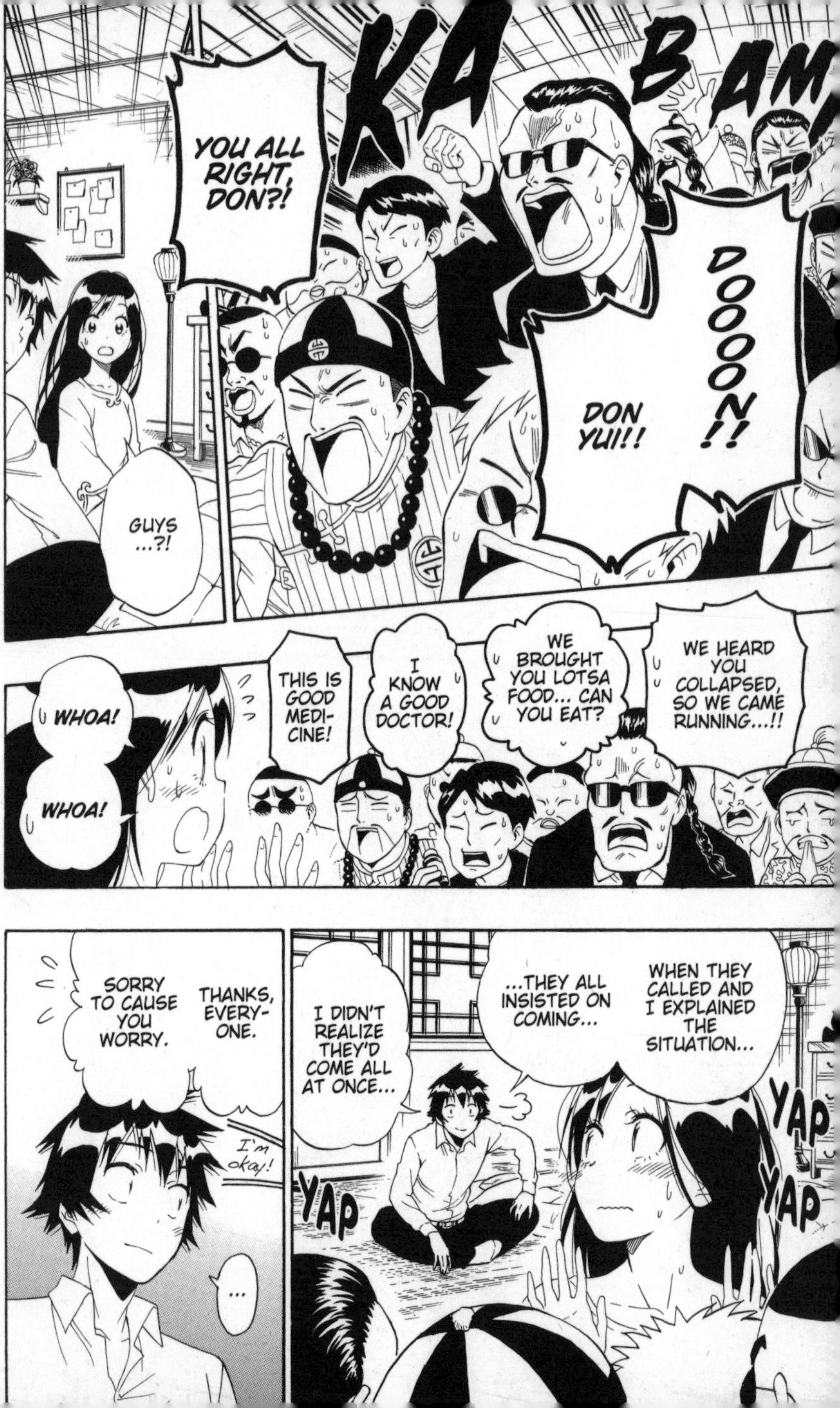
KABAM
DOOOOON!!
DON YUI!!
YOU ALL RIGHT, DON?!
GUYS ...?!
WE HEARD YOU COLLAPSED, SO WE CAME RUNNING...!!
WE BROUGHT YOU LOTSA FOOD... CAN YOU EAT?
I KNOW A GOOD DOCTOR!
THIS IS GOOD MEDI-CINE!
WHOA!
WHOA!
YAP
YAP
WHEN THEY CALLED AND I EXPLAINED THE SITUATION...
...THEY ALL INSISTED ON COMING...
YAP
I DIDN'T REALIZE THEY'D COME ALL AT ONCE...
THANKS, EVERY-ONE.
SORRY TO CAUSE YOU WORRY.
I'm okay!
...

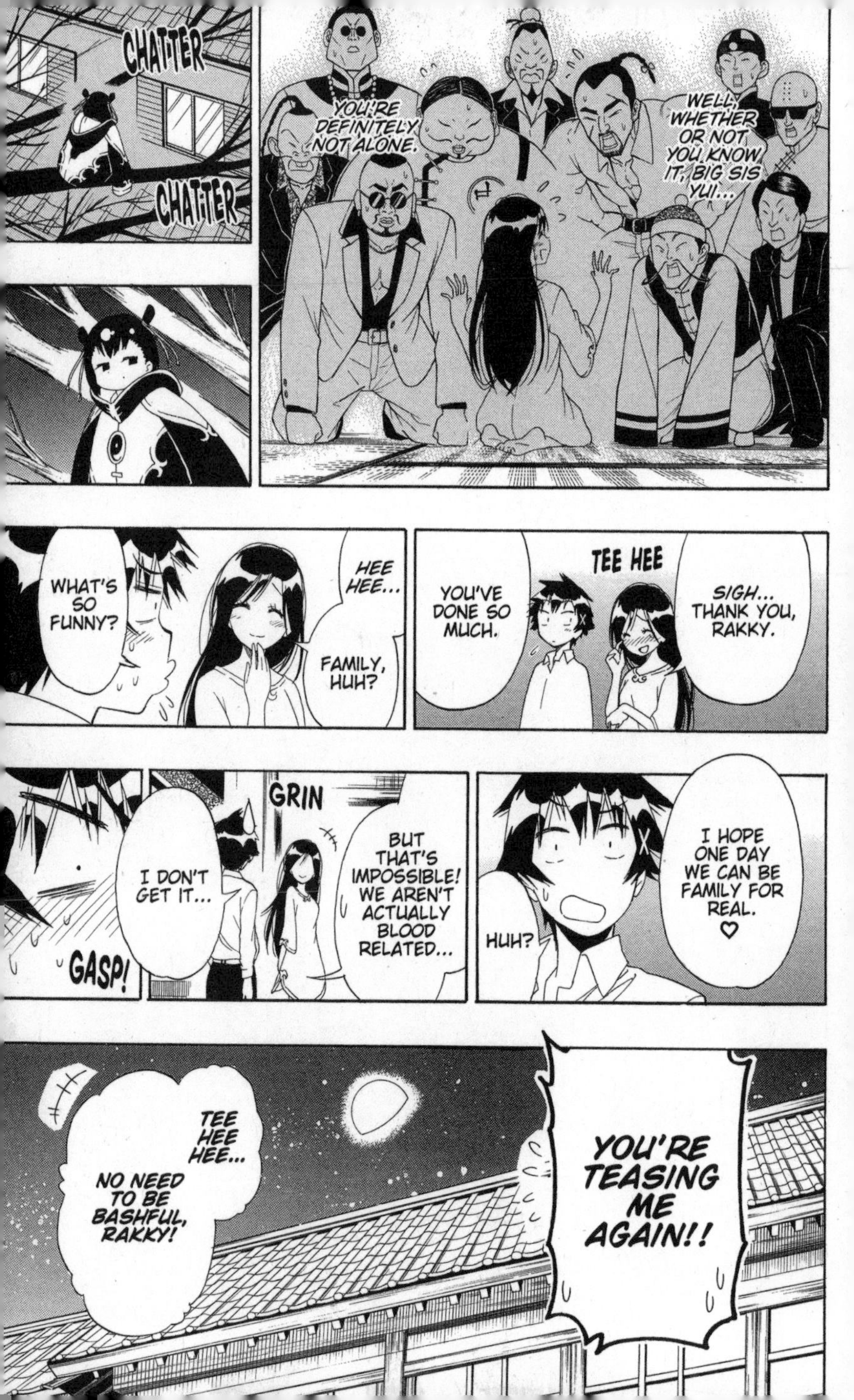
WELL, WHETHER OR NOT YOU KNOW IT, BIG SIS YUI...
YOU'RE DEFINITELY NOT ALONE.
CHATTER
CHATTER
SIGH... THANK YOU, RAKKY.
TEE HEE
YOU'VE DONE SO MUCH.
HEE HEE...
FAMILY, HUH?
WHAT'S SO FUNNY?
I HOPE ONE DAY WE CAN BE FAMILY FOR REAL. ♡
HUH?
BUT THAT'S IMPOSSIBLE! WE AREN'T ACTUALLY BLOOD RELATED...
GRIN
I DON'T GET IT...
GASP!
YOU'RE TEASING ME AGAIN!!
TEE HEE HEE...
NO NEED TO BE BASHFUL, RAKKY!

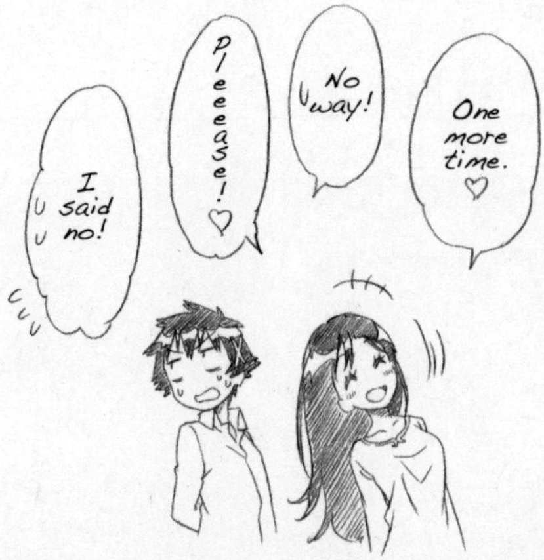
One more time. ♡
No way!
Pleeease! ♡
I said no!

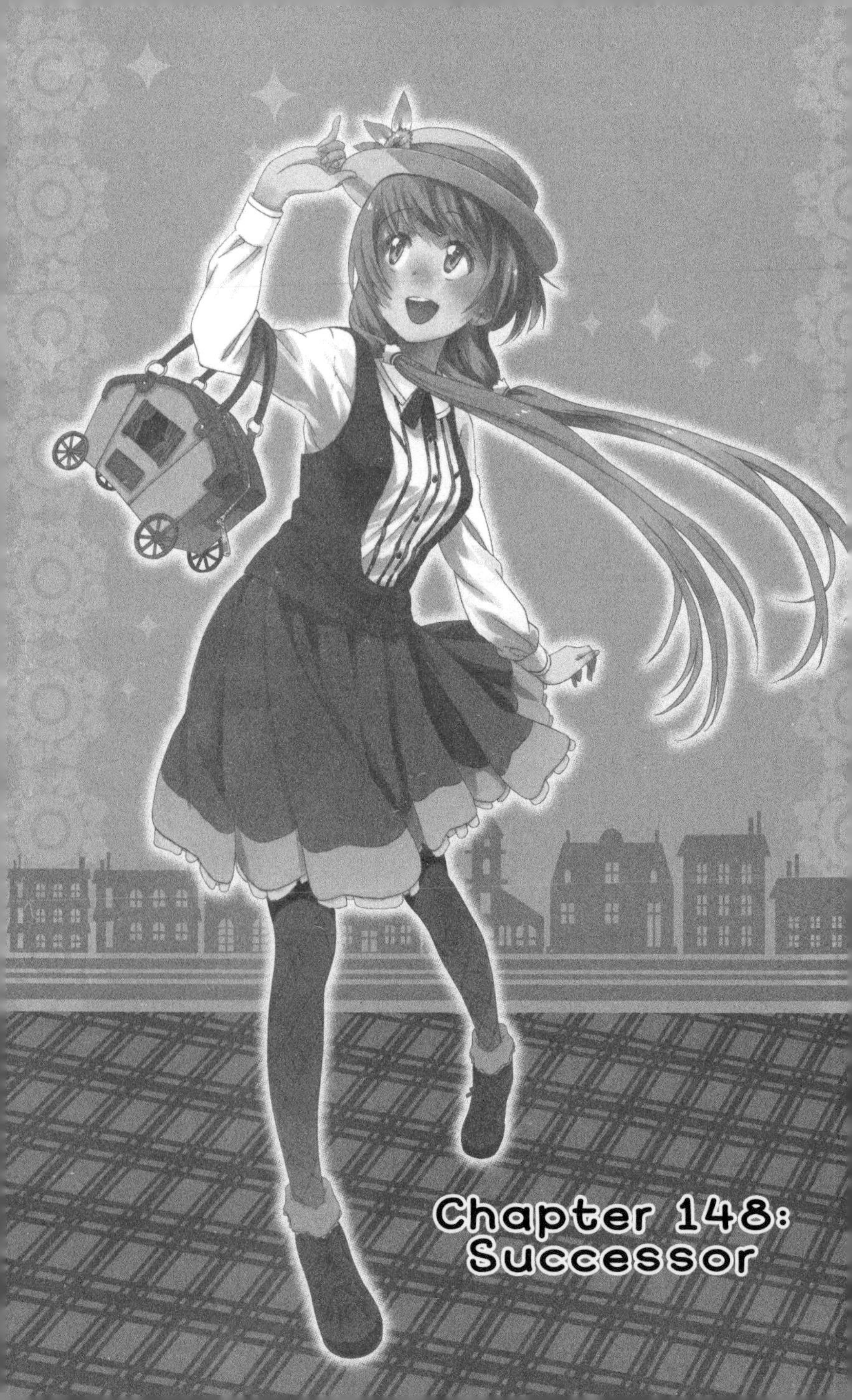
Chapter 148:
Successor

What?!
I'm the one on the front page!!
How come the story's about Yui again?!
They'll pay for this!! They'll be sorry!!

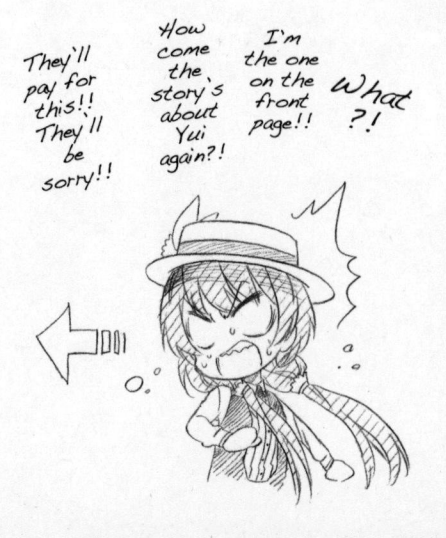

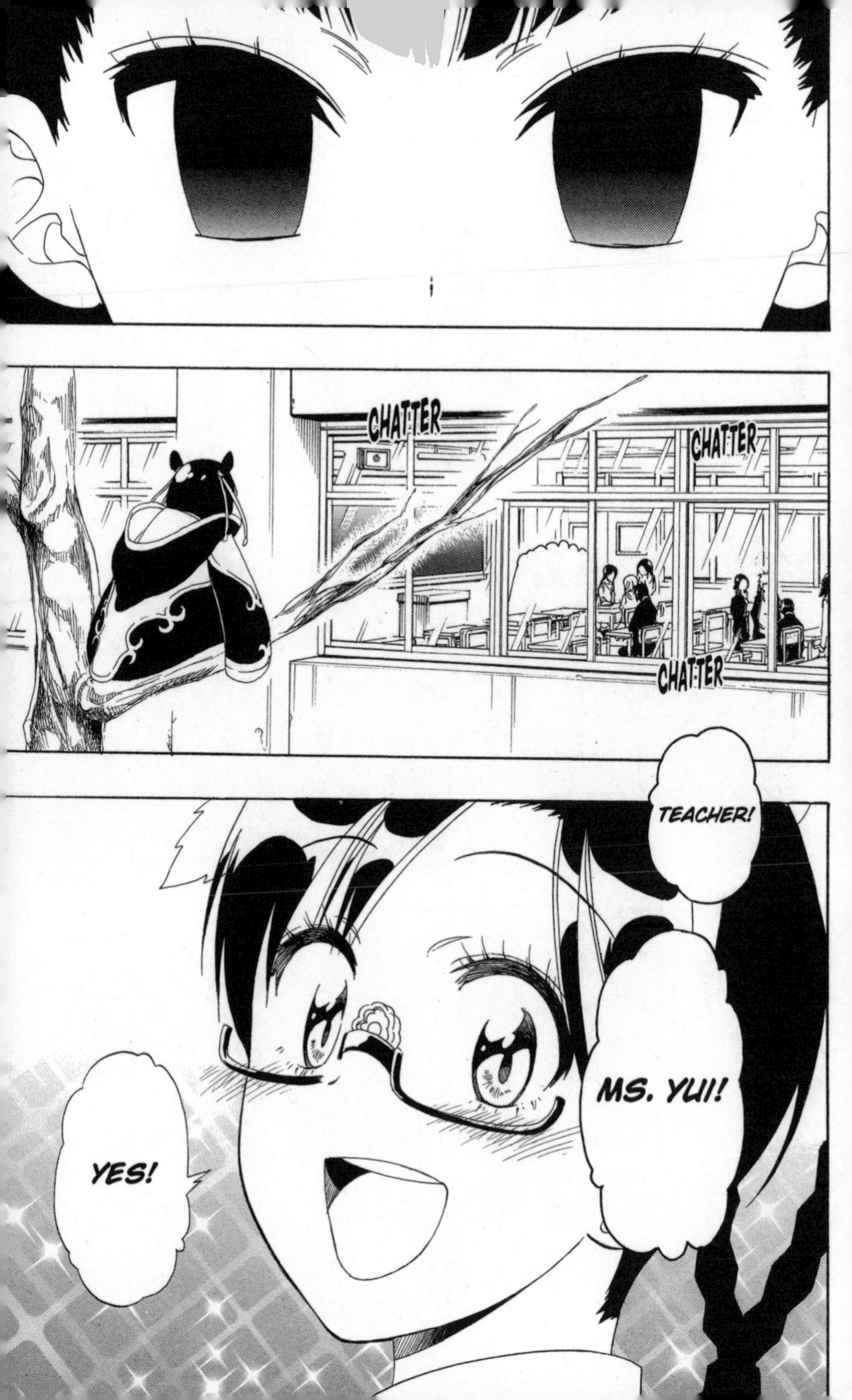
CHATTER
CHATTER
CHATTER
TEACHER!
MS. YUI!
YES!

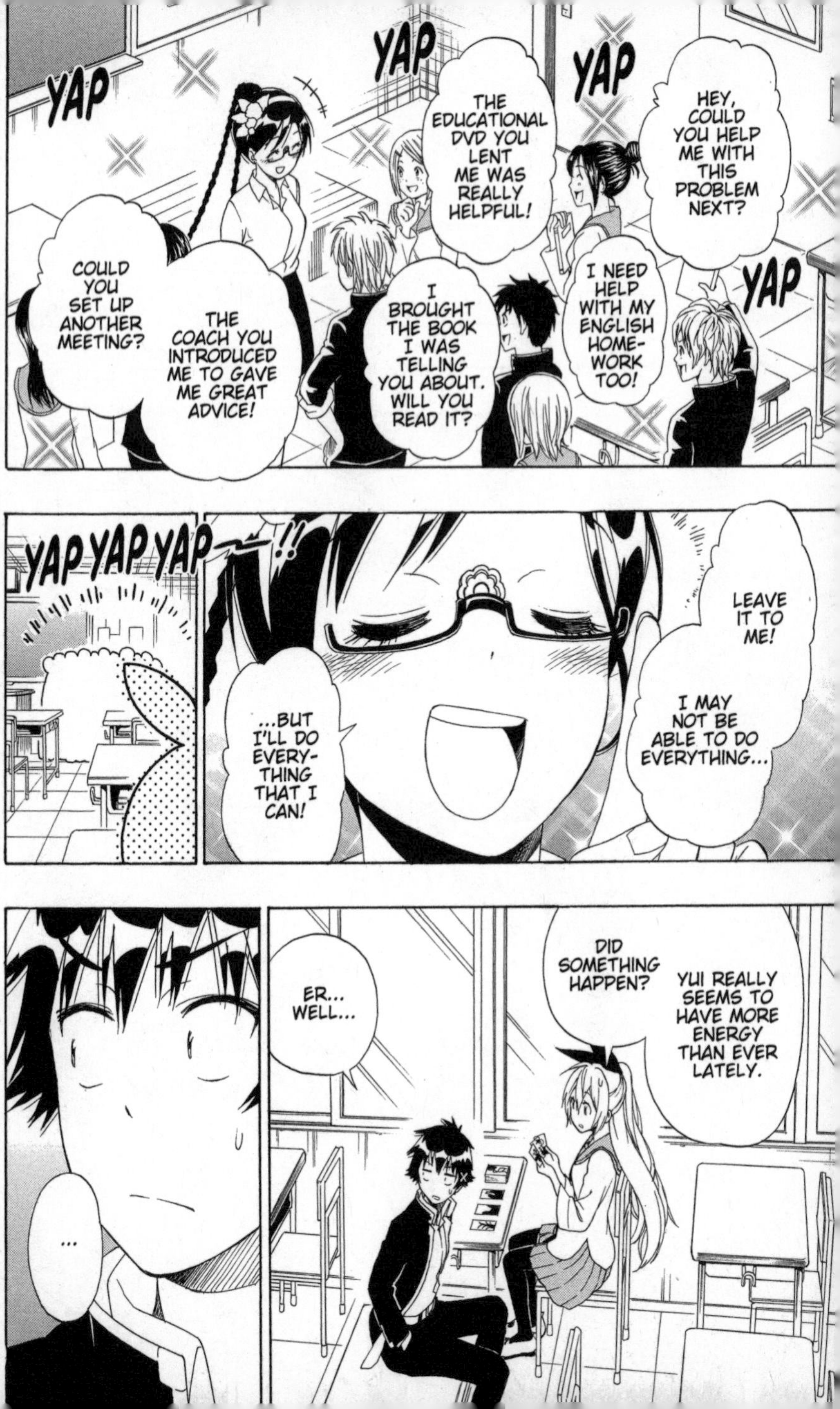
HEY, COULD YOU HELP ME WITH THIS PROBLEM NEXT?
YAP
THE EDUCATIONAL DVD YOU LENT ME WAS REALLY HELPFUL!
YAP
YAP
YAP
I NEED HELP WITH MY ENGLISH HOME-WORK TOO!
I BROUGHT THE BOOK I WAS TELLING YOU ABOUT. WILL YOU READ IT?
THE COACH YOU INTRODUCED ME TO GAVE ME GREAT ADVICE!
COULD YOU SET UP ANOTHER MEETING?
LEAVE IT TO ME!
I MAY NOT BE ABLE TO DO EVERYTHING...
...BUT I'LL DO EVERY-THING THAT I CAN!
YAP YAP YAP!!
DID SOMETHING HAPPEN?
YUI REALLY SEEMS TO HAVE MORE ENERGY THAN EVER LATELY.
ER... WELL...
...

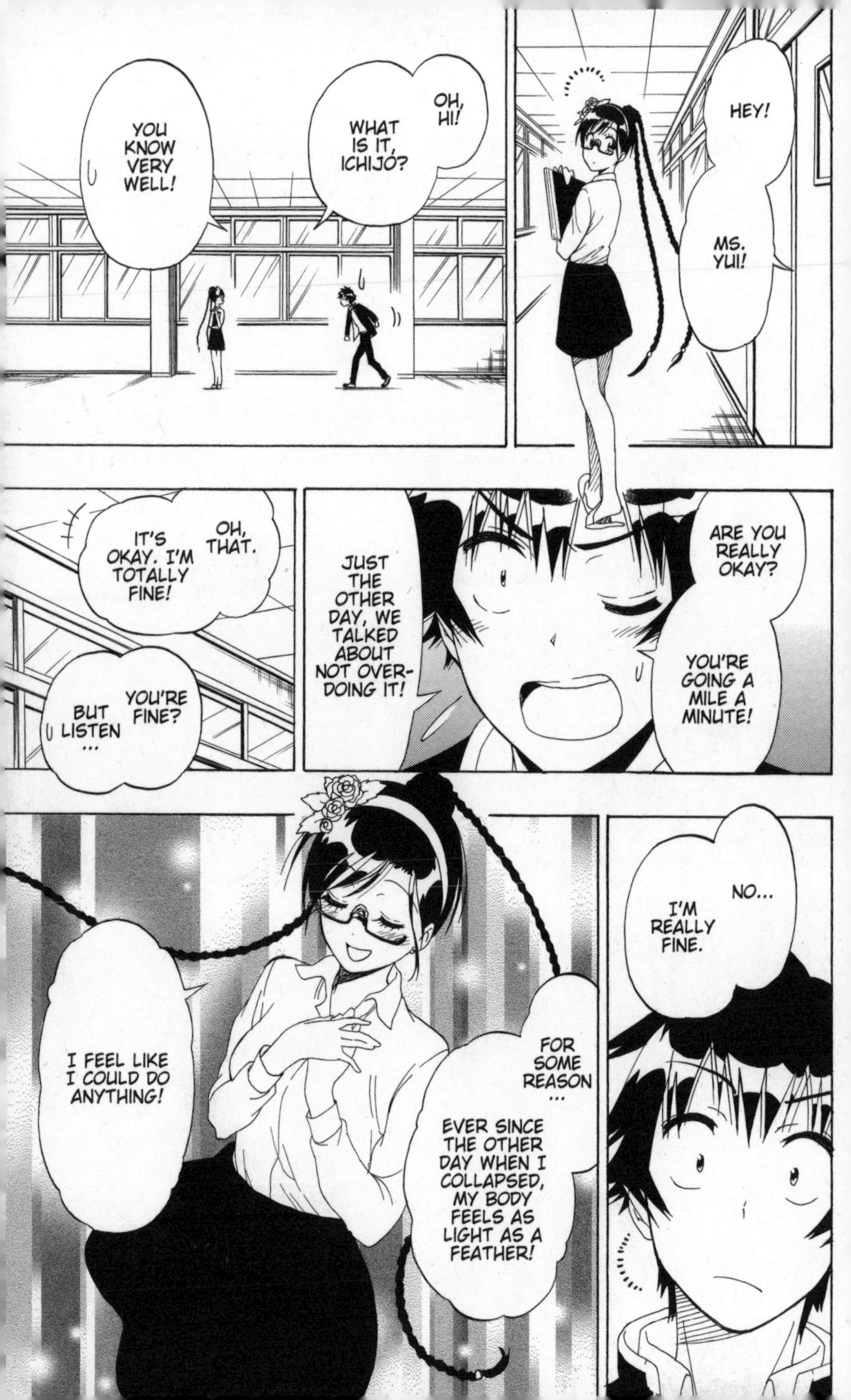
HEY!
MS. YUI!
OH, HI!
WHAT IS IT, ICHIJO?
YOU KNOW VERY WELL!
ARE YOU REALLY OKAY?
YOU'RE GOING A MILE A MINUTE!
JUST THE OTHER DAY, WE TALKED ABOUT NOT OVER-DOING IT!
OH, THAT.
IT'S OKAY. I'M TOTALLY FINE!
YOU'RE FINE?
BUT LISTEN...
NO...
I'M REALLY FINE.
FOR SOME REASON...
EVER SINCE THE OTHER DAY WHEN I COLLAPSED, MY BODY FEELS AS LIGHT AS A FEATHER!
I FEEL LIKE I COULD DO ANYTHING!

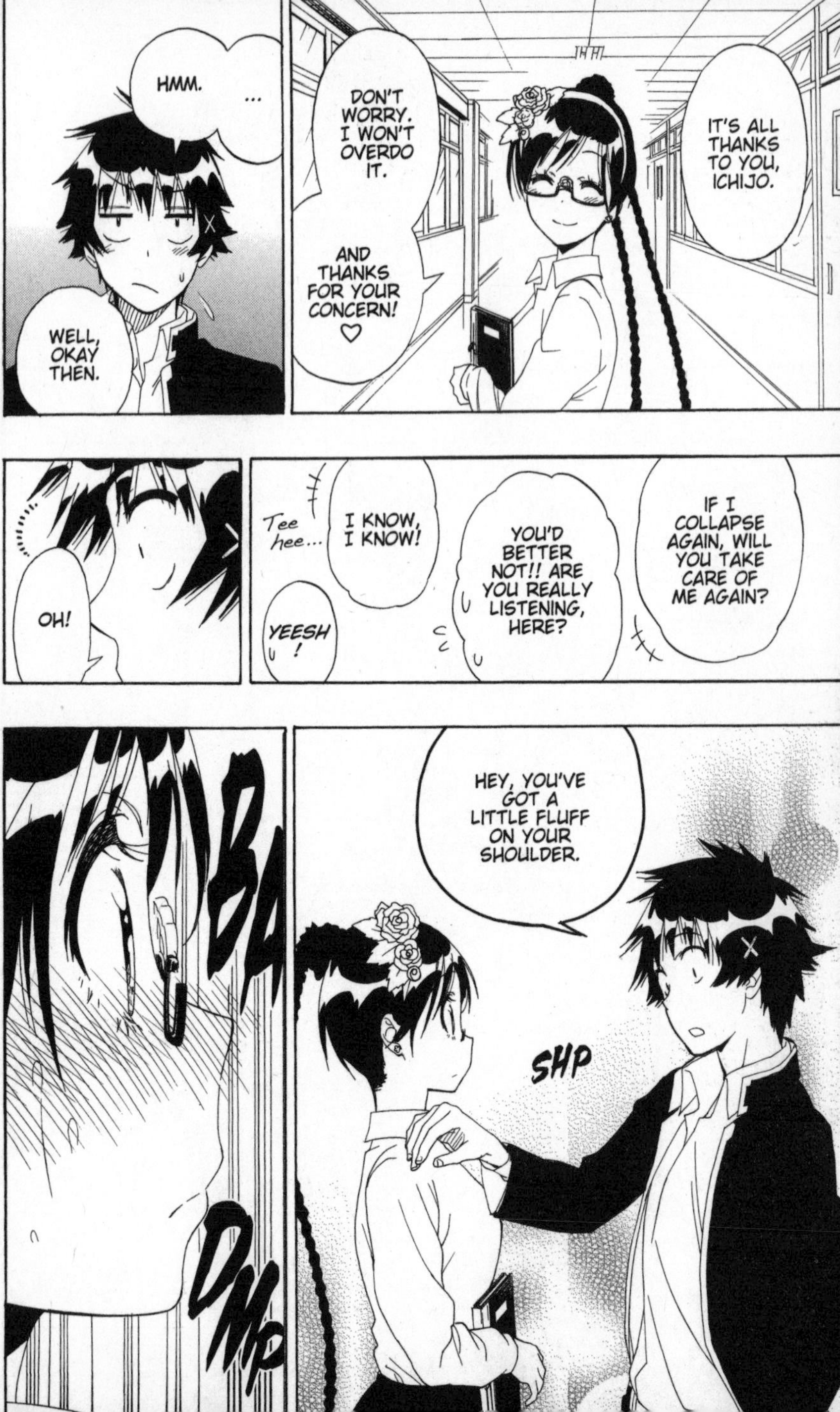
IT'S ALL THANKS TO YOU, ICHIJO.
DON'T WORRY. I WON'T OVERDO IT.
AND THANKS FOR YOUR CONCERN! ♡
HMM.
...
WELL, OKAY THEN.
IF I COLLAPSE AGAIN, WILL YOU TAKE CARE OF ME AGAIN?
YOU'D BETTER NOT!! ARE YOU REALLY LISTENING, HERE?
I KNOW, I KNOW!
Tee hee...
YEESH!
OH!
HEY, YOU'VE GOT A LITTLE FLUFF ON YOUR SHOULDER.
SHP
BA
DMP

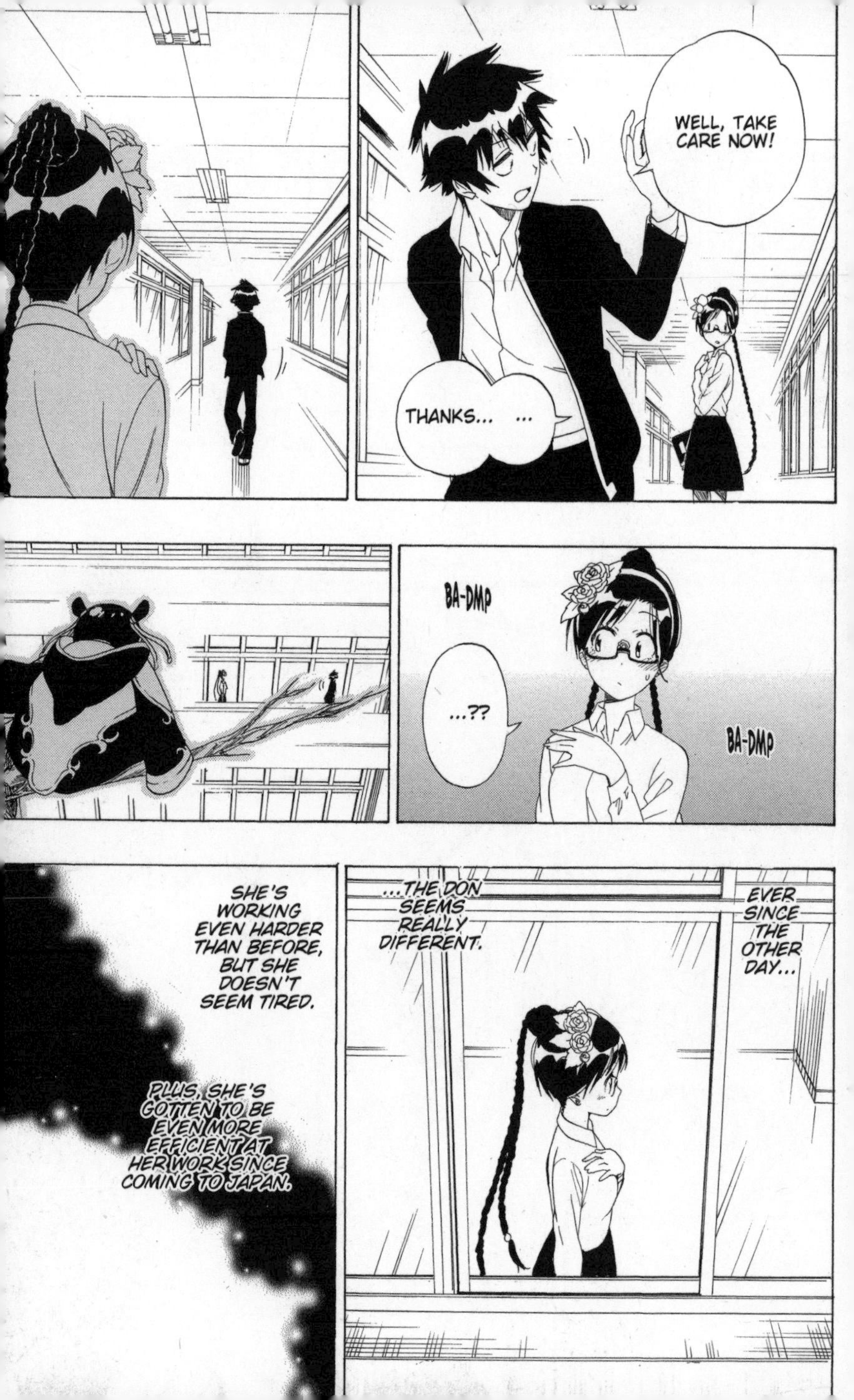
WELL, TAKE CARE NOW!
THANKS... ...
BA-DMP
...??
BA-DMP
EVER SINCE THE OTHER DAY...
...THE DON SEEMS REALLY DIFFERENT.
SHE'S WORKING EVEN HARDER THAN BEFORE, BUT SHE DOESN'T SEEM TIRED.
PLUS, SHE'S GOTTEN TO BE EVEN MORE EFFICIENT AT HER WORK SINCE COMING TO JAPAN.

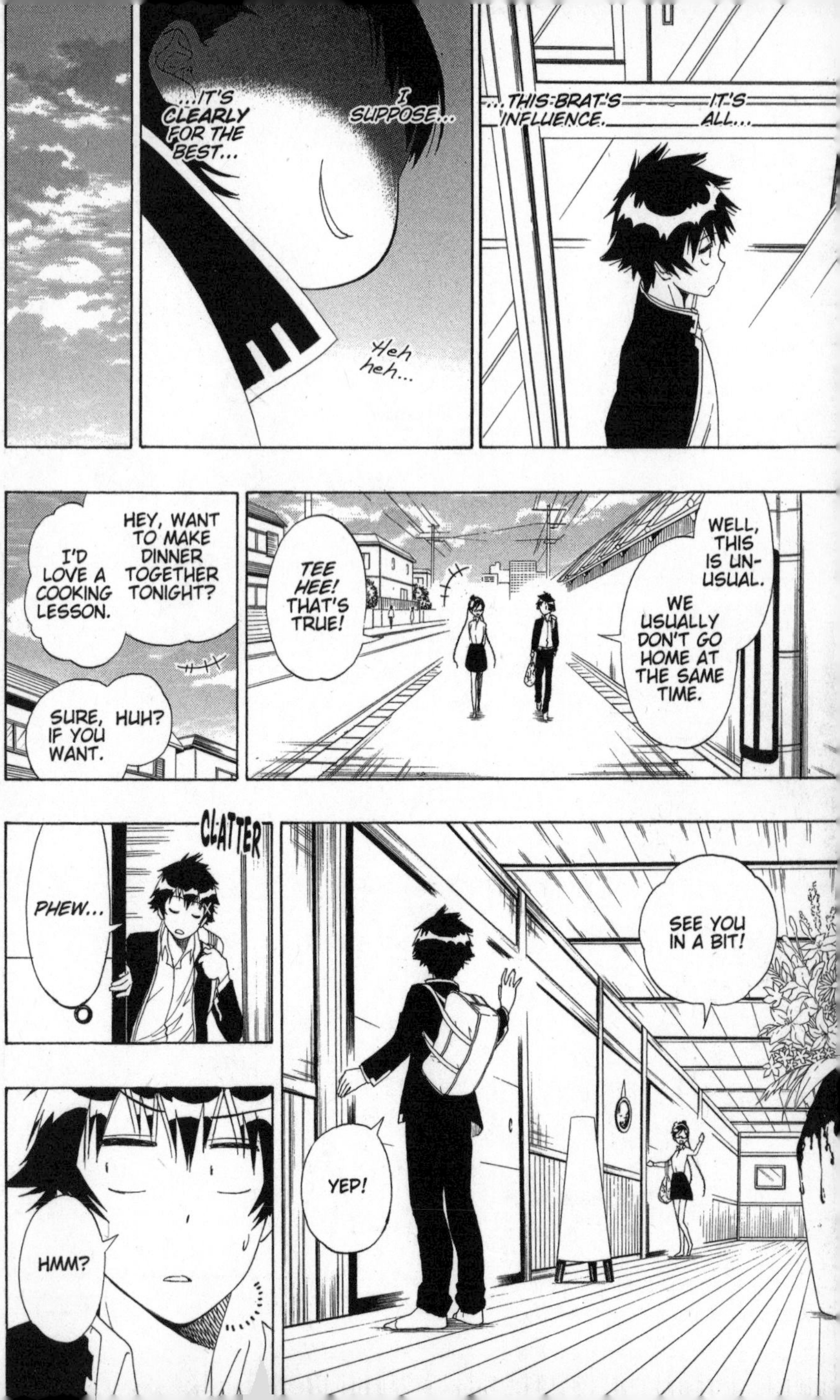
IT'S ALL...
...THIS BRAT'S INFLUENCE.
I SUPPOSE...
...IT'S CLEARLY FOR THE BEST...
Heh heh...
WELL, THIS IS UN-USUAL.
WE USUALLY DON'T GO HOME AT THE SAME TIME.
TEE HEE! THAT'S TRUE!
HEY, WANT TO MAKE DINNER TOGETHER TONIGHT?
I'D LOVE A COOKING LESSON.
HUH?
SURE, IF YOU WANT.
SEE YOU IN A BIT!
YEP!
CLATTER
PHEW...
HMM?

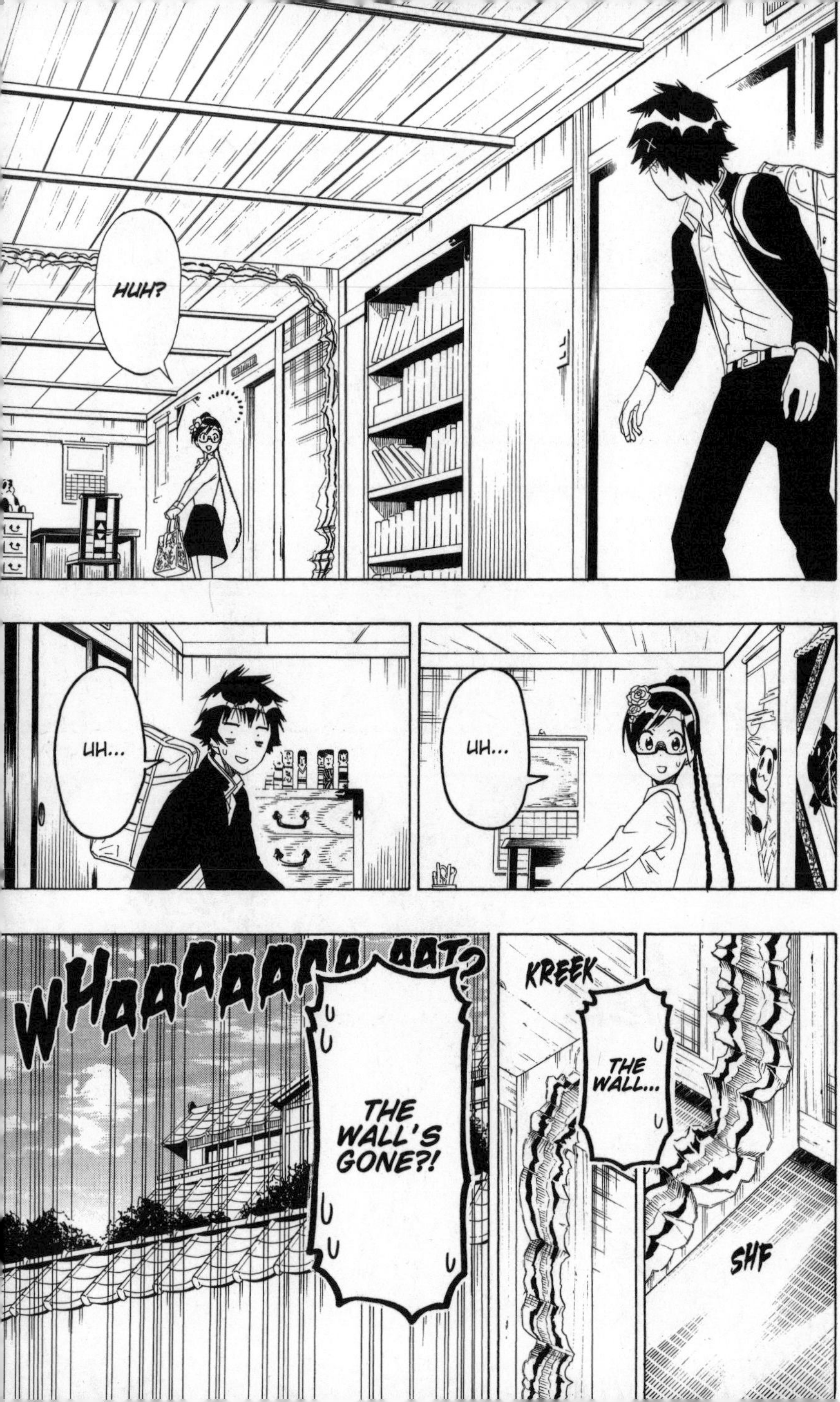
HUH?
UH...
UH...
KREEK
THE WALL...
SHF
THE WALL'S GONE?!
WHAAAAAAAAAT?

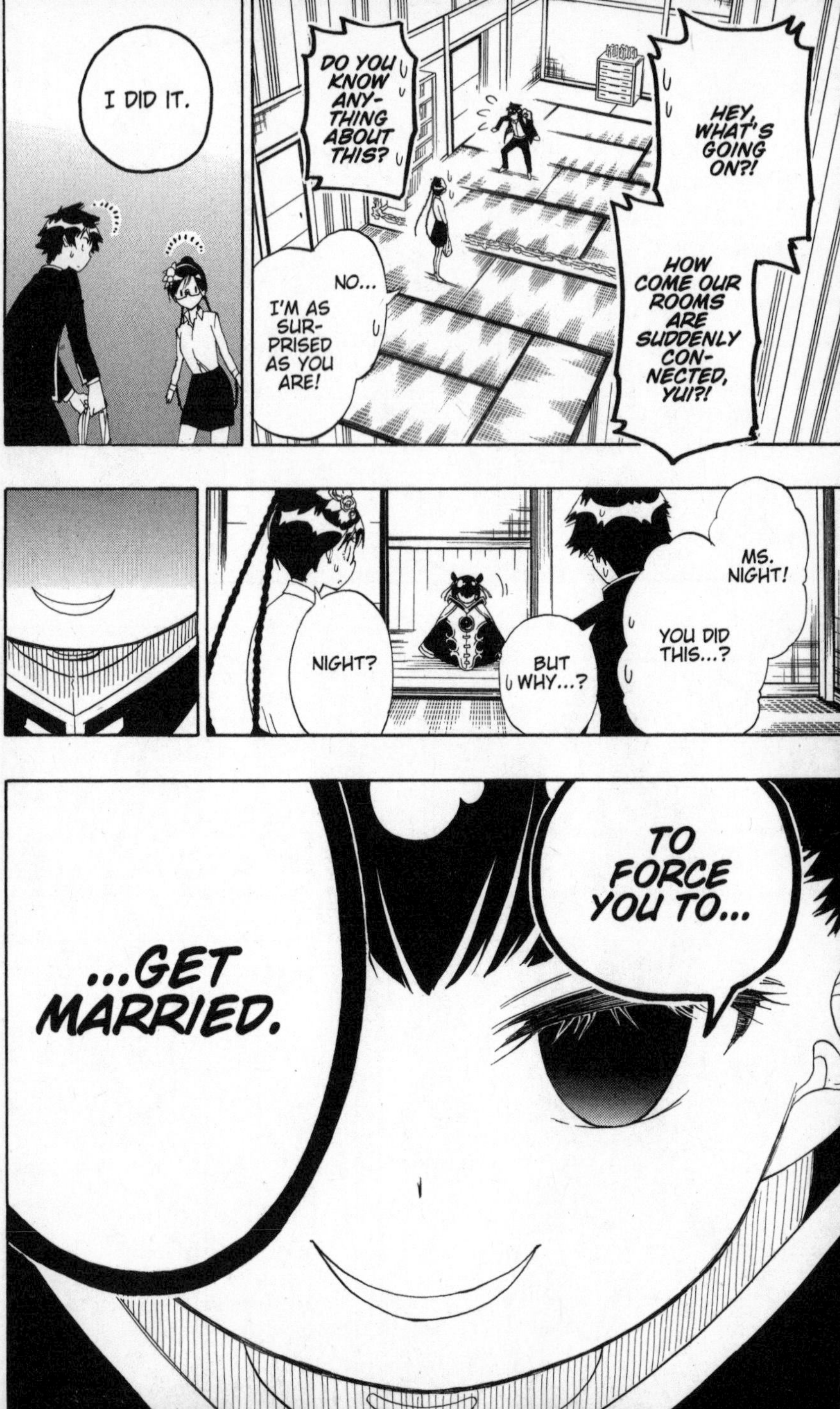
HEY, WHAT'S GOING ON?!
HOW COME OUR ROOMS ARE SUDDENLY CON-NECTED, YUI?!
DO YOU KNOW ANY-THING ABOUT THIS?
NO...
I'M AS SUR-PRISED AS YOU ARE!
I DID IT.
MS. NIGHT!
YOU DID THIS...?
BUT WHY...?
NIGHT?
TO FORCE YOU TO...
...GET MARRIED.

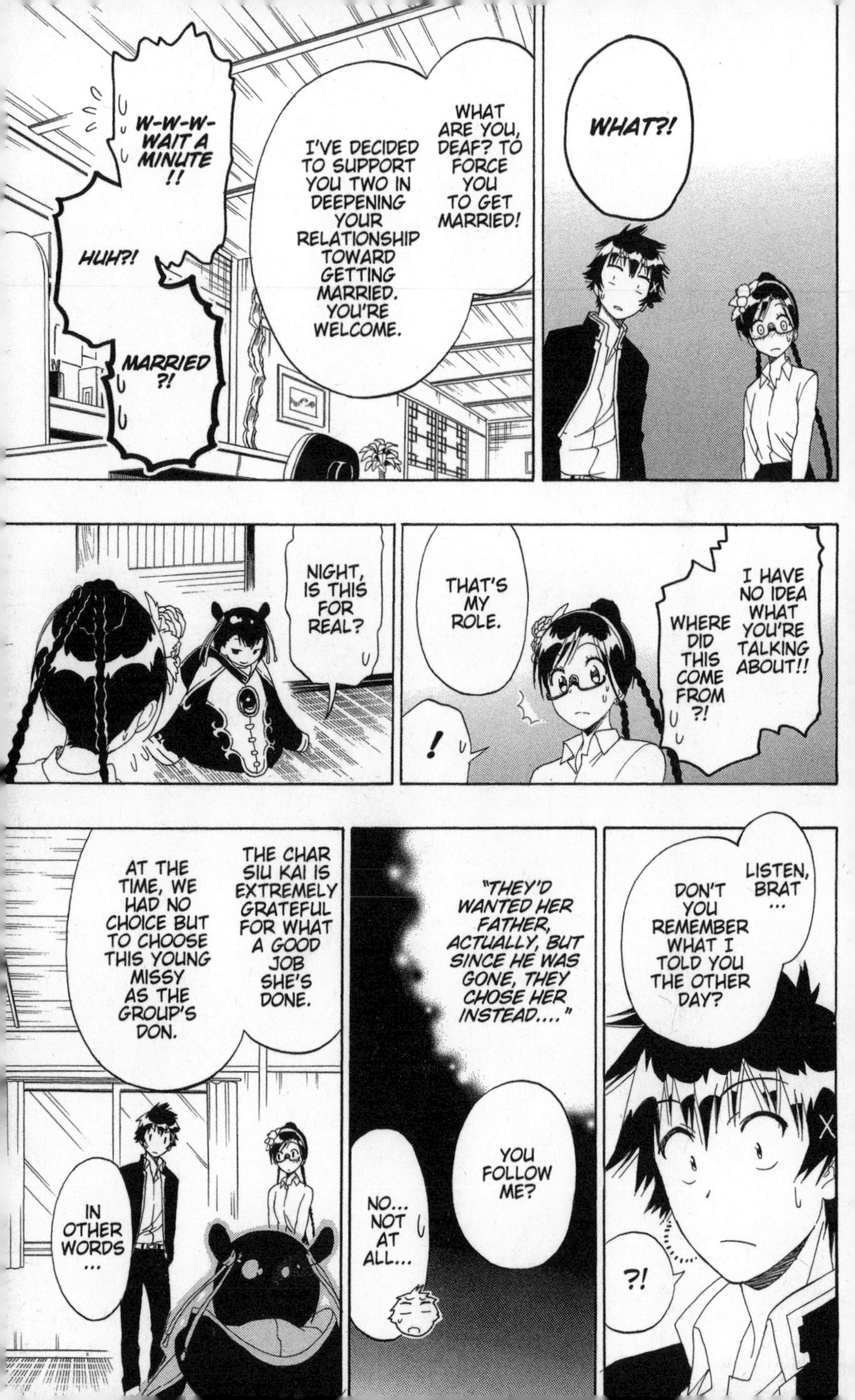
WHAT?!
WHAT ARE YOU, DEAF? TO FORCE YOU TO GET MARRIED!
I'VE DECIDED TO SUPPORT YOU TWO IN DEEPENING YOUR RELATIONSHIP TOWARD GETTING MARRIED. YOU'RE WELCOME.
W-W-W-WAIT A MINUTE!!
HUH?!
MARRIED?!
I HAVE NO IDEA WHAT YOU'RE TALKING ABOUT!!
WHERE DID THIS COME FROM?!
THAT'S MY ROLE.
!
NIGHT, IS THIS FOR REAL?
LISTEN, BRAT...
DON'T YOU REMEMBER WHAT I TOLD YOU THE OTHER DAY?
?!
"THEY'D WANTED HER FATHER, ACTUALLY, BUT SINCE HE WAS GONE, THEY CHOSE HER INSTEAD...."
YOU FOLLOW ME?
NO... NOT AT ALL...
THE CHAR SIU KAI IS EXTREMELY GRATEFUL FOR WHAT A GOOD JOB SHE'S DONE.
AT THE TIME, WE HAD NO CHOICE BUT TO CHOOSE THIS YOUNG MISSY AS THE GROUP'S DON.
IN OTHER WORDS...

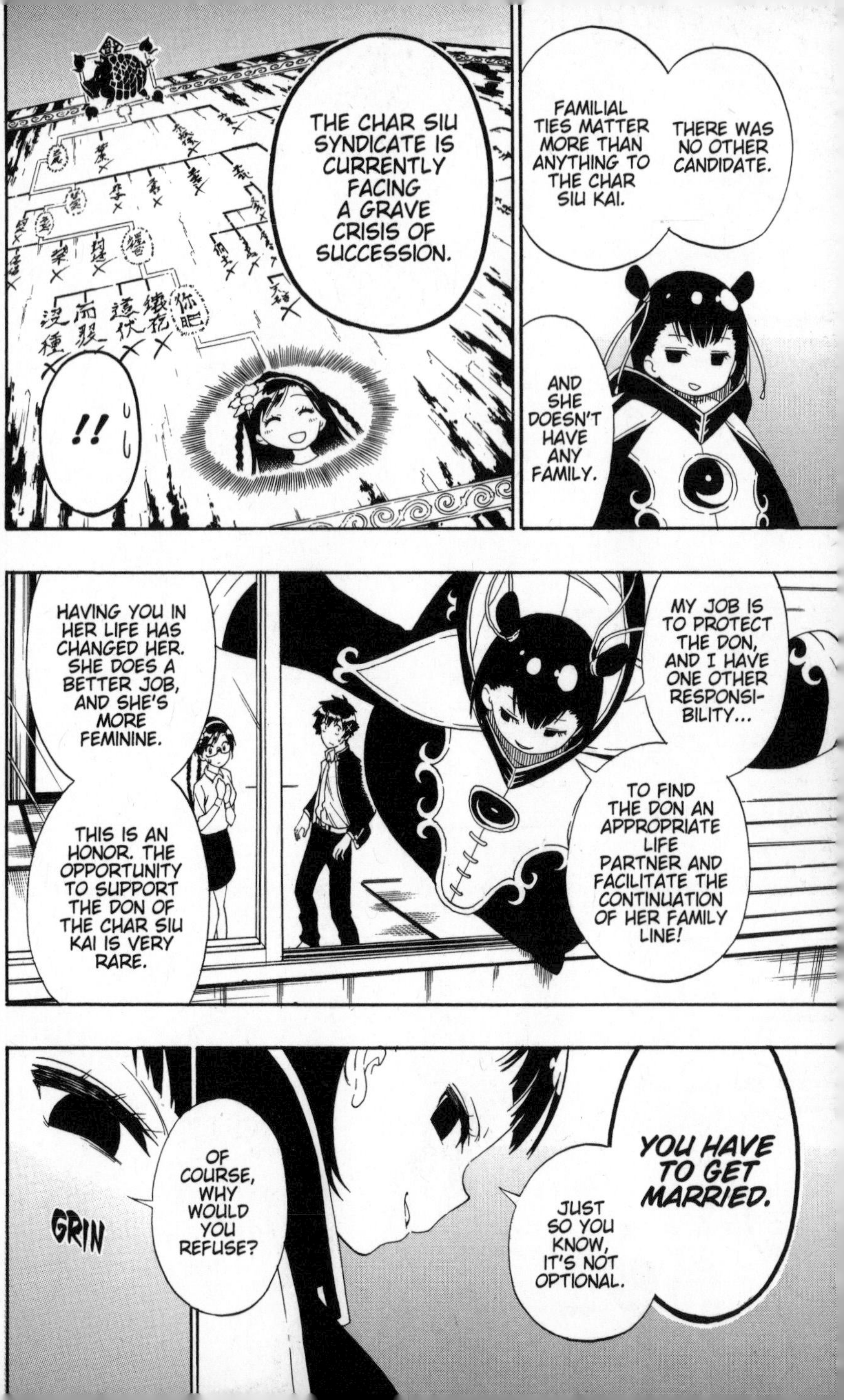

There was no other candidate.
Familial ties matter more than anything to the Char Siu Kai.
And she doesn't have any family.
The Char Siu Syndicate is currently facing a grave crisis of succession.
!!
My job is to protect the Don, and I have one other responsibility...
To find the Don an appropriate life partner and facilitate the continuation of her family line!
Having you in her life has changed her. She does a better job, and she's more feminine.
This is an honor. The opportunity to support the Don of the Char Siu Kai is very rare.
You have to get married.
Just so you know, it's not optional.
Of course, why would you refuse?
GRIN

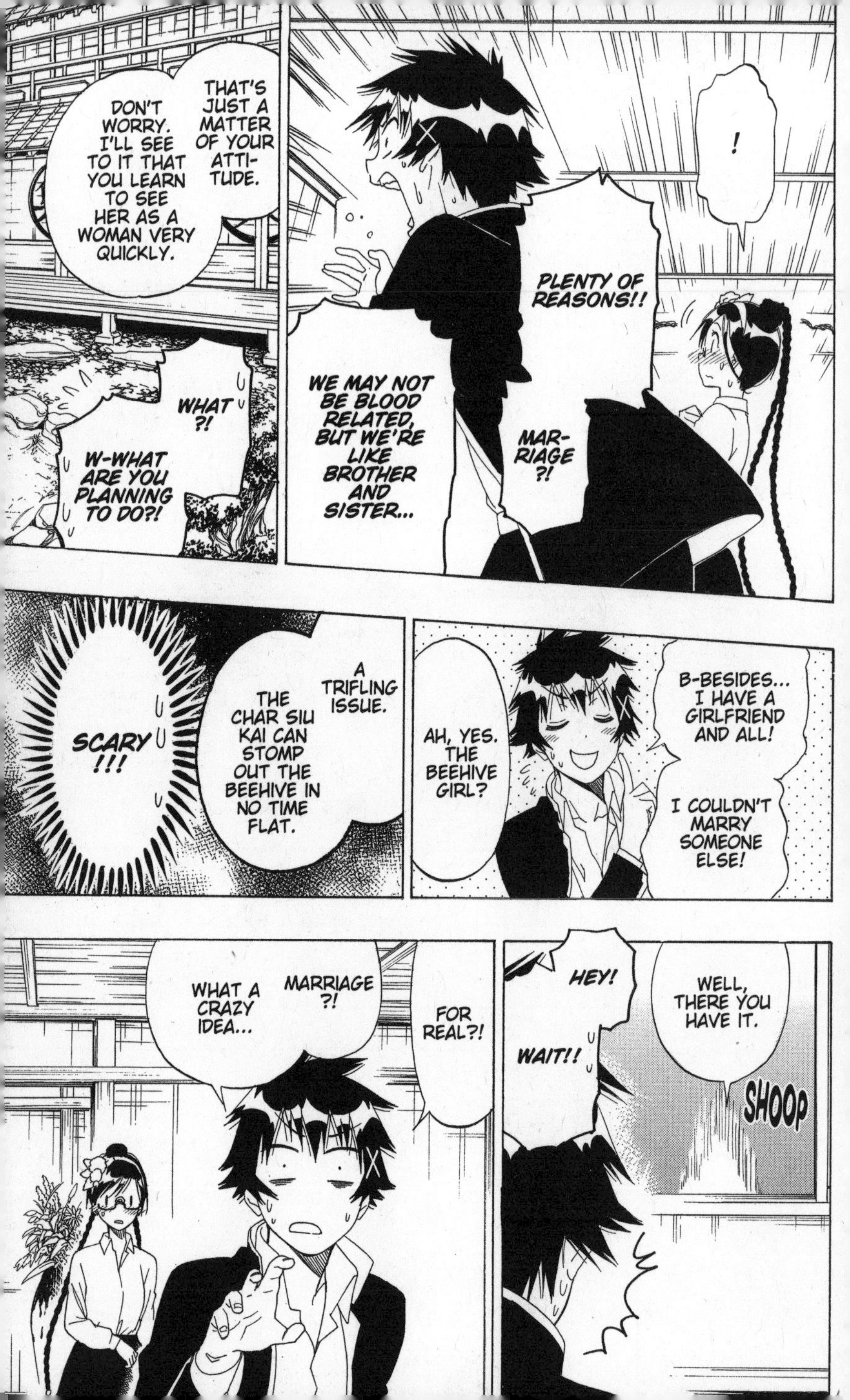
!
PLENTY OF REASONS!!
MAR-RIAGE ?!
WE MAY NOT BE BLOOD RELATED, BUT WE'RE LIKE BROTHER AND SISTER...
THAT'S JUST A MATTER OF YOUR ATTI-TUDE.
DON'T WORRY. I'LL SEE TO IT THAT YOU LEARN TO SEE HER AS A WOMAN VERY QUICKLY.
WHAT ?!
W-WHAT ARE YOU PLANNING TO DO?!
B-BESIDES... I HAVE A GIRLFRIEND AND ALL!
I COULDN'T MARRY SOMEONE ELSE!
AH, YES. THE BEEHIVE GIRL?
A TRIFLING ISSUE.
THE CHAR SIU KAI CAN STOMP OUT THE BEEHIVE IN NO TIME FLAT.
SCARY !!!
WELL, THERE YOU HAVE IT.
SHOOP
HEY!
WAIT!!
FOR REAL?!
MARRIAGE ?!
WHAT A CRAZY IDEA...

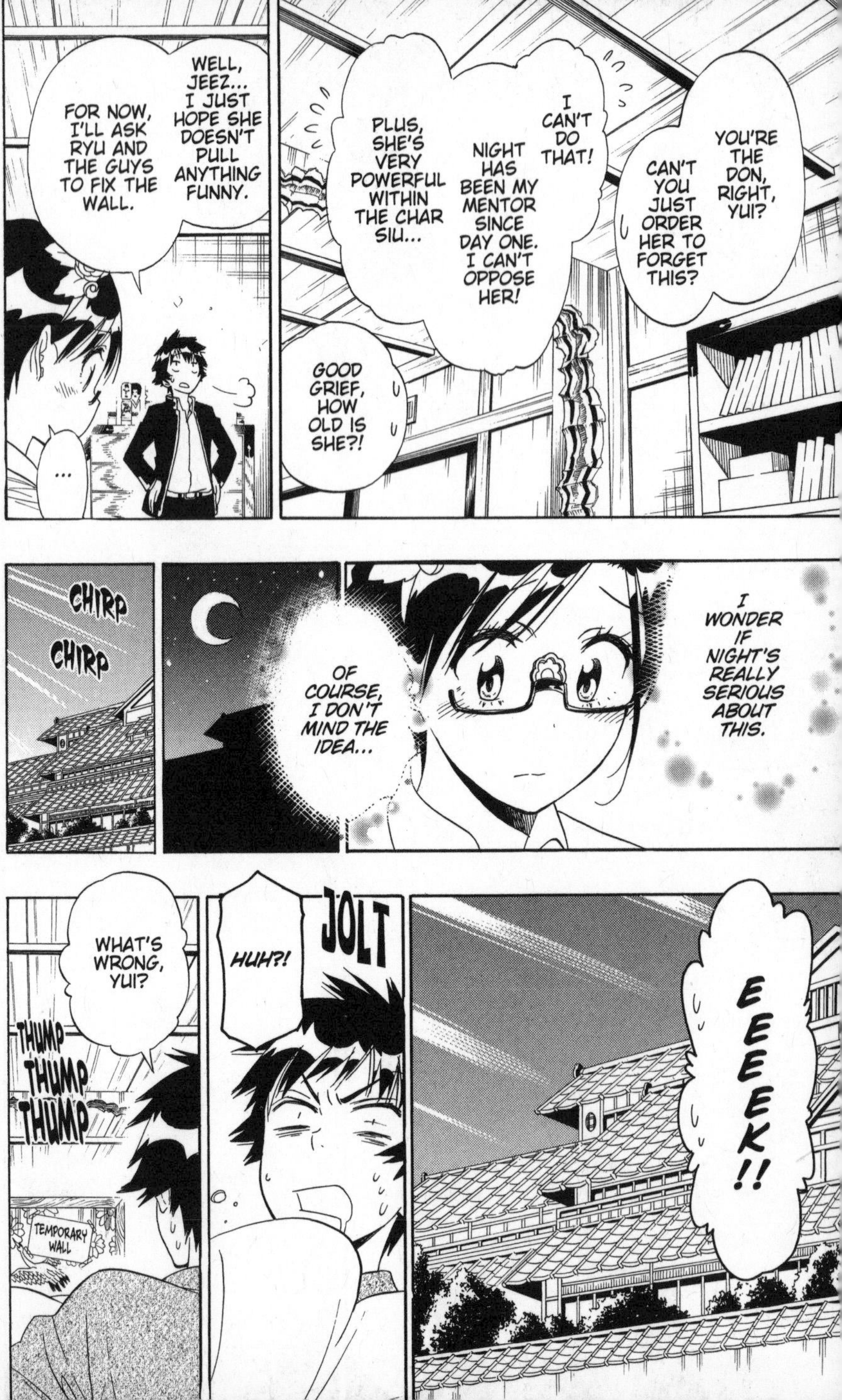
YOU'RE THE DON, RIGHT, YUI?
CAN'T YOU JUST ORDER HER TO FORGET THIS?
I CAN'T DO THAT!
NIGHT HAS BEEN MY MENTOR SINCE DAY ONE. I CAN'T OPPOSE HER!
PLUS, SHE'S VERY POWERFUL WITHIN THE CHAR SIU...
GOOD GRIEF, HOW OLD IS SHE?!
WELL, JEEZ... I JUST HOPE SHE DOESN'T PULL ANYTHING FUNNY.
FOR NOW, I'LL ASK RYU AND THE GUYS TO FIX THE WALL.
...
I WONDER IF NIGHT'S REALLY SERIOUS ABOUT THIS.
OF COURSE, I DON'T MIND THE IDEA...
CHIRP
CHIRP
EEEEEK!!
JOLT
HUH?!
WHAT'S WRONG, YUI?
THUMP THUMP THUMP
TEMPORARY WALL

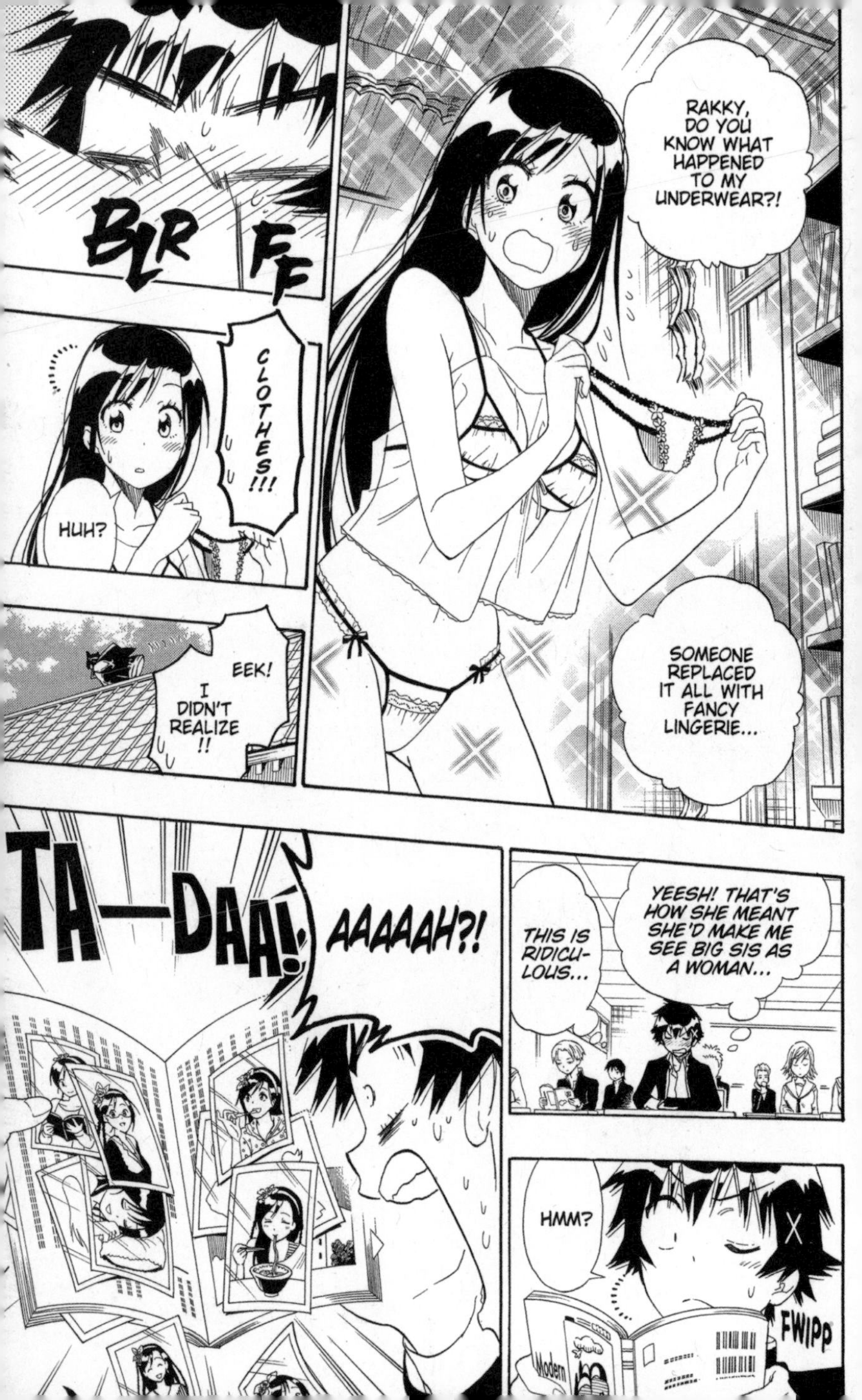
RAKKY, DO YOU KNOW WHAT HAPPENED TO MY UNDERWEAR?!
SOMEONE REPLACED IT ALL WITH FANCY LINGERIE...
BLR FF
CLOTHES!!!
HUH?
EEK! I DIDN'T REALIZE!!
HMM?
FWIPP
YEESH! THAT'S HOW SHE MEANT SHE'D MAKE ME SEE BIG SIS AS A WOMAN...
THIS IS RIDICULOUS...
TA-DAA!
AAAAAH?!
Modern

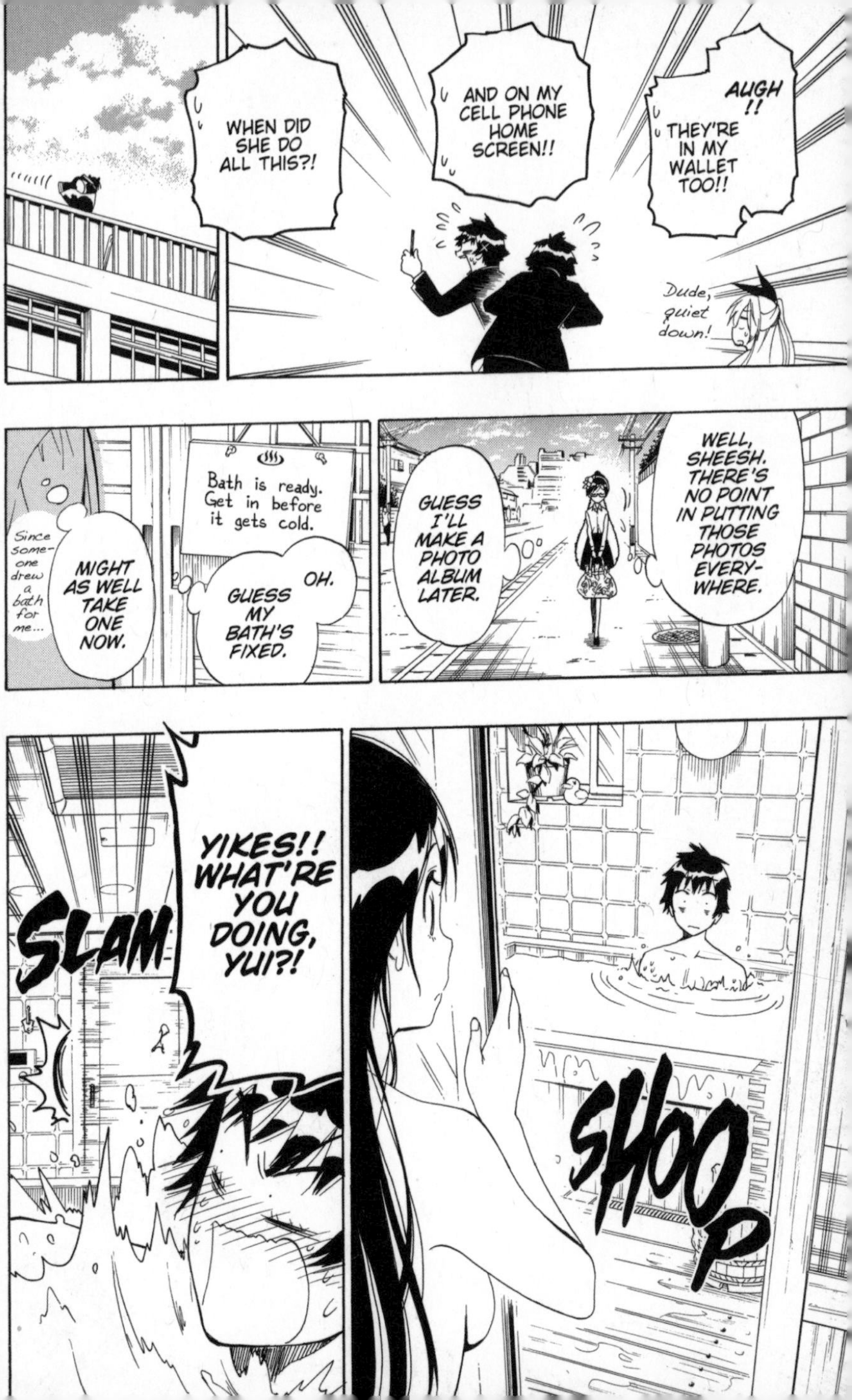
AUGH!! THEY'RE IN MY WALLET TOO!!
Dude, quiet down!
AND ON MY CELL PHONE HOME SCREEN!!
WHEN DID SHE DO ALL THIS?!
WELL, SHEESH. THERE'S NO POINT IN PUTTING THOSE PHOTOS EVERYWHERE.
GUESS I'LL MAKE A PHOTO ALBUM LATER.
Bath is ready. Get in before it gets cold.
OH. GUESS MY BATH'S FIXED.
MIGHT AS WELL TAKE ONE NOW.
Since someone drew a bath for me...
SHOOP
YIKES!! WHAT'RE YOU DOING, YUI?!
SLAM

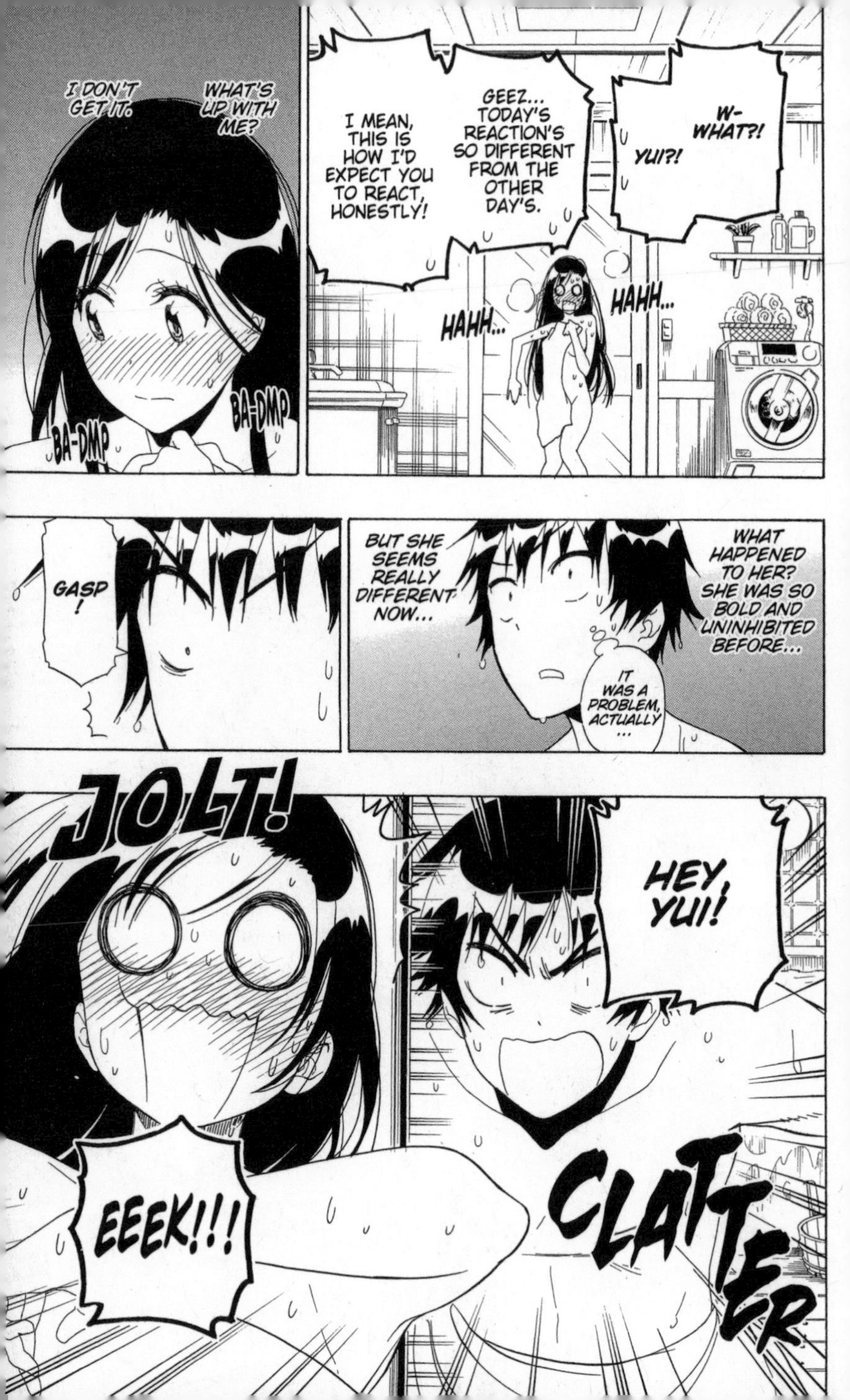
W-
WHAT?!
YUI?!
GEEZ... TODAY'S REACTION'S SO DIFFERENT FROM THE OTHER DAY'S.
I MEAN, THIS IS HOW I'D EXPECT YOU TO REACT, HONESTLY!
HAHH...
HAHH...
WHAT'S UP WITH ME?
I DON'T GET IT.
BA-DMP
BA-DMP
WHAT HAPPENED TO HER? SHE WAS SO BOLD AND UNINHIBITED BEFORE...
IT WAS A PROBLEM, ACTUALLY...
BUT SHE SEEMS REALLY DIFFERENT NOW...
GASP!
HEY, YUI!
CLATTER
JOLT!
EEEK!!!

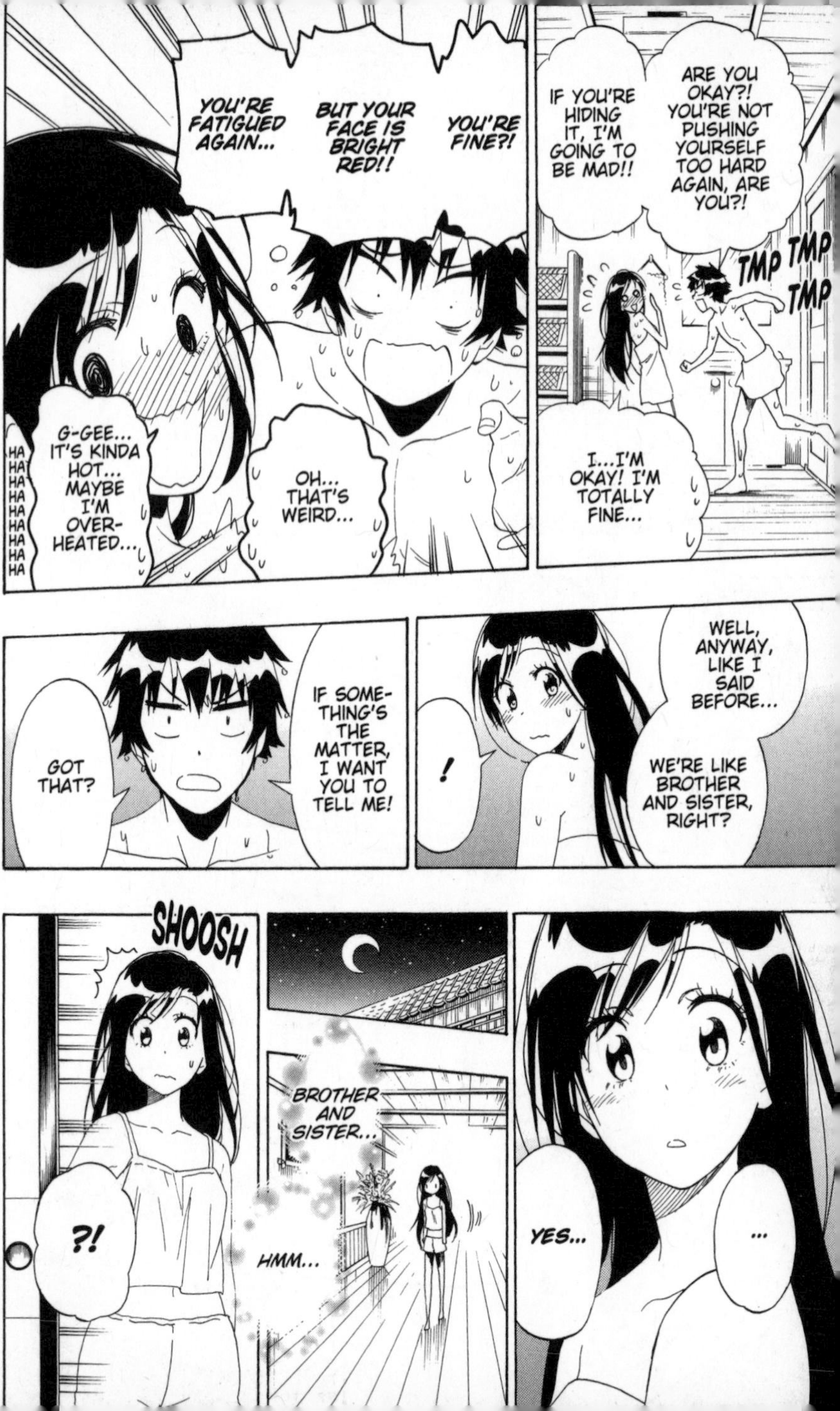
ARE YOU OKAY?! YOU'RE NOT PUSHING YOURSELF TOO HARD AGAIN, ARE YOU?!
IF YOU'RE HIDING IT, I'M GOING TO BE MAD!!
TMP TMP TMP
I...I'M OKAY! I'M TOTALLY FINE...
YOU'RE FINE?!
BUT YOUR FACE IS BRIGHT RED!!
YOU'RE FATIGUED AGAIN...
OH... THAT'S WEIRD...
G-GEE... IT'S KINDA HOT... MAYBE I'M OVER-HEATED...
HA HA HA HA HA HA HA HA HA
WELL, ANYWAY, LIKE I SAID BEFORE...
WE'RE LIKE BROTHER AND SISTER, RIGHT?
!
IF SOME-THING'S THE MATTER, I WANT YOU TO TELL ME!
GOT THAT?
YES...
...
BROTHER AND SISTER...
HMM...
SHOOSH
?!

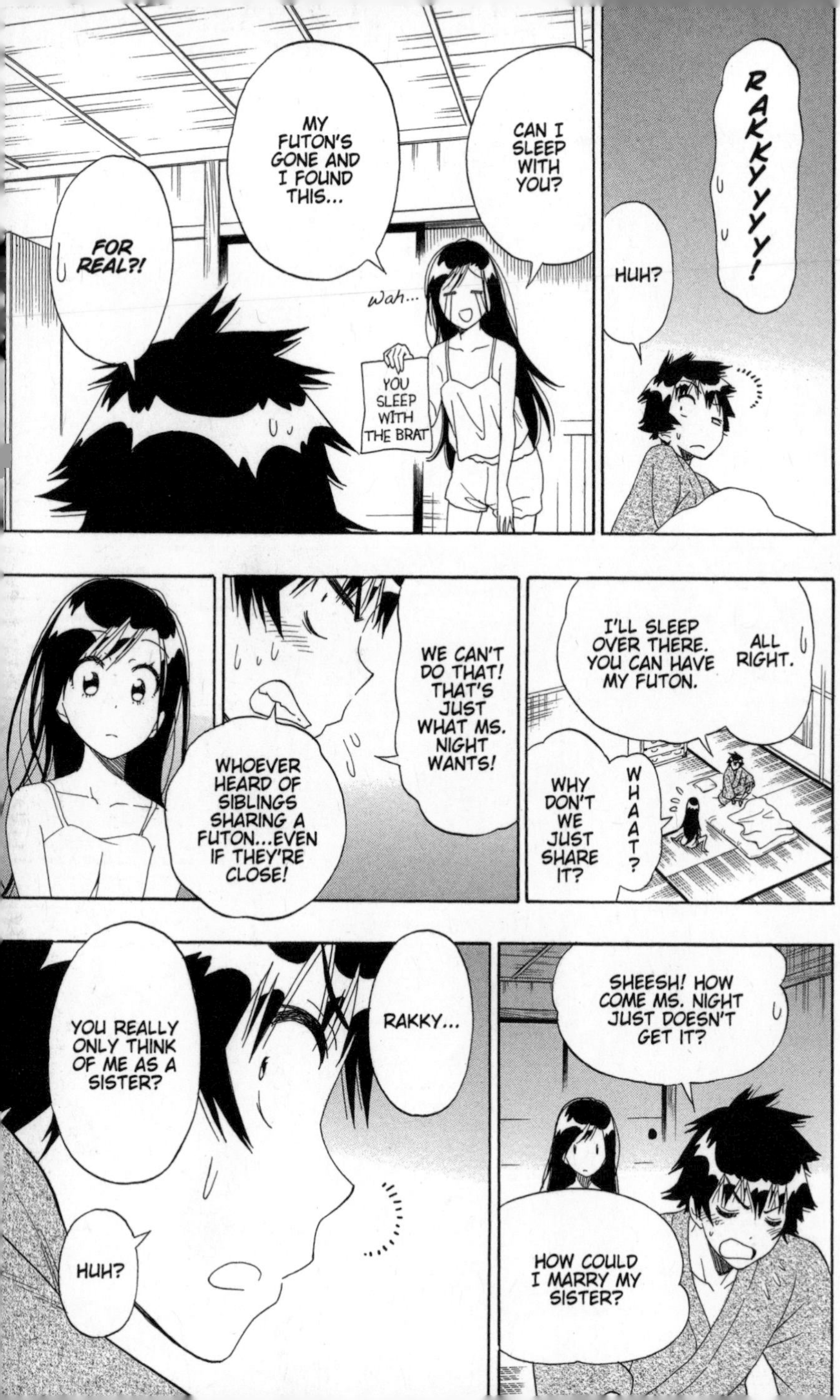
RAKKYYYY!
HUH?
CAN I SLEEP WITH YOU?
MY FUTON'S GONE AND I FOUND THIS...
Wah...
YOU SLEEP WITH THE BRAT
FOR REAL?!
ALL RIGHT.
I'LL SLEEP OVER THERE. YOU CAN HAVE MY FUTON.
WHAAAT?
WHY DON'T WE JUST SHARE IT?
WE CAN'T DO THAT! THAT'S JUST WHAT MS. NIGHT WANTS!
WHOEVER HEARD OF SIBLINGS SHARING A FUTON...EVEN IF THEY'RE CLOSE!
SHEESH! HOW COME MS. NIGHT JUST DOESN'T GET IT?
HOW COULD I MARRY MY SISTER?
RAKKY...
YOU REALLY ONLY THINK OF ME AS A SISTER?
HUH?

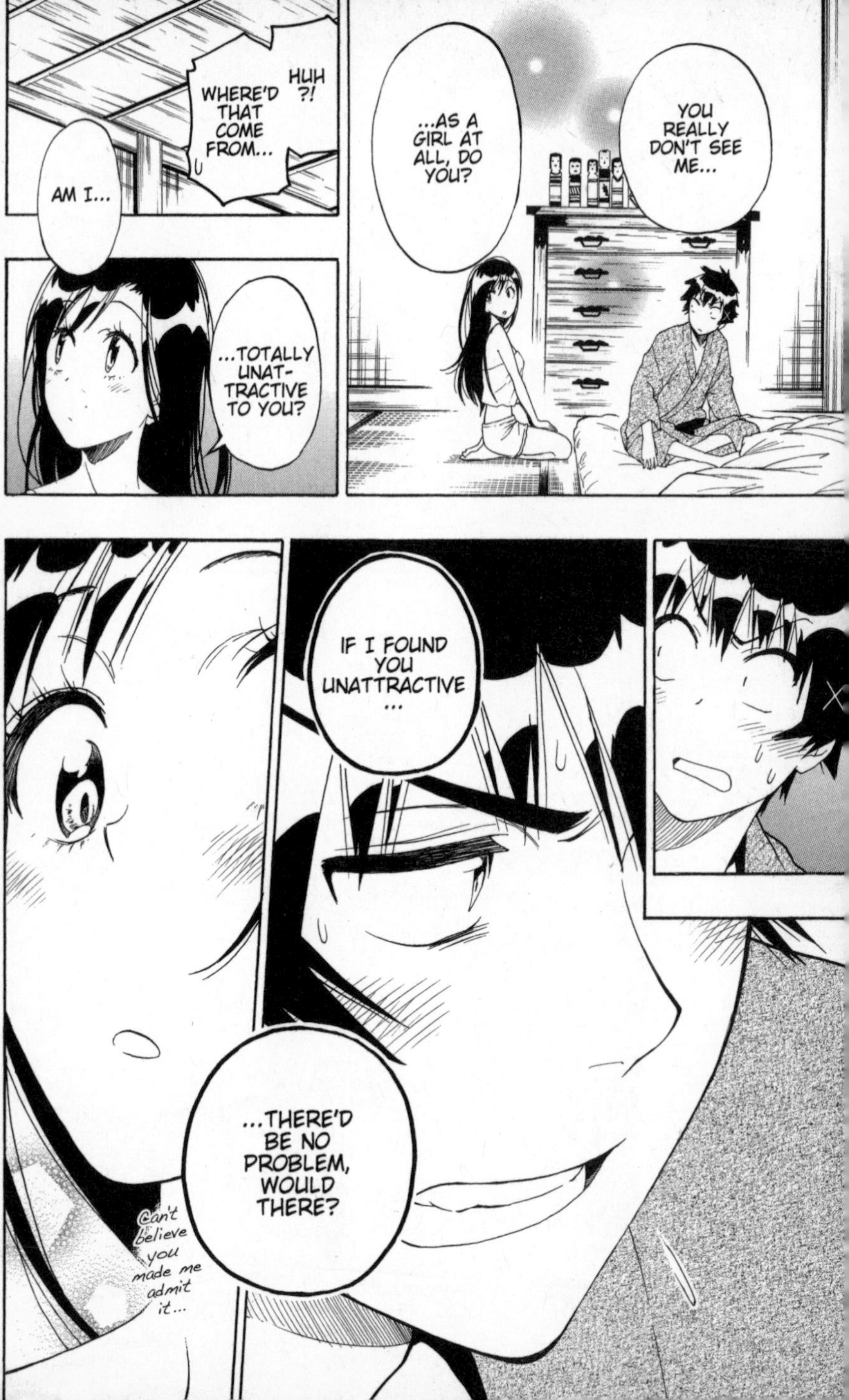
YOU REALLY DON'T SEE ME...
...AS A GIRL AT ALL, DO YOU?
HUH ?!
WHERE'D THAT COME FROM...
AM I...
...TOTALLY UNAT-TRACTIVE TO YOU?
IF I FOUND YOU UNATTRACTIVE ...
...THERE'D BE NO PROBLEM, WOULD THERE?
Can't believe you made me admit it...

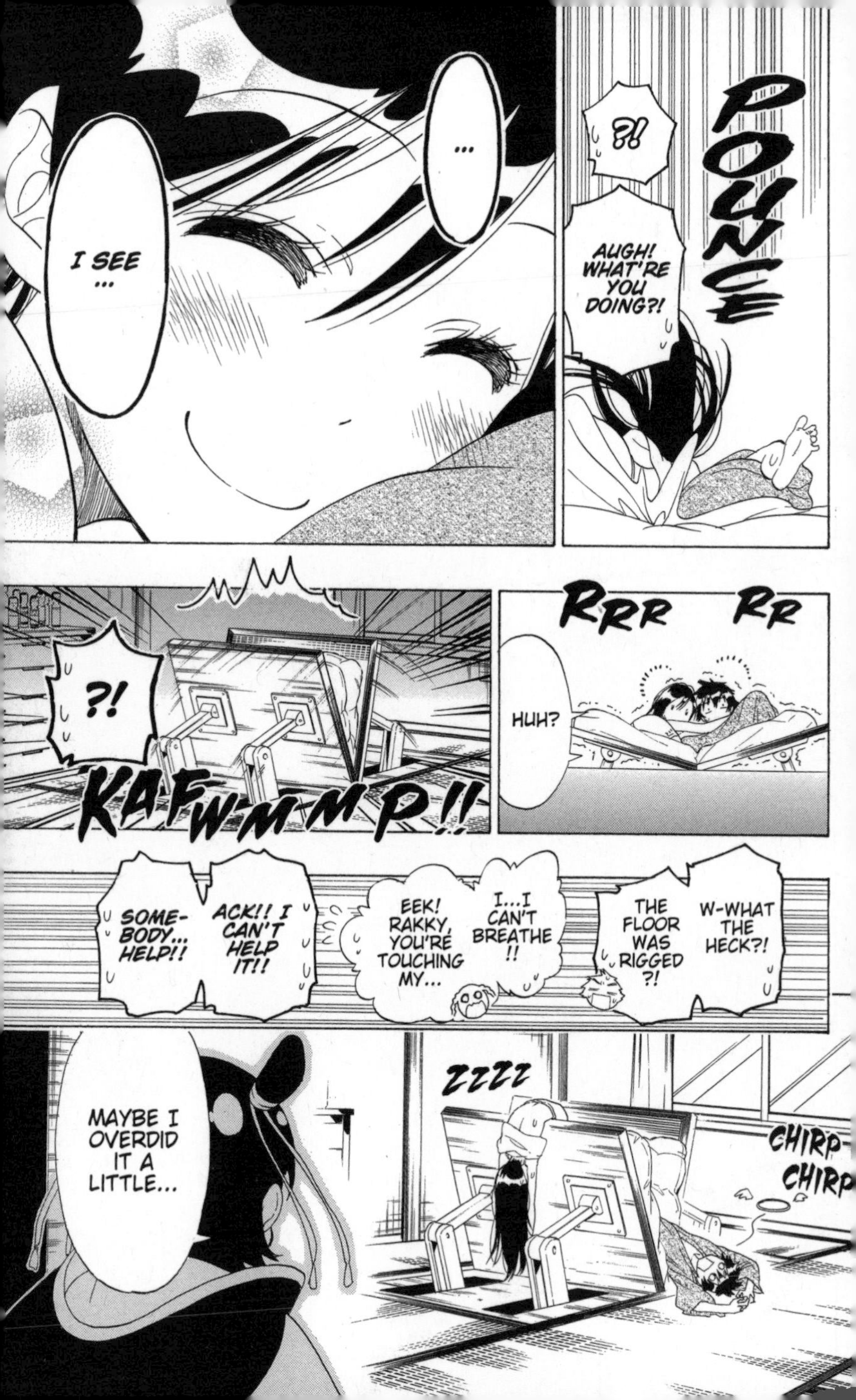
POUNCE
?!
AUGH! WHAT'RE YOU DOING?!
...
I SEE ...
RRR RR
HUH?
?!
KAFWMMP!!
W-WHAT THE HECK?!
THE FLOOR WAS RIGGED ?!
I...I CAN'T BREATHE !!
EEK! RAKKY, YOU'RE TOUCHING MY...
ACK!! I CAN'T HELP IT!!
SOME-BODY... HELP!!
CHIRP-CHIRP
ZZZZ
MAYBE I OVERDID IT A LITTLE...

Heh heh... Heh heh heh heh heh heh...

Not one panel.

I didn't appear in a single panel.

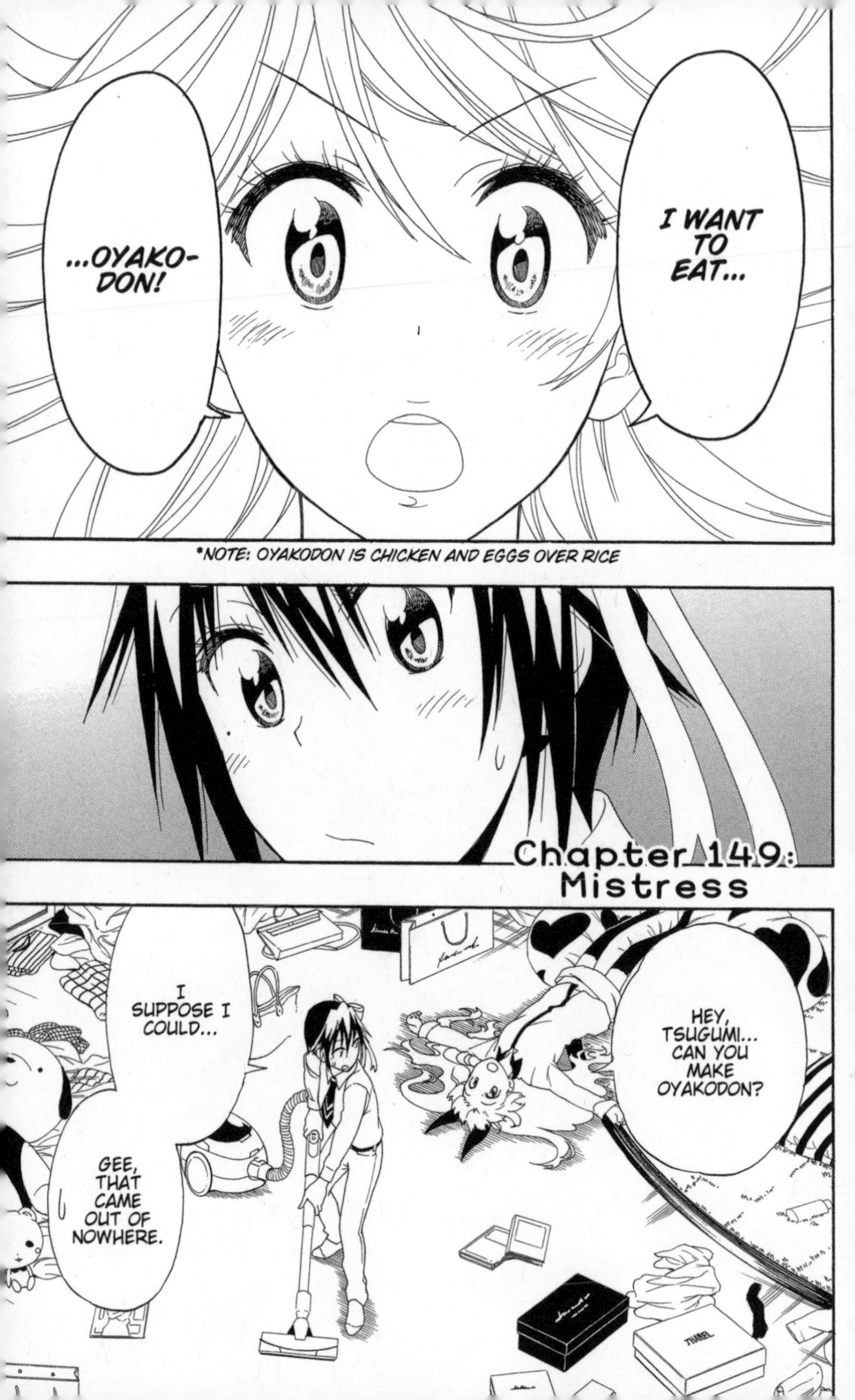
I WANT TO EAT...
...OYAKO-DON!
*NOTE: OYAKODON IS CHICKEN AND EGGS OVER RICE
Chapter 149: Mistress
HEY, TSUGUMI... CAN YOU MAKE OYAKODON?
I SUPPOSE I COULD...
GEE, THAT CAME OUT OF NOWHERE.
THANEL

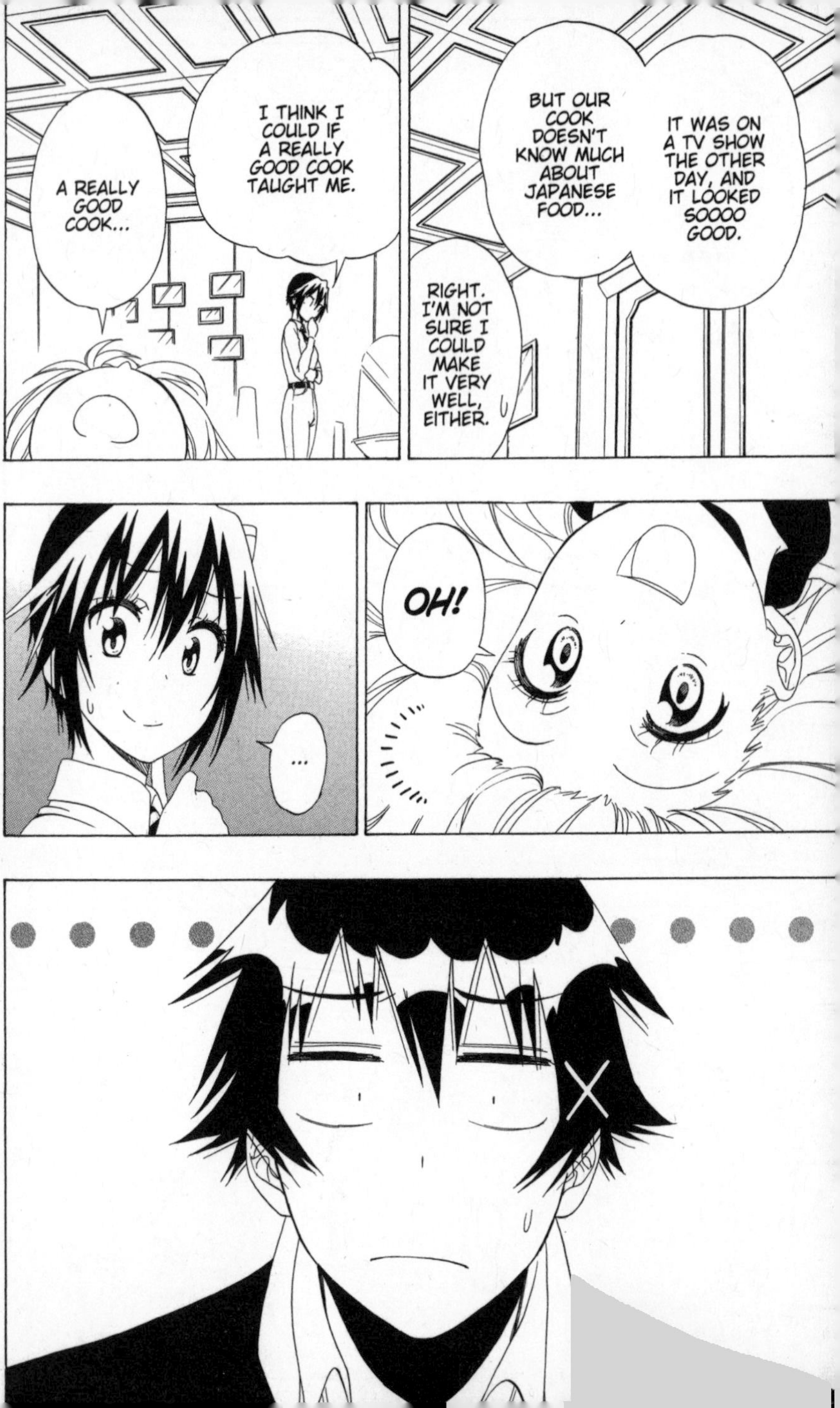
IT WAS ON A TV SHOW THE OTHER DAY, AND IT LOOKED SOOOO GOOD.
BUT OUR COOK DOESN'T KNOW MUCH ABOUT JAPANESE FOOD...
RIGHT. I'M NOT SURE I COULD MAKE IT VERY WELL, EITHER.
I THINK I COULD IF A REALLY GOOD COOK TAUGHT ME.
A REALLY GOOD COOK...
OH!
...

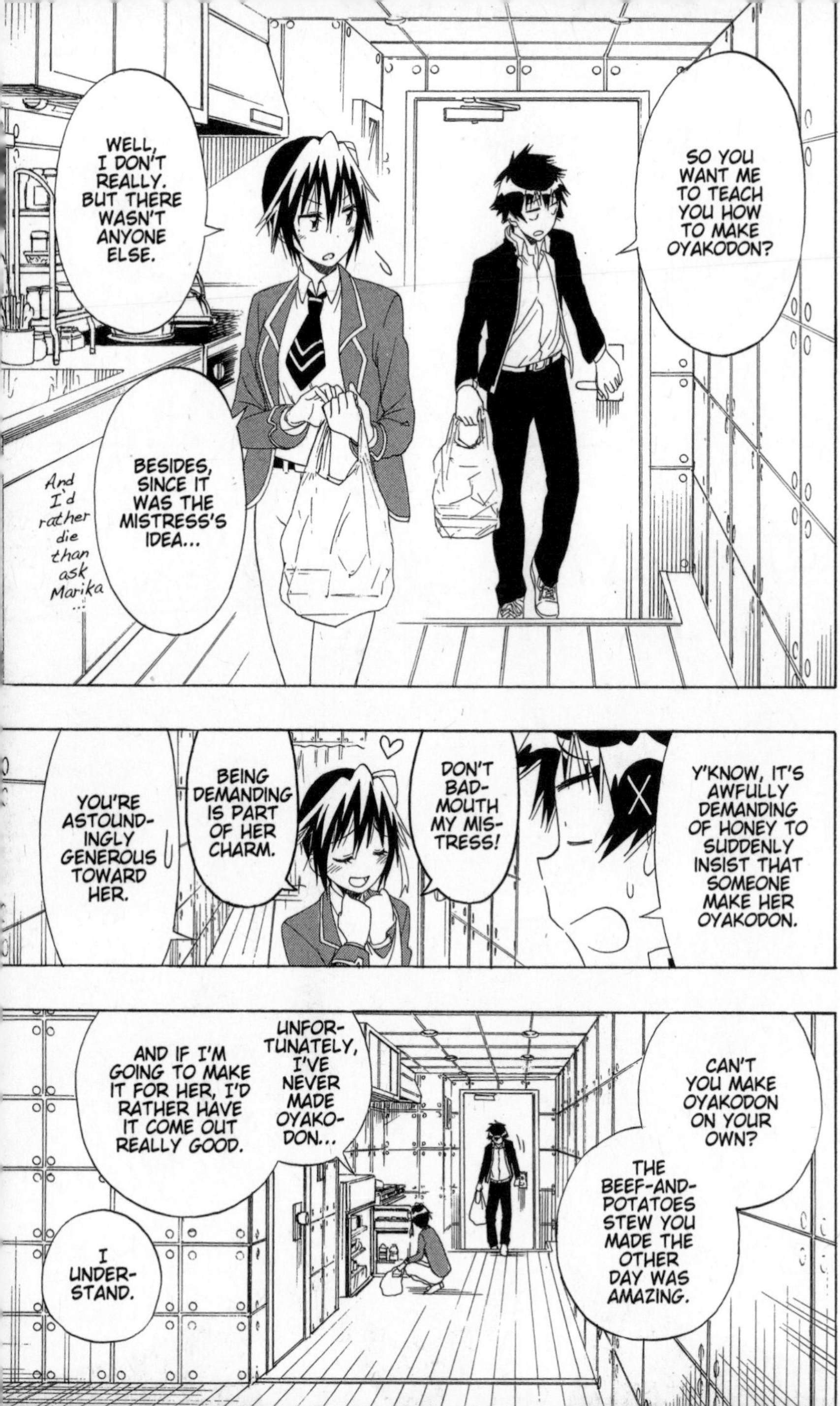
SO YOU WANT ME TO TEACH YOU HOW TO MAKE OYAKODON?
WELL, I DON'T REALLY. BUT THERE WASN'T ANYONE ELSE.
BESIDES, SINCE IT WAS THE MISTRESS'S IDEA...
And I'd rather die than ask Marika...
Y'KNOW, IT'S AWFULLY DEMANDING OF HONEY TO SUDDENLY INSIST THAT SOMEONE MAKE HER OYAKODON.
DON'T BAD-MOUTH MY MIS-TRESS!
BEING DEMANDING IS PART OF HER CHARM.
YOU'RE ASTOUND-INGLY GENEROUS TOWARD HER.
CAN'T YOU MAKE OYAKODON ON YOUR OWN?
THE BEEF-AND-POTATOES STEW YOU MADE THE OTHER DAY WAS AMAZING.
UNFOR-TUNATELY, I'VE NEVER MADE OYAKO-DON...
AND IF I'M GOING TO MAKE IT FOR HER, I'D RATHER HAVE IT COME OUT REALLY GOOD.
I UNDER-STAND.

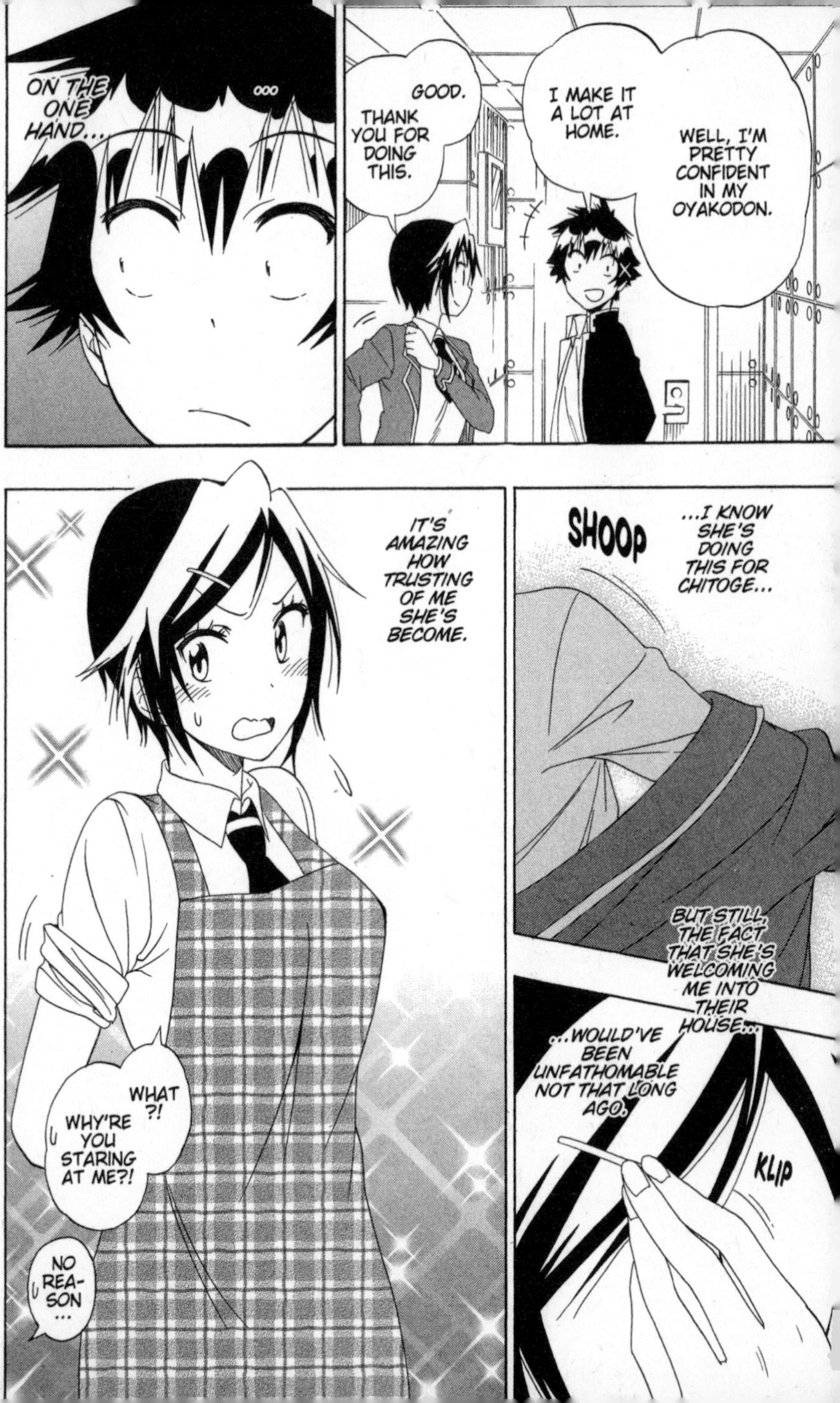
WELL, I'M PRETTY CONFIDENT IN MY OYAKODON.
I MAKE IT A LOT AT HOME.
GOOD.
THANK YOU FOR DOING THIS.
ON THE ONE HAND...
ooo
SHOOP
...I KNOW SHE'S DOING THIS FOR CHITOGE...
BUT STILL, THE FACT THAT SHE'S WELCOMING ME INTO THEIR HOUSE...
...WOULD'VE BEEN UNFATHOMABLE NOT THAT LONG AGO.
KLIP
IT'S AMAZING HOW TRUSTING OF ME SHE'S BECOME.
WHAT ?!
WHY'RE YOU STARING AT ME?!
NO REA-SON...

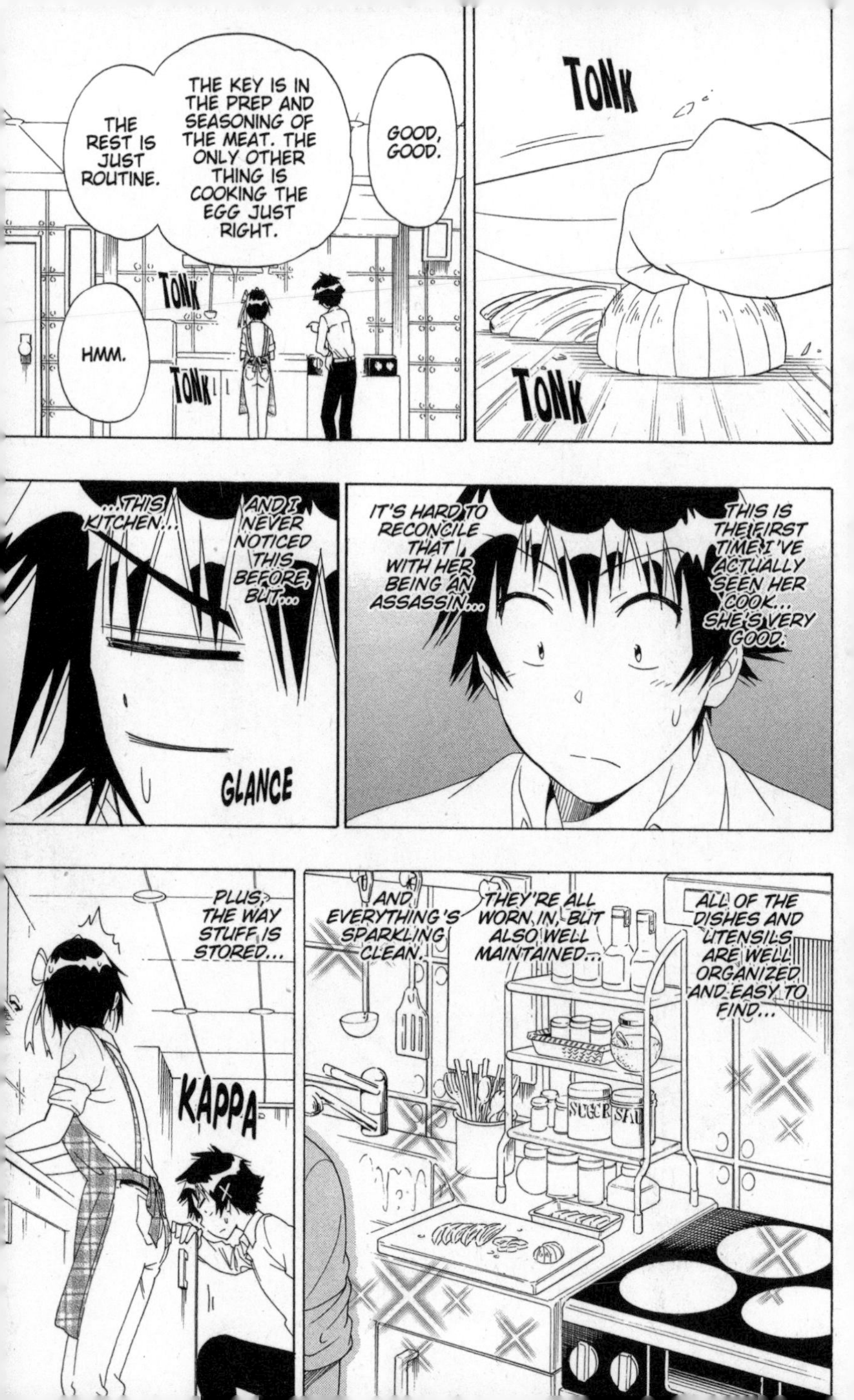
TONK
TONK
GOOD, GOOD.
THE KEY IS IN THE PREP AND SEASONING OF THE MEAT. THE ONLY OTHER THING IS COOKING THE EGG JUST RIGHT.
THE REST IS JUST ROUTINE.
TONK
HMM.
TONK
THIS IS THE FIRST TIME I'VE ACTUALLY SEEN HER COOK... SHE'S VERY GOOD.
IT'S HARD TO RECONCILE THAT WITH HER BEING AN ASSASSIN...
...THIS KITCHEN...
AND I NEVER NOTICED THIS BEFORE, BUT...
GLANCE
ALL OF THE DISHES AND UTENSILS ARE WELL ORGANIZED AND EASY TO FIND...
THEY'RE ALL WORN IN, BUT ALSO WELL MAINTAINED...
AND EVERYTHING'S SPARKLING CLEAN.
PLUS, THE WAY STUFF IS STORED...
KAPPA

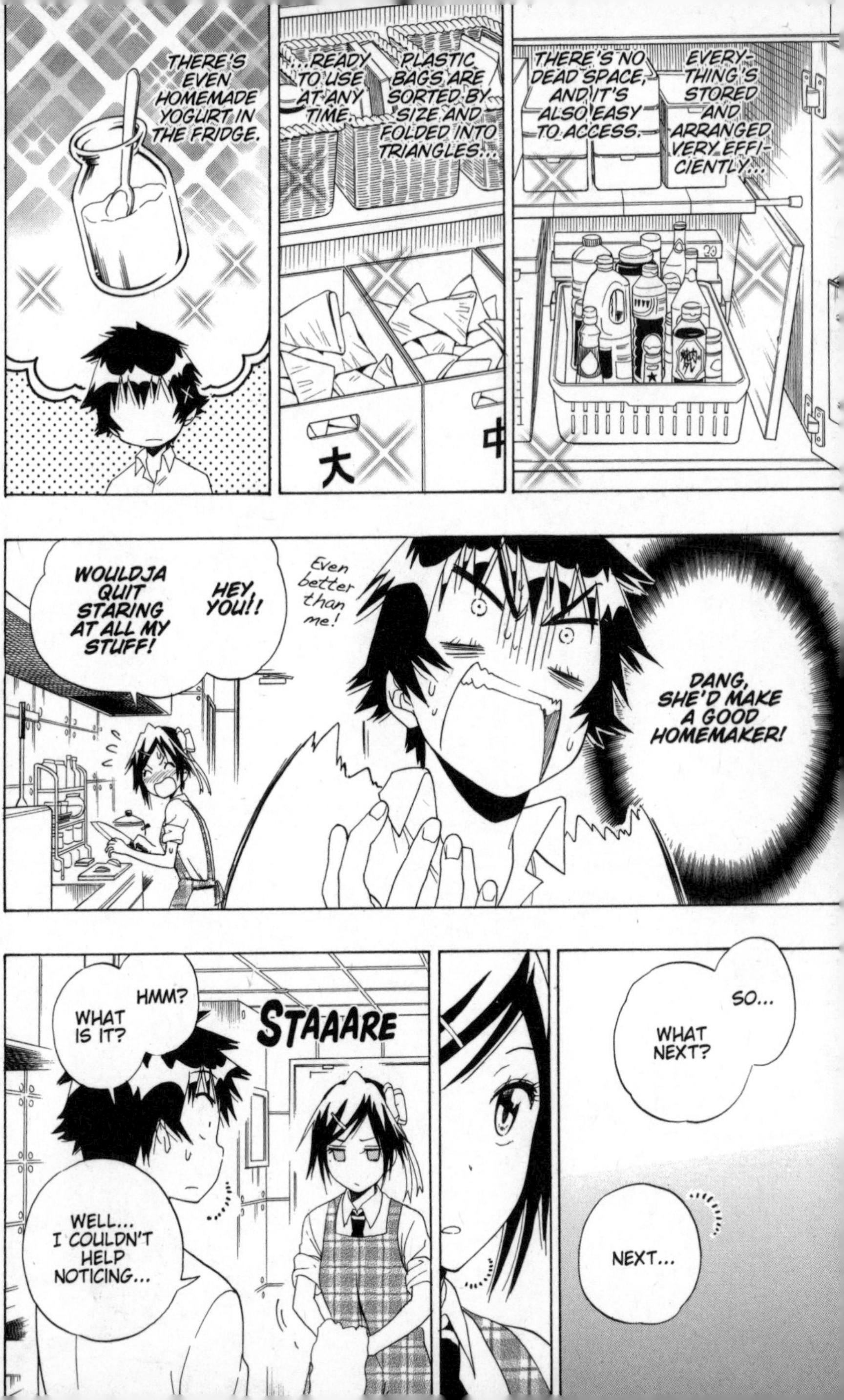

EVERYTHING'S STORED AND ARRANGED VERY EFFICIENTLY...
THERE'S NO DEAD SPACE, AND IT'S ALSO EASY TO ACCESS.
大
中
PLASTIC BAGS ARE SORTED BY SIZE AND FOLDED INTO TRIANGLES...
...READY TO USE AT ANY TIME.
THERE'S EVEN HOMEMADE YOGURT IN THE FRIDGE.
DANG, SHE'D MAKE A GOOD HOMEMAKER!
Even better than me!
HEY, YOU!!
WOULDJA QUIT STARING AT ALL MY STUFF!
SO...
WHAT NEXT?
NEXT...
HMM?
WHAT IS IT?
STAAARE
WELL... I COULDN'T HELP NOTICING...

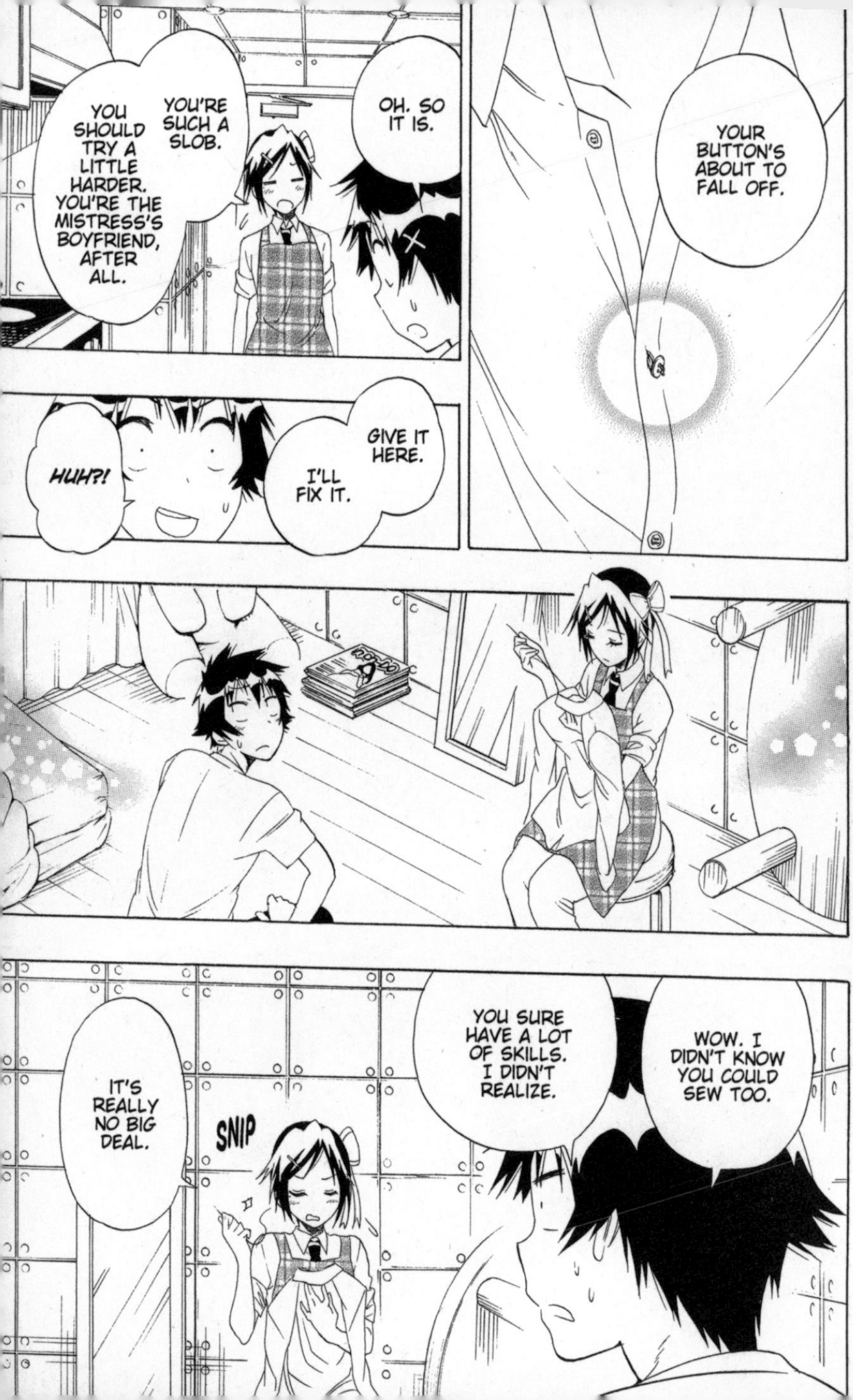
YOUR BUTTON'S ABOUT TO FALL OFF.
OH. SO IT IS.
YOU'RE SUCH A SLOB.
YOU SHOULD TRY A LITTLE HARDER. YOU'RE THE MISTRESS'S BOYFRIEND, AFTER ALL.
GIVE IT HERE.
I'LL FIX IT.
HUH?!
WOW. I DIDN'T KNOW YOU COULD SEW TOO.
YOU SURE HAVE A LOT OF SKILLS. I DIDN'T REALIZE.
SNIP
IT'S REALLY NO BIG DEAL.

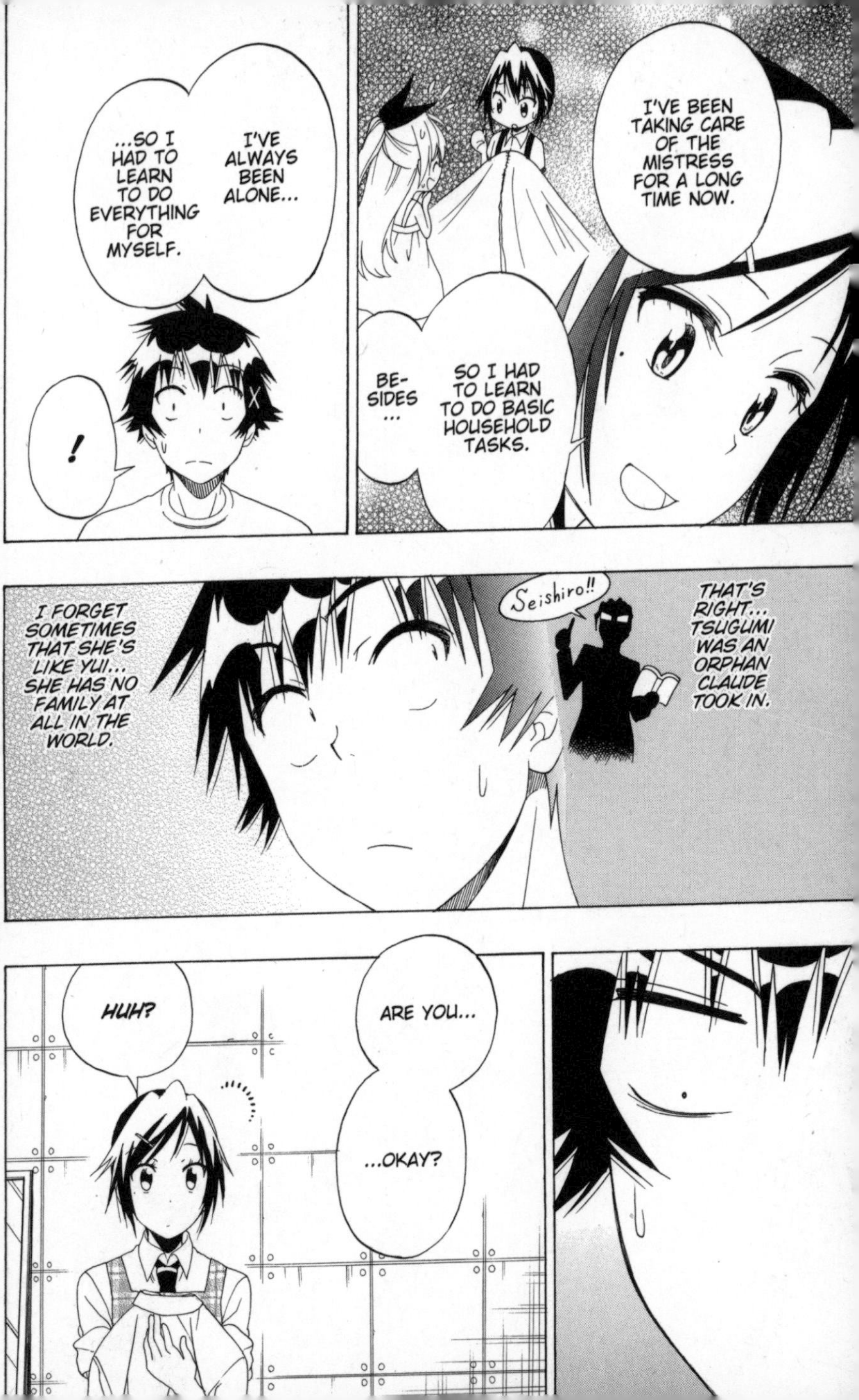
I'VE BEEN TAKING CARE OF THE MISTRESS FOR A LONG TIME NOW.
SO I HAD TO LEARN TO DO BASIC HOUSEHOLD TASKS.
BE-SIDES...
I'VE ALWAYS BEEN ALONE...
...SO I HAD TO LEARN TO DO EVERYTHING FOR MYSELF.
!
THAT'S RIGHT... TSUGUMI WAS AN ORPHAN CLAUDE TOOK IN.
Seishiro!!
I FORGET SOMETIMES THAT SHE'S LIKE YUI... SHE HAS NO FAMILY AT ALL IN THE WORLD.
ARE YOU...
...OKAY?
HUH?

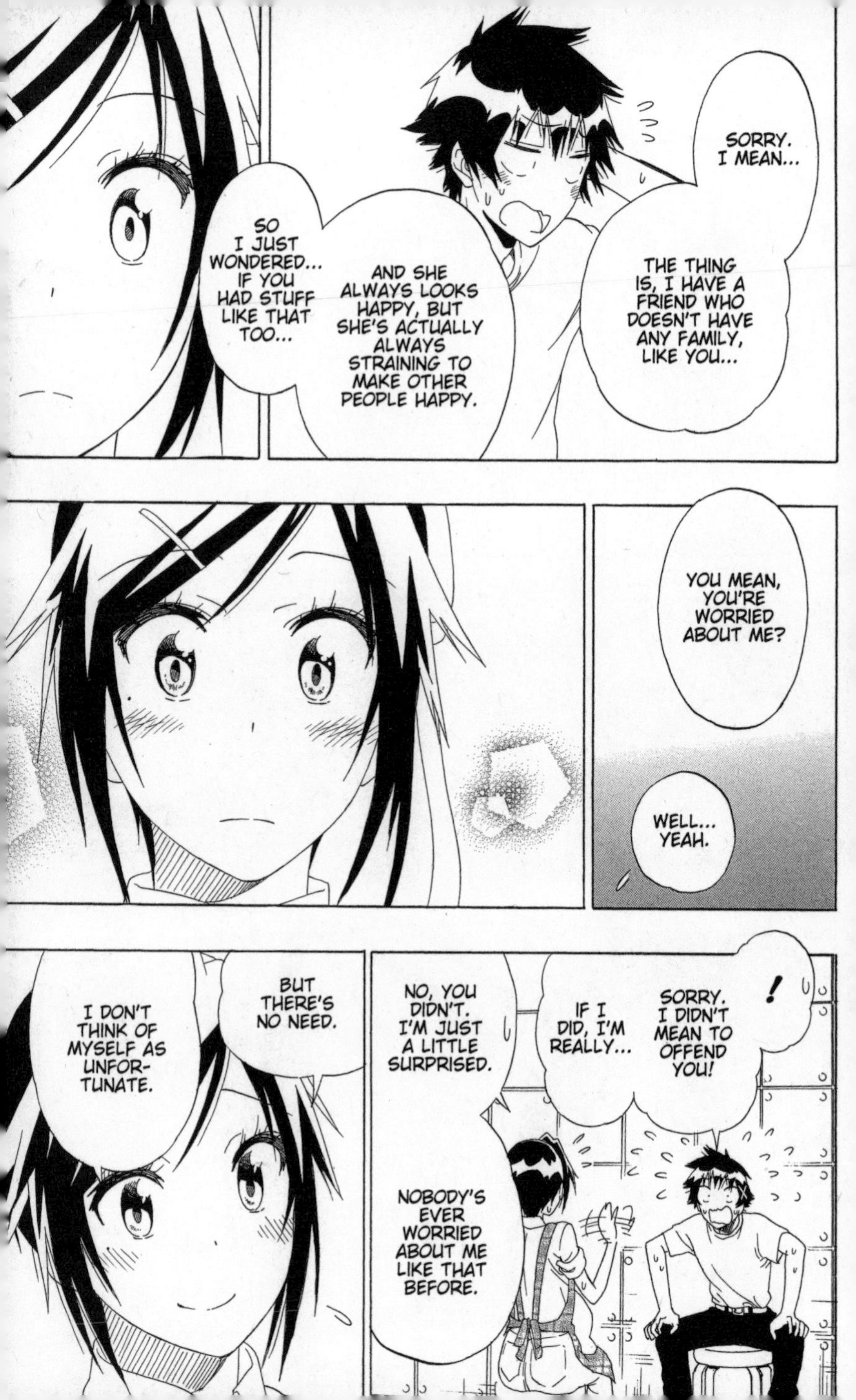
SORRY. I MEAN...
THE THING IS, I HAVE A FRIEND WHO DOESN'T HAVE ANY FAMILY, LIKE YOU...
AND SHE ALWAYS LOOKS HAPPY, BUT SHE'S ACTUALLY ALWAYS STRAINING TO MAKE OTHER PEOPLE HAPPY.
SO I JUST WONDERED... IF YOU HAD STUFF LIKE THAT TOO...
YOU MEAN, YOU'RE WORRIED ABOUT ME?
WELL... YEAH.
!
SORRY. I DIDN'T MEAN TO OFFEND YOU!
IF I DID, I'M REALLY...
NO, YOU DIDN'T. I'M JUST A LITTLE SURPRISED.
NOBODY'S EVER WORRIED ABOUT ME LIKE THAT BEFORE.
BUT THERE'S NO NEED.
I DON'T THINK OF MYSELF AS UNFOR-TUNATE.

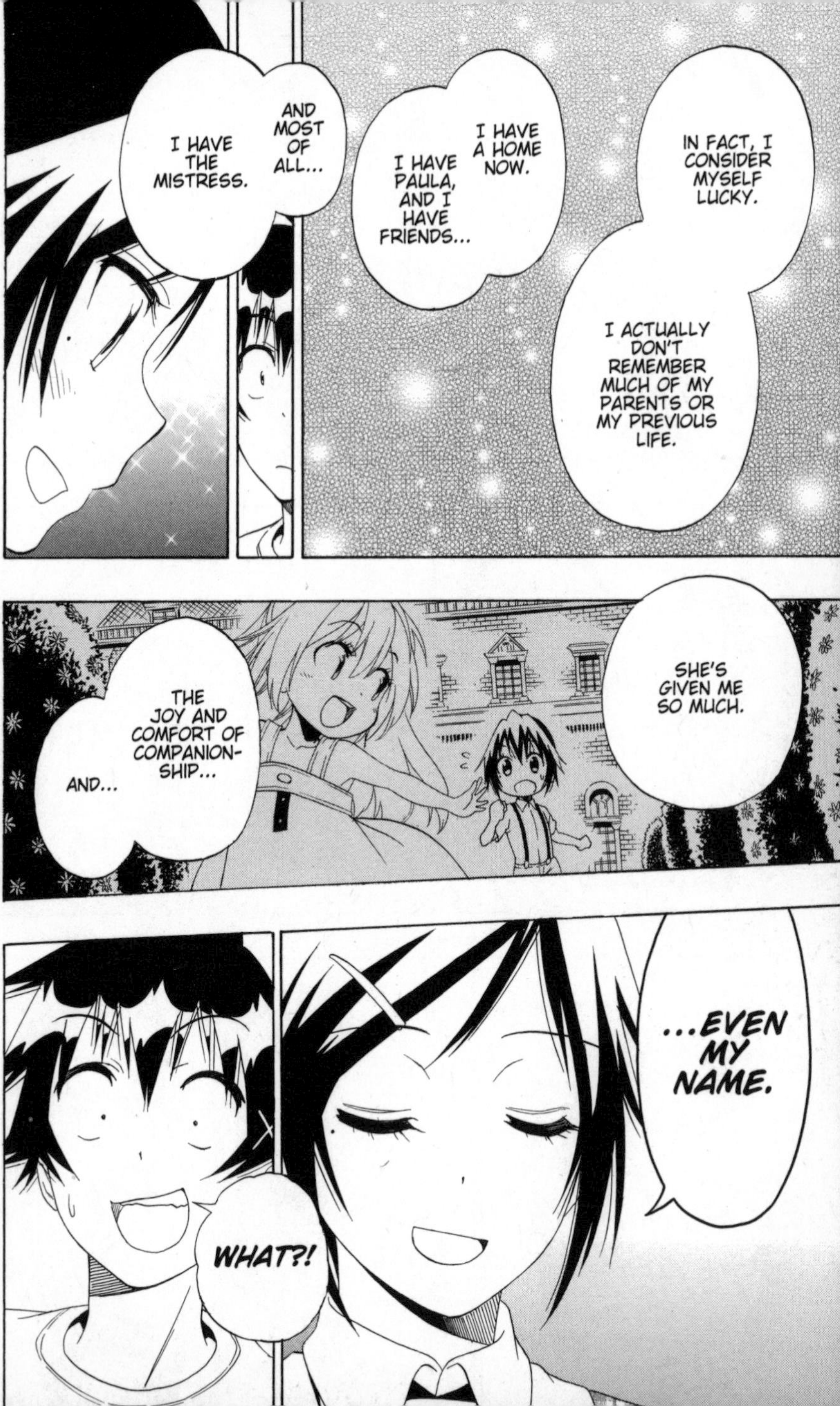
IN FACT, I CONSIDER MYSELF LUCKY.
I ACTUALLY DON'T REMEMBER MUCH OF MY PARENTS OR MY PREVIOUS LIFE.
I HAVE A HOME NOW.
I HAVE PAULA, AND I HAVE FRIENDS...
AND MOST OF ALL...
I HAVE THE MISTRESS.
SHE'S GIVEN ME SO MUCH.
THE JOY AND COMFORT OF COMPANIONSHIP...
AND...
...EVEN MY NAME.
WHAT?!

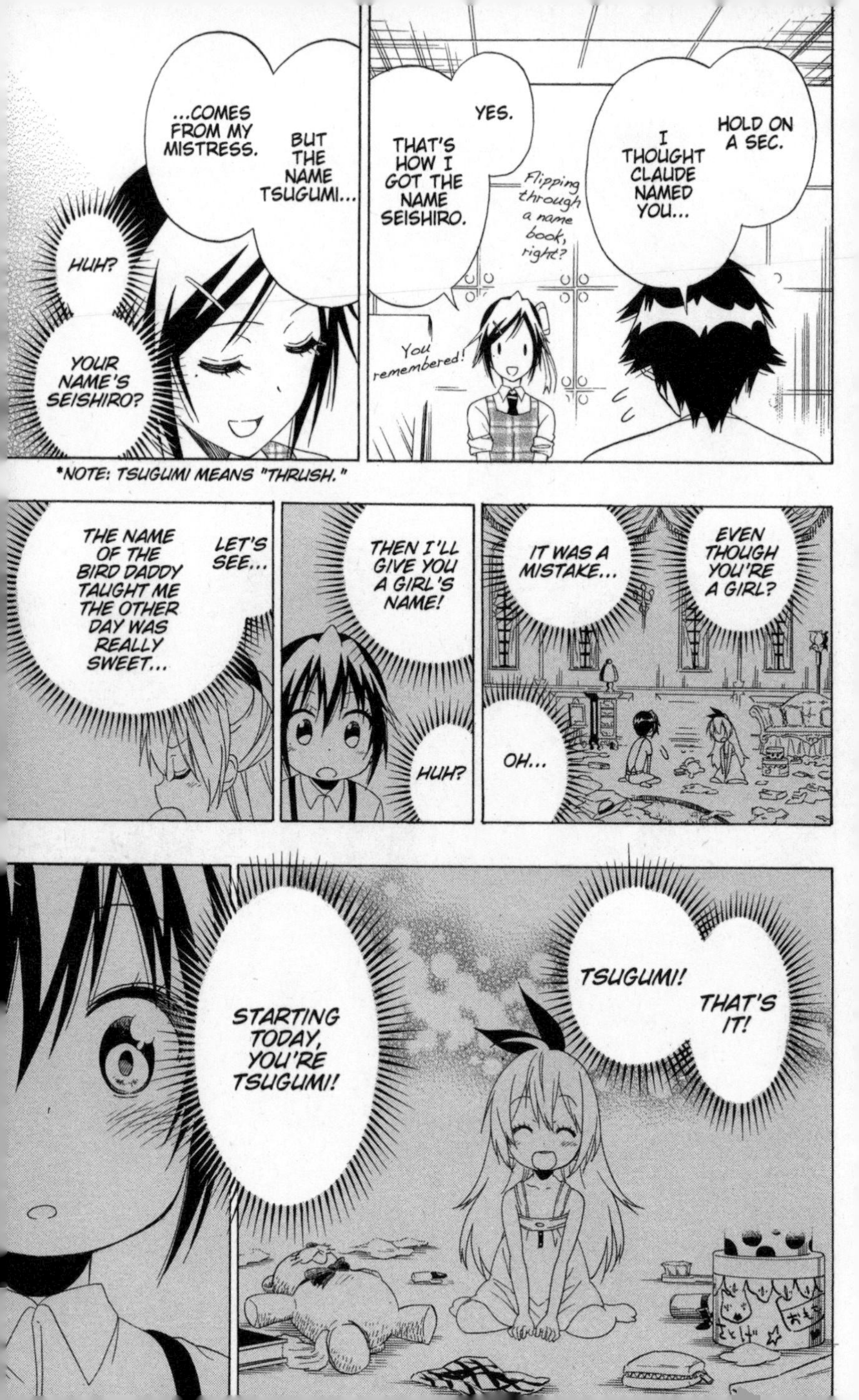
HOLD ON A SEC.
I THOUGHT CLAUDE NAMED YOU...
YES.
THAT'S HOW I GOT THE NAME SEISHIRO.
Flipping through a name book, right?
You remembered!
YOUR NAME'S SEISHIRO?
HUH?
BUT THE NAME TSUGUMI...
...COMES FROM MY MISTRESS.
*NOTE: TSUGUMI MEANS "THRUSH."
EVEN THOUGH YOU'RE A GIRL?
IT WAS A MISTAKE...
OH...
THEN I'LL GIVE YOU A GIRL'S NAME!
HUH?
LET'S SEE...
THE NAME OF THE BIRD DADDY TAUGHT ME THE OTHER DAY WAS REALLY SWEET...
TSUGUMI!
THAT'S IT!
STARTING TODAY, YOU'RE TSUGUMI!

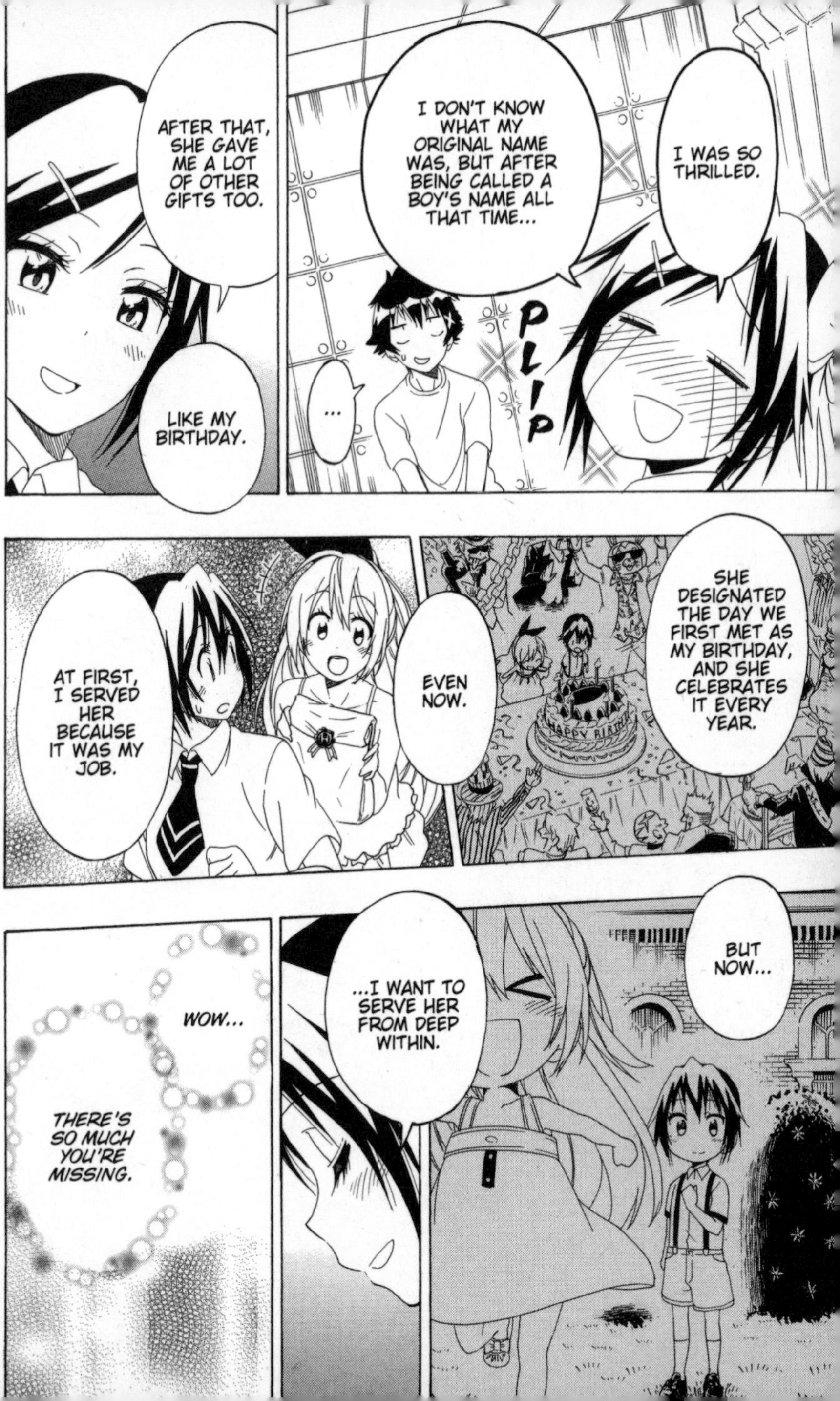
I WAS SO THRILLED.
I DON'T KNOW WHAT MY ORIGINAL NAME WAS, BUT AFTER BEING CALLED A BOY'S NAME ALL THAT TIME...
PLIP
...
AFTER THAT, SHE GAVE ME A LOT OF OTHER GIFTS TOO.
LIKE MY BIRTHDAY.
SHE DESIGNATED THE DAY WE FIRST MET AS MY BIRTHDAY, AND SHE CELEBRATES IT EVERY YEAR.
HAPPY BIRTH
EVEN NOW.
AT FIRST, I SERVED HER BECAUSE IT WAS MY JOB.
BUT NOW...
...I WANT TO SERVE HER FROM DEEP WITHIN.
WOW...
THERE'S SO MUCH YOU'RE MISSING.

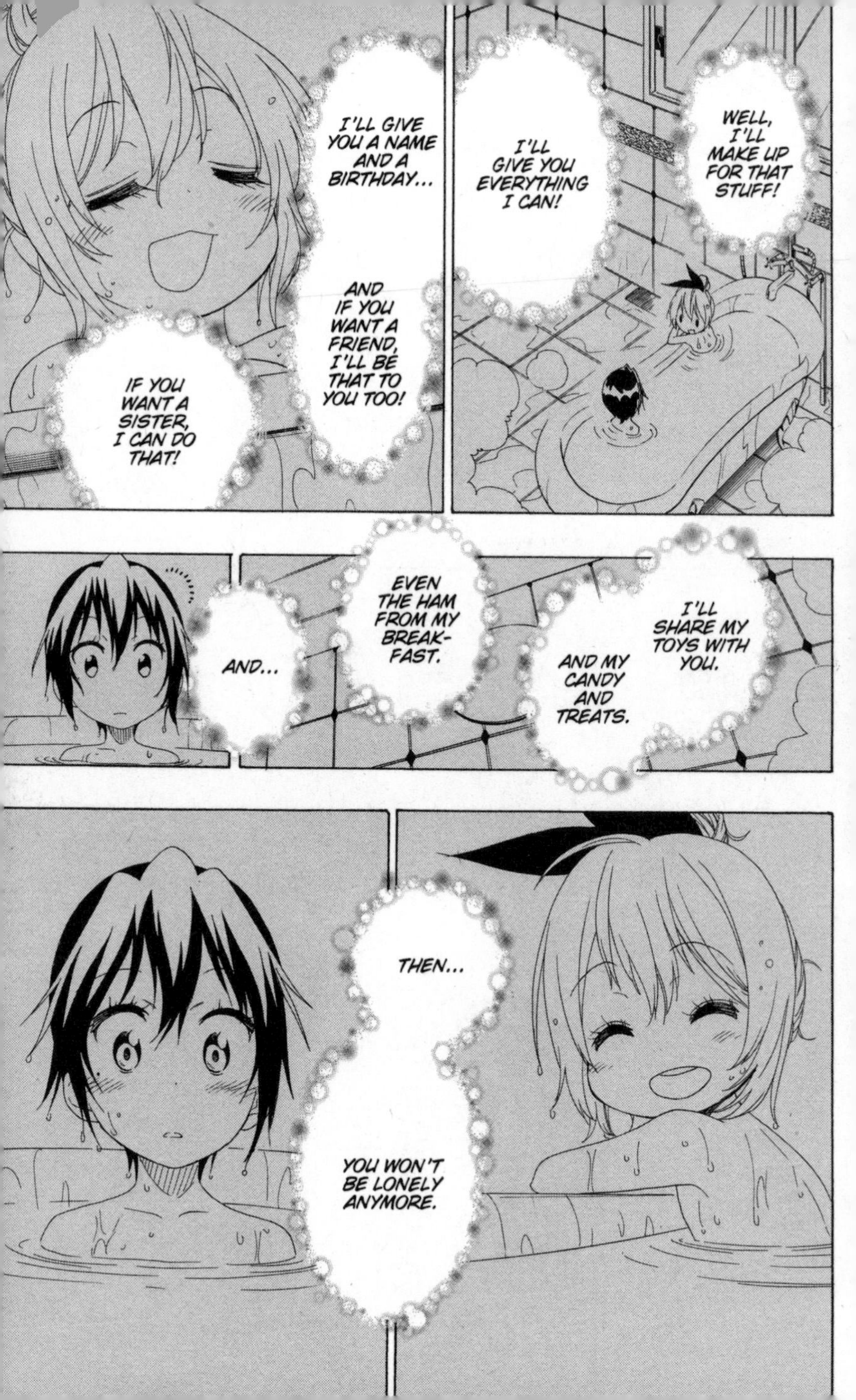
WELL, I'LL MAKE UP FOR THAT STUFF!
I'LL GIVE YOU EVERYTHING I CAN!
I'LL GIVE YOU A NAME AND A BIRTHDAY...
AND IF YOU WANT A FRIEND, I'LL BE THAT TO YOU TOO!
IF YOU WANT A SISTER, I CAN DO THAT!
I'LL SHARE MY TOYS WITH YOU.
AND MY CANDY AND TREATS.
EVEN THE HAM FROM MY BREAK-FAST.
AND...
THEN...
YOU WON'T BE LONELY ANYMORE.

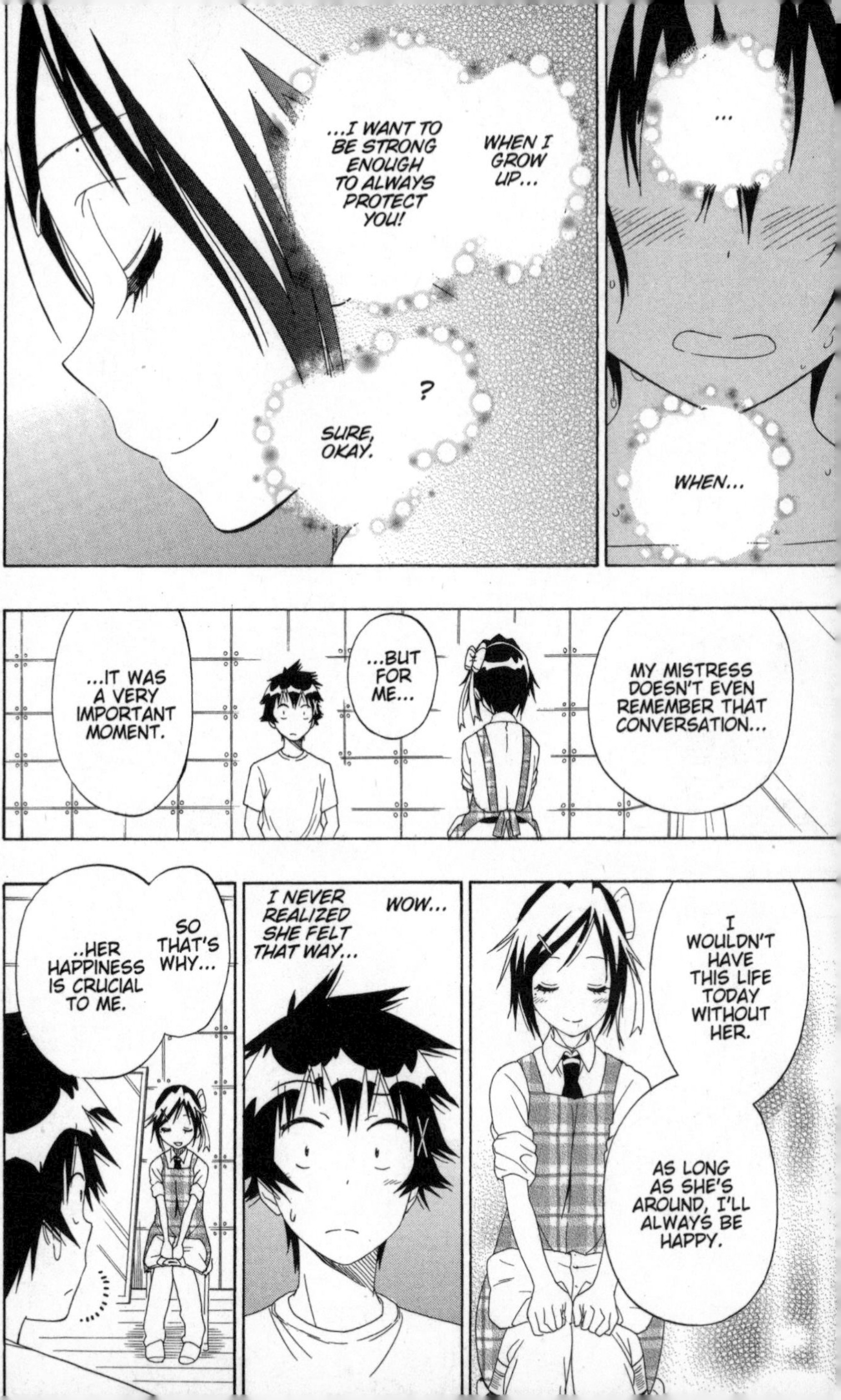
WHEN...
...
WHEN I GROW UP...
...I WANT TO BE STRONG ENOUGH TO ALWAYS PROTECT YOU!
?
SURE, OKAY.
MY MISTRESS DOESN'T EVEN REMEMBER THAT CONVERSATION...
...BUT FOR ME...
...IT WAS A VERY IMPORTANT MOMENT.
I WOULDN'T HAVE THIS LIFE TODAY WITHOUT HER.
AS LONG AS SHE'S AROUND, I'LL ALWAYS BE HAPPY.
WOW...
I NEVER REALIZED SHE FELT THAT WAY...
SO THAT'S WHY...
..HER HAPPINESS IS CRUCIAL TO ME.

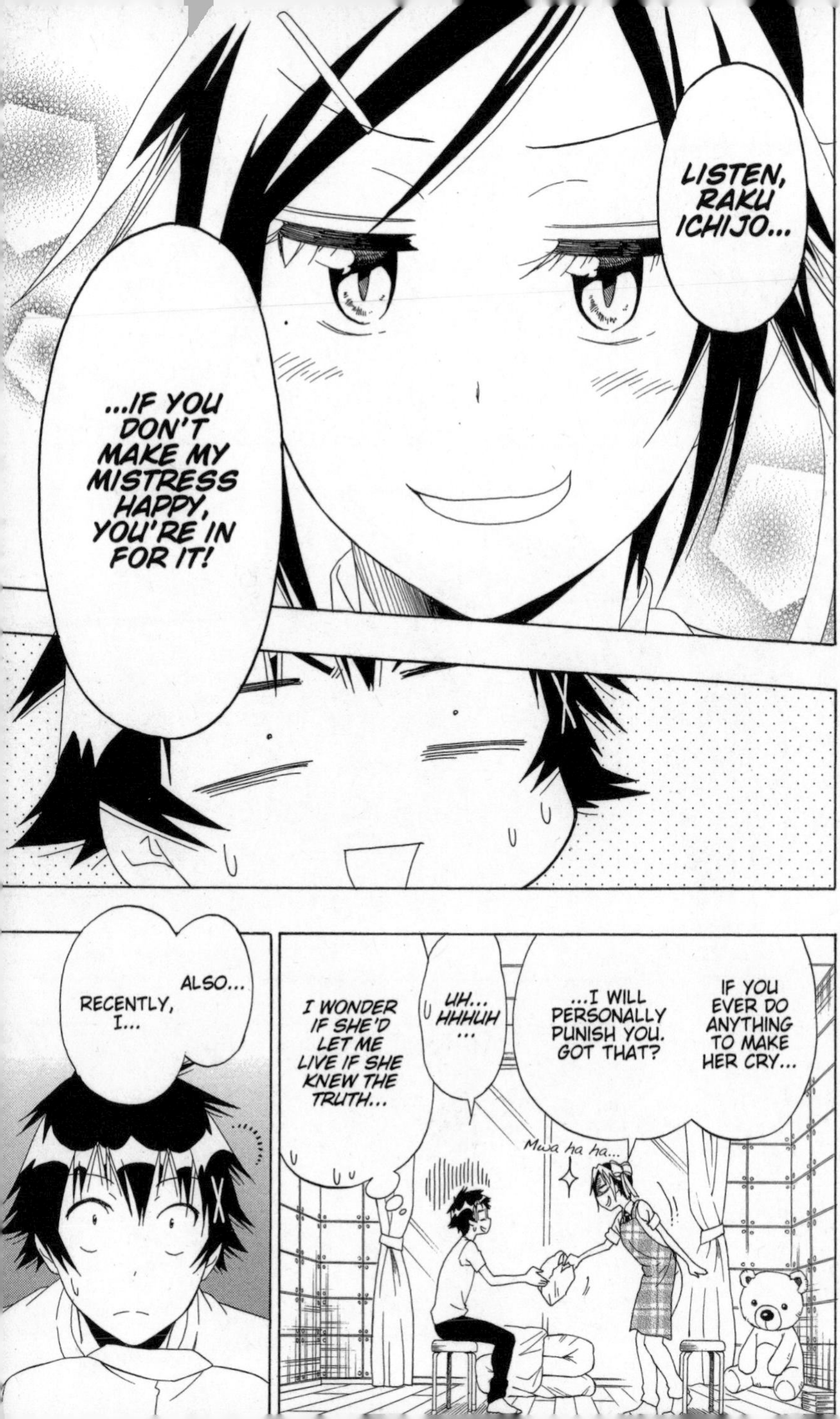
LISTEN, RAKU ICHIJO...
...IF YOU DON'T MAKE MY MISTRESS HAPPY, YOU'RE IN FOR IT!
IF YOU EVER DO ANYTHING TO MAKE HER CRY...
...I WILL PERSONALLY PUNISH YOU. GOT THAT?
Mwa ha ha...
UH... HHHUH...
I WONDER IF SHE'D LET ME LIVE IF SHE KNEW THE TRUTH...
ALSO... RECENTLY, I...

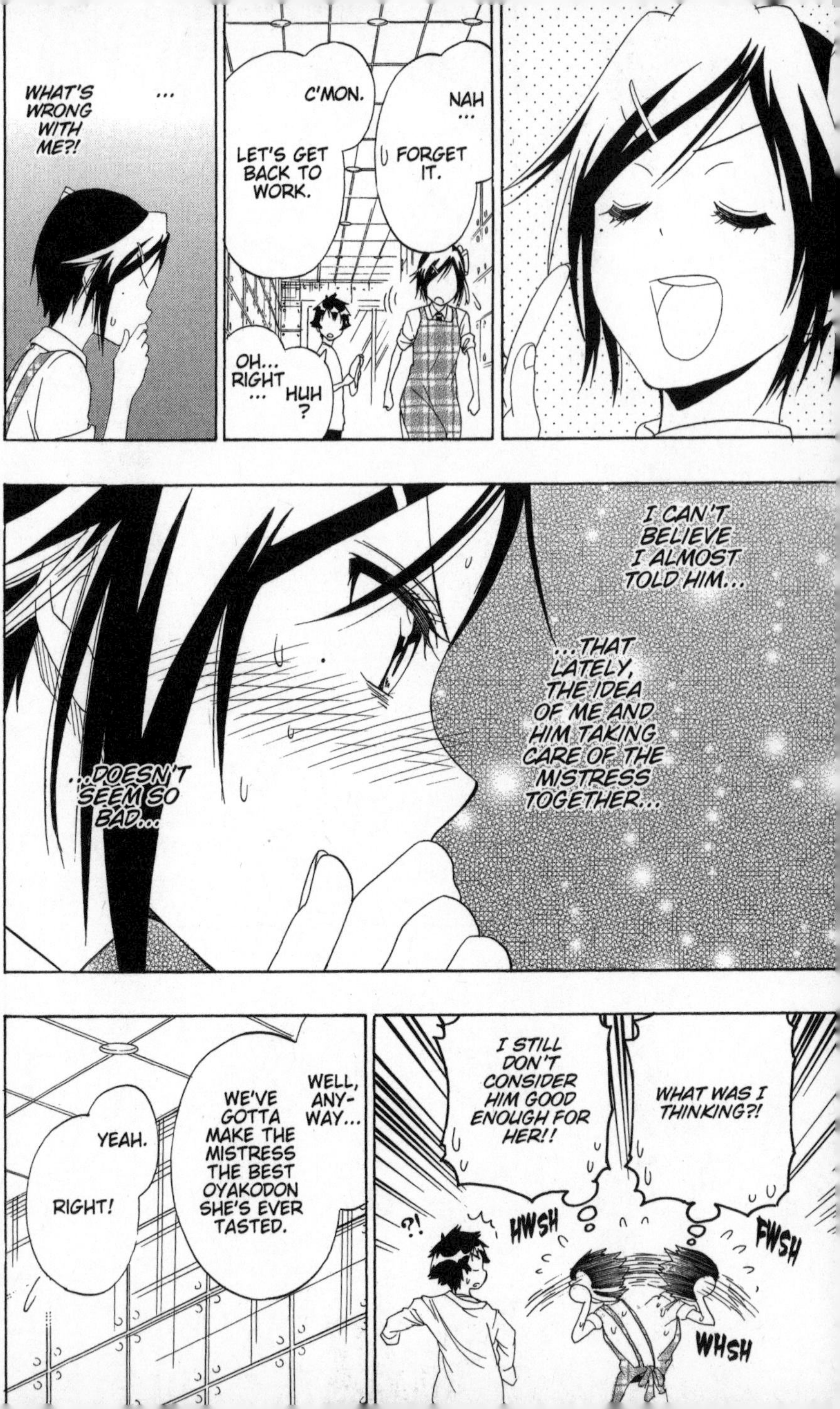
NAH ... FORGET IT.
C'MON. LET'S GET BACK TO WORK.
OH... RIGHT ... HUH ?
WHAT'S WRONG WITH ME?!
...
I CAN'T BELIEVE I ALMOST TOLD HIM...
...THAT LATELY, THE IDEA OF ME AND HIM TAKING CARE OF THE MISTRESS TOGETHER...
...DOESN'T SEEM SO BAD...
I STILL DON'T CONSIDER HIM GOOD ENOUGH FOR HER!!
WHAT WAS I THINKING?!
FWSH
HWSH
?!
WHSH
WELL, ANY-WAY...
WE'VE GOTTA MAKE THE MISTRESS THE BEST OYAKODON SHE'S EVER TASTED.
YEAH.
RIGHT!

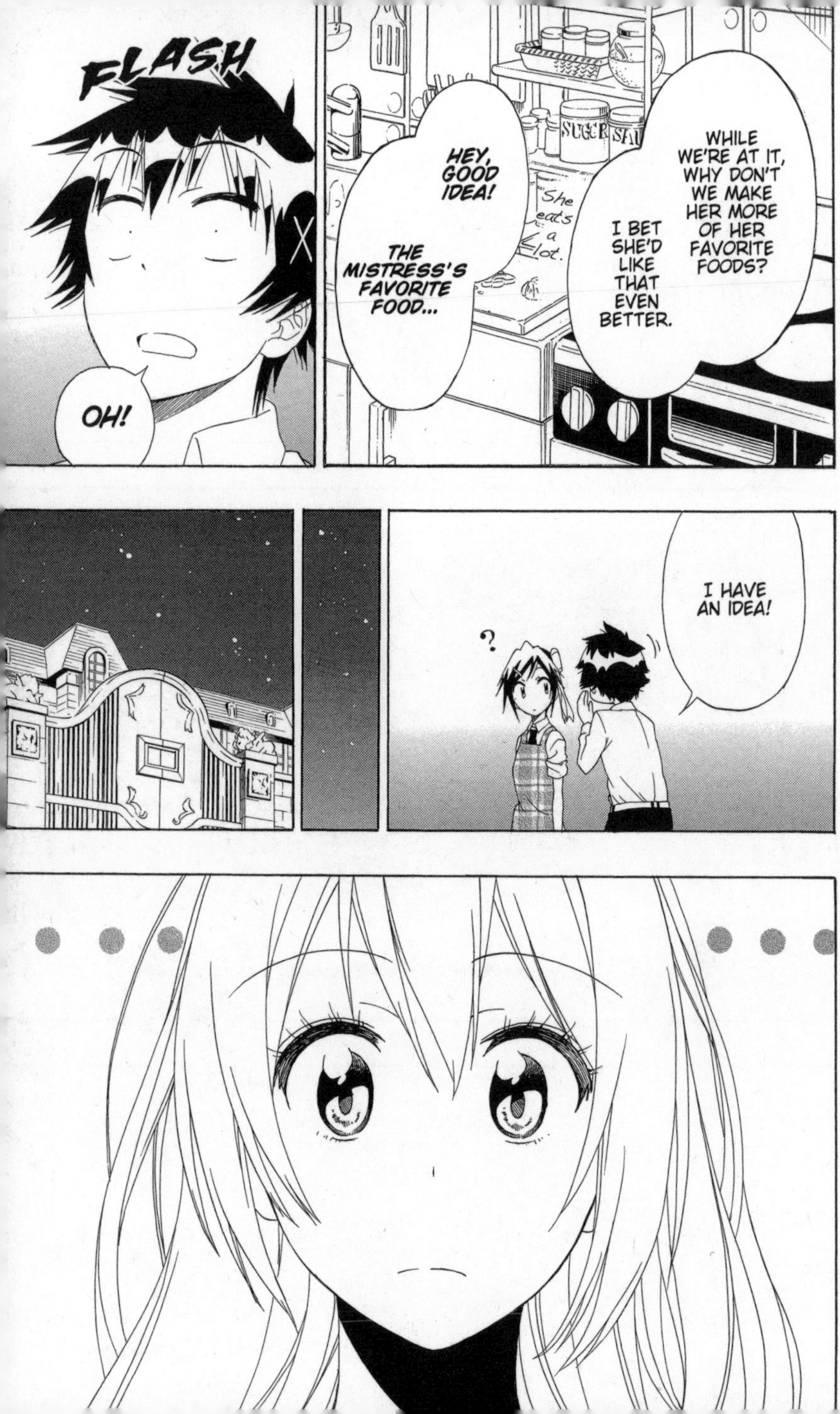
WHILE WE'RE AT IT, WHY DON'T WE MAKE HER MORE OF HER FAVORITE FOODS?
I BET SHE'D LIKE THAT EVEN BETTER.
HEY, GOOD IDEA!
THE MISTRESS'S FAVORITE FOOD...
She eats a lot.
FLASH
OH!
I HAVE AN IDEA!
?

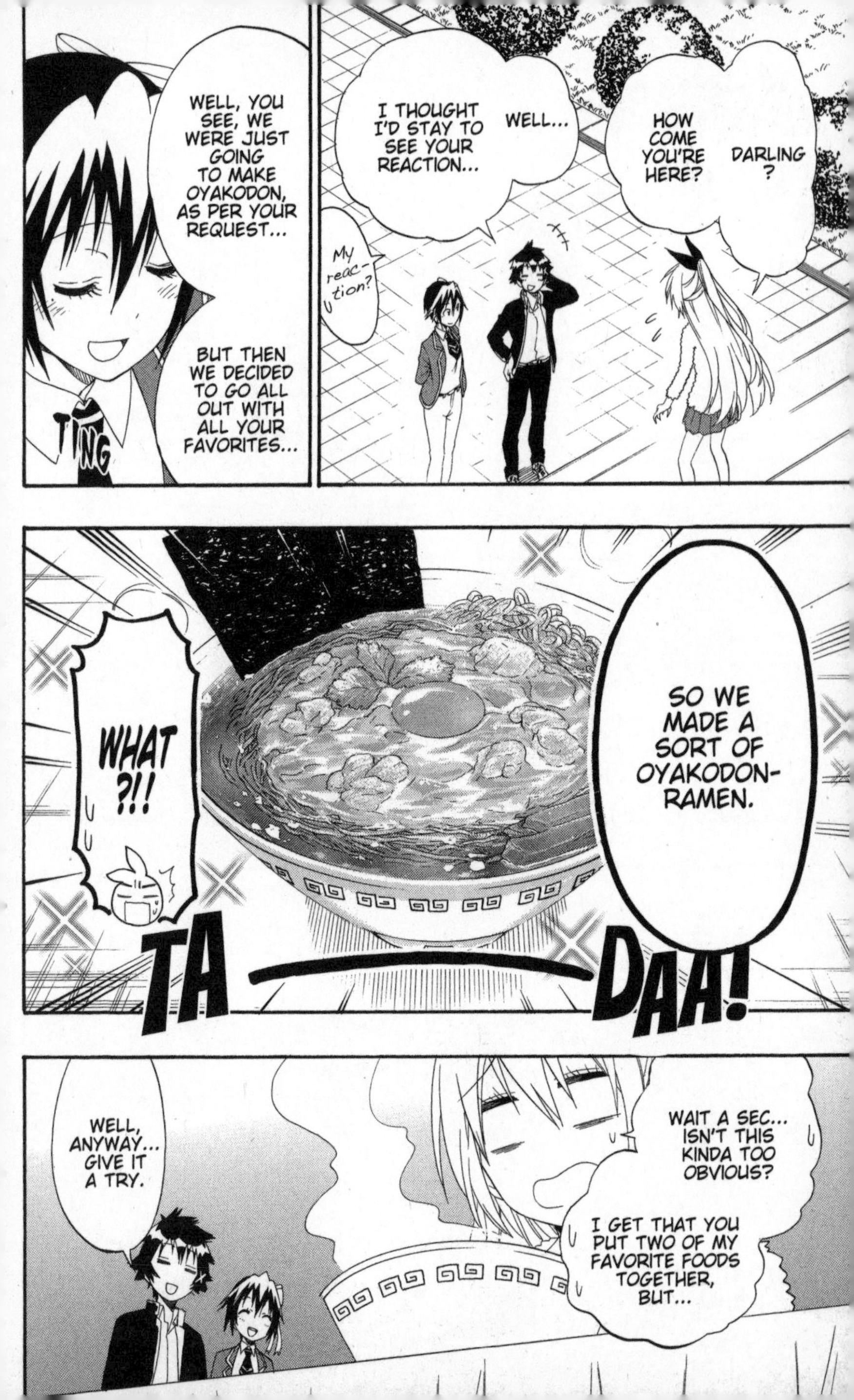
DARLING?
HOW COME YOU'RE HERE?
WELL...
I THOUGHT I'D STAY TO SEE YOUR REACTION...
My reac-tion?
WELL, YOU SEE, WE WERE JUST GOING TO MAKE OYAKODON, AS PER YOUR REQUEST...
BUT THEN WE DECIDED TO GO ALL OUT WITH ALL YOUR FAVORITES...
TING
SO WE MADE A SORT OF OYAKODON-RAMEN.
TA—DAA!
WHAT?!!
WAIT A SEC... ISN'T THIS KINDA TOO OBVIOUS?
I GET THAT YOU PUT TWO OF MY FAVORITE FOODS TOGETHER, BUT...
WELL, ANYWAY... GIVE IT A TRY.

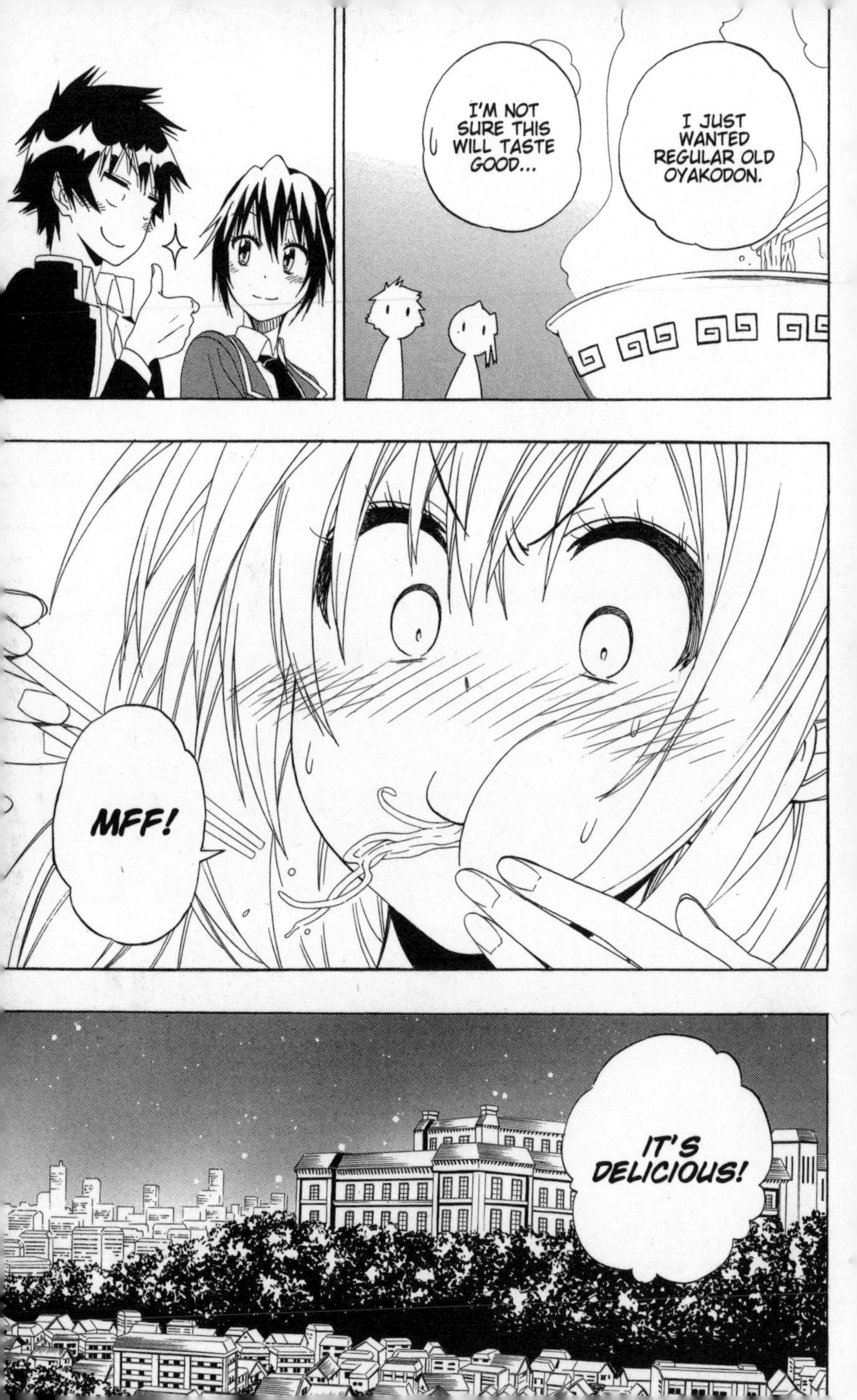
I JUST WANTED REGULAR OLD OYAKODON.
I'M NOT SURE THIS WILL TASTE GOOD...
MFF!
IT'S DELICIOUS!

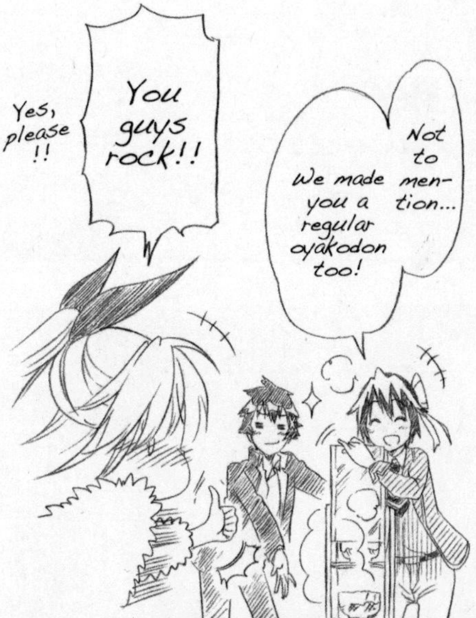
Not to mention... We made you a regular oyakodon too!
You guys rock!!
Yes, please!!
FWAA...

Chapter 150: Groups

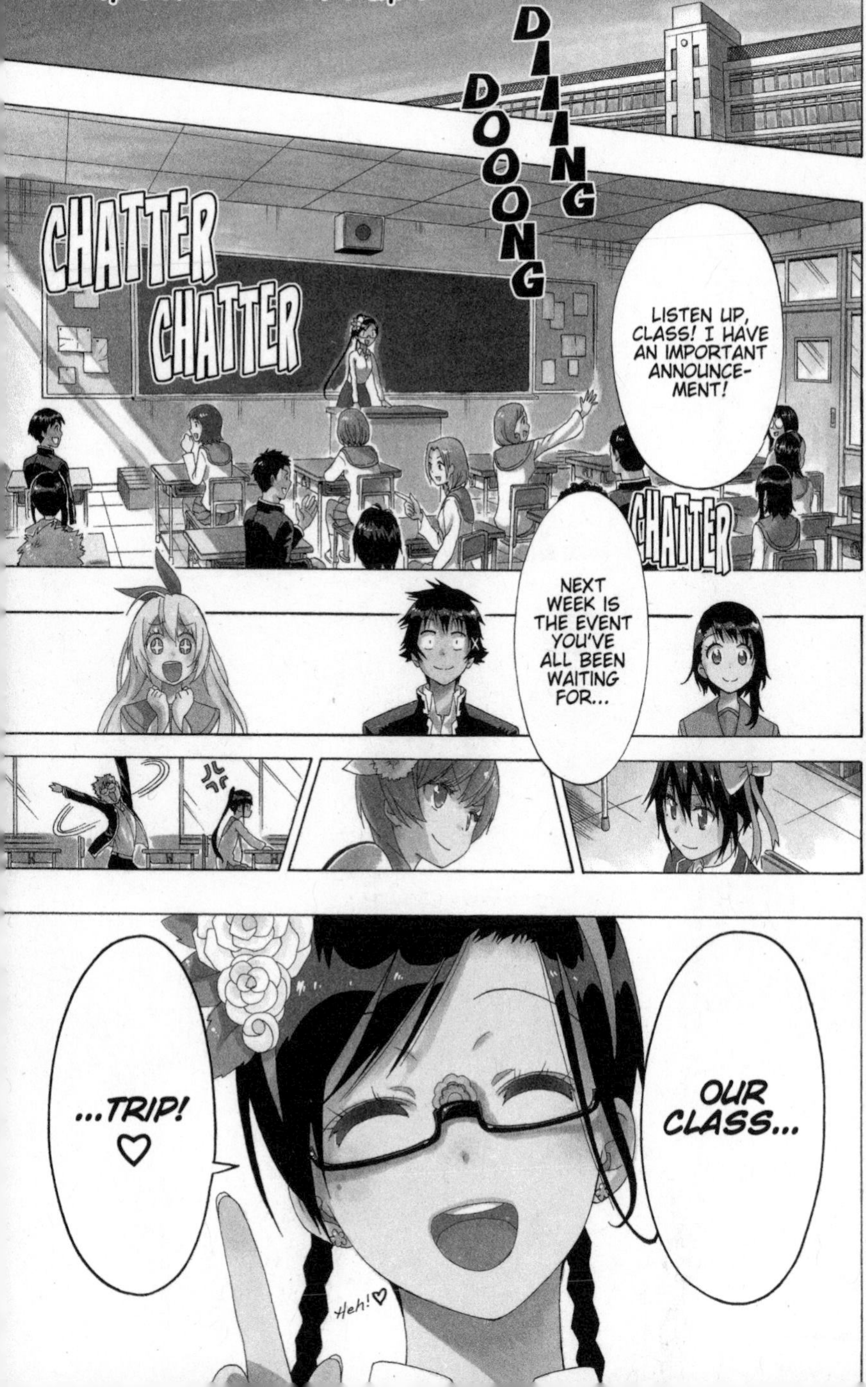
DIIING
DOOONG
LISTEN UP, CLASS! I HAVE AN IMPORTANT ANNOUNCE-MENT!
CHATTER
CHATTER
CHATTER
NEXT WEEK IS THE EVENT YOU'VE ALL BEEN WAITING FOR...
OUR CLASS...
...TRIP! ♡
Heh!♡

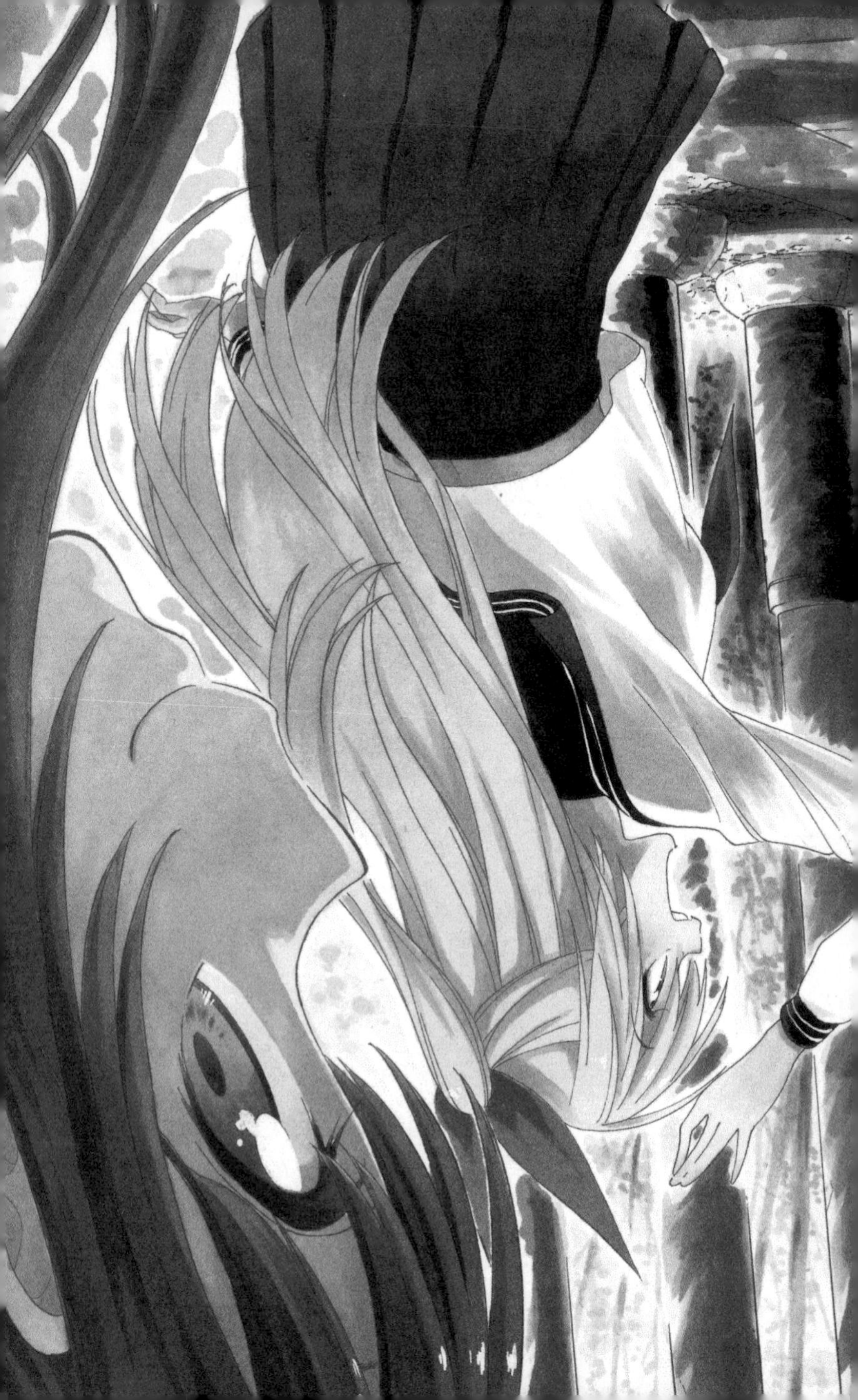

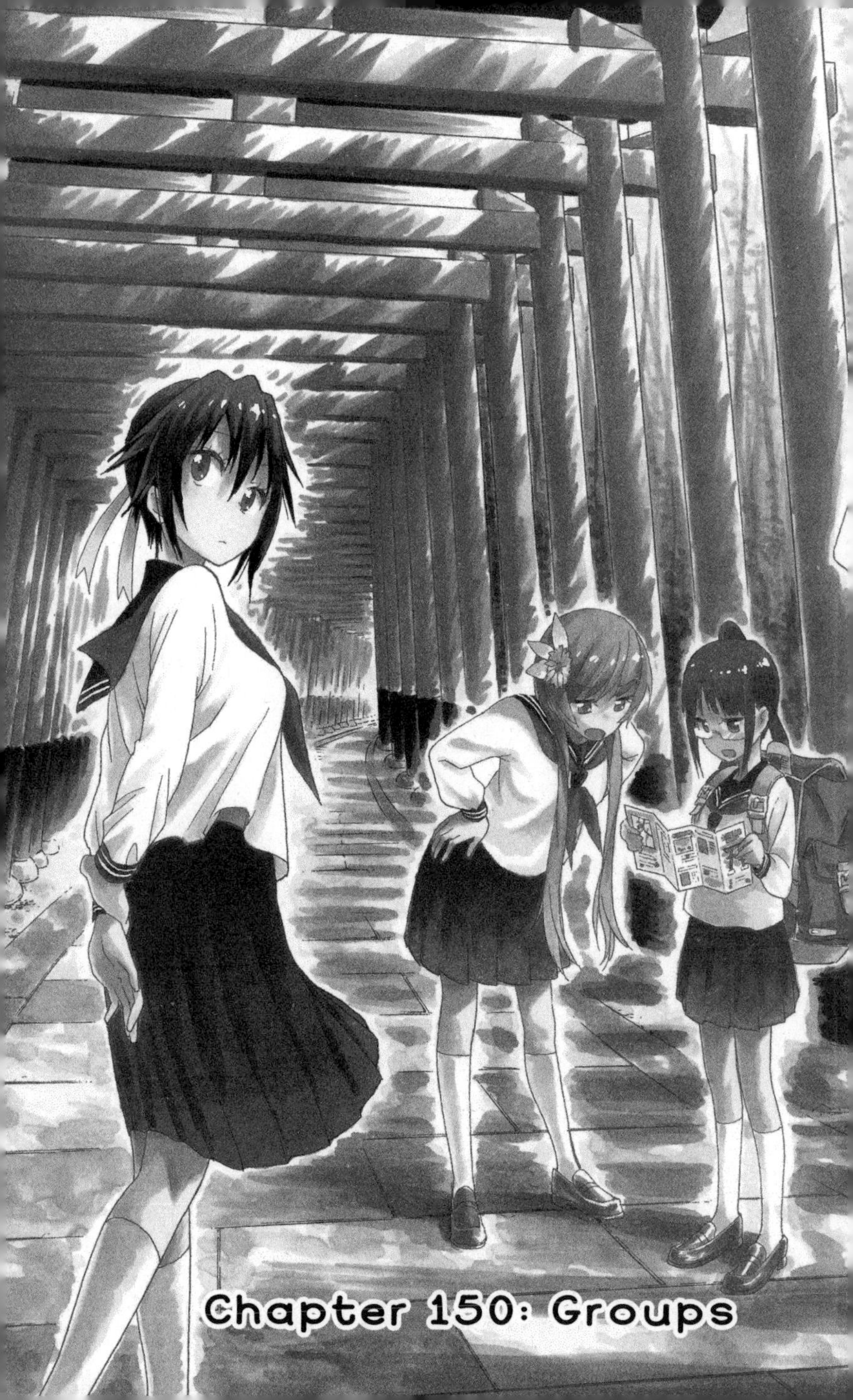
Chapter 150: Groups

How come it seems like I'm the only one without fresh costumes?
Is it my imagination?
Or is that a real thing?
Marika...

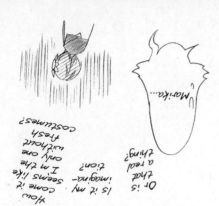

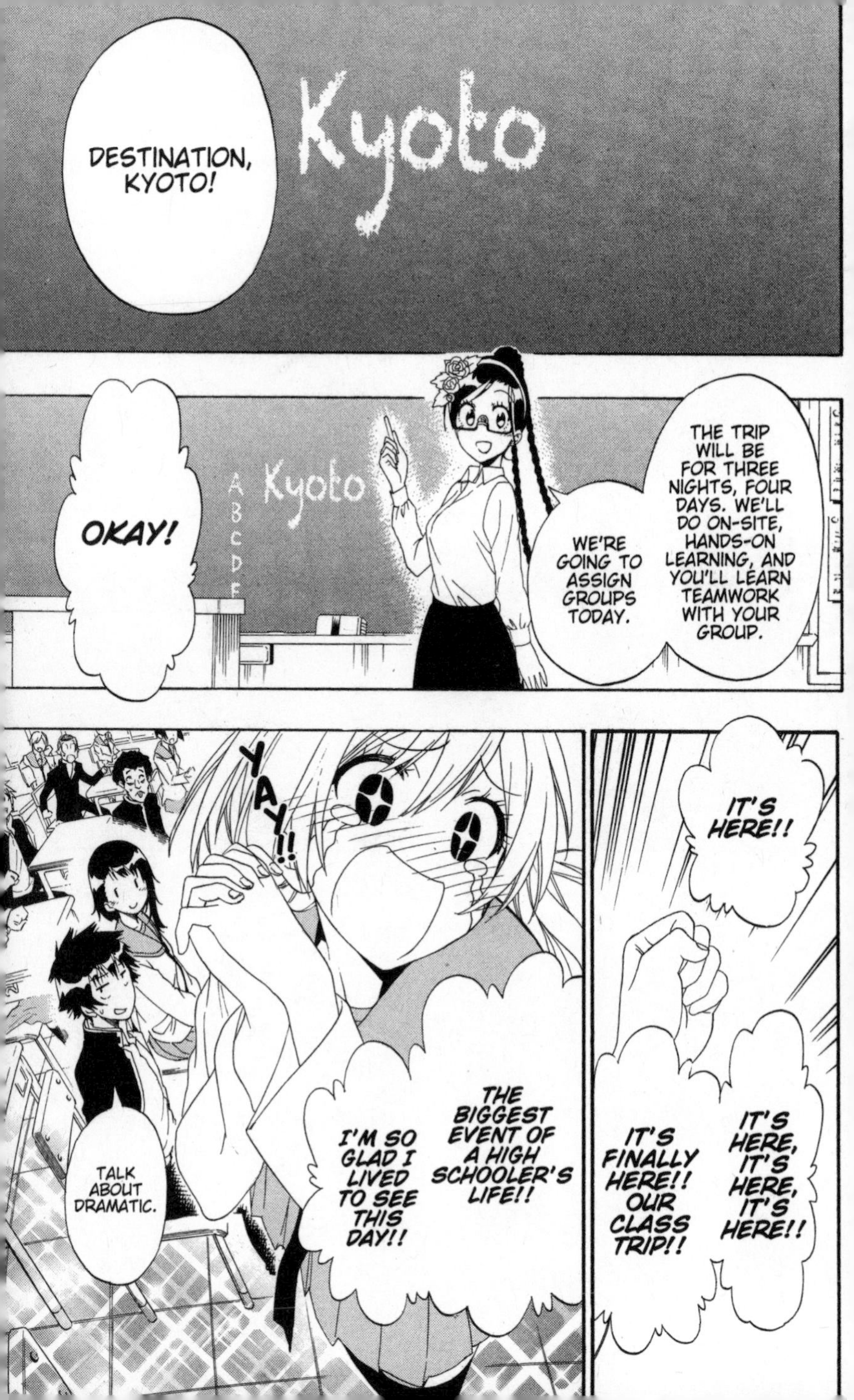
Kyoto
DESTINATION, KYOTO!
THE TRIP WILL BE FOR THREE NIGHTS, FOUR DAYS. WE'LL DO ON-SITE, HANDS-ON LEARNING, AND YOU'LL LEARN TEAMWORK WITH YOUR GROUP.
WE'RE GOING TO ASSIGN GROUPS TODAY.
Kyoto
A B C D E
OKAY!
IT'S HERE!!
IT'S HERE, IT'S HERE, IT'S HERE!!
IT'S FINALLY HERE!! OUR CLASS TRIP!!
YAY!!
THE BIGGEST EVENT OF A HIGH SCHOOLER'S LIFE!!
I'M SO GLAD I LIVED TO SEE THIS DAY!!
TALK ABOUT DRAMATIC.

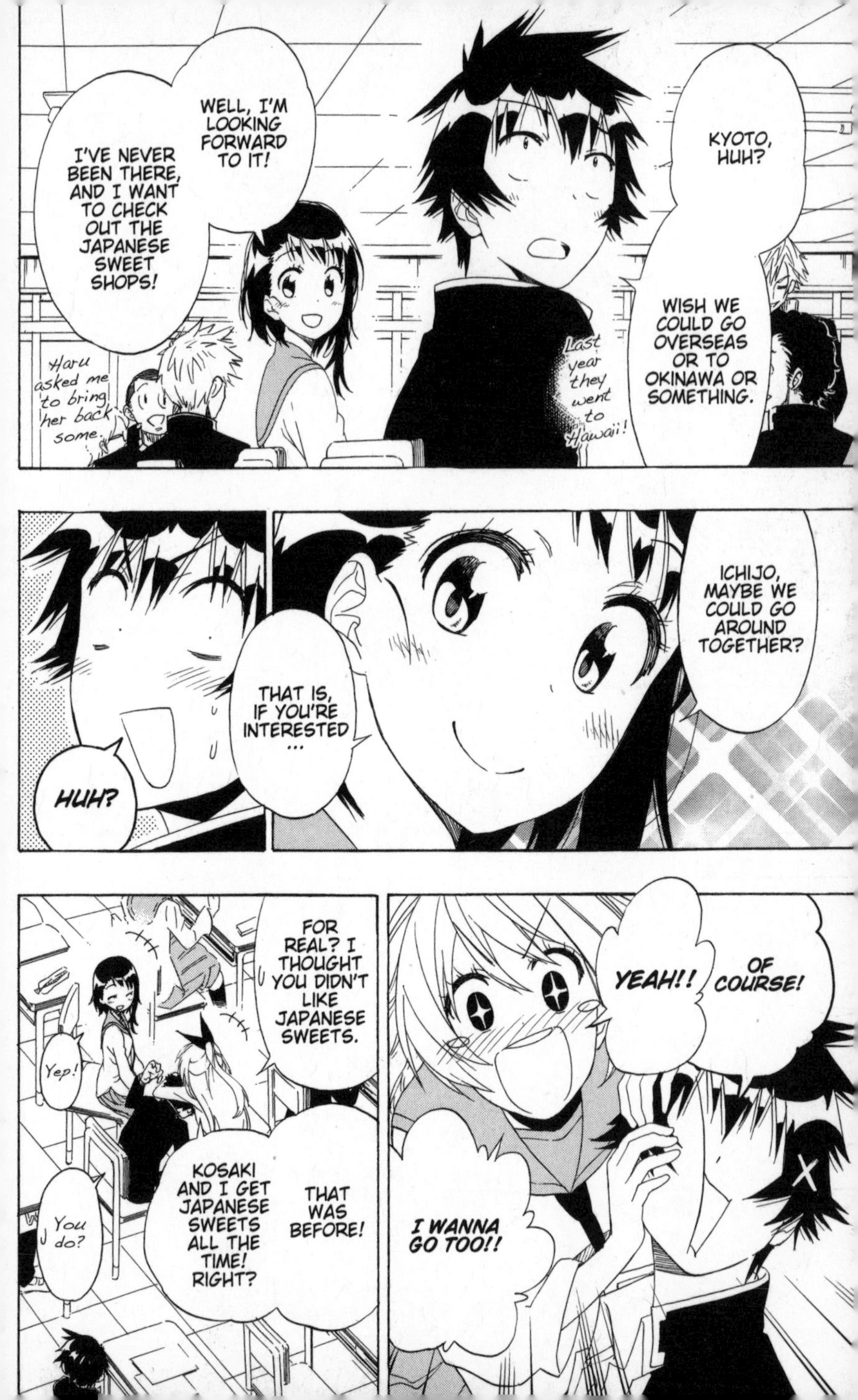
KYOTO, HUH?
WISH WE COULD GO OVERSEAS OR TO OKINAWA OR SOMETHING.
Last year they went to Hawaii!
WELL, I'M LOOKING FORWARD TO IT!
I'VE NEVER BEEN THERE, AND I WANT TO CHECK OUT THE JAPANESE SWEET SHOPS!
Haru asked me to bring her back some.
ICHIJO, MAYBE WE COULD GO AROUND TOGETHER?
THAT IS, IF YOU'RE INTERESTED ...
HUH?
OF COURSE!
YEAH!!
I WANNA GO TOO!!
FOR REAL? I THOUGHT YOU DIDN'T LIKE JAPANESE SWEETS.
THAT WAS BEFORE!
KOSAKI AND I GET JAPANESE SWEETS ALL THE TIME! RIGHT?
Yep!
You do?

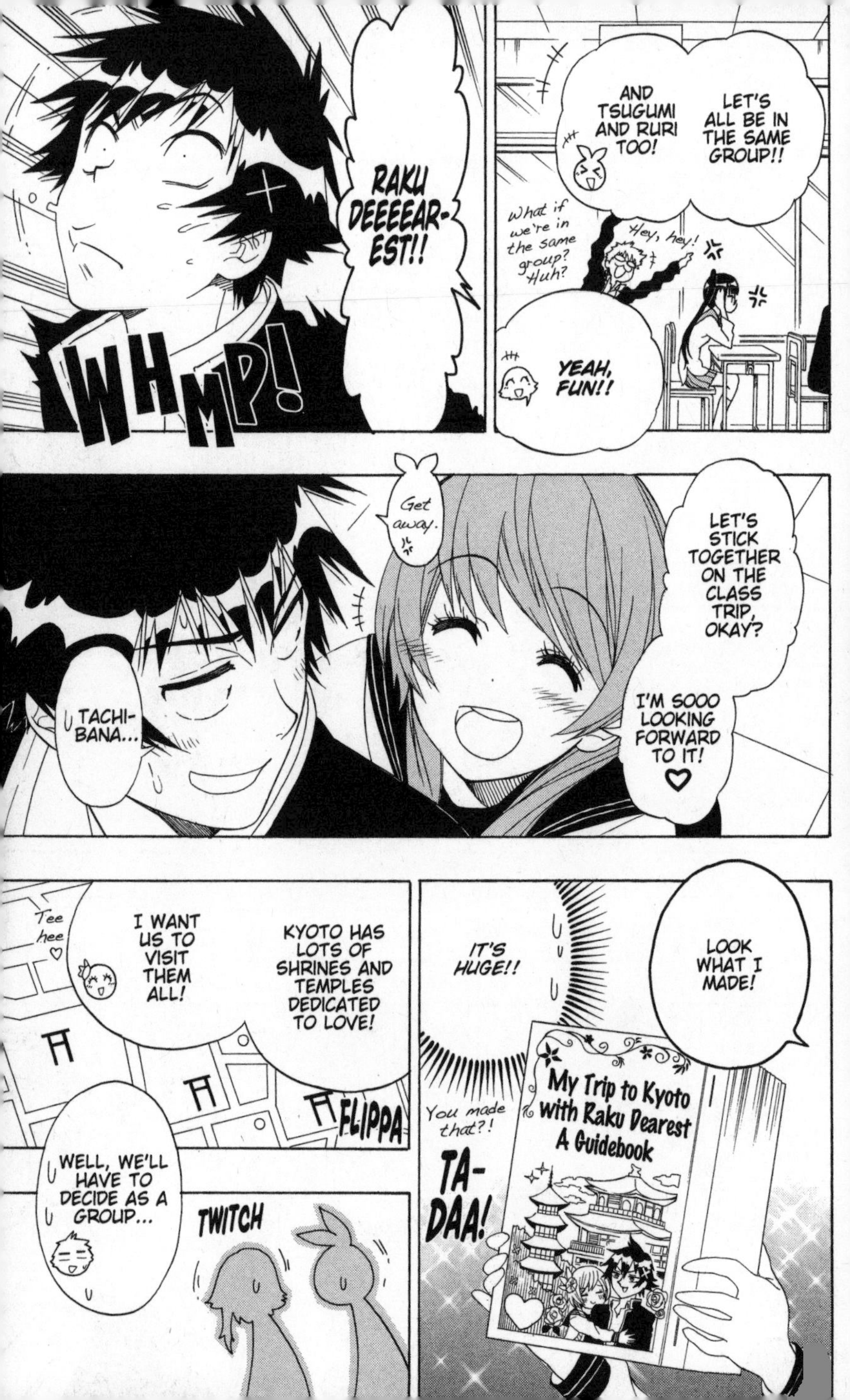
LET'S ALL BE IN THE SAME GROUP!!
AND TSUGUMI AND RURI TOO!
What if we're in the same group? Huh?
Hey, hey!
YEAH, FUN!!
RAKU DEEEEAR-EST!!
WHMP!
LET'S STICK TOGETHER ON THE CLASS TRIP, OKAY?
I'M SOOO LOOKING FORWARD TO IT!
Get away.
TACHI-BANA...
KYOTO HAS LOTS OF SHRINES AND TEMPLES DEDICATED TO LOVE!
I WANT US TO VISIT THEM ALL!
Tee hee
FLIPPA
WELL, WE'LL HAVE TO DECIDE AS A GROUP...
TWITCH
LOOK WHAT I MADE!
IT'S HUGE!!
TA-DAA!
You made that?!
My Trip to Kyoto with Raku Dearest A Guidebook

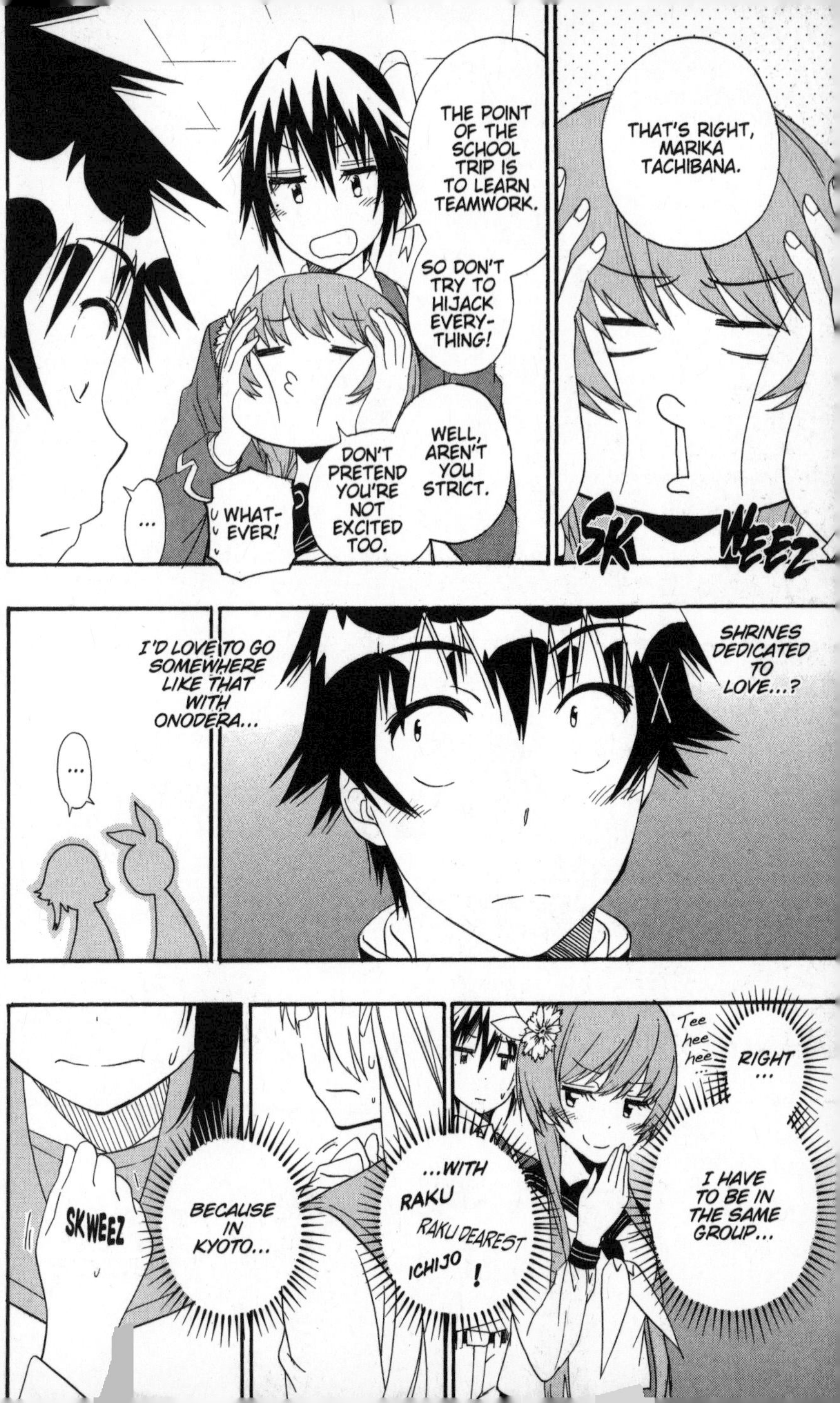
THAT'S RIGHT, MARIKA TACHIBANA.
SKWEEZ
THE POINT OF THE SCHOOL TRIP IS TO LEARN TEAMWORK.
SO DON'T TRY TO HIJACK EVERY-THING!
WELL, AREN'T YOU STRICT.
DON'T PRETEND YOU'RE NOT EXCITED TOO.
WHAT-EVER!
...
SHRINES DEDICATED TO LOVE...?
I'D LOVE TO GO SOMEWHERE LIKE THAT WITH ONODERA...
...
Tee hee hee...
RIGHT...
I HAVE TO BE IN THE SAME GROUP...
...WITH RAKU
RAKU DEAREST
ICHIJO
!
BECAUSE IN KYOTO...
SKWEEZ

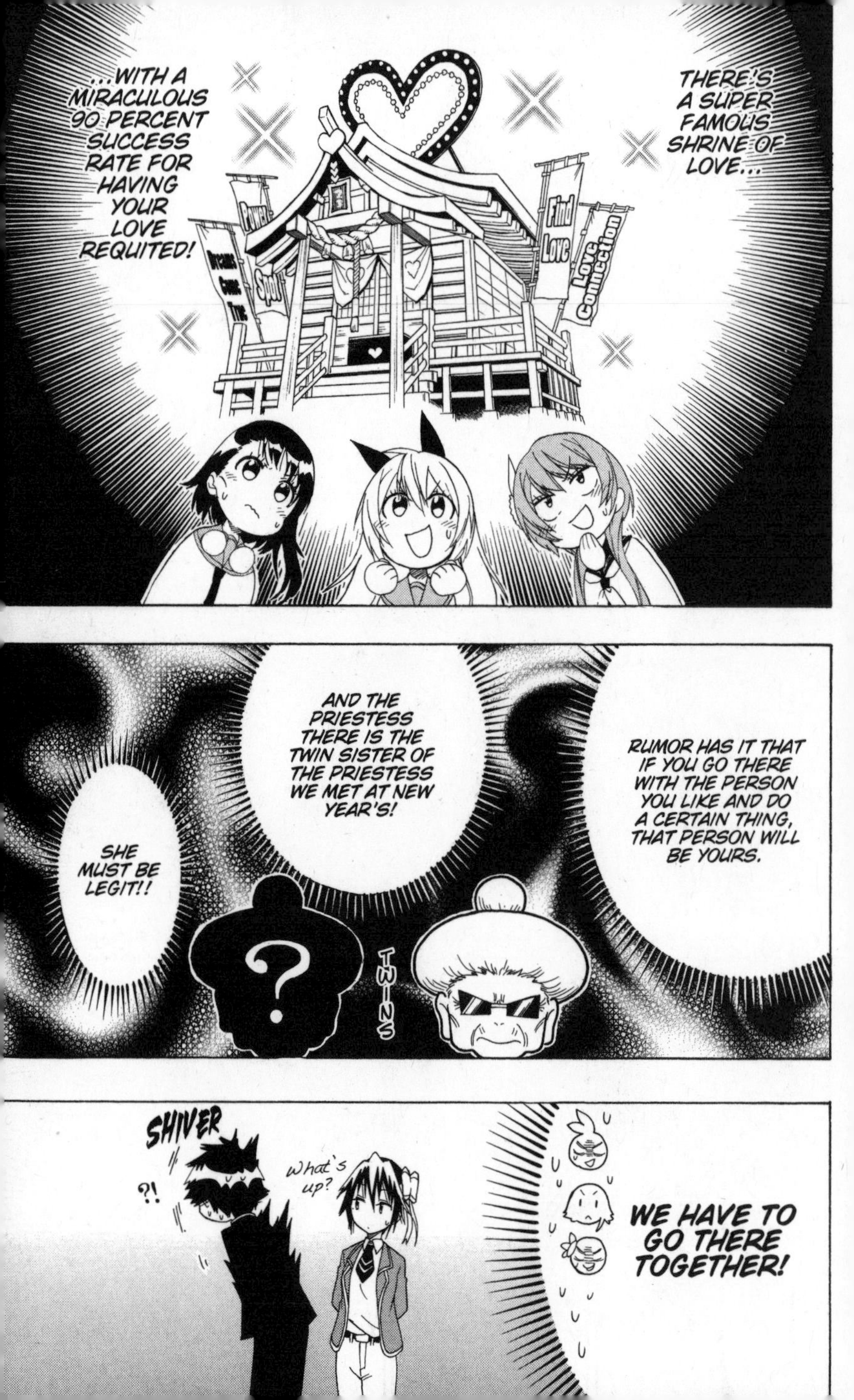
THERE'S A SUPER FAMOUS SHRINE OF LOVE...
...WITH A MIRACULOUS 90 PERCENT SUCCESS RATE FOR HAVING YOUR LOVE REQUITED!
Power
Dreams Come True
Spot
Find Love
Love Connection
RUMOR HAS IT THAT IF YOU GO THERE WITH THE PERSON YOU LIKE AND DO A CERTAIN THING, THAT PERSON WILL BE YOURS.
AND THE PRIESTESS THERE IS THE TWIN SISTER OF THE PRIESTESS WE MET AT NEW YEAR'S!
TWINS
?
SHE MUST BE LEGIT!!
WE HAVE TO GO THERE TOGETHER!
What's up?
SHIVER
?!

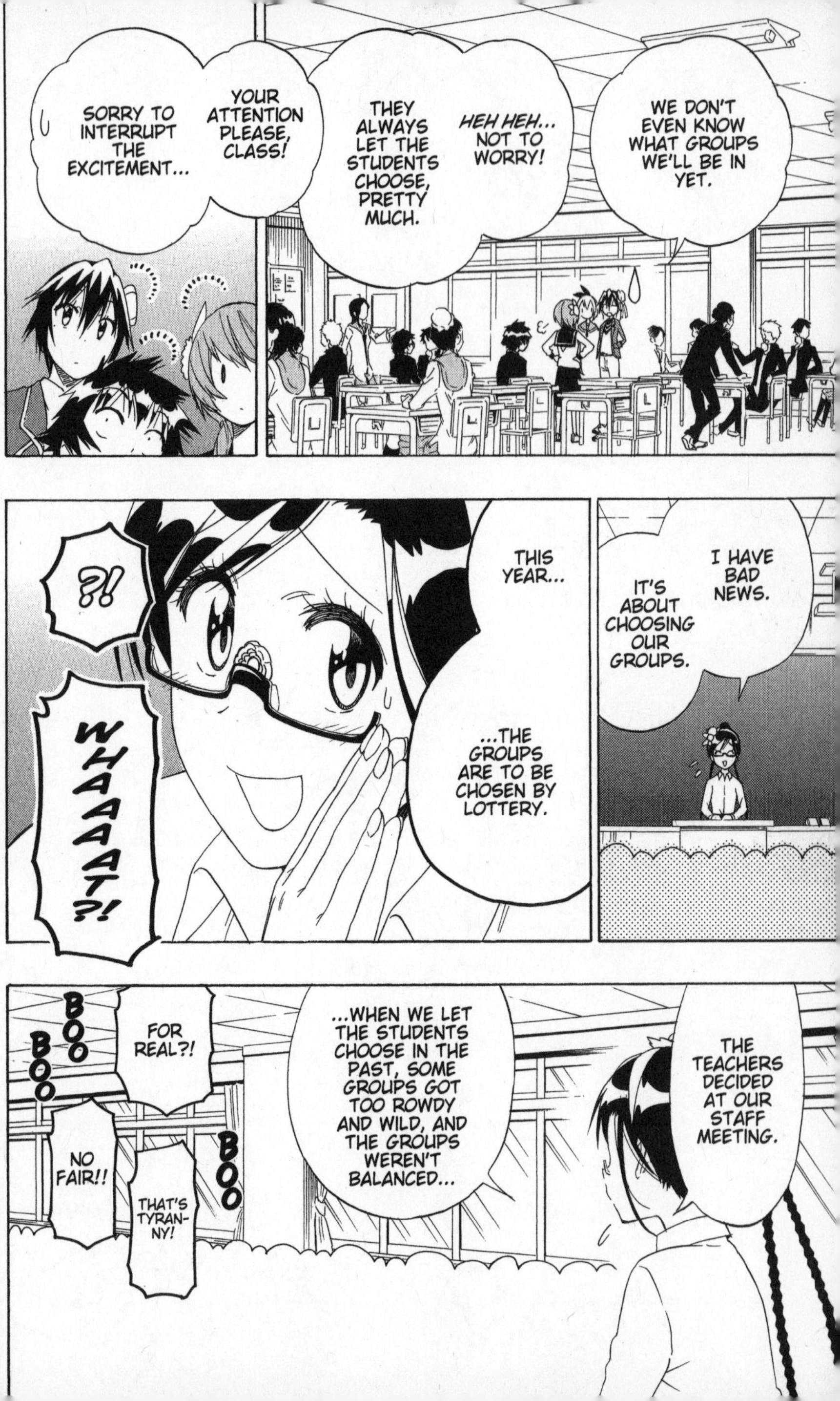
WE DON'T EVEN KNOW WHAT GROUPS WE'LL BE IN YET.
HEH HEH... NOT TO WORRY!
THEY ALWAYS LET THE STUDENTS CHOOSE, PRETTY MUCH.
YOUR ATTENTION PLEASE, CLASS!
SORRY TO INTERRUPT THE EXCITEMENT...
I HAVE BAD NEWS.
IT'S ABOUT CHOOSING OUR GROUPS.
THIS YEAR...
...THE GROUPS ARE TO BE CHOSEN BY LOTTERY.
?!
WHAAAAAT?!
THE TEACHERS DECIDED AT OUR STAFF MEETING.
...WHEN WE LET THE STUDENTS CHOOSE IN THE PAST, SOME GROUPS GOT TOO ROWDY AND WILD, AND THE GROUPS WEREN'T BALANCED...
BOO
FOR REAL?!
BOO
BOO
NO FAIR!!
THAT'S TYRAN-NY!
BOO

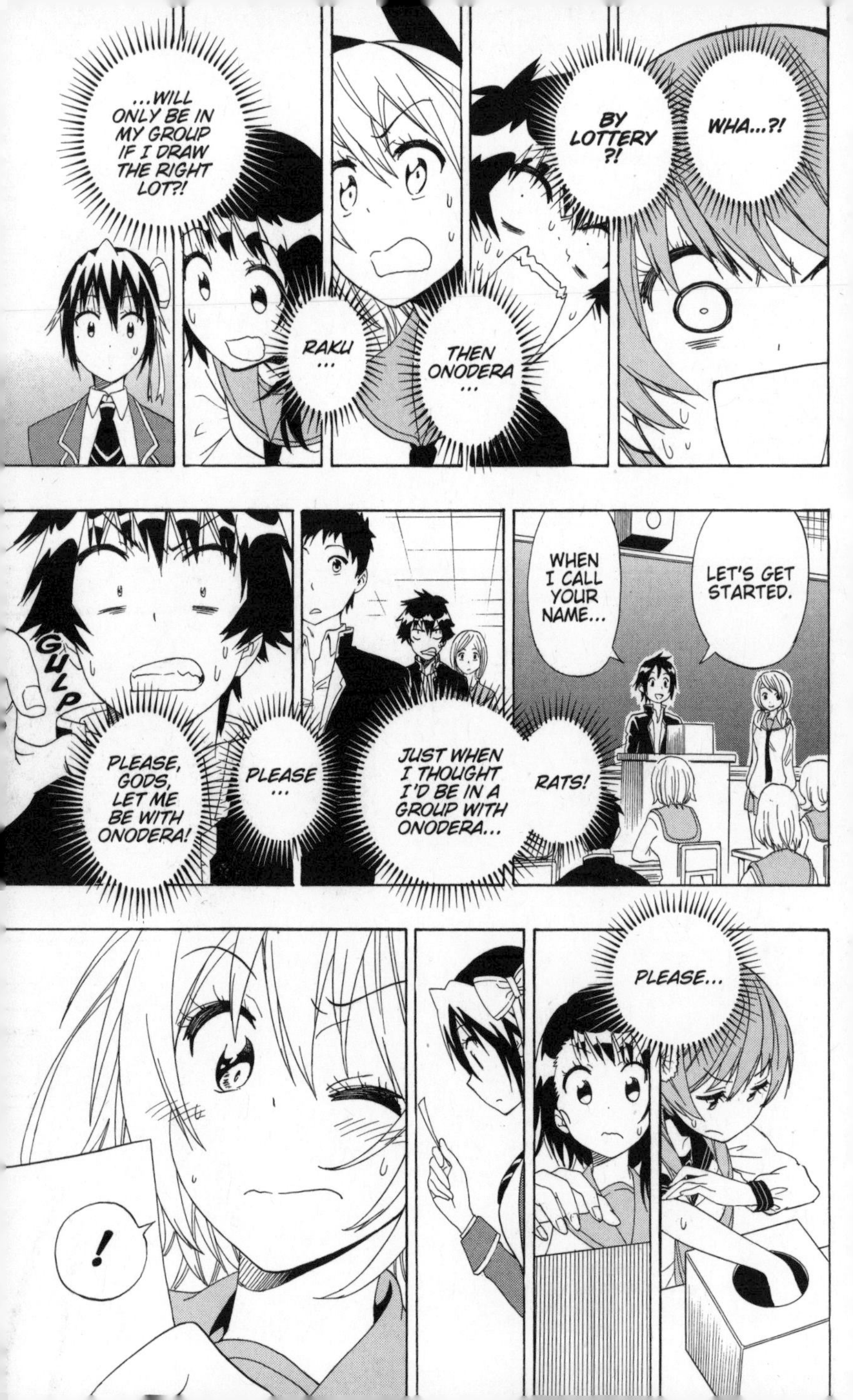
WHA...?!
BY LOTTERY ?!
THEN ONODERA ...
RAKU ...
...WILL ONLY BE IN MY GROUP IF I DRAW THE RIGHT LOT?!
LET'S GET STARTED.
WHEN I CALL YOUR NAME...
RATS!
JUST WHEN I THOUGHT I'D BE IN A GROUP WITH ONODERA...
PLEASE ...
PLEASE, GODS, LET ME BE WITH ONODERA!
GULP
PLEASE...
!

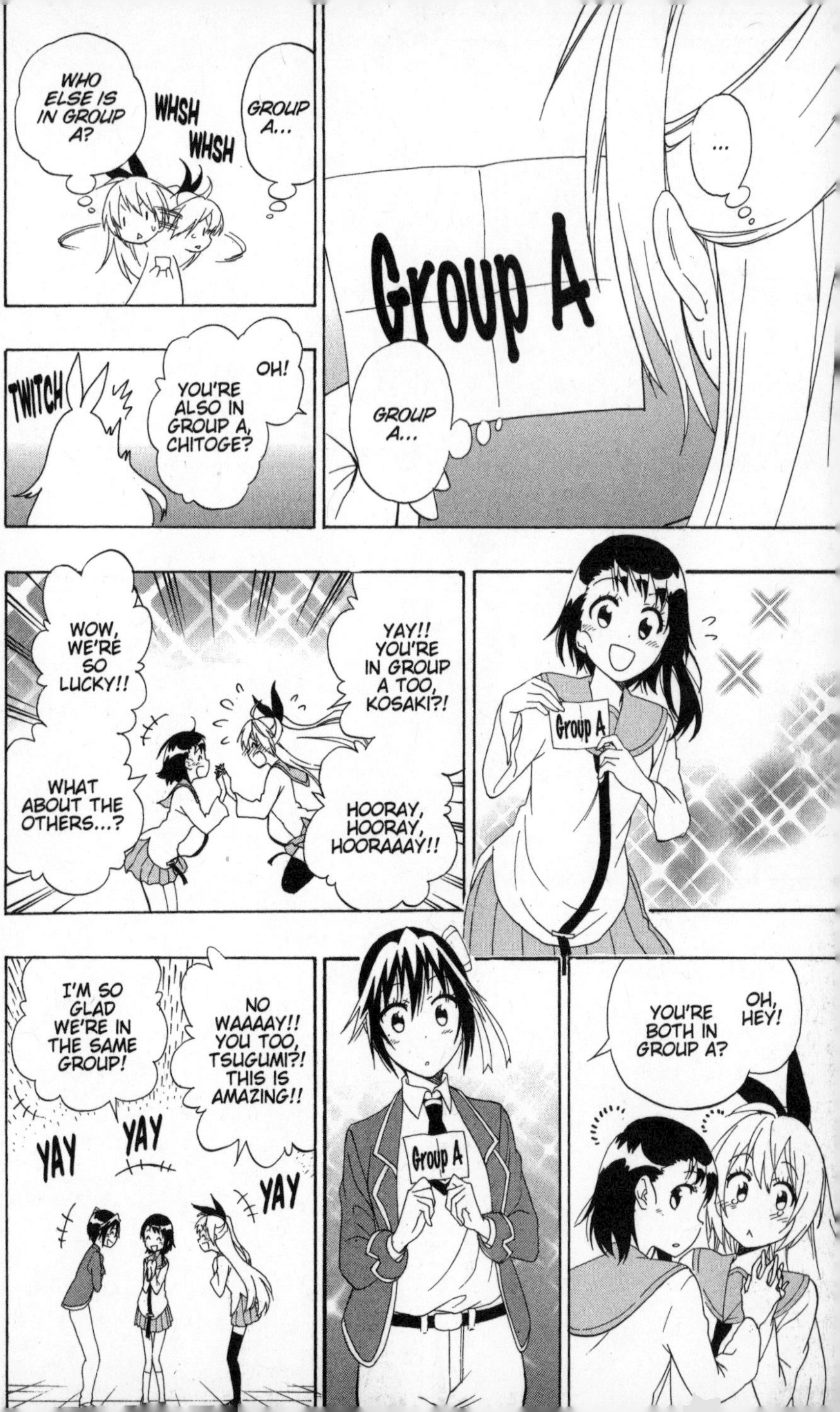
...
Group A
GROUP A...
WHO ELSE IS IN GROUP A?
WHSH
WHSH
GROUP A...
OH!
YOU'RE ALSO IN GROUP A, CHITOGE?
TWITCH
Group A
YAY!! YOU'RE IN GROUP A TOO, KOSAKI?!
HOORAY, HOORAY, HOORAAAY!!
WOW, WE'RE SO LUCKY!!
WHAT ABOUT THE OTHERS...?
OH, HEY!
YOU'RE BOTH IN GROUP A?
Group A
NO WAAAAY!! YOU TOO, TSUGUMI?! THIS IS AMAZING!!
I'M SO GLAD WE'RE IN THE SAME GROUP!
YAY
YAY
YAY

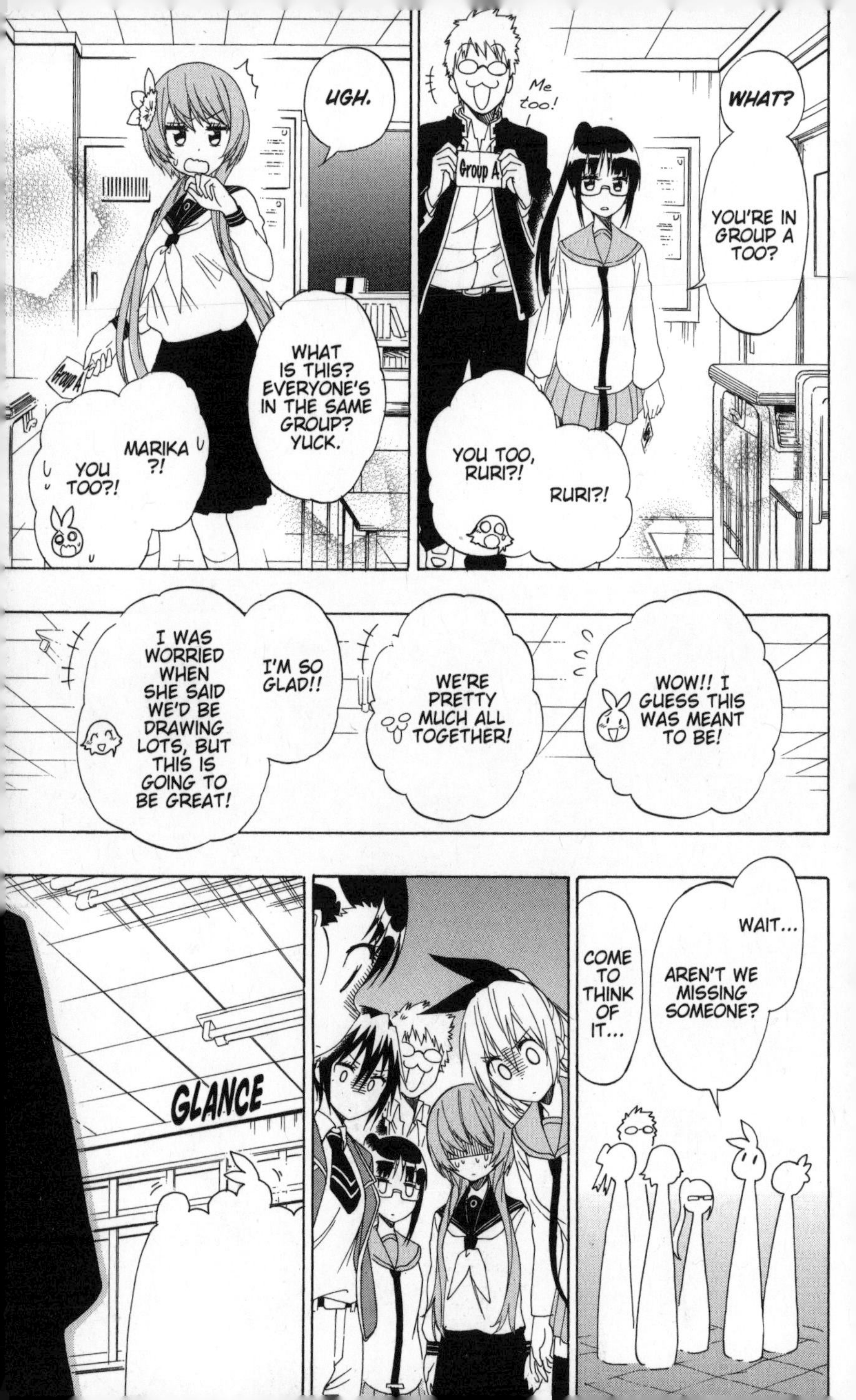
WHAT?
YOU'RE IN GROUP A TOO?
Me too!
Group A
YOU TOO, RURI?!
RURI?!
UGH.
WHAT IS THIS? EVERYONE'S IN THE SAME GROUP? YUCK.
MARIKA ?!
YOU TOO?!
Group A
WOW!! I GUESS THIS WAS MEANT TO BE!
WE'RE PRETTY MUCH ALL TOGETHER!
I'M SO GLAD!!
I WAS WORRIED WHEN SHE SAID WE'D BE DRAWING LOTS, BUT THIS IS GOING TO BE GREAT!
WAIT...
AREN'T WE MISSING SOMEONE?
COME TO THINK OF IT...
GLANCE

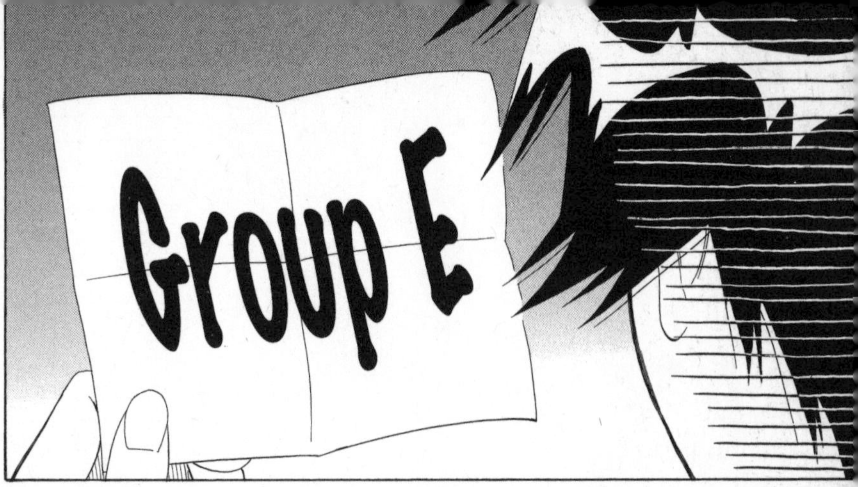
Group E

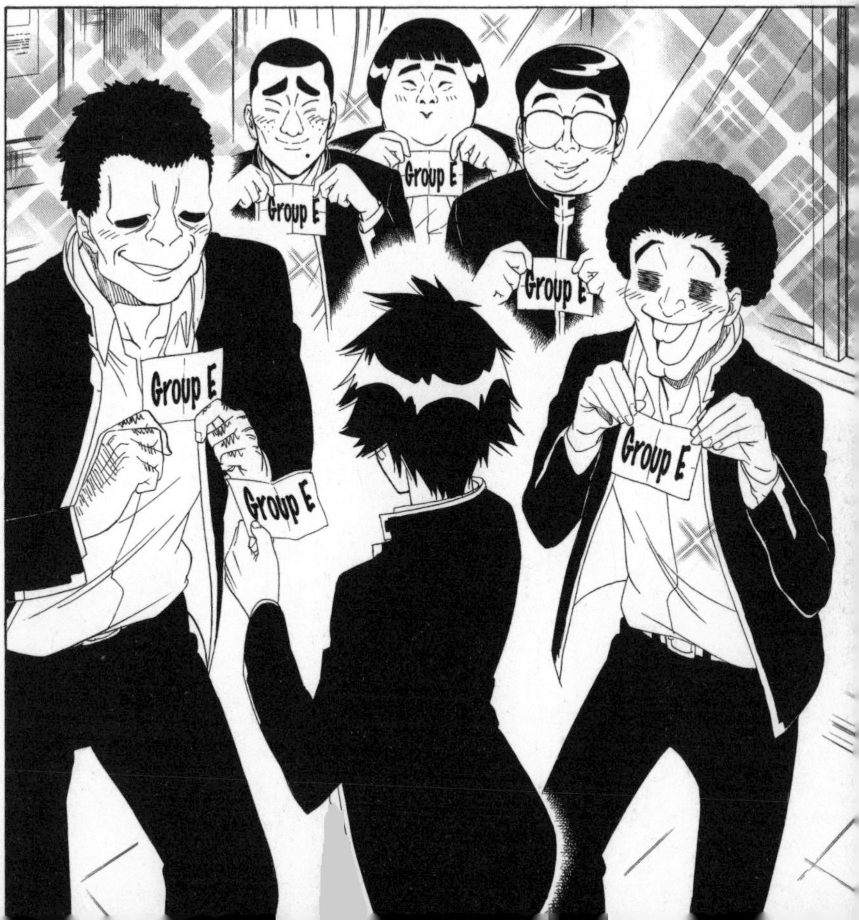
Group E
Group E
Group E
Group E
Group E
Group E
Group E

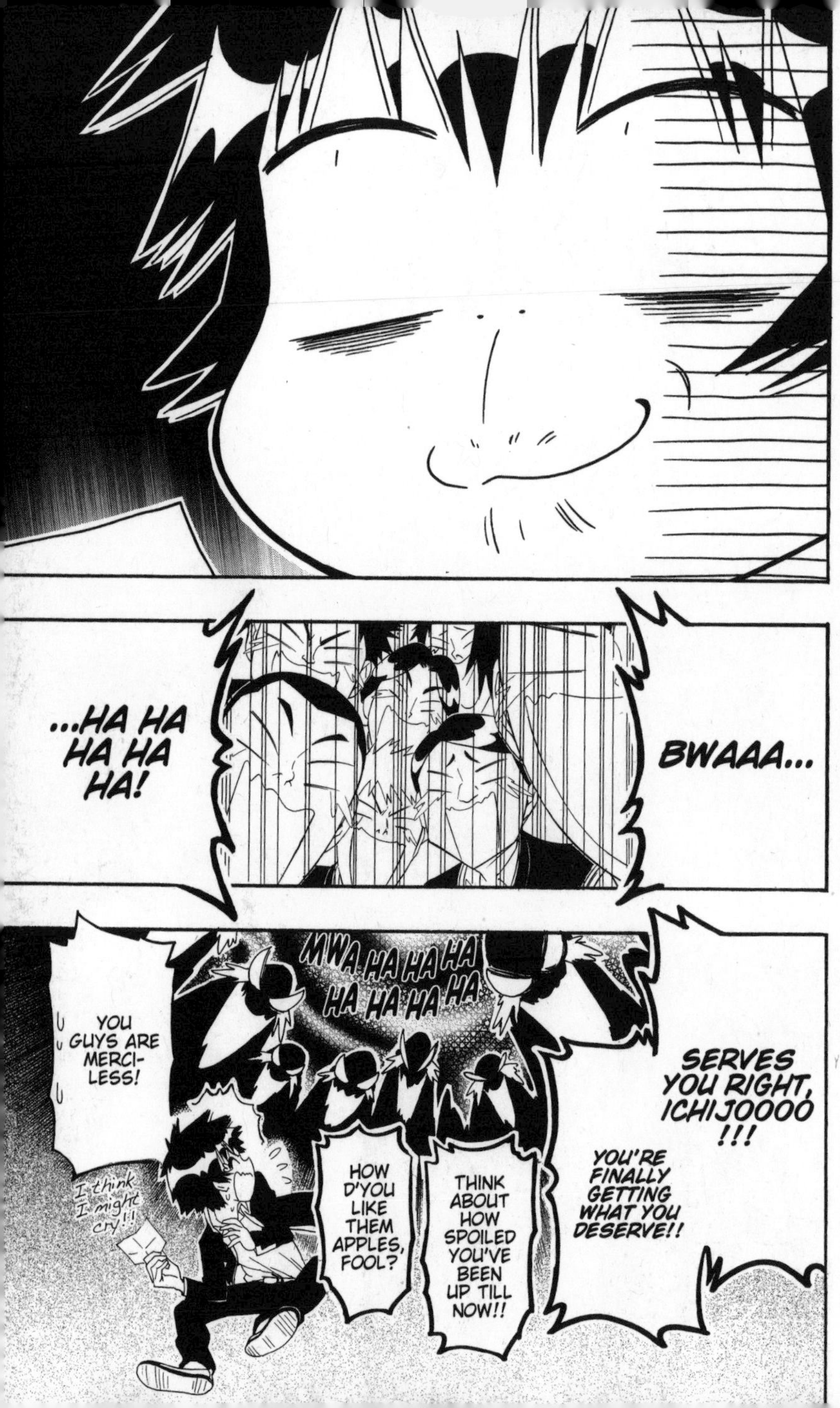
BWAAA...
...HA HA HA HA HA!
SERVES YOU RIGHT, ICHIJOOOO!!!
YOU'RE FINALLY GETTING WHAT YOU DESERVE!!
MWA HA HA HA HA HA HA HA HA
THINK ABOUT HOW SPOILED YOU'VE BEEN UP TILL NOW!!
HOW D'YOU LIKE THEM APPLES, FOOL?
YOU GUYS ARE MERCI-LESS!
I think I might cry!!

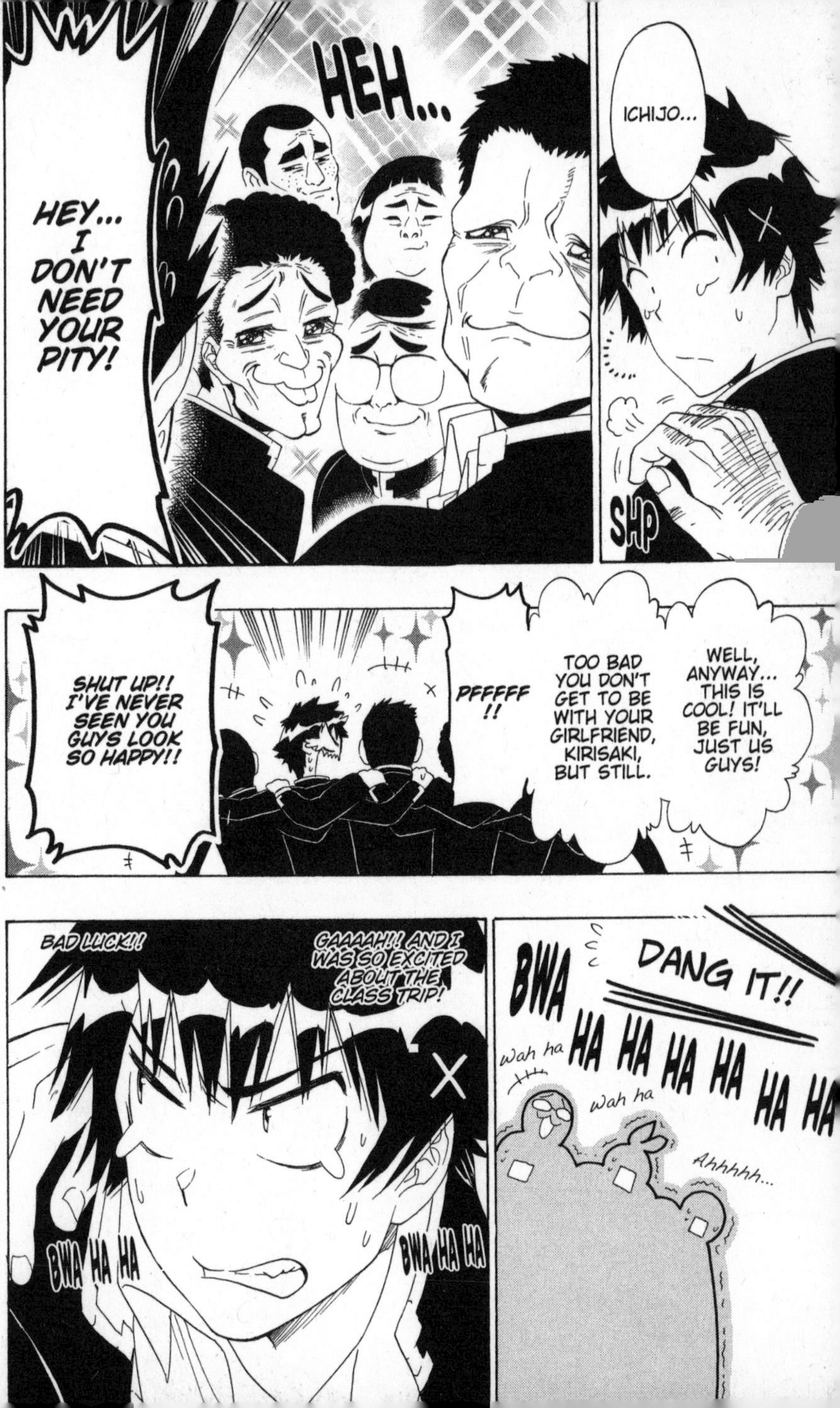
ICHIJO...
SHP
HEH...
HEY... I DON'T NEED YOUR PITY!
WELL, ANYWAY... THIS IS COOL! IT'LL BE FUN, JUST US GUYS!
TOO BAD YOU DON'T GET TO BE WITH YOUR GIRLFRIEND, KIRISAKI, BUT STILL.
PFFFFF!!
SHUT UP!! I'VE NEVER SEEN YOU GUYS LOOK SO HAPPY!!
DANG IT!!
BWA HA HA HA HA HA HA HA
Wah ha
Wah ha
Ahhhhh...
GAAAAH!! AND I WAS SO EXCITED ABOUT THE CLASS TRIP!
BAD LUCK!!
BWA HA HA
BWA HA HA

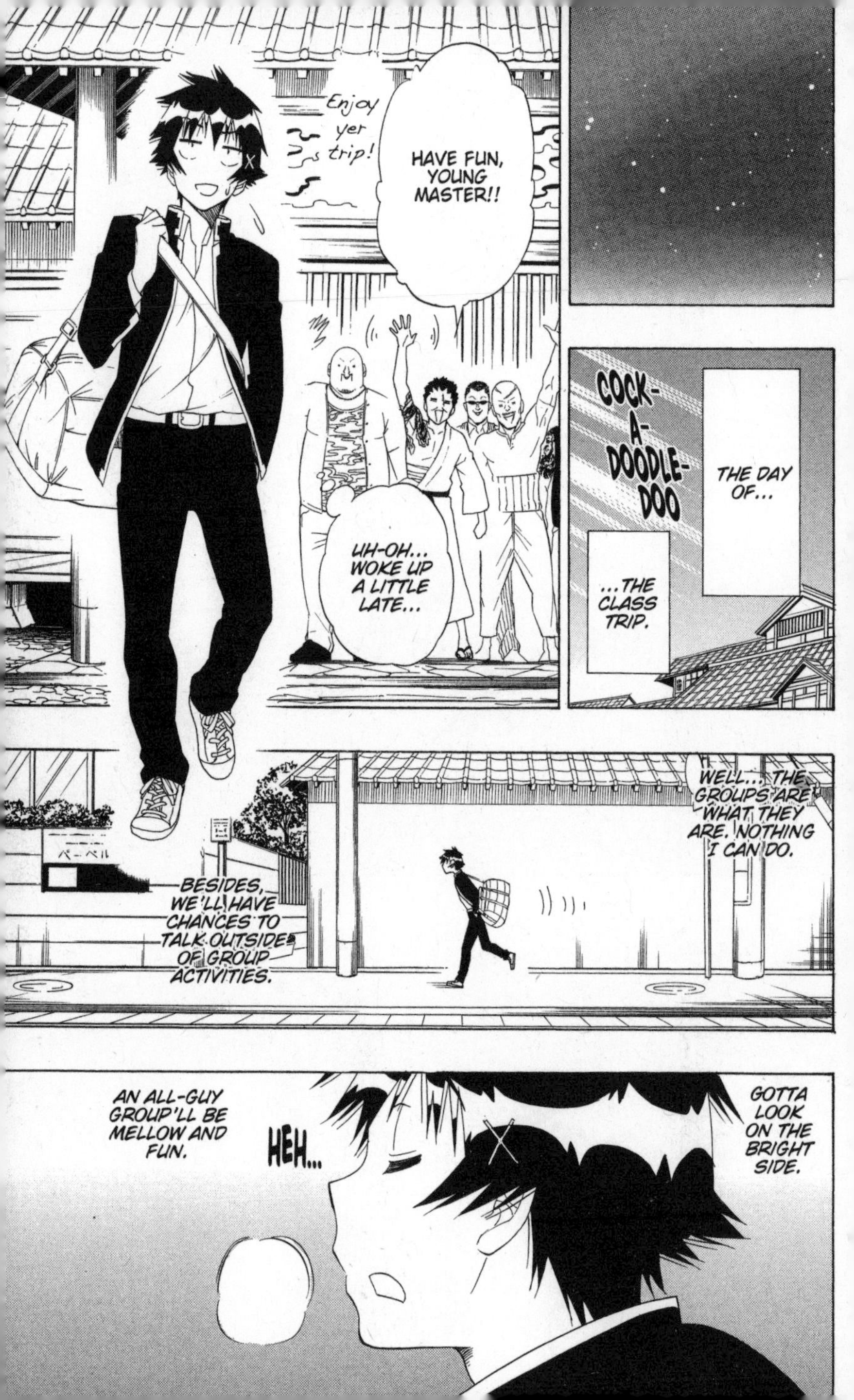
THE DAY OF...
...THE CLASS TRIP.
COCK-A-DOODLE-DOO
HAVE FUN, YOUNG MASTER!!
Enjoy yer trip!
UH-OH... WOKE UP A LITTLE LATE...
WELL... THE GROUPS ARE WHAT THEY ARE. NOTHING I CAN DO.
BESIDES, WE'LL HAVE CHANCES TO TALK OUTSIDE OF GROUP ACTIVITIES.
GOTTA LOOK ON THE BRIGHT SIDE.
HEH...
AN ALL-GUY GROUP'LL BE MELLOW AND FUN.

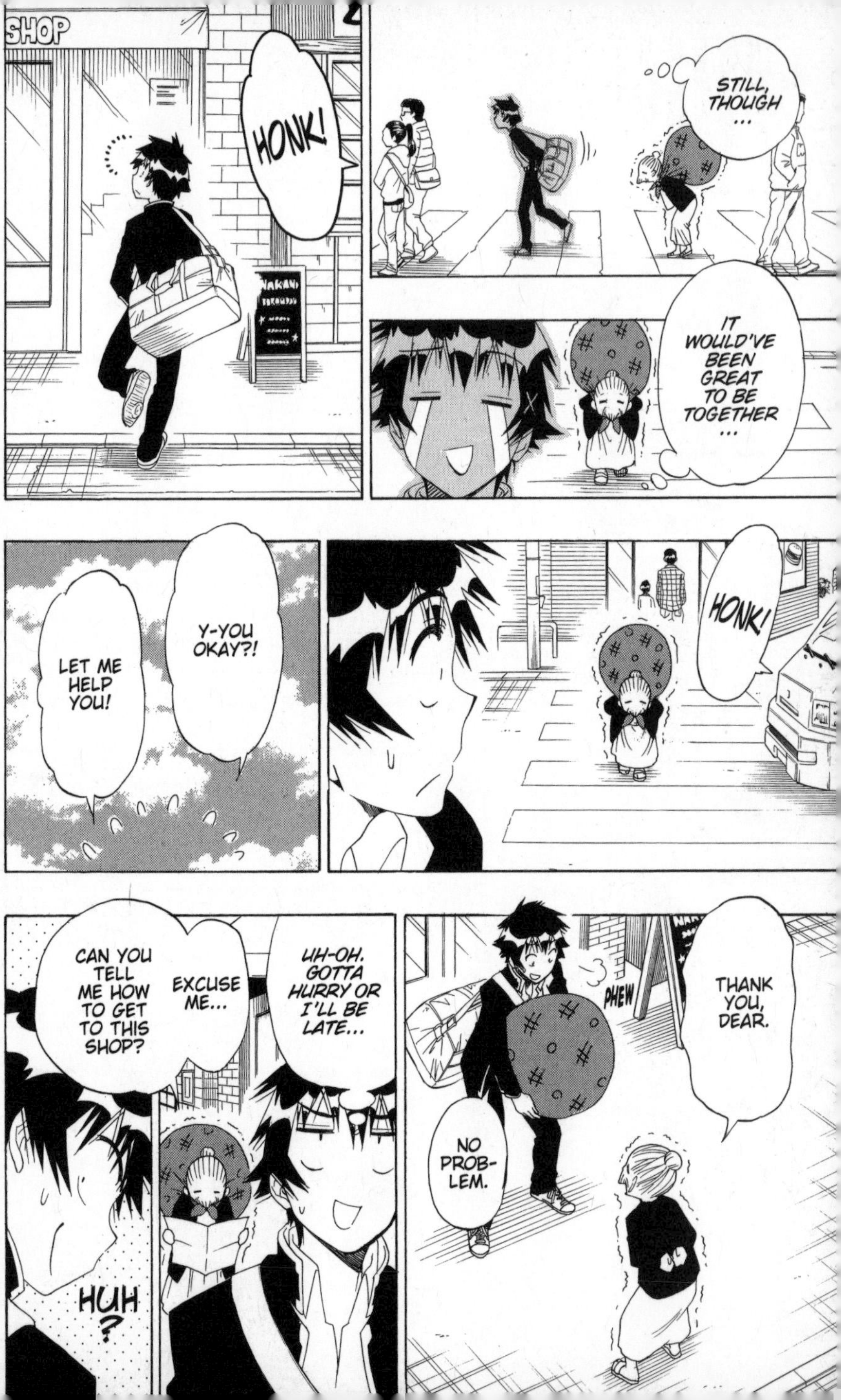
STILL, THOUGH...
IT WOULD'VE BEEN GREAT TO BE TOGETHER...
SHOP
HONK!
HONK!
Y-YOU OKAY?!
LET ME HELP YOU!
THANK YOU, DEAR.
PHEW
NO PROB-LEM.
UH-OH. GOTTA HURRY OR I'LL BE LATE...
EXCUSE ME...
CAN YOU TELL ME HOW TO GET TO THIS SHOP?
HUH?

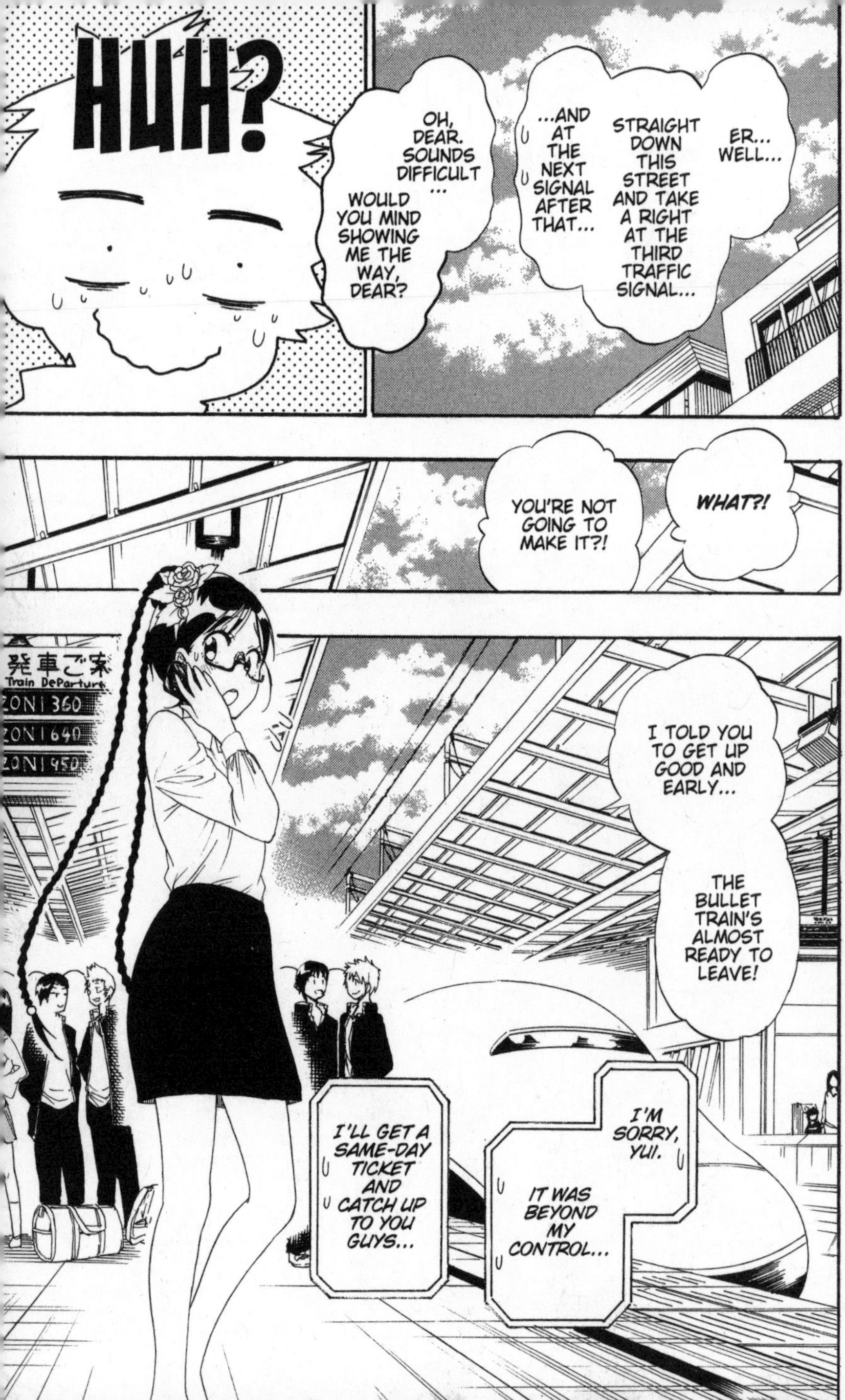
ER... WELL...
STRAIGHT DOWN THIS STREET AND TAKE A RIGHT AT THE THIRD TRAFFIC SIGNAL...
...AND AT THE NEXT SIGNAL AFTER THAT...
OH, DEAR. SOUNDS DIFFICULT...
WOULD YOU MIND SHOWING ME THE WAY, DEAR?
HUH?
WHAT?!
YOU'RE NOT GOING TO MAKE IT?!
I TOLD YOU TO GET UP GOOD AND EARLY...
THE BULLET TRAIN'S ALMOST READY TO LEAVE!
I'M SORRY, YUI.
IT WAS BEYOND MY CONTROL...
I'LL GET A SAME-DAY TICKET AND CATCH UP TO YOU GUYS...
発車ご案
Train Departure
ZONI 360
ZONI 640
ZONI 950

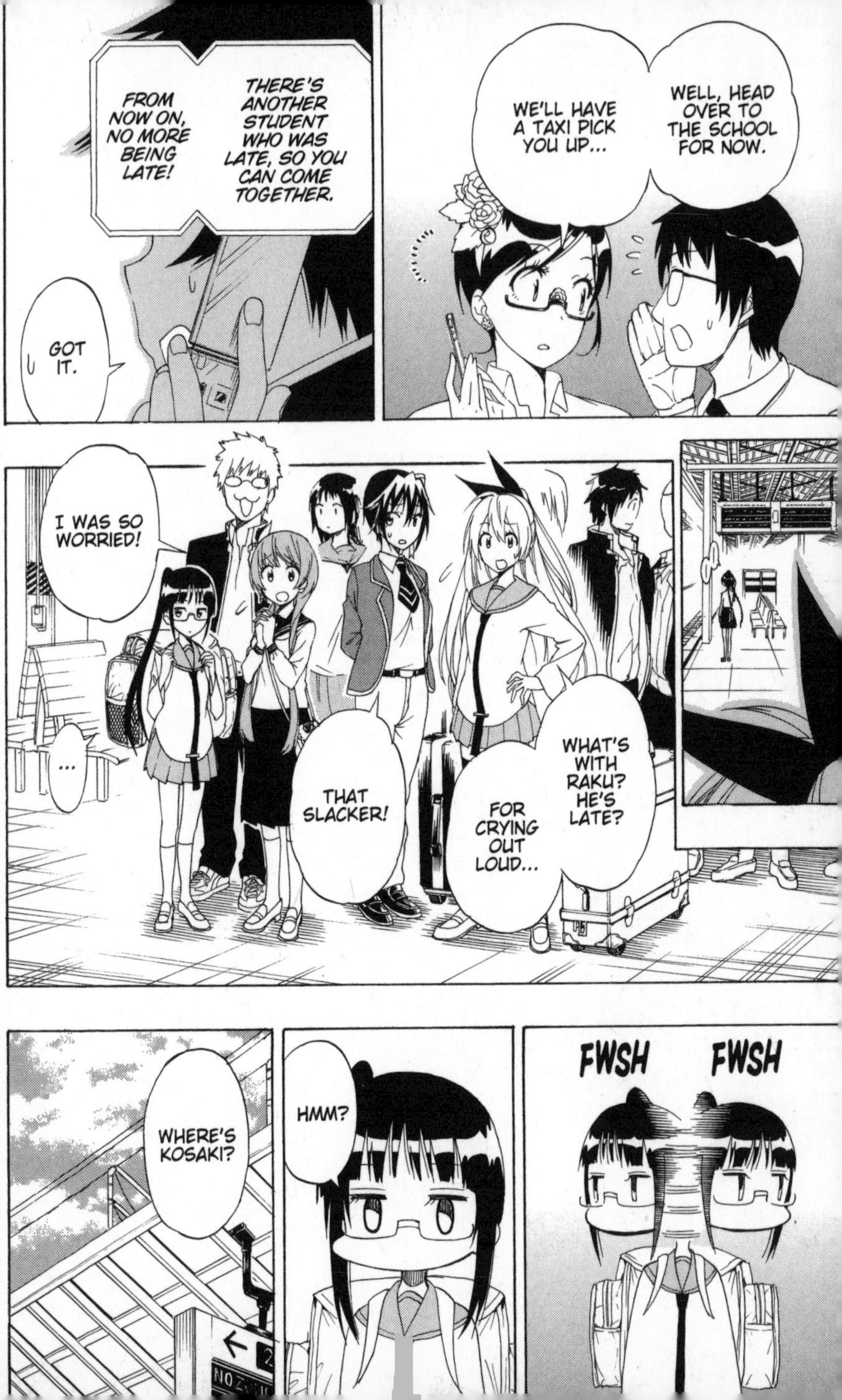
WELL, HEAD OVER TO THE SCHOOL FOR NOW.
WE'LL HAVE A TAXI PICK YOU UP...
THERE'S ANOTHER STUDENT WHO WAS LATE, SO YOU CAN COME TOGETHER.
FROM NOW ON, NO MORE BEING LATE!
GOT IT.
WHAT'S WITH RAKU? HE'S LATE?
FOR CRYING OUT LOUD...
THAT SLACKER!
I WAS SO WORRIED!
...
FWSH
FWSH
HMM?
WHERE'S KOSAKI?

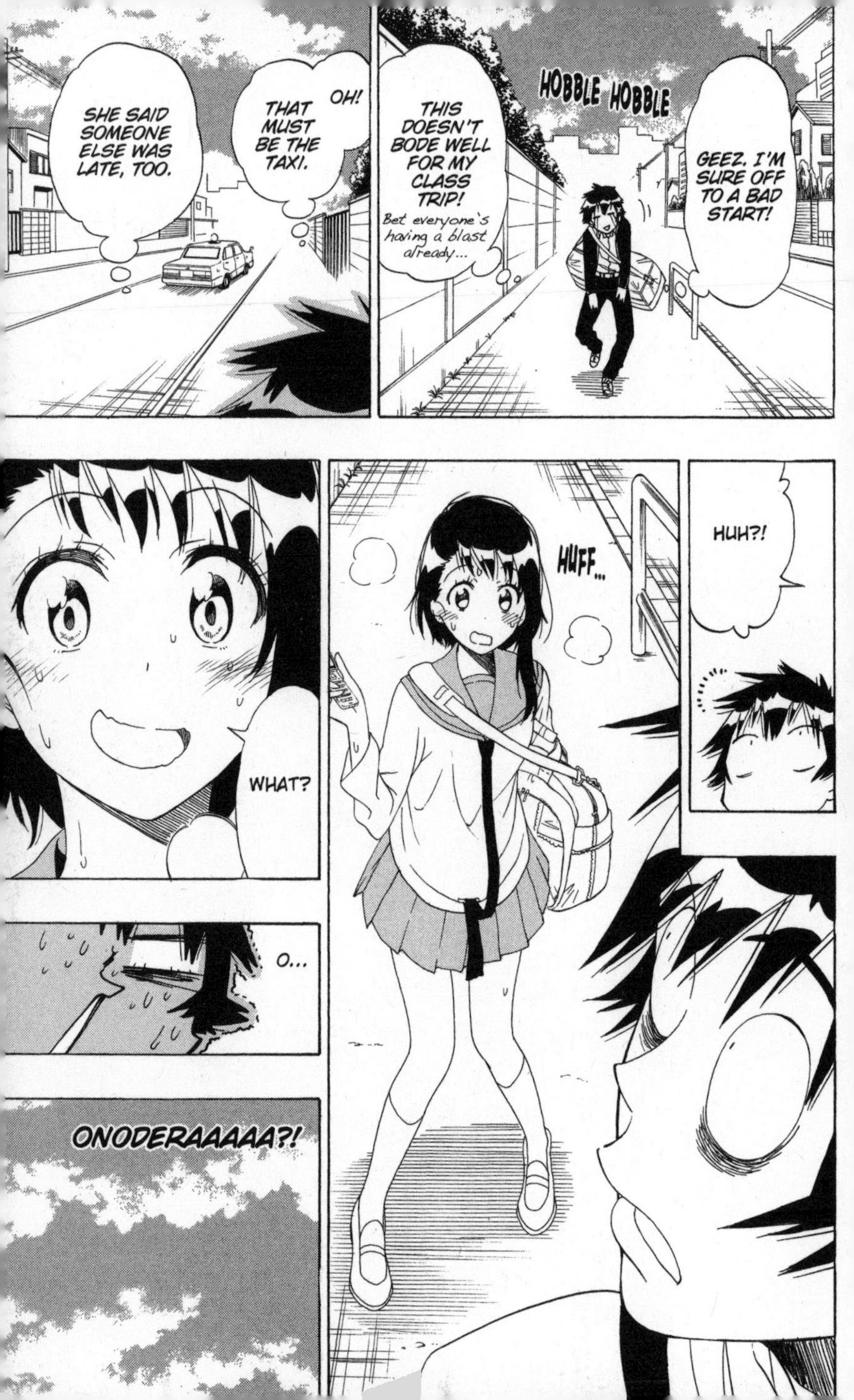
GEEZ. I'M SURE OFF TO A BAD START!
HOBBLE HOBBLE
THIS DOESN'T BODE WELL FOR MY CLASS TRIP!
Bet everyone's having a blast already...
OH!
THAT MUST BE THE TAXI.
SHE SAID SOMEONE ELSE WAS LATE, TOO.
HUH?!
HUFF...
WHAT?
O...
ONODERAAAAA?!

Next stop is the knife shop on 3rd street...
And then the rice store...
Thanks so much...

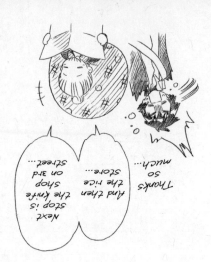

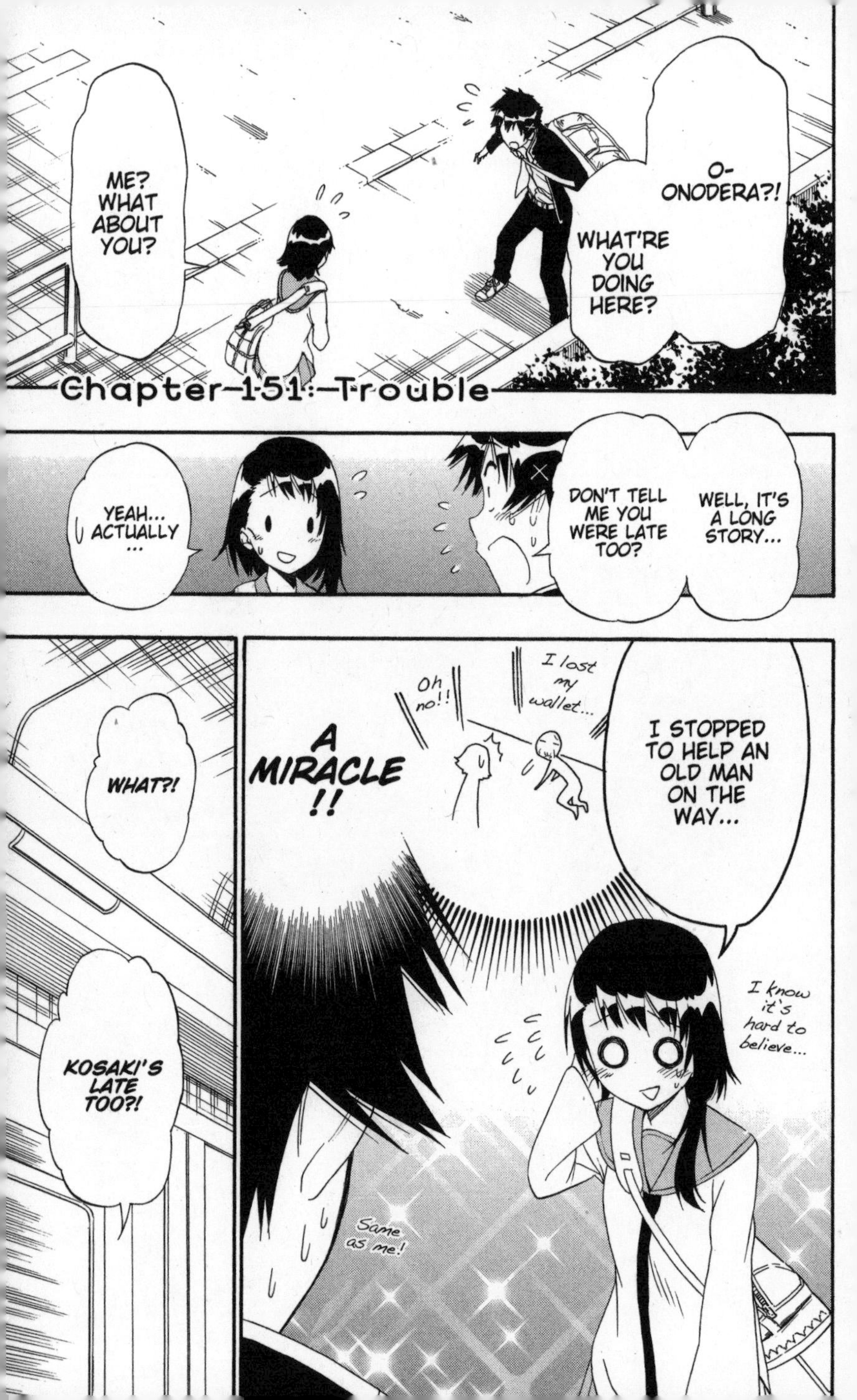
O-ONODERA?!
WHAT'RE YOU DOING HERE?
ME? WHAT ABOUT YOU?
Chapter 151: Trouble
WELL, IT'S A LONG STORY...
DON'T TELL ME YOU WERE LATE TOO?
YEAH... ACTUALLY ...
I STOPPED TO HELP AN OLD MAN ON THE WAY...
I lost my wallet...
Oh no!!
A MIRACLE !!
I know it's hard to believe...
Same as me!
WHAT?!
KOSAKI'S LATE TOO?!

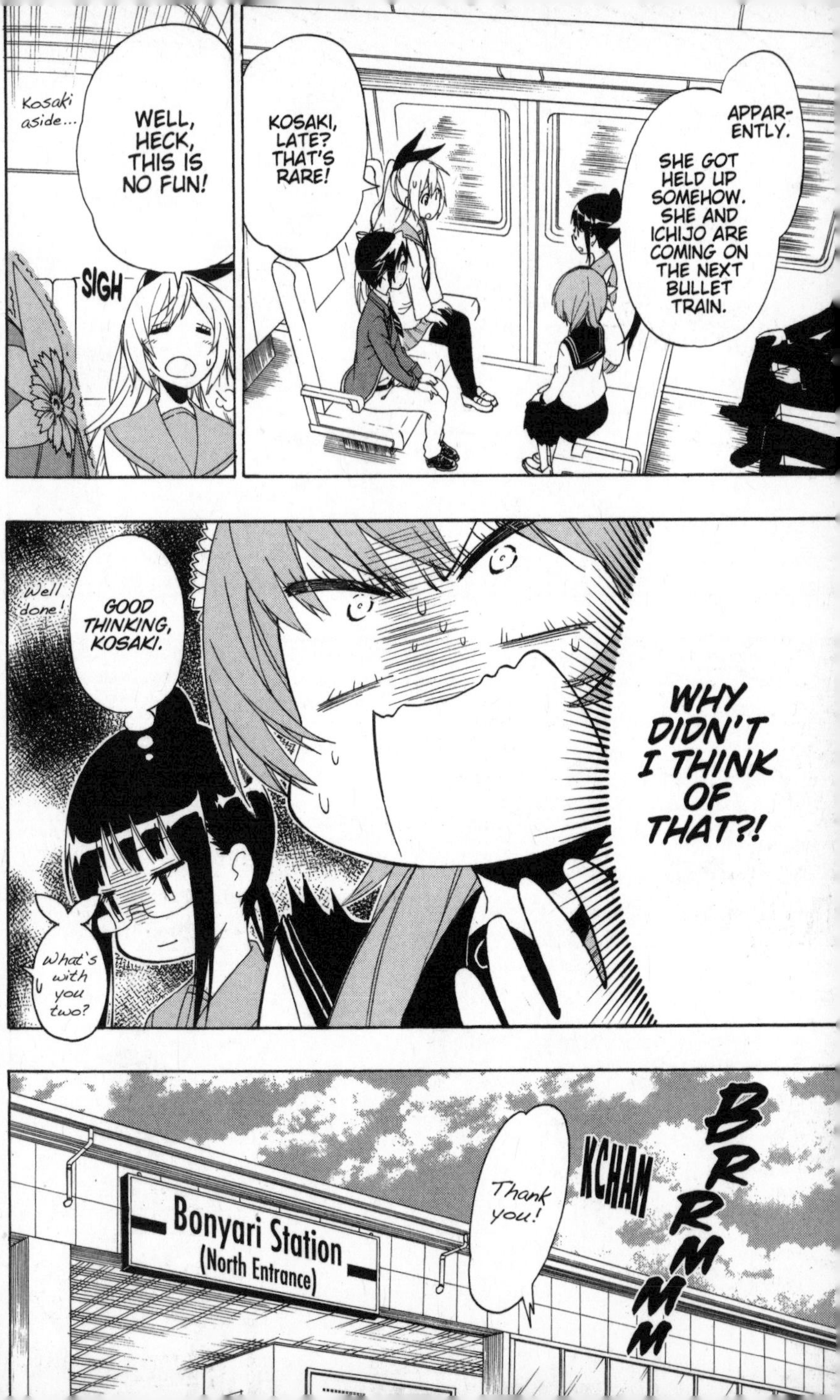
APPARENTLY.
SHE GOT HELD UP SOMEHOW. SHE AND ICHIJO ARE COMING ON THE NEXT BULLET TRAIN.
KOSAKI, LATE? THAT'S RARE!
WELL, HECK, THIS IS NO FUN!
Kosaki aside...
SIGH
WHY DIDN'T I THINK OF THAT?!
GOOD THINKING, KOSAKI.
Well done!
What's with you two?
BRRMMMM
KCHAM
Thank you!
Bonyari Station
(North Entrance)

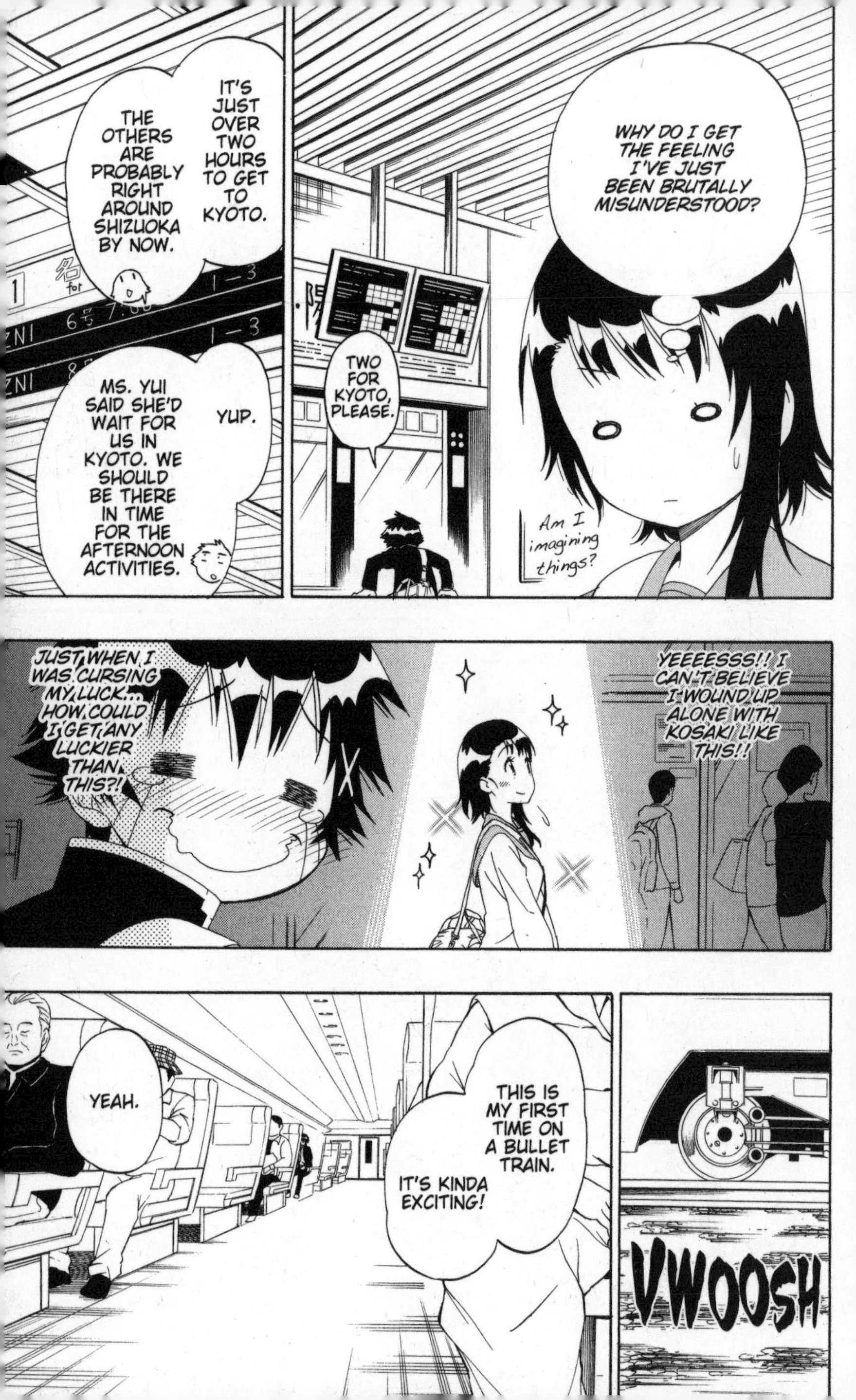
WHY DO I GET THE FEELING I'VE JUST BEEN BRUTALLY MISUNDERSTOOD?
Am I imagining things?
TWO FOR KYOTO, PLEASE.
IT'S JUST OVER TWO HOURS TO GET TO KYOTO.
THE OTHERS ARE PROBABLY RIGHT AROUND SHIZUOKA BY NOW.
MS. YUI SAID SHE'D WAIT FOR US IN KYOTO. WE SHOULD BE THERE IN TIME FOR THE AFTERNOON ACTIVITIES.
YUP.
YEEEESSS!! I CAN'T BELIEVE I WOUND UP ALONE WITH KOSAKI LIKE THIS!!
JUST WHEN I WAS CURSING MY LUCK... HOW COULD I GET ANY LUCKIER THAN THIS?!
VWOOSH
THIS IS MY FIRST TIME ON A BULLET TRAIN.
IT'S KINDA EXCITING!
YEAH.

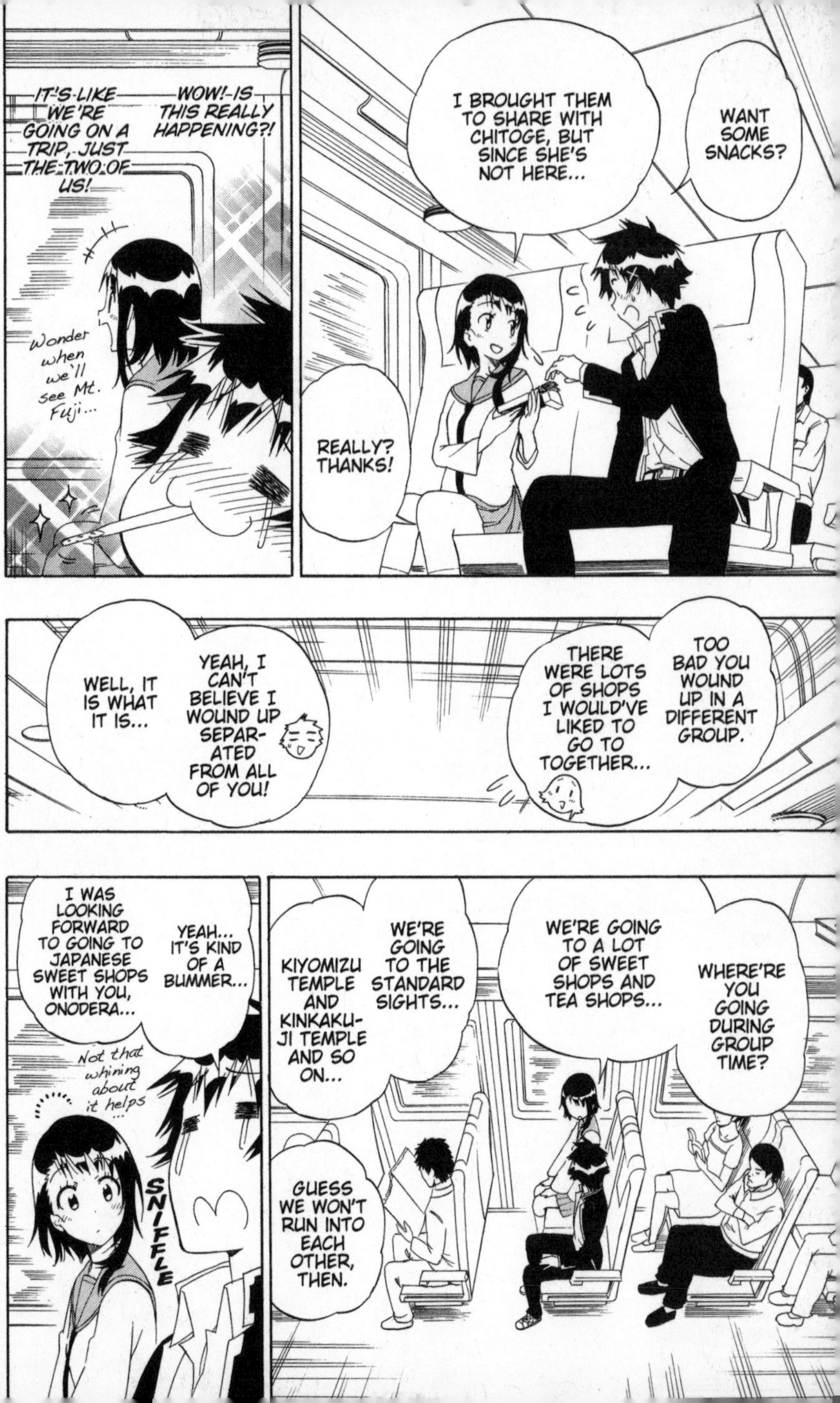
WANT SOME SNACKS?
I BROUGHT THEM TO SHARE WITH CHITOGE, BUT SINCE SHE'S NOT HERE...
REALLY? THANKS!
WOW! IS THIS REALLY HAPPENING?!
IT'S LIKE WE'RE GOING ON A TRIP, JUST THE TWO OF US!
Wonder when we'll see Mt. Fuji...
TOO BAD YOU WOUND UP IN A DIFFERENT GROUP.
THERE WERE LOTS OF SHOPS I WOULD'VE LIKED TO GO TO TOGETHER...
YEAH, I CAN'T BELIEVE I WOUND UP SEPARATED FROM ALL OF YOU!
WELL, IT IS WHAT IT IS...
WHERE'RE YOU GOING DURING GROUP TIME?
WE'RE GOING TO A LOT OF SWEET SHOPS AND TEA SHOPS...
WE'RE GOING TO THE STANDARD SIGHTS...
KIYOMIZU TEMPLE AND KINKAKUJI TEMPLE AND SO ON...
GUESS WE WON'T RUN INTO EACH OTHER, THEN.
YEAH... IT'S KIND OF A BUMMER...
I WAS LOOKING FORWARD TO GOING TO JAPANESE SWEET SHOPS WITH YOU, ONODERA...
Not that whining about it helps...
SNIFFLE

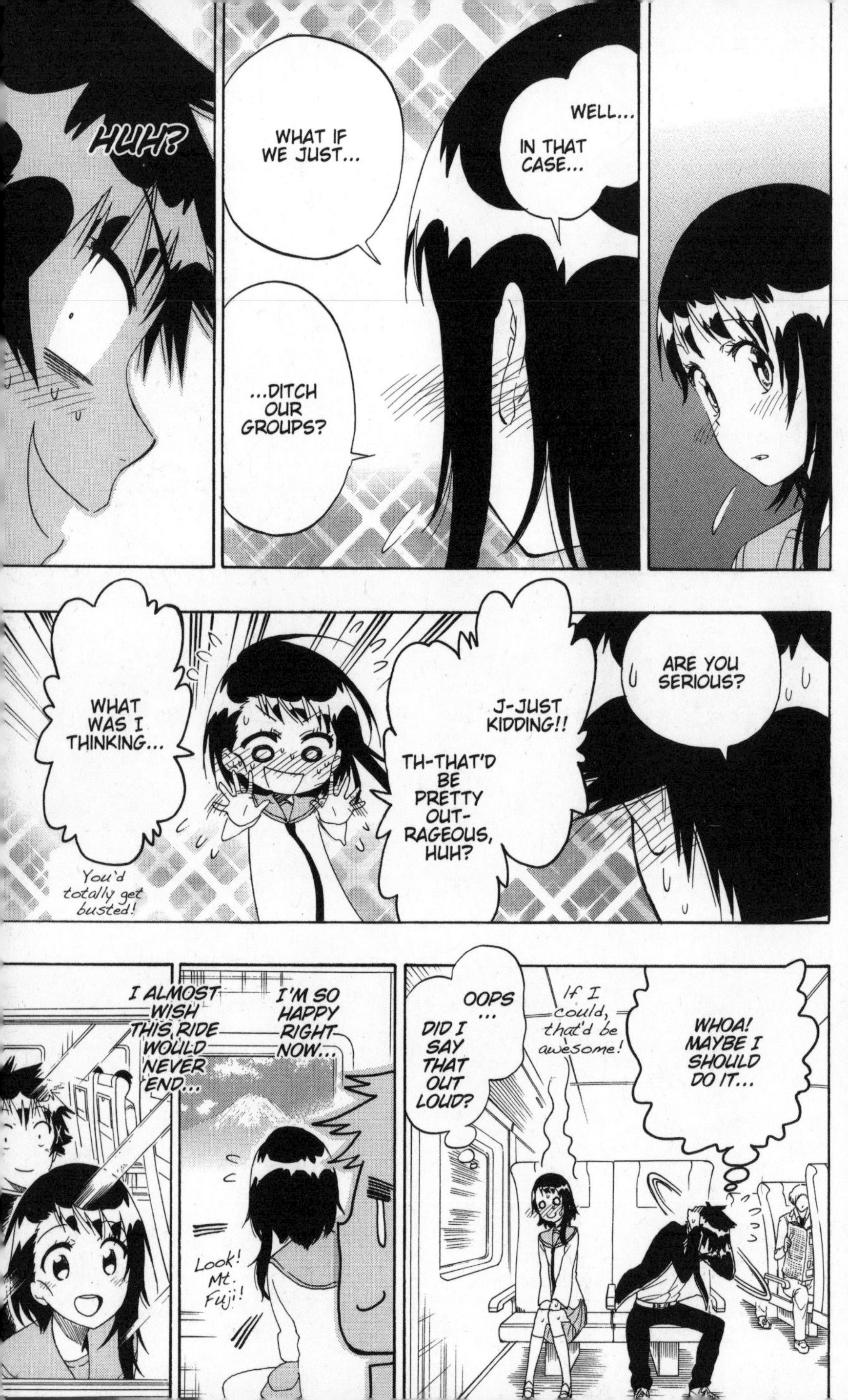
WELL...
IN THAT CASE...
WHAT IF WE JUST...
...DITCH OUR GROUPS?
HUH?
ARE YOU SERIOUS?
J-JUST KIDDING!!
TH-THAT'D BE PRETTY OUT-RAGEOUS, HUH?
WHAT WAS I THINKING...
You'd totally get busted!
WHOA! MAYBE I SHOULD DO IT...
If I could, that'd be awesome!
OOPS...
DID I SAY THAT OUT LOUD?
I'M SO HAPPY RIGHT NOW...
I ALMOST WISH THIS RIDE WOULD NEVER END...
Look! Mt. Fuji!

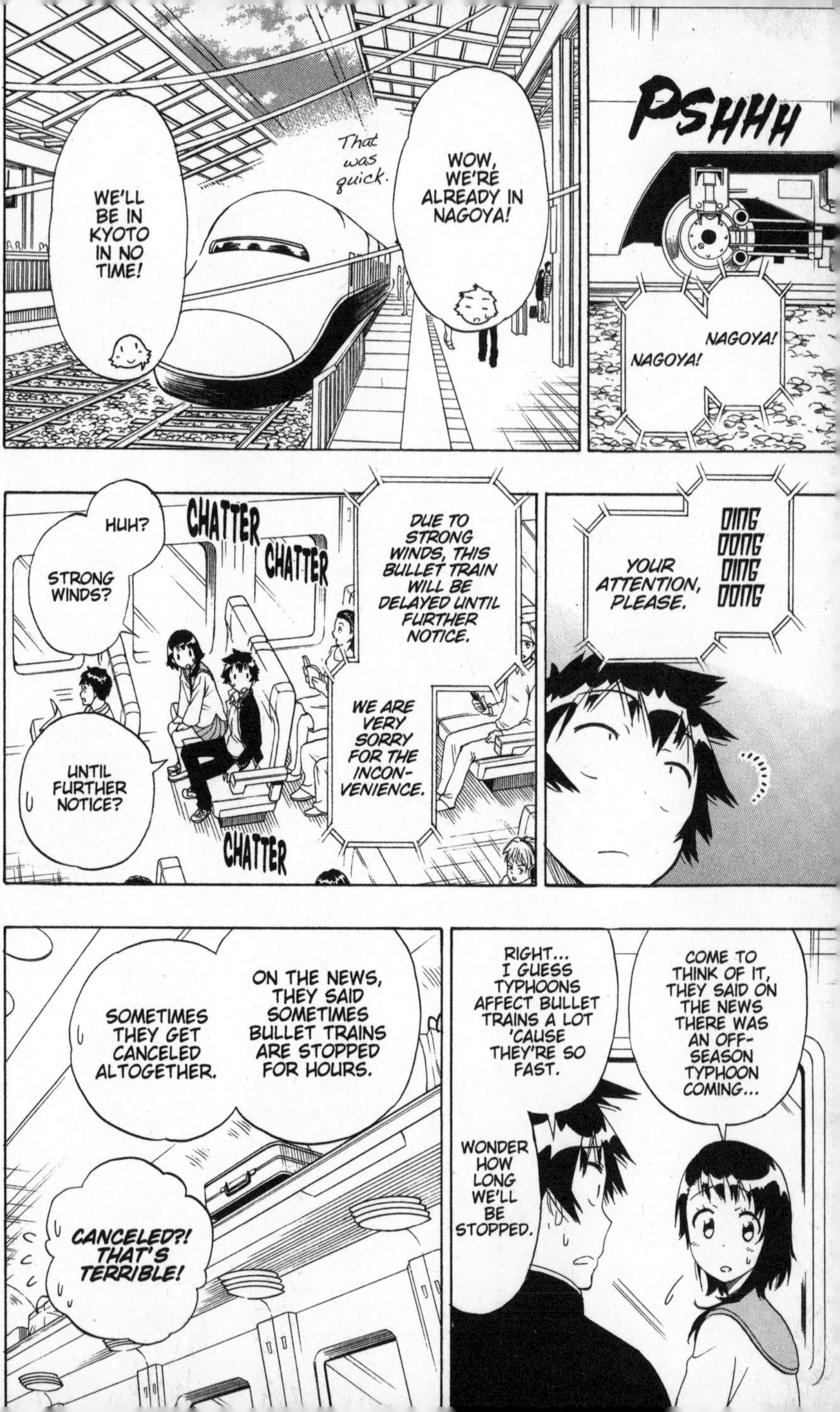
PSHHH
NAGOYA!
NAGOYA!
WOW, WE'RE ALREADY IN NAGOYA!
That was quick.
WE'LL BE IN KYOTO IN NO TIME!
DING DONG DING DONG
YOUR ATTENTION, PLEASE.
DUE TO STRONG WINDS, THIS BULLET TRAIN WILL BE DELAYED UNTIL FURTHER NOTICE.
WE ARE VERY SORRY FOR THE INCONVENIENCE.
CHATTER
CHATTER
HUH?
STRONG WINDS?
UNTIL FURTHER NOTICE?
CHATTER
COME TO THINK OF IT, THEY SAID ON THE NEWS THERE WAS AN OFF-SEASON TYPHOON COMING...
RIGHT... I GUESS TYPHOONS AFFECT BULLET TRAINS A LOT 'CAUSE THEY'RE SO FAST.
WONDER HOW LONG WE'LL BE STOPPED.
ON THE NEWS, THEY SAID SOMETIMES BULLET TRAINS ARE STOPPED FOR HOURS.
SOMETIMES THEY GET CANCELED ALTOGETHER.
CANCELED?! THAT'S TERRIBLE!

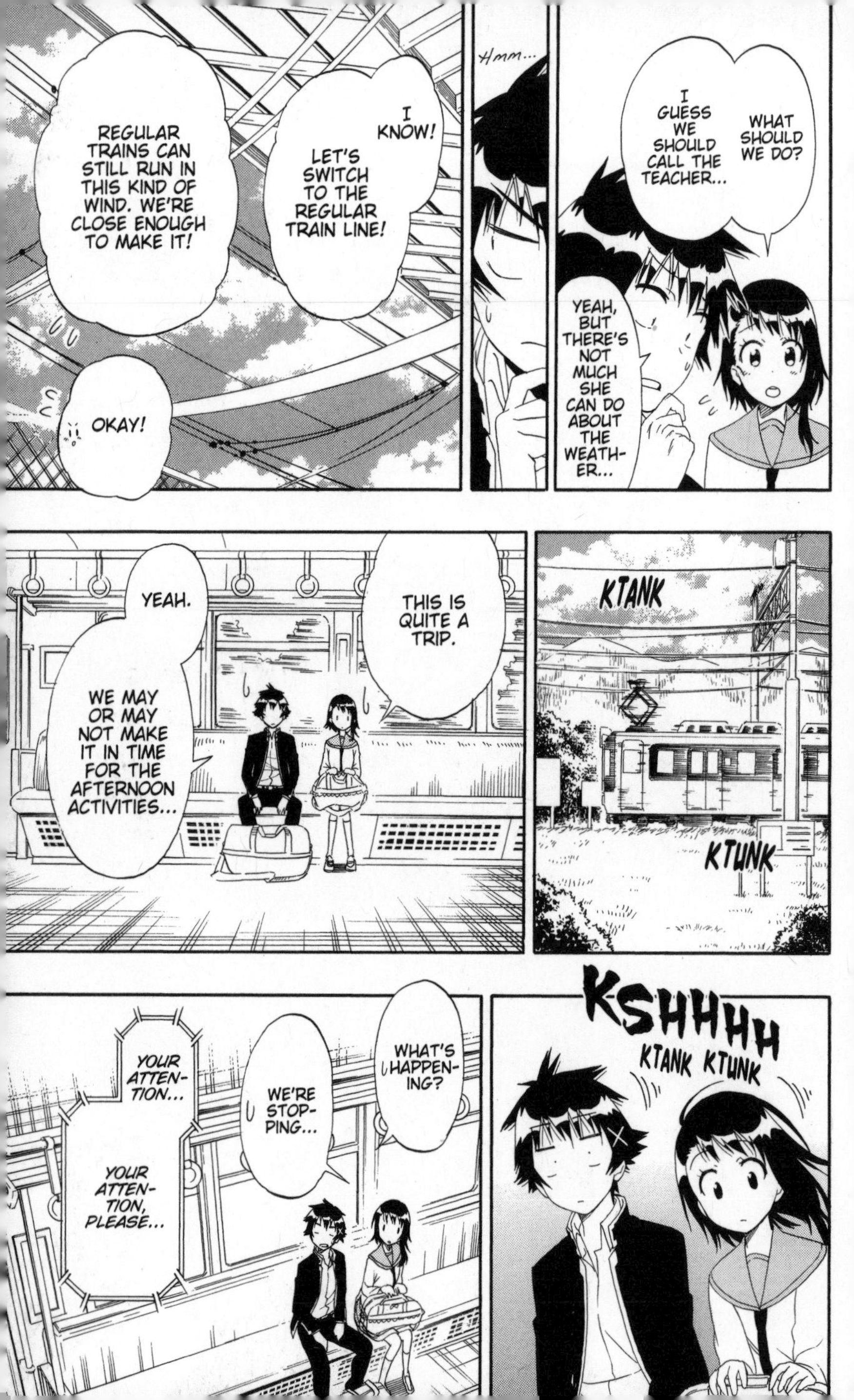
I GUESS WE SHOULD CALL THE TEACHER...
WHAT SHOULD WE DO?
YEAH, BUT THERE'S NOT MUCH SHE CAN DO ABOUT THE WEATH-ER...
Hmm...
I KNOW!
LET'S SWITCH TO THE REGULAR TRAIN LINE!
REGULAR TRAINS CAN STILL RUN IN THIS KIND OF WIND. WE'RE CLOSE ENOUGH TO MAKE IT!
OKAY!
KTANK
KTUNK
THIS IS QUITE A TRIP.
YEAH.
WE MAY OR MAY NOT MAKE IT IN TIME FOR THE AFTERNOON ACTIVITIES...
KSHHHH
KTANK KTUNK
WHAT'S HAPPEN-ING?
WE'RE STOP-PING...
YOUR ATTEN-TION...
YOUR ATTEN-TION, PLEASE...

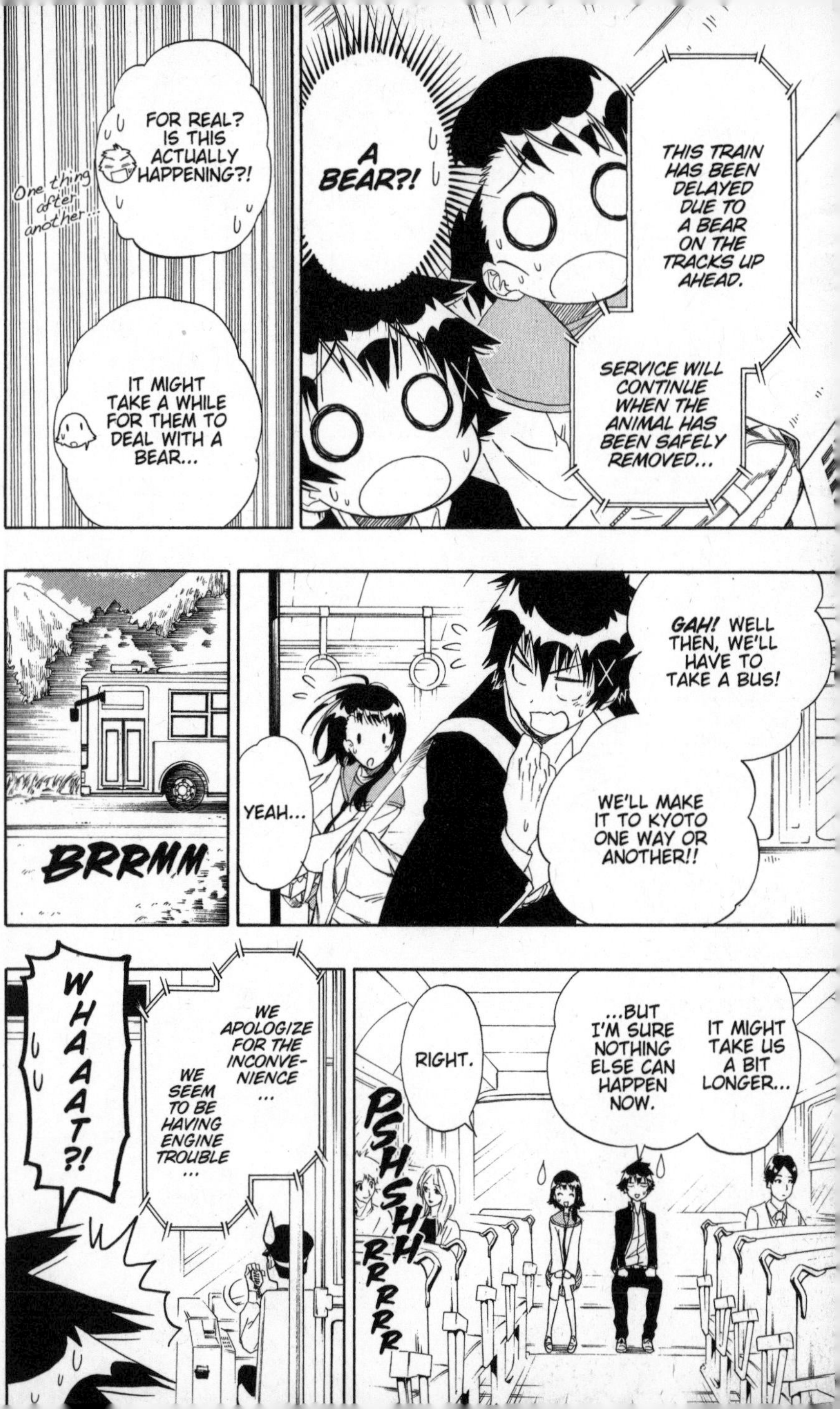
THIS TRAIN HAS BEEN DELAYED DUE TO A BEAR ON THE TRACKS UP AHEAD.
SERVICE WILL CONTINUE WHEN THE ANIMAL HAS BEEN SAFELY REMOVED...
A BEAR?!
FOR REAL? IS THIS ACTUALLY HAPPENING?!
One thing after another...
IT MIGHT TAKE A WHILE FOR THEM TO DEAL WITH A BEAR...
GAH! WELL THEN, WE'LL HAVE TO TAKE A BUS!
WE'LL MAKE IT TO KYOTO ONE WAY OR ANOTHER!!
YEAH...
BRRMM
IT MIGHT TAKE US A BIT LONGER...
...BUT I'M SURE NOTHING ELSE CAN HAPPEN NOW.
RIGHT.
PSHSHH RRRRR
WE APOLOGIZE FOR THE INCONVE-NIENCE...
WE SEEM TO BE HAVING ENGINE TROUBLE...
WHAAAT?!

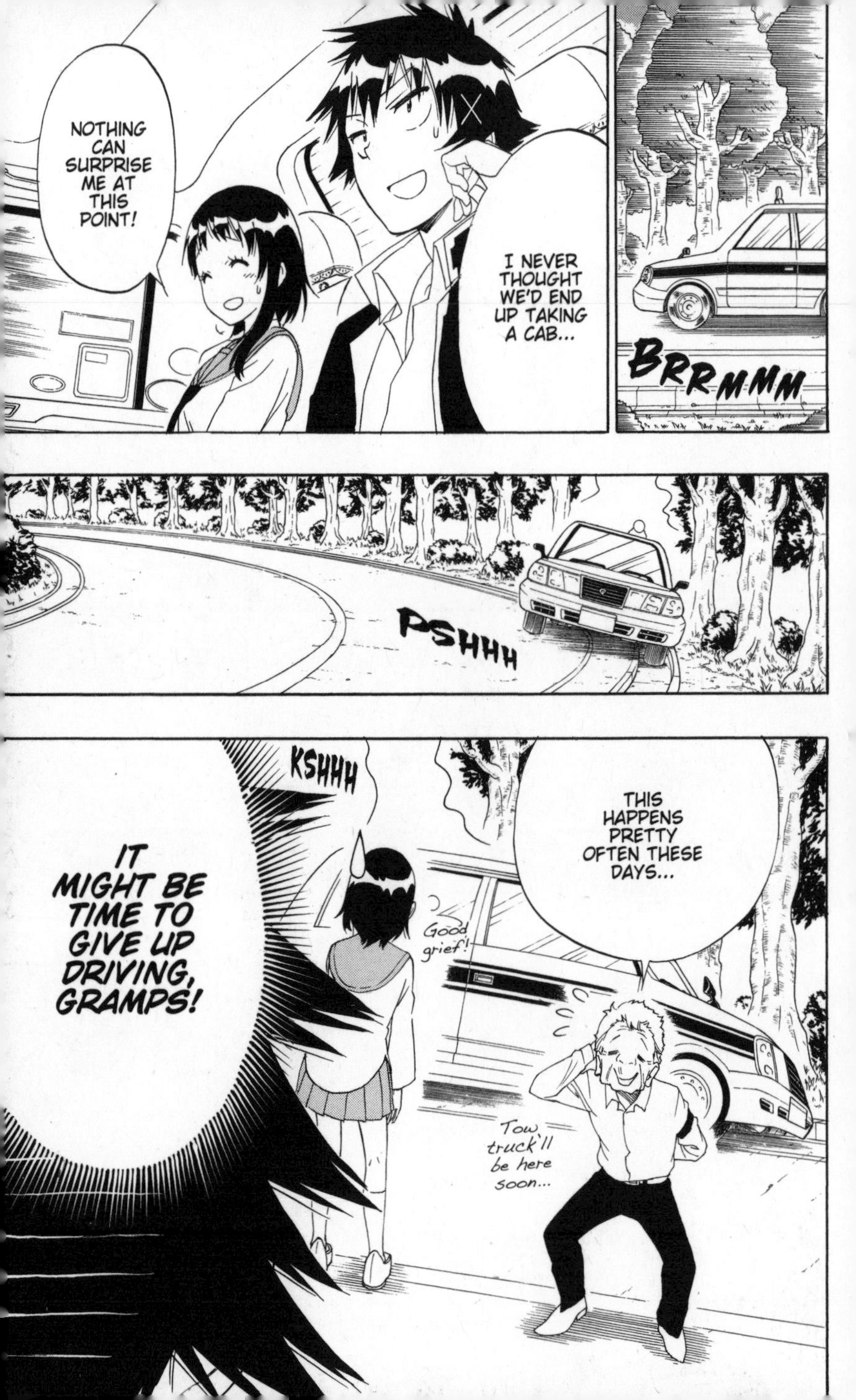
BRRMMM
I NEVER THOUGHT WE'D END UP TAKING A CAB...
NOTHING CAN SURPRISE ME AT THIS POINT!
PSHHH
THIS HAPPENS PRETTY OFTEN THESE DAYS...
KSHHH
Good grief!
Tow truck'll be here soon...
IT MIGHT BE TIME TO GIVE UP DRIVING, GRAMPS!

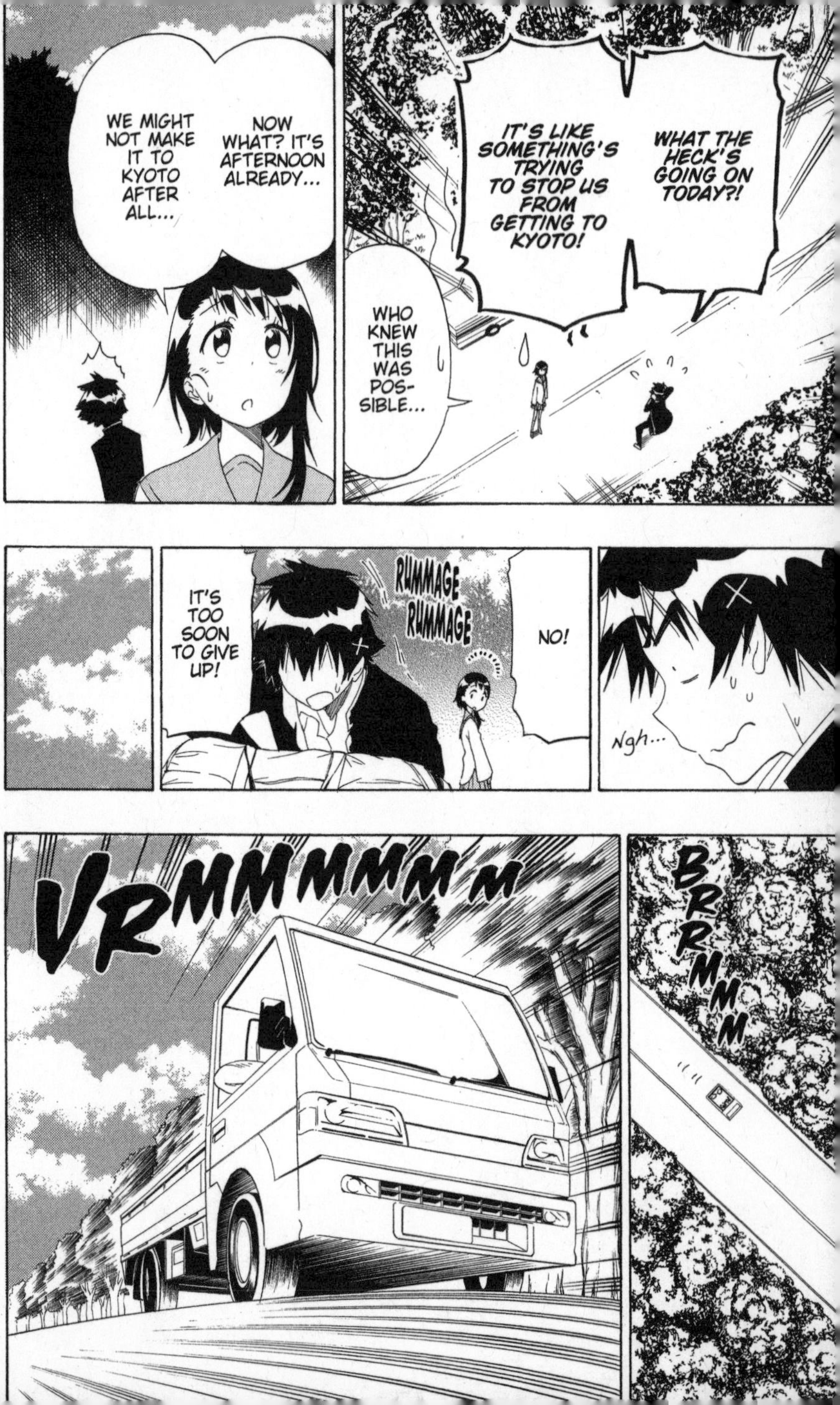
WHAT THE HECK'S GOING ON TODAY?!
IT'S LIKE SOMETHING'S TRYING TO STOP US FROM GETTING TO KYOTO!
WHO KNEW THIS WAS POS-SIBLE...
NOW WHAT? IT'S AFTERNOON ALREADY...
WE MIGHT NOT MAKE IT TO KYOTO AFTER ALL...
Ngh...
NO!
RUMMAGE RUMMAGE
IT'S TOO SOON TO GIVE UP!
BRRMMM
VRMMMMMM M

WHERE'D YOU TWO COME FROM?
I'LL BE DARNED! DIDN'T EXPECT TO PICK UP A PAIR OF TEENAGERS OUT HERE IN THE WOODS!
BWA HA HA HA
ER...
FROM BONYARI CITY.
Need a lift to Kyoto. Please hel
BON-YARI CITY ?!
THAT FAR?!
THANK GOODNESS FOR THE KINDNESS OF STRANGERS ...
I SURE DIDN'T EXPECT TO BE HITCHHIKING ON OUR CLASS TRIP!
ACHOO !
YOU OKAY? IT'S PRETTY COLD TO BE RIDING OUTSIDE IN THIS SEASON.
I'M FINE!
I'M SORRY, ONO-DERA.
IF WE'D JUST STAYED ON THE BULLET TRAIN, WE'D PROBABLY BE IN KYOTO BY NOW...
PFF...
TEE HEE HEE

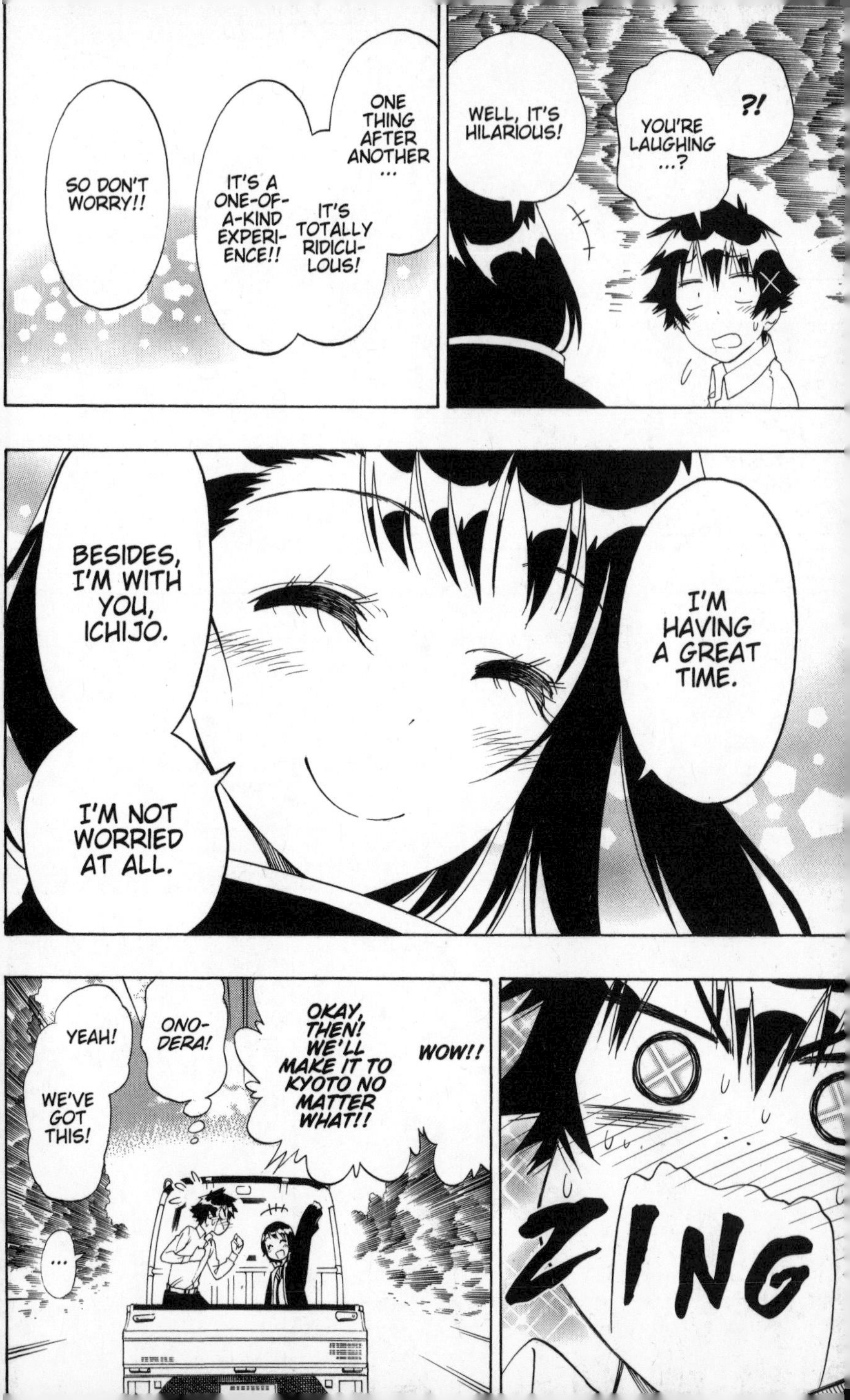
?!
YOU'RE LAUGHING ...?
WELL, IT'S HILARIOUS!
ONE THING AFTER ANOTHER ...
IT'S TOTALLY RIDICU-LOUS!
IT'S A ONE-OF-A-KIND EXPERI-ENCE!!
SO DON'T WORRY!!
I'M HAVING A GREAT TIME.
BESIDES, I'M WITH YOU, ICHIJO.
I'M NOT WORRIED AT ALL.
ZING
WOW!!
OKAY, THEN! WE'LL MAKE IT TO KYOTO NO MATTER WHAT!!
ONO-DERA!
YEAH!
WE'VE GOT THIS!
...

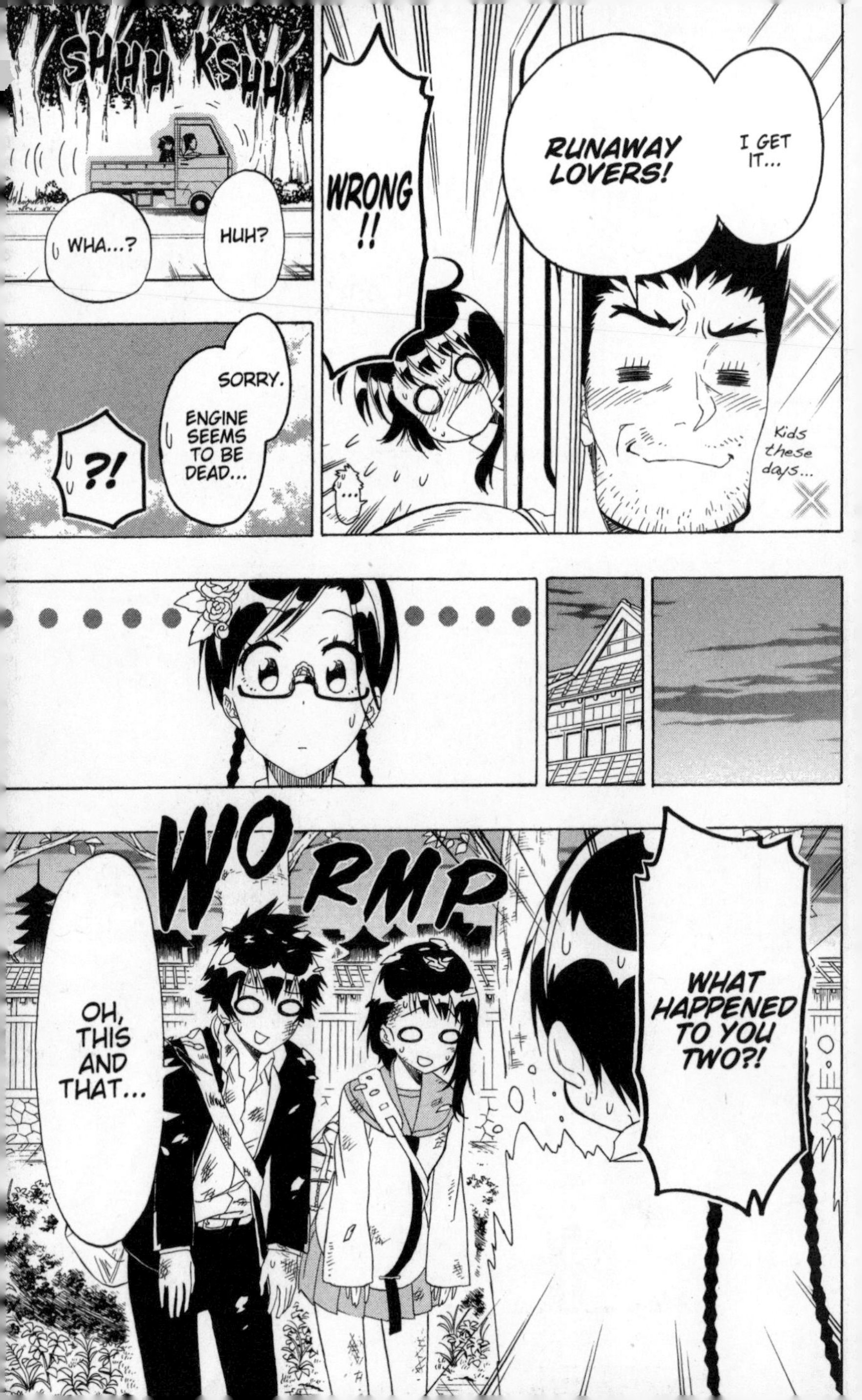
I GET IT...
RUNAWAY LOVERS!
Kids these days...
WRONG!!
SHHH KSHHH
HUH?
WHA...?
SORRY.
ENGINE SEEMS TO BE DEAD...
?!
....
WORMP
WHAT HAPPENED TO YOU TWO?!
OH, THIS AND THAT...

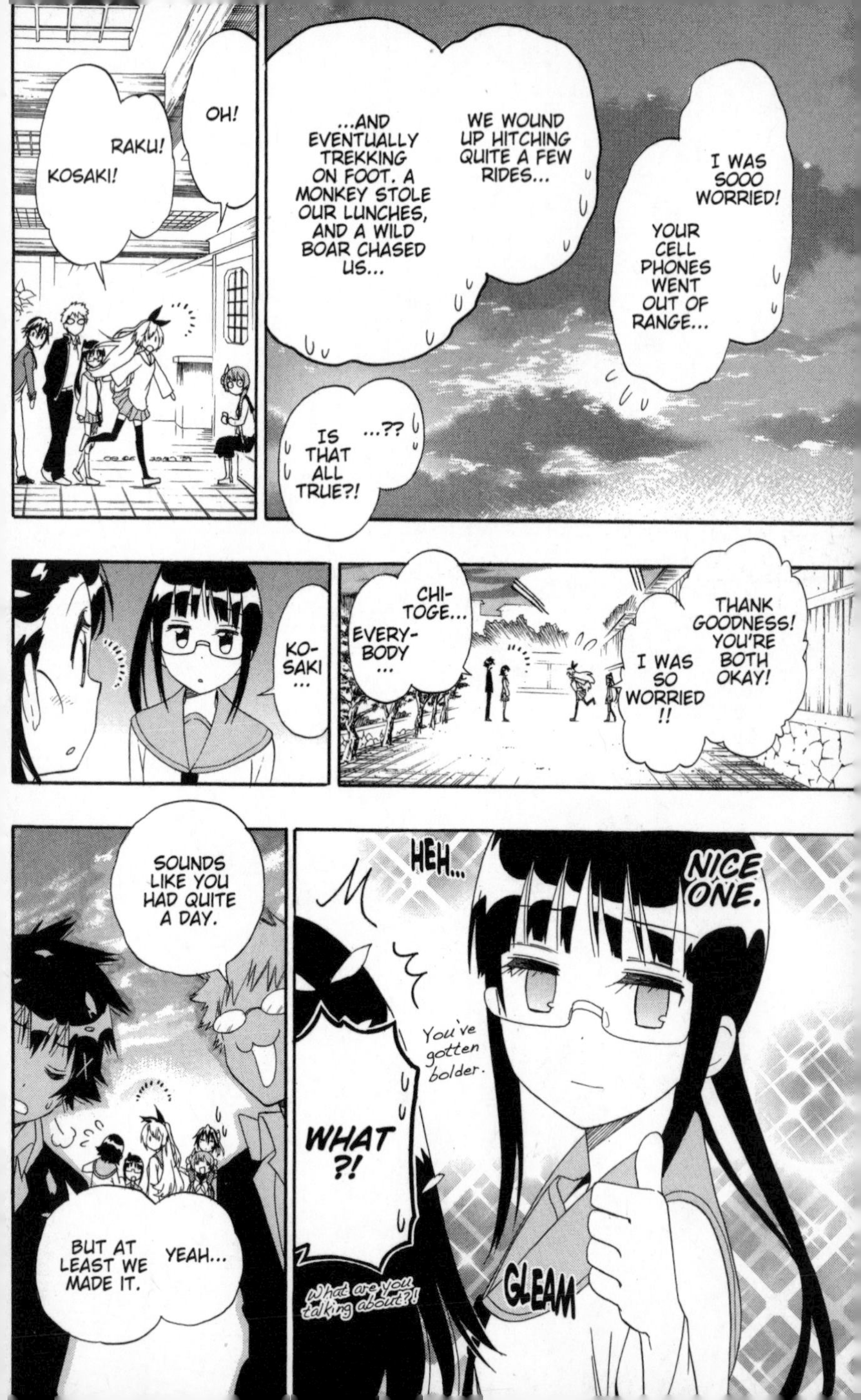
I WAS SOOO WORRIED!
YOUR CELL PHONES WENT OUT OF RANGE...
WE WOUND UP HITCHING QUITE A FEW RIDES...
...AND EVENTUALLY TREKKING ON FOOT. A MONKEY STOLE OUR LUNCHES, AND A WILD BOAR CHASED US...
...??
IS THAT ALL TRUE?!
OH!
RAKU!
KOSAKI!
THANK GOODNESS! YOU'RE BOTH OKAY!
I WAS SO WORRIED!!
CHI-TOGE...
EVERY-BODY...
KO-SAKI...
NICE ONE.
HEH...
You've gotten bolder.
WHAT?!
What are you talking about?!
GLEAM
SOUNDS LIKE YOU HAD QUITE A DAY.
YEAH...
BUT AT LEAST WE MADE IT.

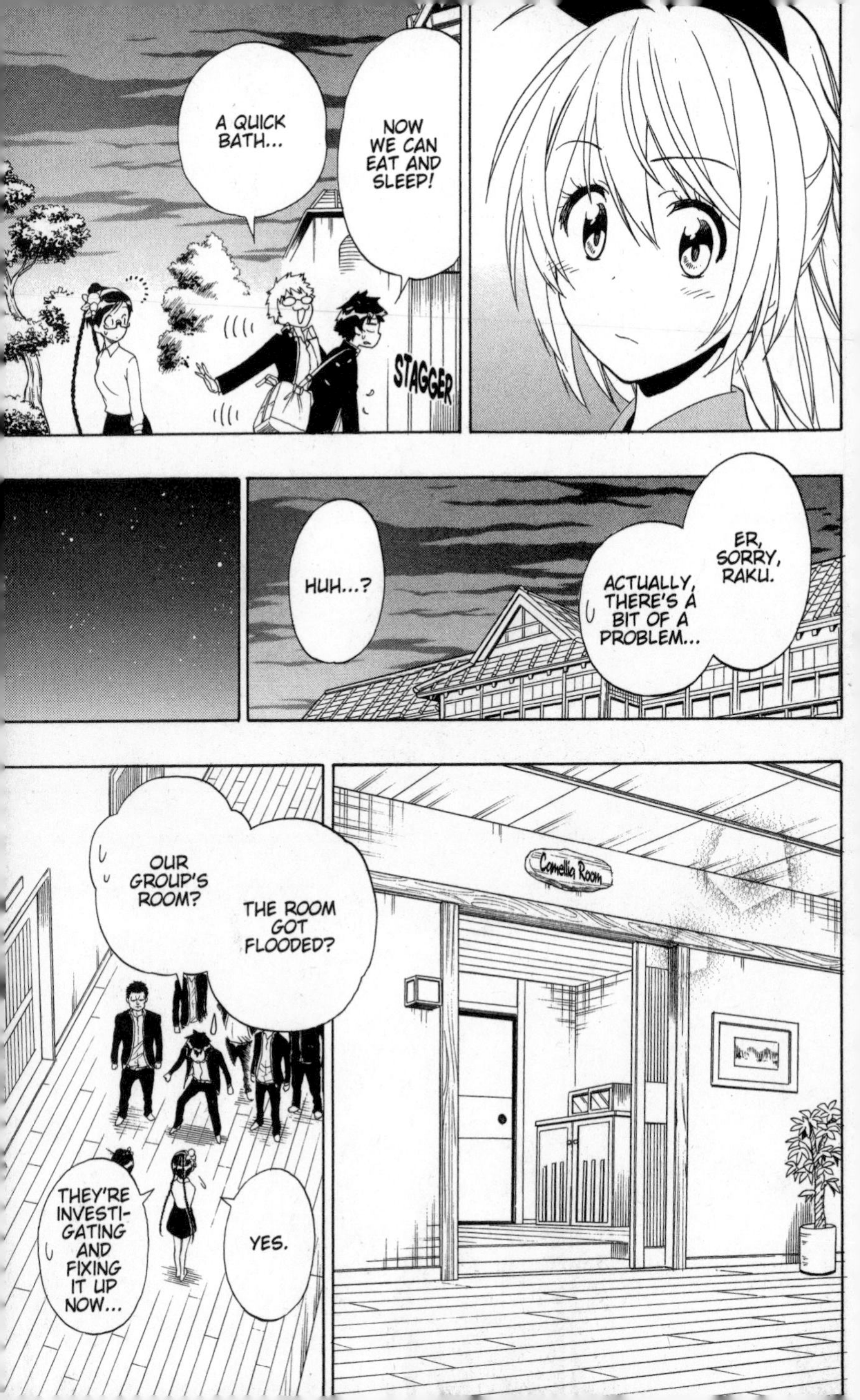
NOW WE CAN EAT AND SLEEP!
A QUICK BATH...
STAGGER
ER, SORRY, RAKU.
ACTUALLY, THERE'S A BIT OF A PROBLEM...
HUH...?
Camellia Room
OUR GROUP'S ROOM?
THE ROOM GOT FLOODED?
YES.
THEY'RE INVESTI-GATING AND FIXING IT UP NOW...

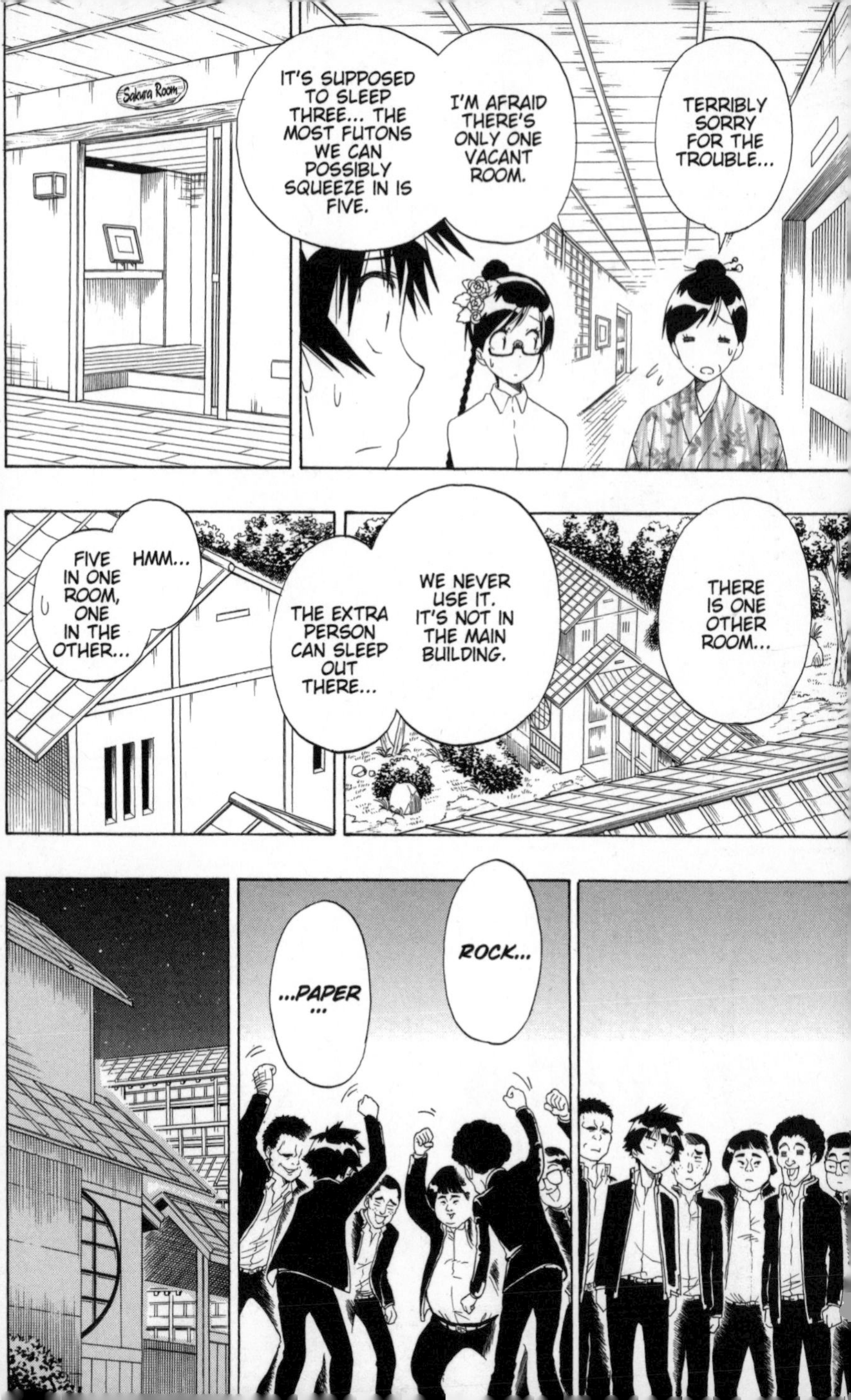
TERRIBLY SORRY FOR THE TROUBLE...
I'M AFRAID THERE'S ONLY ONE VACANT ROOM.
IT'S SUPPOSED TO SLEEP THREE... THE MOST FUTONS WE CAN POSSIBLY SQUEEZE IN IS FIVE.
Sakura Room
THERE IS ONE OTHER ROOM...
WE NEVER USE IT. IT'S NOT IN THE MAIN BUILDING.
THE EXTRA PERSON CAN SLEEP OUT THERE...
HMM...
FIVE IN ONE ROOM, ONE IN THE OTHER...
ROCK...
...PAPER ...

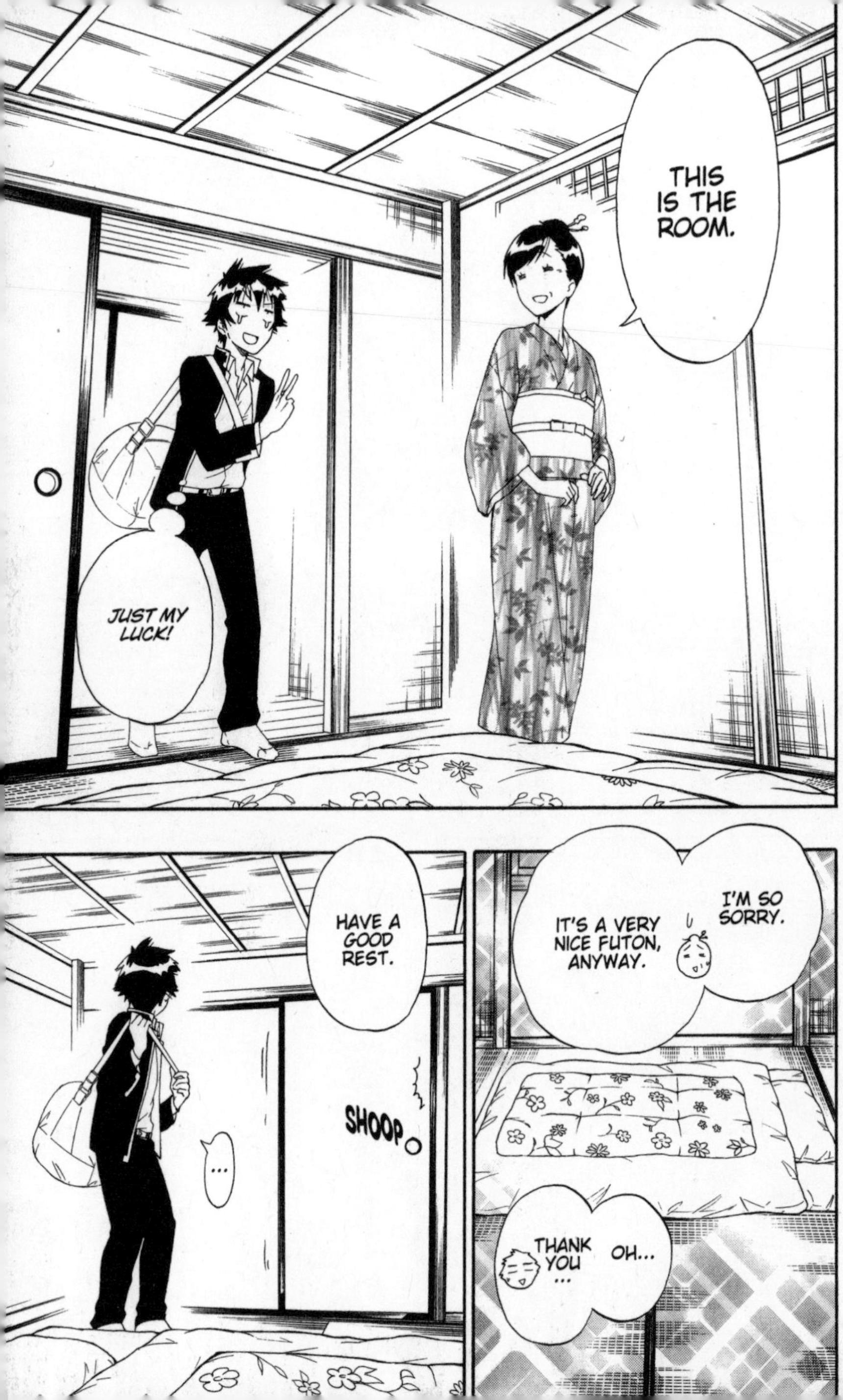
THIS IS THE ROOM.
JUST MY LUCK!
I'M SO SORRY.
IT'S A VERY NICE FUTON, ANYWAY.
OH...
THANK YOU ...
HAVE A GOOD REST.
SHOOP
...

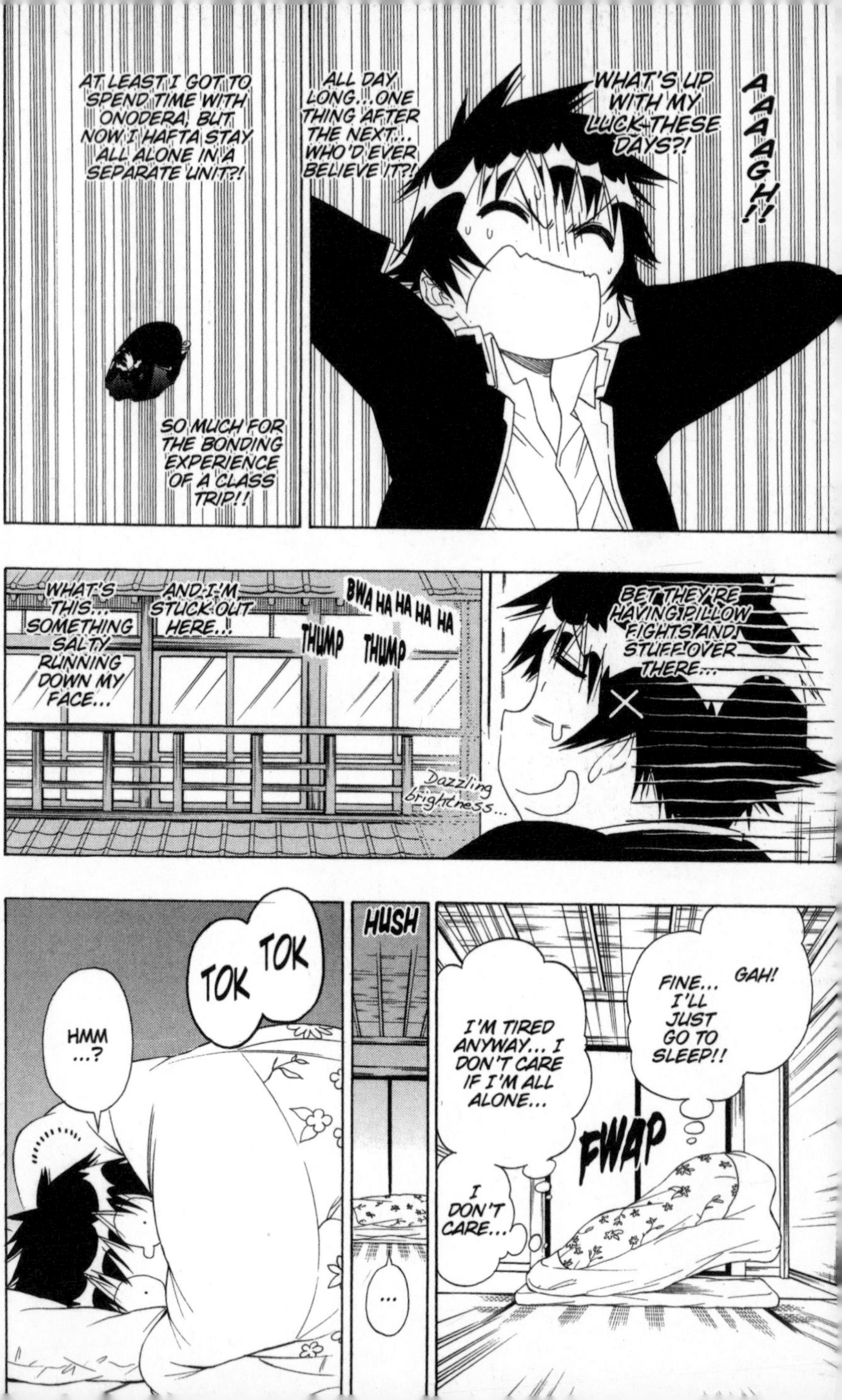
AAAAAGH!!
WHAT'S UP WITH MY LUCK THESE DAYS?!
ALL DAY LONG... ONE THING AFTER THE NEXT... WHO'D EVER BELIEVE IT?!
AT LEAST I GOT TO SPEND TIME WITH ONODERA, BUT NOW I HAFTA STAY ALL ALONE IN A SEPARATE UNIT?!
SO MUCH FOR THE BONDING EXPERIENCE OF A CLASS TRIP!!
BET THEY'RE HAVING PILLOW FIGHTS AND STUFF OVER THERE...
Dazzling brightness...
BWA HA HA HA HA
THUMP THUMP
AND I'M STUCK OUT HERE...!
WHAT'S THIS... SOMETHING SALTY RUNNING DOWN MY FACE...
GAH!
FINE... I'LL JUST GO TO SLEEP!!
FWAP
I'M TIRED ANYWAY... I DON'T CARE IF I'M ALL ALONE...
I DON'T CARE...
HUSH
...
TOK TOK
HMM ...?

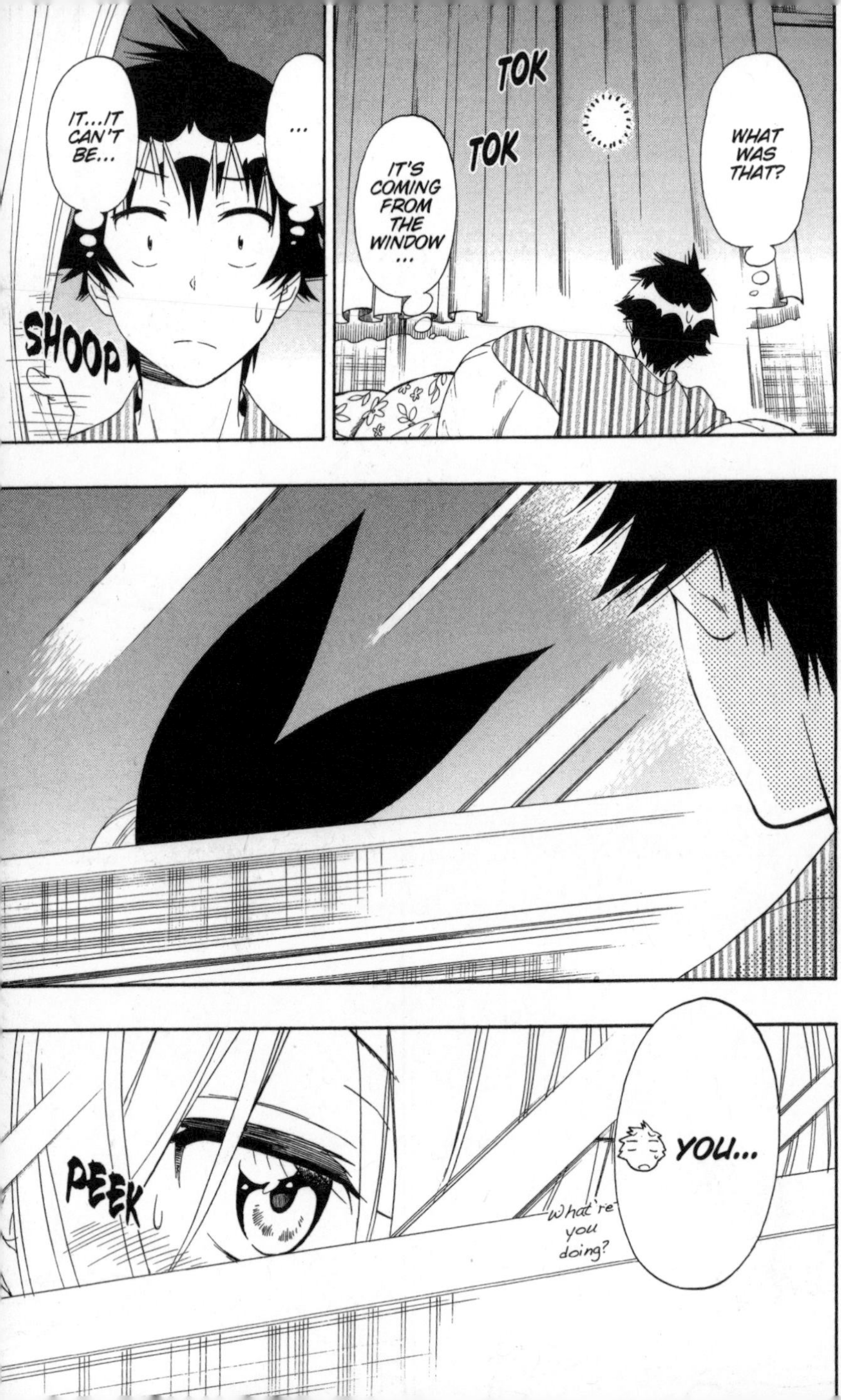
WHAT WAS THAT?
TOK
TOK
IT'S COMING FROM THE WINDOW...
...
IT...IT CAN'T BE...
SHOOP
YOU...
What're you doing?
PEEK

So?
You were alone together. How far did you go?
Spill it!
Um... It really wasn't like that...
I'm telling you, it was rough. Really...

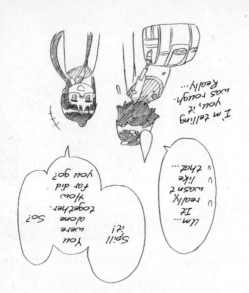

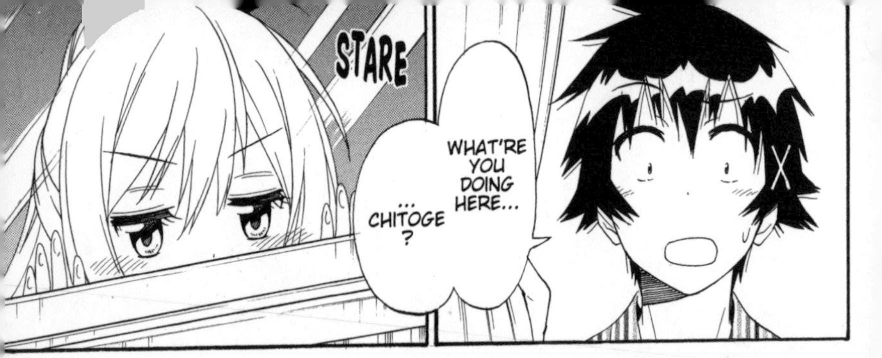
WHAT'RE YOU DOING HERE... ...CHITOGE?
STARE

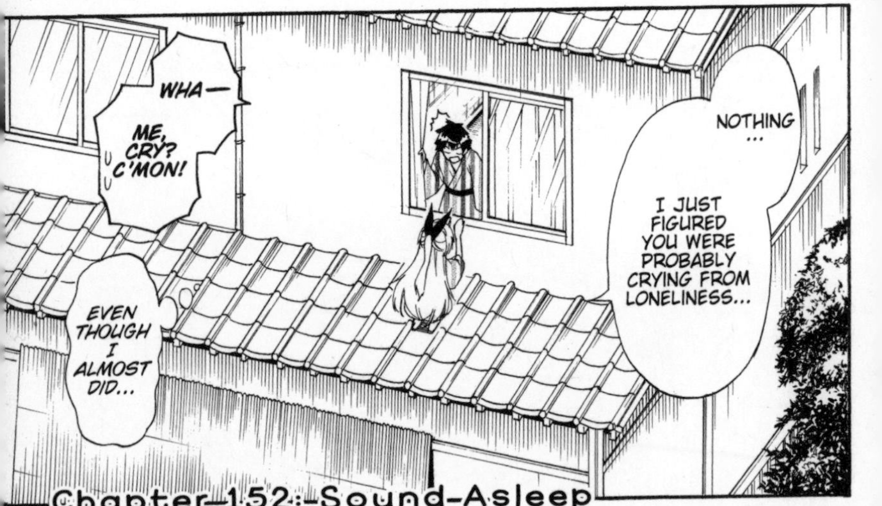
NOTHING ...
I JUST FIGURED YOU WERE PROBABLY CRYING FROM LONELINESS...
WHA— ME, CRY? C'MON!
EVEN THOUGH I ALMOST DID...

Chapter 152: Sound Asleep

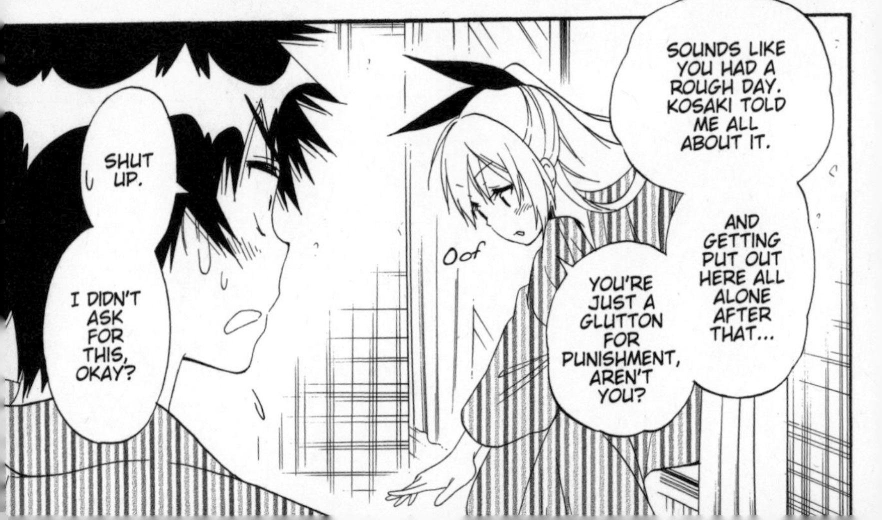
SOUNDS LIKE YOU HAD A ROUGH DAY. KOSAKI TOLD ME ALL ABOUT IT.
AND GETTING PUT OUT HERE ALL ALONE AFTER THAT...
YOU'RE JUST A GLUTTON FOR PUNISHMENT, AREN'T YOU?
Oof
SHUT UP.
I DIDN'T ASK FOR THIS, OKAY?

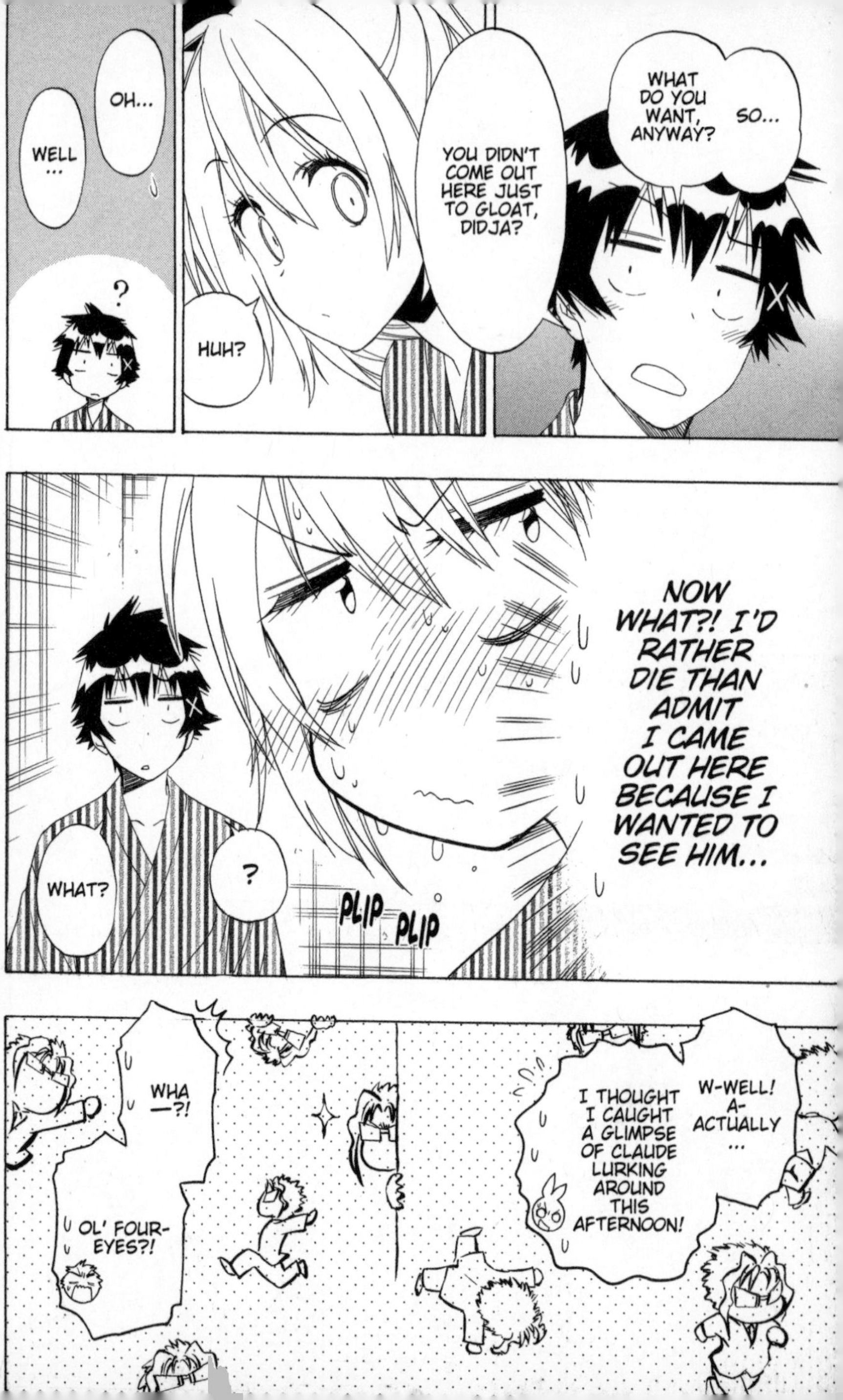
SO...
WHAT DO YOU WANT, ANYWAY?
YOU DIDN'T COME OUT HERE JUST TO GLOAT, DIDJA?
HUH?
OH...
WELL...
?
NOW WHAT?! I'D RATHER DIE THAN ADMIT I CAME OUT HERE BECAUSE I WANTED TO SEE HIM...
PLIP PLIP
?
WHAT?
W-WELL! A-ACTUALLY...
I THOUGHT I CAUGHT A GLIMPSE OF CLAUDE LURKING AROUND THIS AFTERNOON!
WHA—?!
OL' FOUR-EYES?!

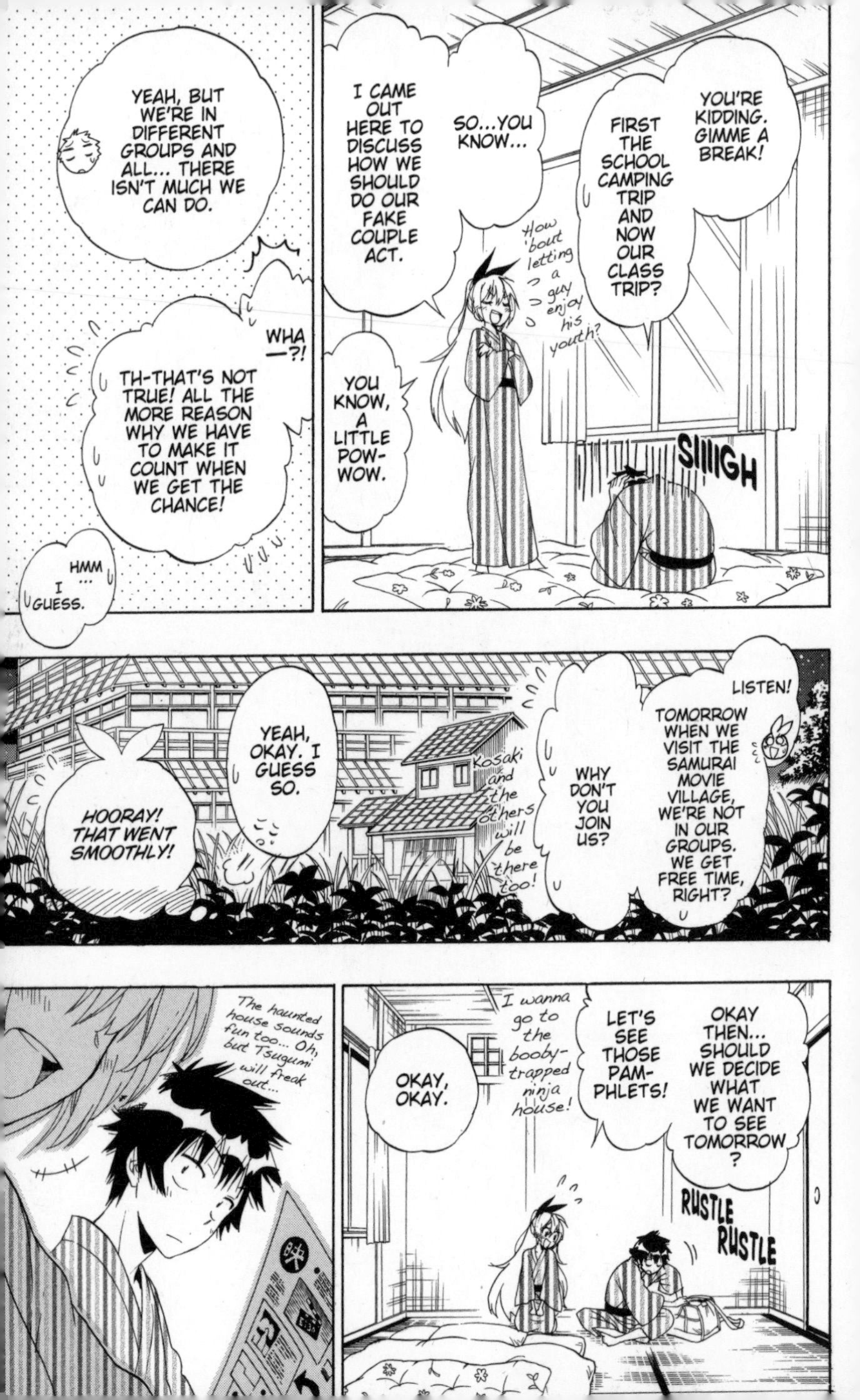
YOU'RE KIDDING. GIMME A BREAK!
FIRST THE SCHOOL CAMPING TRIP AND NOW OUR CLASS TRIP?
SIIIIGH
How 'bout letting a guy enjoy his youth?
SO...YOU KNOW...
I CAME OUT HERE TO DISCUSS HOW WE SHOULD DO OUR FAKE COUPLE ACT.
YOU KNOW, A LITTLE POW-WOW.
YEAH, BUT WE'RE IN DIFFERENT GROUPS AND ALL... THERE ISN'T MUCH WE CAN DO.
WHA—?!
TH-THAT'S NOT TRUE! ALL THE MORE REASON WHY WE HAVE TO MAKE IT COUNT WHEN WE GET THE CHANCE!
HMM... I GUESS.
LISTEN!
TOMORROW WHEN WE VISIT THE SAMURAI MOVIE VILLAGE, WE'RE NOT IN OUR GROUPS. WE GET FREE TIME, RIGHT?
WHY DON'T YOU JOIN US?
Kosaki and the others will be there too!
YEAH, OKAY. I GUESS SO.
HOORAY! THAT WENT SMOOTHLY!
OKAY THEN... SHOULD WE DECIDE WHAT WE WANT TO SEE TOMORROW?
LET'S SEE THOSE PAM-PHLETS!
RUSTLE RUSTLE
I wanna go to the booby-trapped ninja house!
OKAY, OKAY.
The haunted house sounds fun too... Oh, but Tsugumi will freak out...

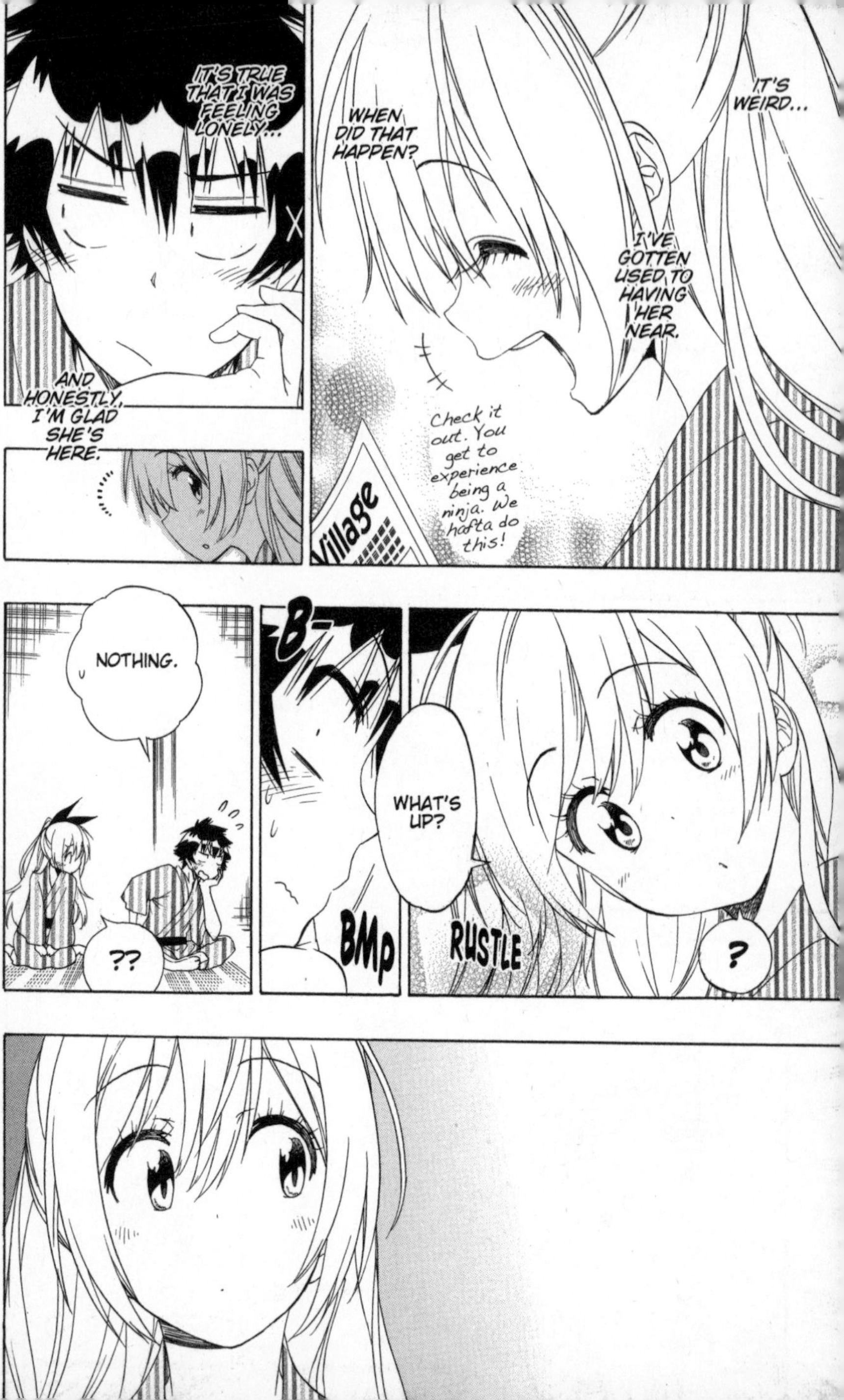
IT'S WEIRD...
WHEN DID THAT HAPPEN?
I'VE GOTTEN USED TO HAVING HER NEAR.
Check it out. You get to experience being a ninja. We hafta do this!
Village
IT'S TRUE THAT I WAS FEELING LONELY...
AND HONESTLY, I'M GLAD SHE'S HERE.
RUSTLE
?
B-
BMP
WHAT'S UP?
NOTHING.
??

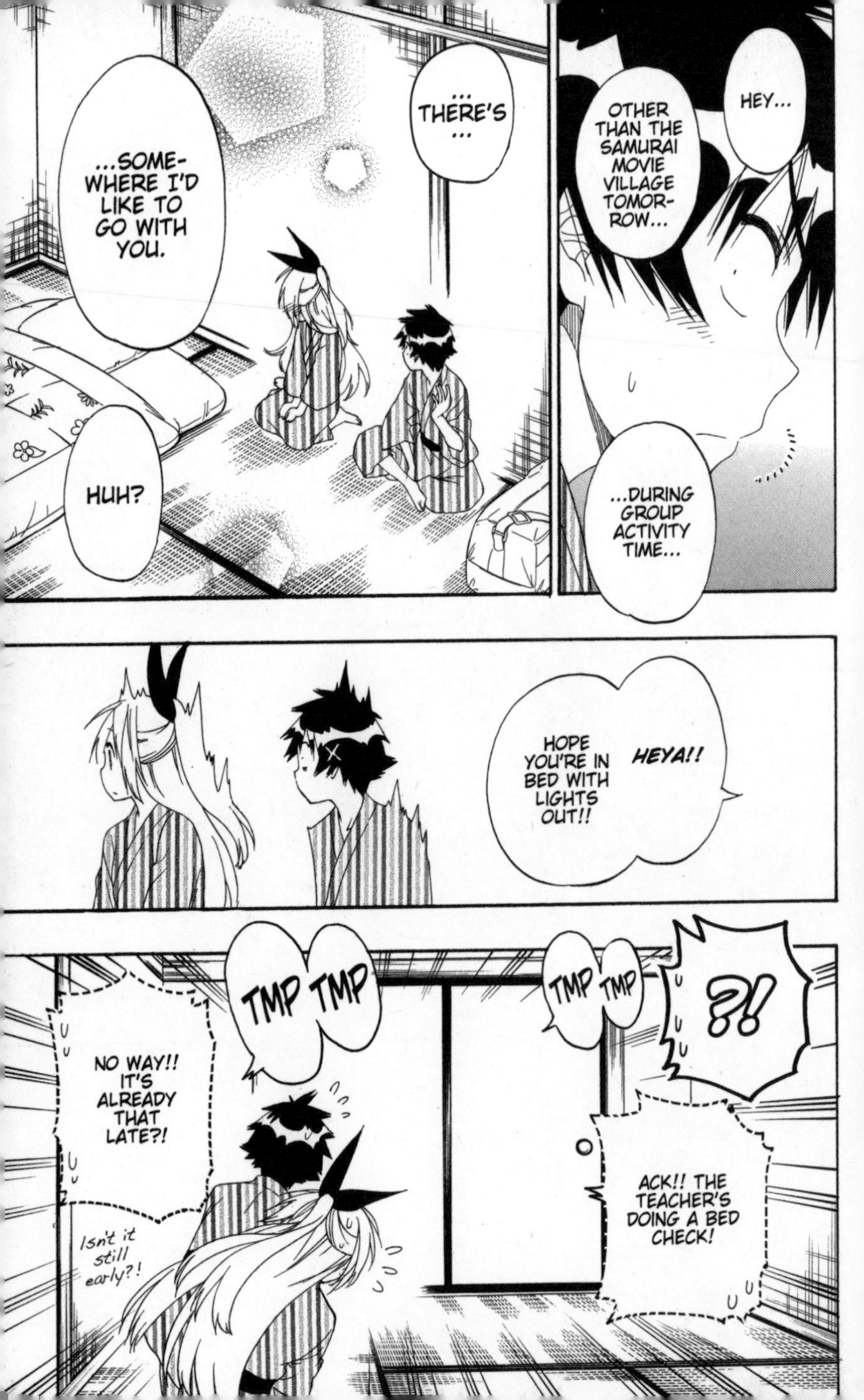
HEY...
OTHER THAN THE SAMURAI MOVIE VILLAGE TOMORROW...
...DURING GROUP ACTIVITY TIME...
...THERE'S...
...SOMEWHERE I'D LIKE TO GO WITH YOU.
HUH?
HEYA!!
HOPE YOU'RE IN BED WITH LIGHTS OUT!!
?!
TMP TMP
ACK!! THE TEACHER'S DOING A BED CHECK!
TMP TMP
NO WAY!! IT'S ALREADY THAT LATE?!
Isn't it still early?!

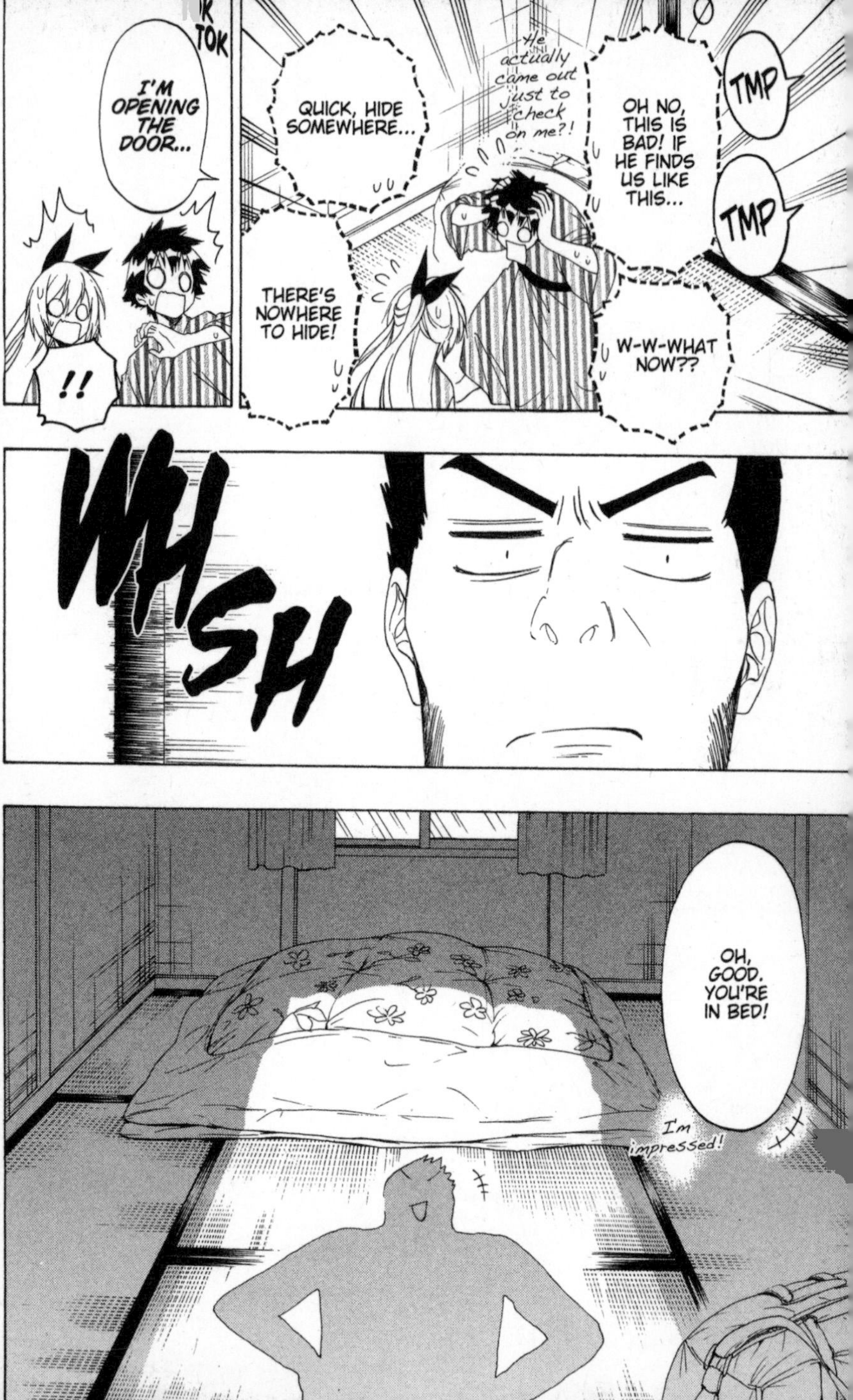
TMP
TMP
OH NO, THIS IS BAD! IF HE FINDS US LIKE THIS...
He actually came out just to check on me?!
W-W-WHAT NOW??
QUICK, HIDE SOMEWHERE...
THERE'S NOWHERE TO HIDE!
TOK TOK
I'M OPENING THE DOOR...
!!
WHSH
OH, GOOD. YOU'RE IN BED!
I'm impressed!

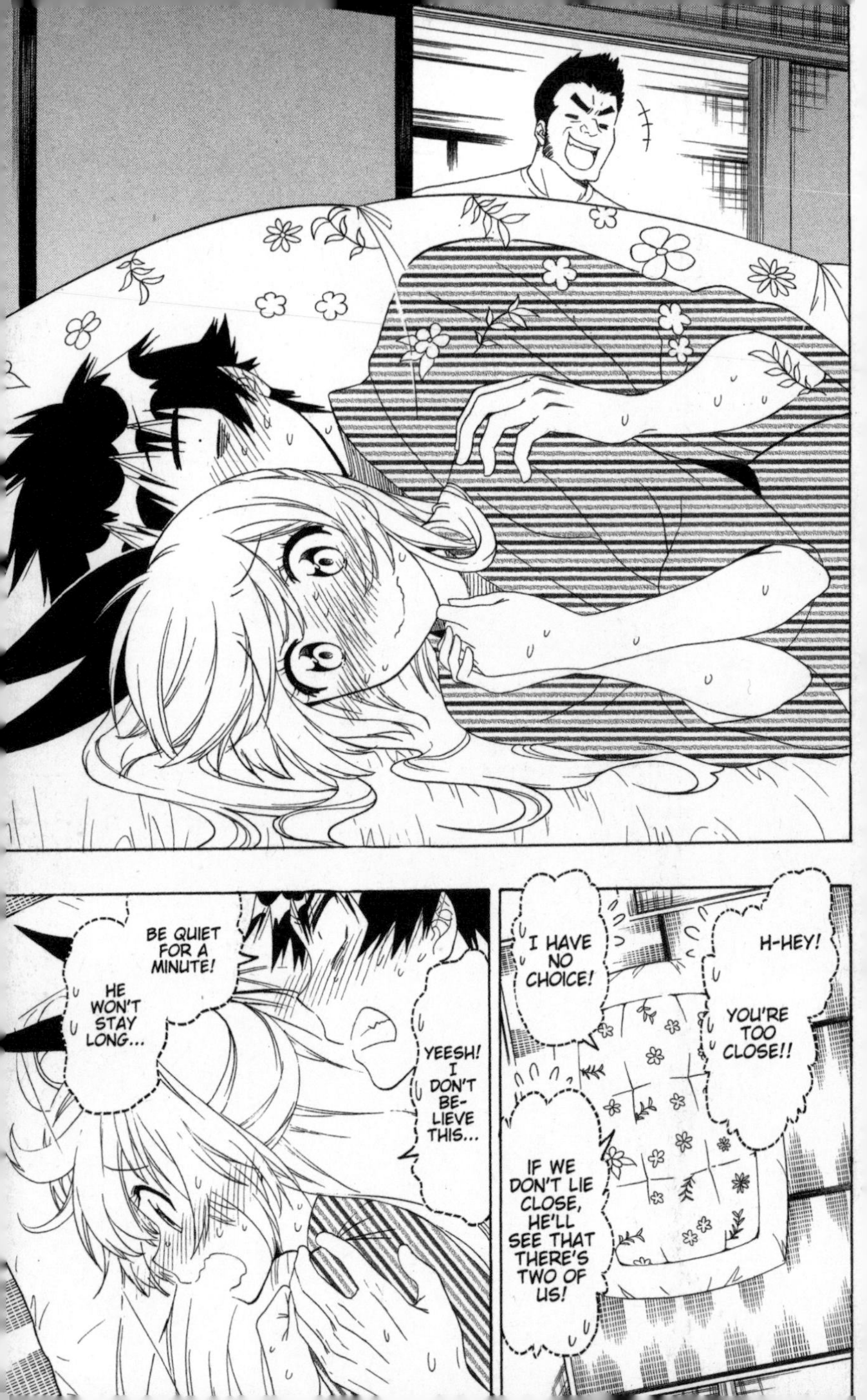
H-HEY!
YOU'RE TOO CLOSE!!
I HAVE NO CHOICE!
IF WE DON'T LIE CLOSE, HE'LL SEE THAT THERE'S TWO OF US!
BE QUIET FOR A MINUTE!
HE WON'T STAY LONG...
YEESH! I DON'T BE-LIEVE THIS...

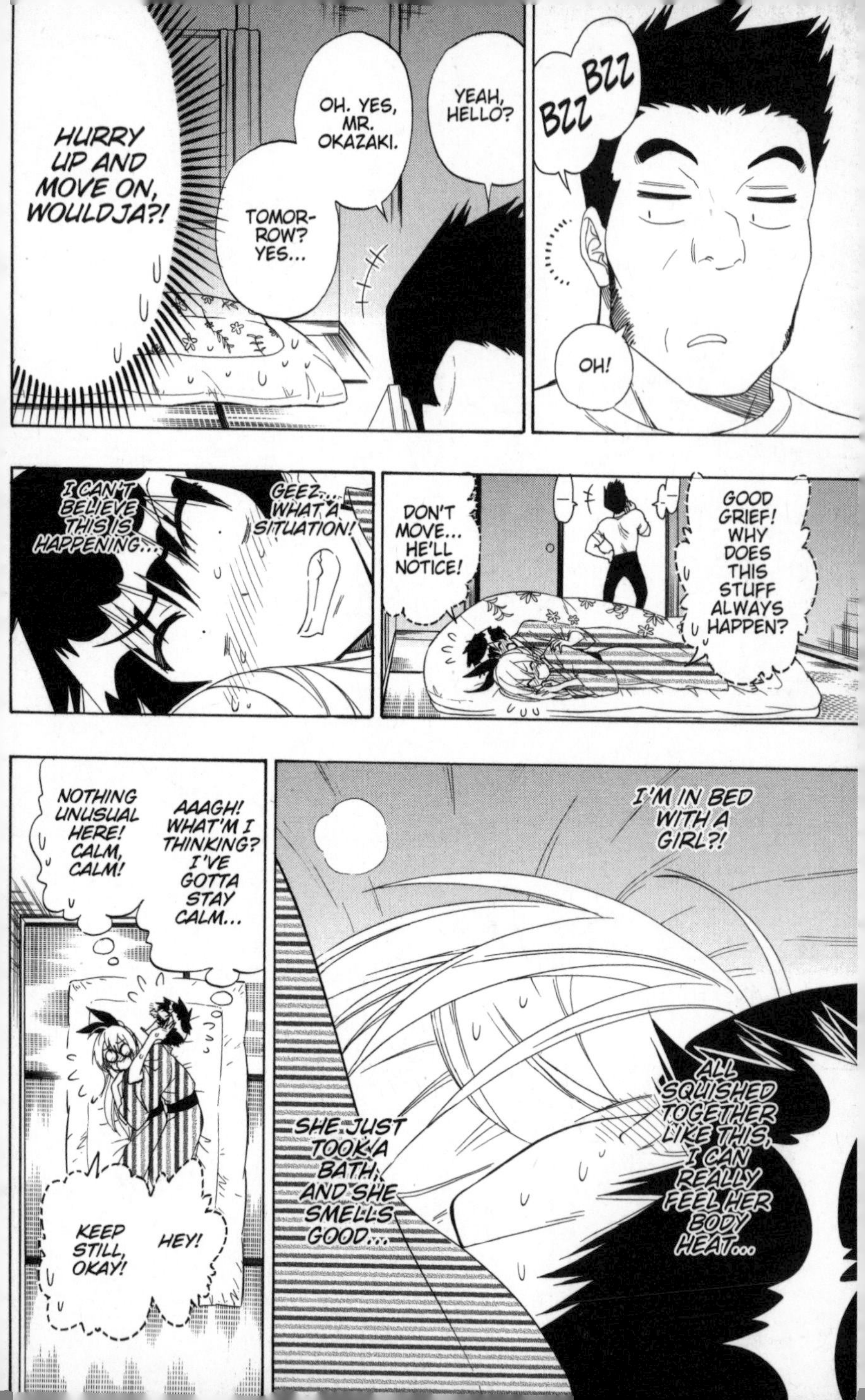
BZZ
BZZ
OH!
YEAH, HELLO?
OH. YES, MR. OKAZAKI.
TOMOR-ROW? YES...
HURRY UP AND MOVE ON, WOULDJA?!
GOOD GRIEF! WHY DOES THIS STUFF ALWAYS HAPPEN?
DON'T MOVE... HE'LL NOTICE!
GEEZ... WHAT A SITUATION!
I CAN'T BELIEVE THIS IS HAPPENING...
I'M IN BED WITH A GIRL?!
ALL SQUISHED TOGETHER LIKE THIS, I CAN REALLY FEEL HER BODY HEAT...
SHE JUST TOOK A BATH, AND SHE SMELLS GOOD...
AAAGH! WHAT'M I THINKING? I'VE GOTTA STAY CALM...
NOTHING UNUSUAL HERE! CALM, CALM!
HEY!
KEEP STILL, OKAY!

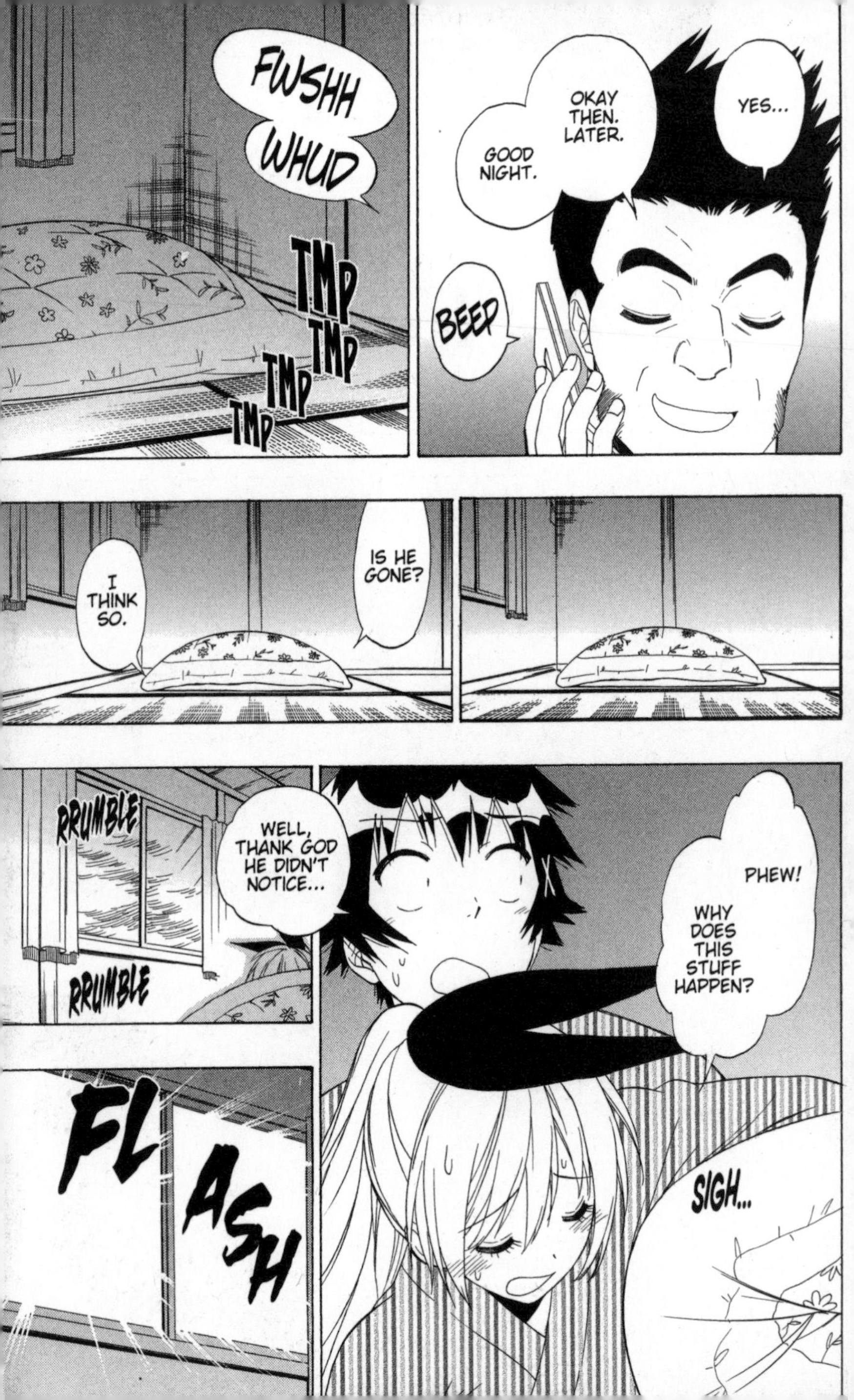
YES...
OKAY THEN. LATER.
GOOD NIGHT.
BEEP
FWSHH
WHUD
TMP TMP TMP TMP
I THINK SO.
IS HE GONE?
PHEW!
WHY DOES THIS STUFF HAPPEN?
SIGH...
WELL, THANK GOD HE DIDN'T NOTICE...
RRUMBLE
RRUMBLE
FLASH

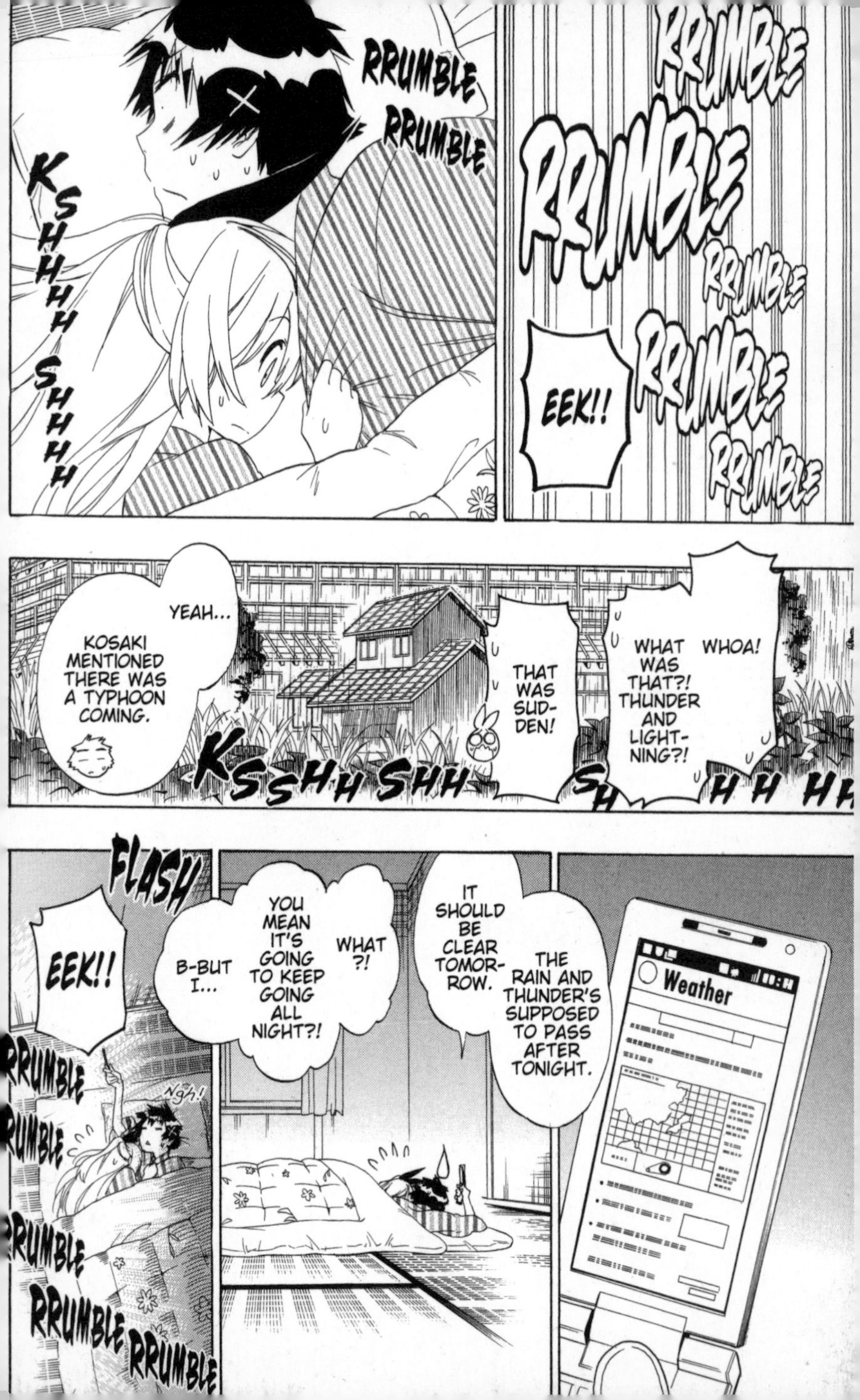
RRUMBLE
RRUMBLE
RRUMBLE
RRUMBLE
RRUMBLE
EEK!!
RRUMBLE
RRUMBLE
KSHHHH SHHHH
WHOA!
WHAT WAS THAT?! THUNDER AND LIGHTNING?!
THAT WAS SUDDEN!
KSSHH SHH SHHH HH
YEAH...
KOSAKI MENTIONED THERE WAS A TYPHOON COMING.
Weather
IT SHOULD BE CLEAR TOMORROW.
THE RAIN AND THUNDER'S SUPPOSED TO PASS AFTER TONIGHT.
WHAT ?!
YOU MEAN IT'S GOING TO KEEP GOING ALL NIGHT?!
B-BUT I...
FLASH
EEK!!
Ngh!
RRUMBLE
RRUMBLE
RRUMBLE
RRUMBLE
RRUMBLE

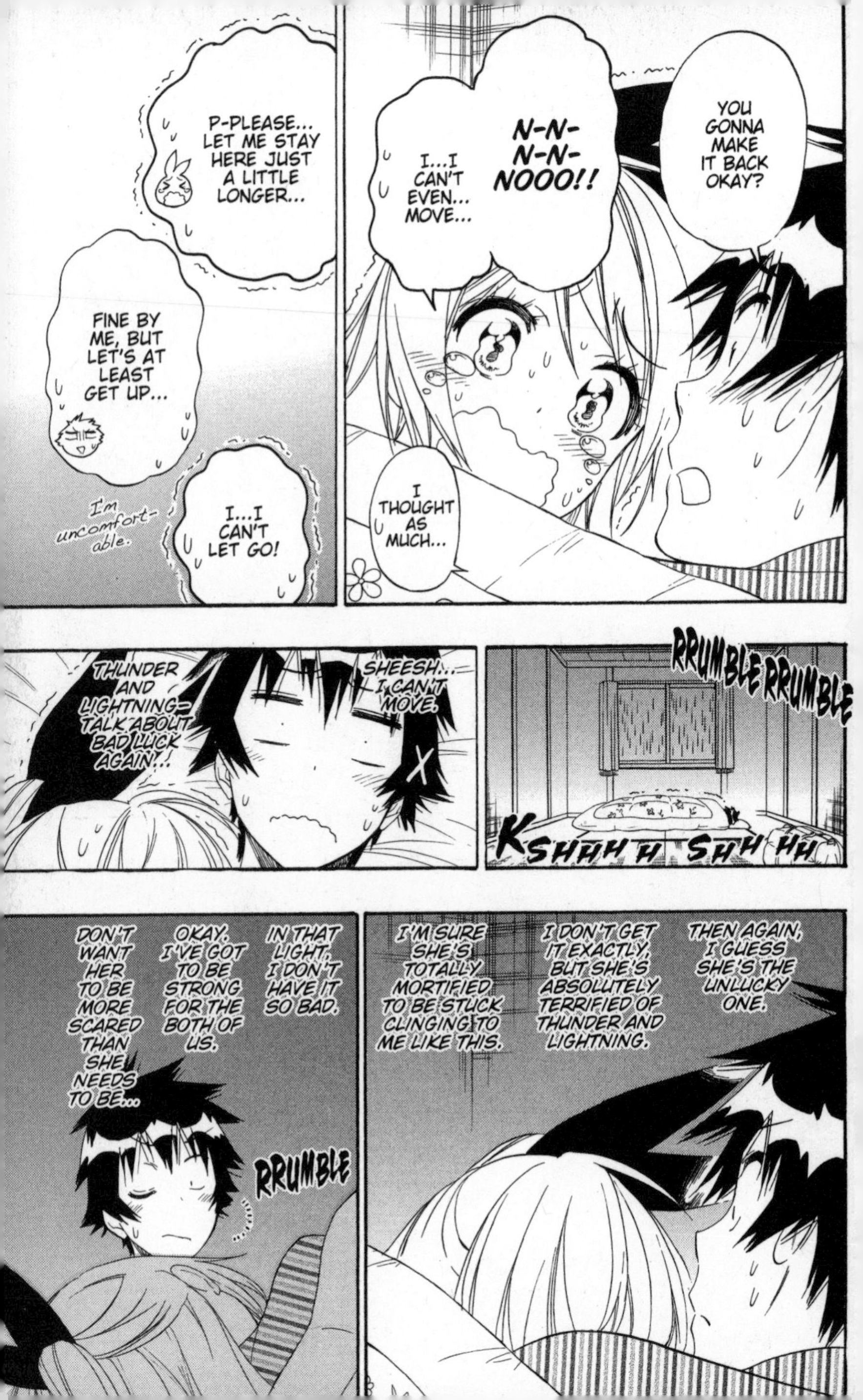
YOU GONNA MAKE IT BACK OKAY?
N-N-N-N-NOOO!!
I...I CAN'T EVEN... MOVE...
I THOUGHT AS MUCH...
P-PLEASE... LET ME STAY HERE JUST A LITTLE LONGER...
FINE BY ME, BUT LET'S AT LEAST GET UP...
I...I CAN'T LET GO!
I'm uncomfort-able.
RRUMBLE RRUMBLE
KSHHH H SHH HH
SHEESH... I CAN'T MOVE.
THUNDER AND LIGHTNING—TALK ABOUT BAD LUCK AGAIN...
THEN AGAIN, I GUESS SHE'S THE UNLUCKY ONE.
I DON'T GET IT EXACTLY, BUT SHE'S ABSOLUTELY TERRIFIED OF THUNDER AND LIGHTNING.
I'M SURE SHE'S TOTALLY MORTIFIED TO BE STUCK CLINGING TO ME LIKE THIS.
IN THAT LIGHT, I DON'T HAVE IT SO BAD.
OKAY. I'VE GOT TO BE STRONG FOR THE BOTH OF US.
DON'T WANT HER TO BE MORE SCARED THAN SHE NEEDS TO BE...
RRUMBLE

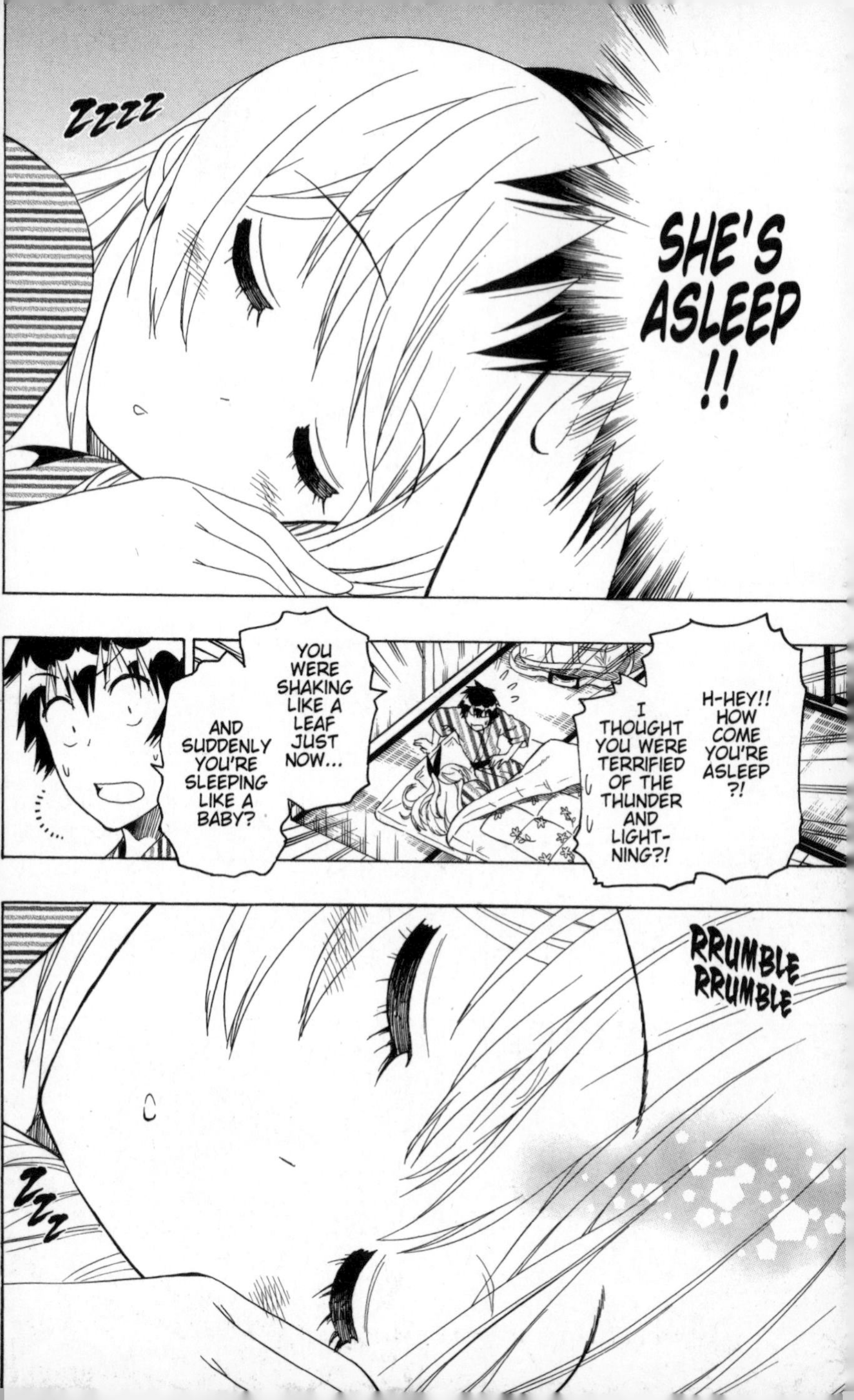
SHE'S ASLEEP!!
ZZZZ
H-HEY!! HOW COME YOU'RE ASLEEP?!
I THOUGHT YOU WERE TERRIFIED OF THE THUNDER AND LIGHT-NING?!
YOU WERE SHAKING LIKE A LEAF JUST NOW...
AND SUDDENLY YOU'RE SLEEPING LIKE A BABY?
RRUMBLE RRUMBLE
ZZZ

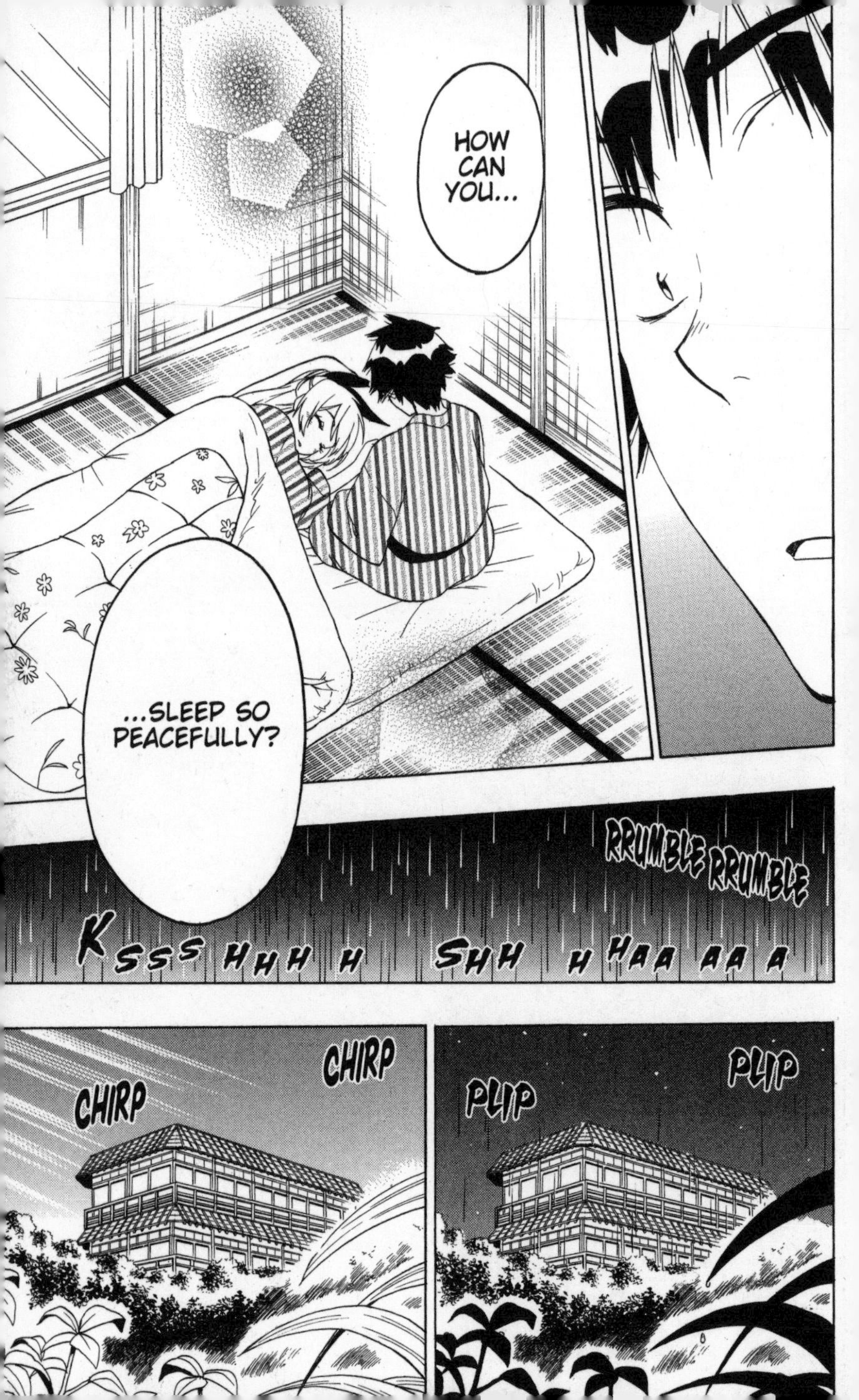
HOW CAN YOU...
...SLEEP SO PEACEFULLY?
RRUMBLE RRUMBLE
KSSSHHHH SHH HHAAAAA
PLIP
PLIP
CHIRP
CHIRP

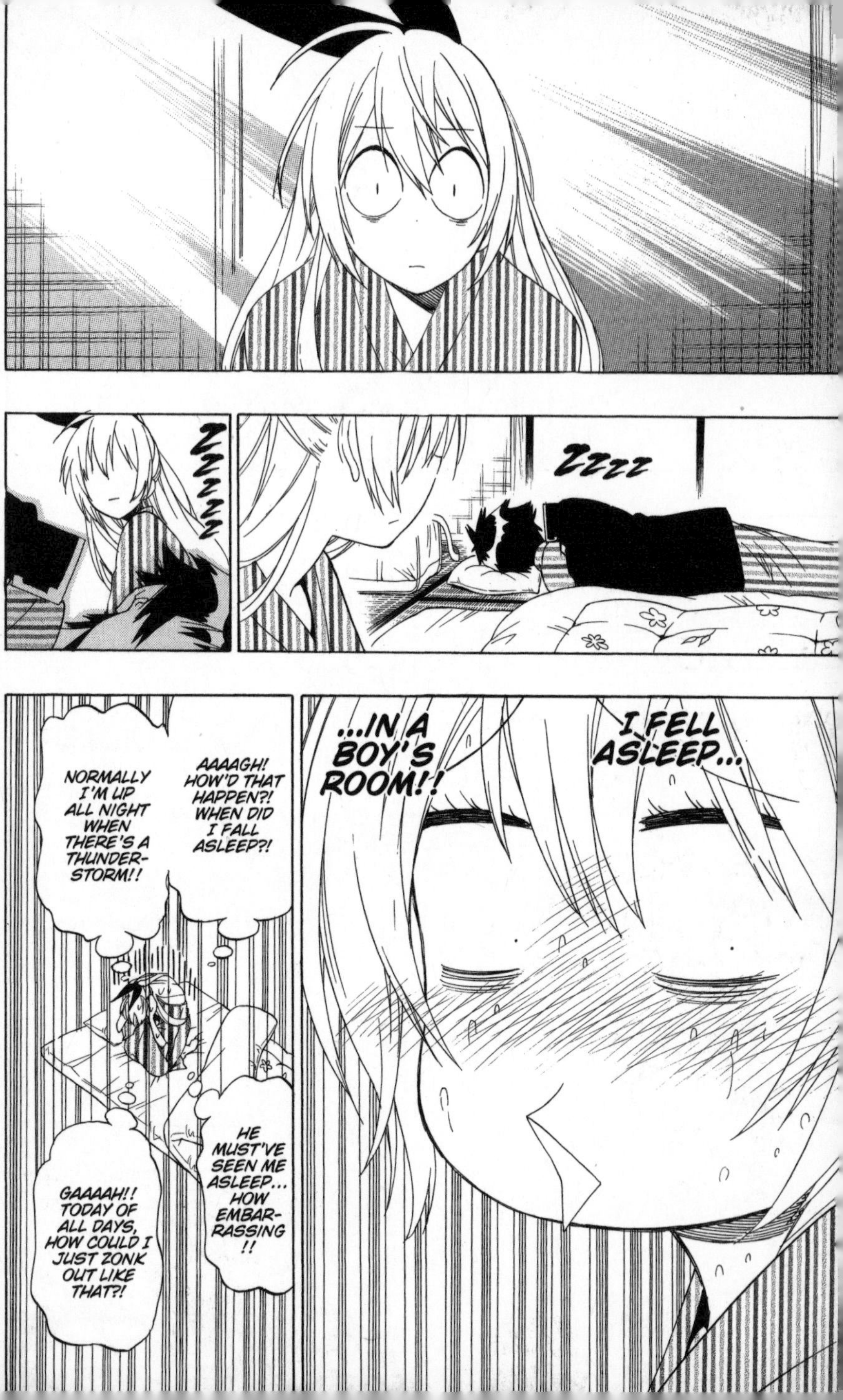
ZZZZ
ZZZZZZ
I FELL ASLEEP...
...IN A BOY'S ROOM!!
NORMALLY I'M UP ALL NIGHT WHEN THERE'S A THUNDER-STORM!!
AAAAGH! HOW'D THAT HAPPEN?! WHEN DID I FALL ASLEEP?!
HE MUST'VE SEEN ME ASLEEP... HOW EMBAR-RASSING!!
GAAAAH!! TODAY OF ALL DAYS, HOW COULD I JUST ZONK OUT LIKE THAT?!

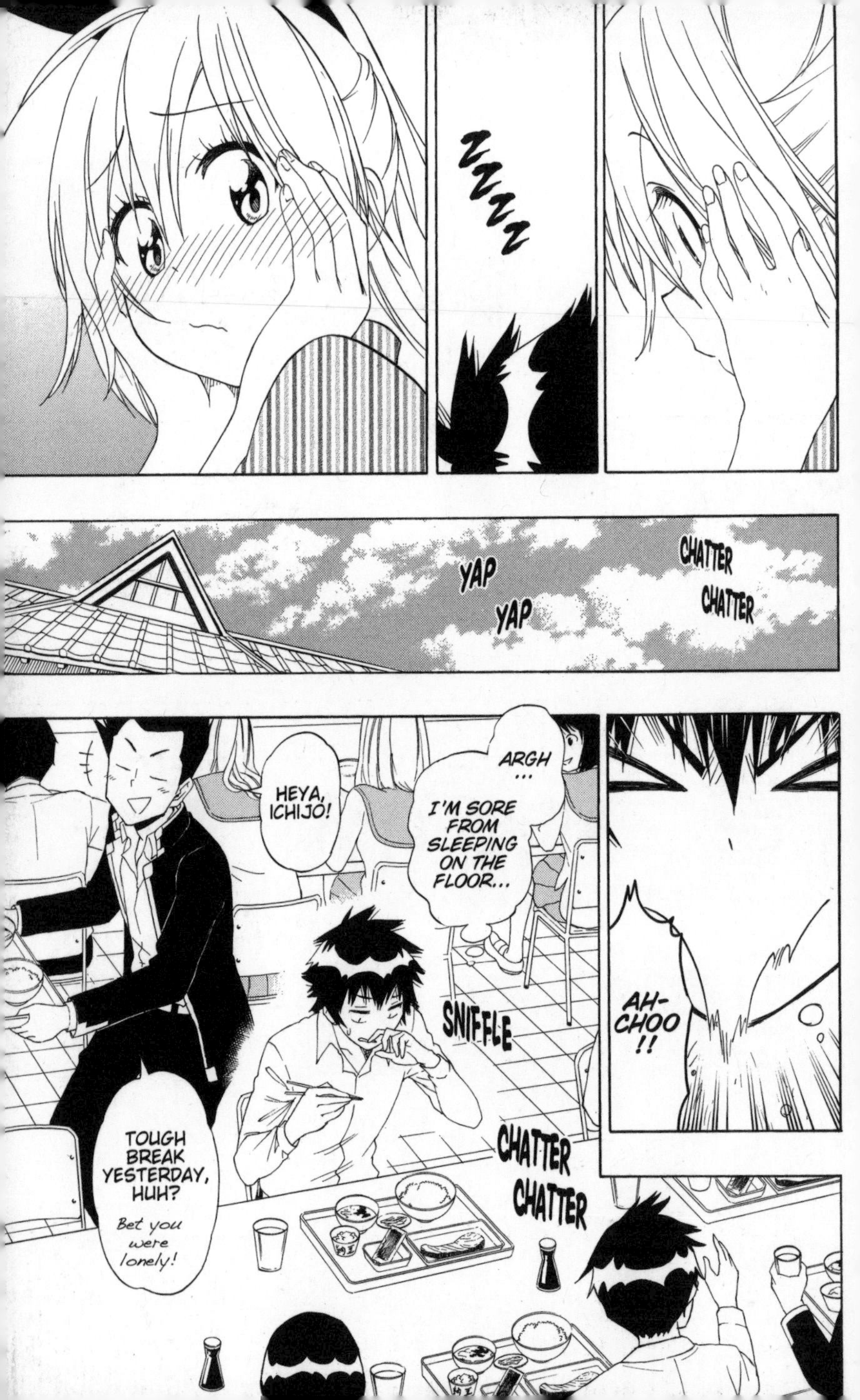
ZZZZ
CHATTER
CHATTER
YAP
YAP
AH-CHOO!!
ARGH...
I'M SORE FROM SLEEPING ON THE FLOOR...
HEYA, ICHIJO!
SNIFFLE
TOUGH BREAK YESTERDAY, HUH?
Bet you were lonely!
CHATTER
CHATTER

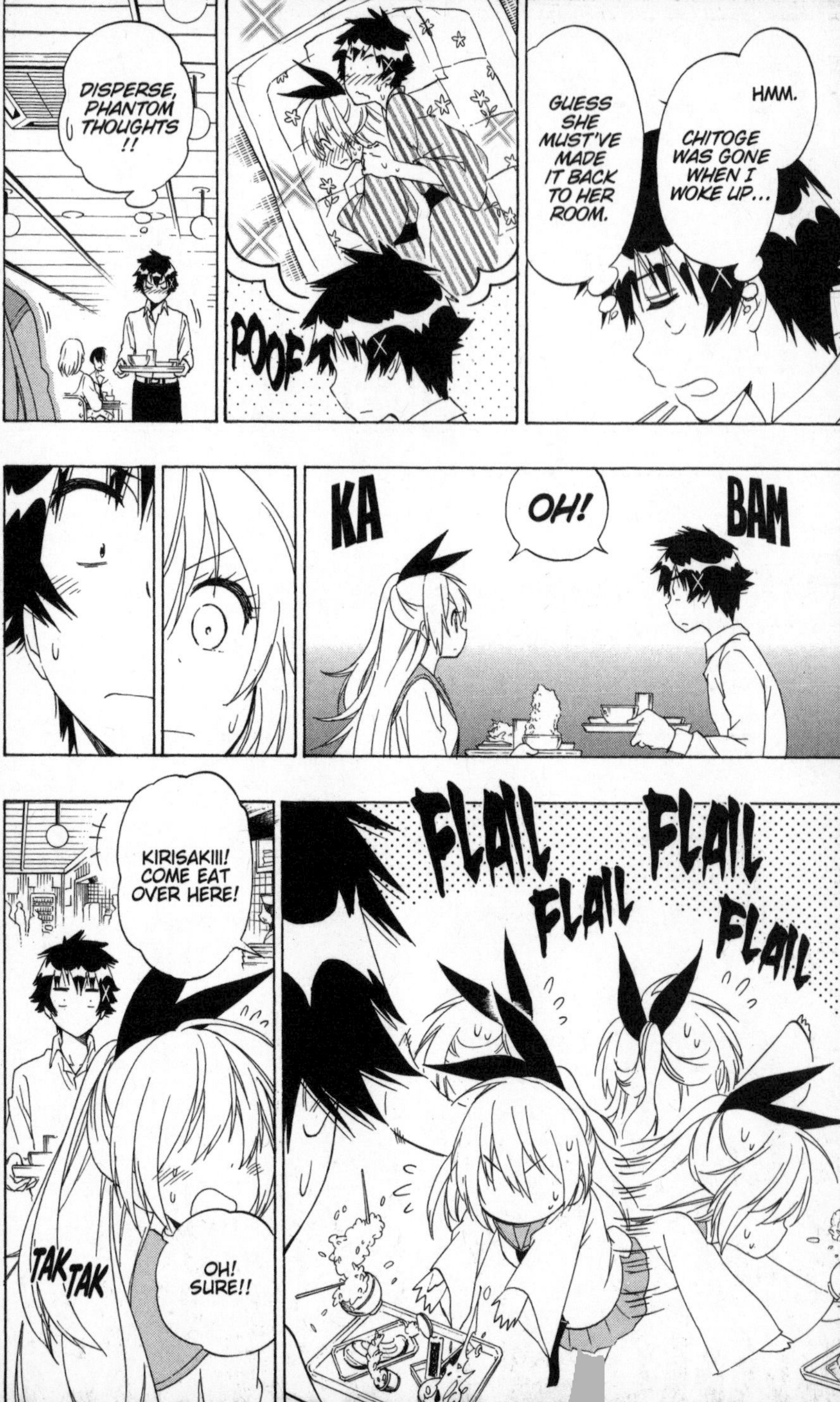
HMM.
CHITOGE WAS GONE WHEN I WOKE UP...
GUESS SHE MUST'VE MADE IT BACK TO HER ROOM.
POOF
DISPERSE, PHANTOM THOUGHTS !!
BAM
OH!
KA
FLAIL
FLAIL
FLAIL
FLAIL
KIRISAKIII! COME EAT OVER HERE!
OH! SURE!!
TAK TAK

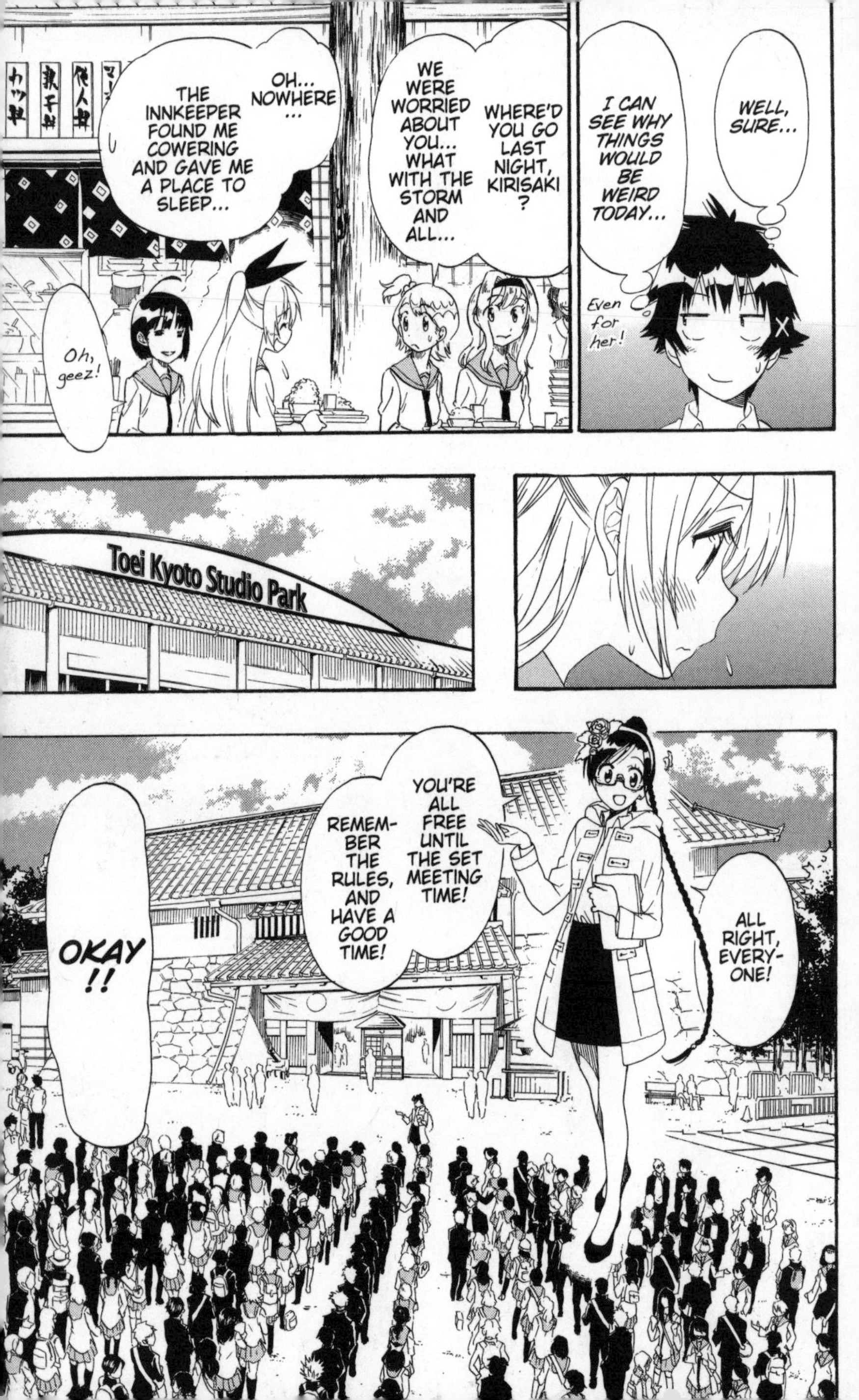
WELL, SURE...
I CAN SEE WHY THINGS WOULD BE WEIRD TODAY...
Even for her!
WHERE'D YOU GO LAST NIGHT, KIRISAKI?
WE WERE WORRIED ABOUT YOU... WHAT WITH THE STORM AND ALL...
OH... NOWHERE...
THE INNKEEPER FOUND ME COWERING AND GAVE ME A PLACE TO SLEEP...
Oh, geez!
Toei Kyoto Studio Park
ALL RIGHT, EVERY-ONE!
YOU'RE ALL FREE UNTIL THE SET MEETING TIME!
REMEM-BER THE RULES, AND HAVE A GOOD TIME!
OKAY!!

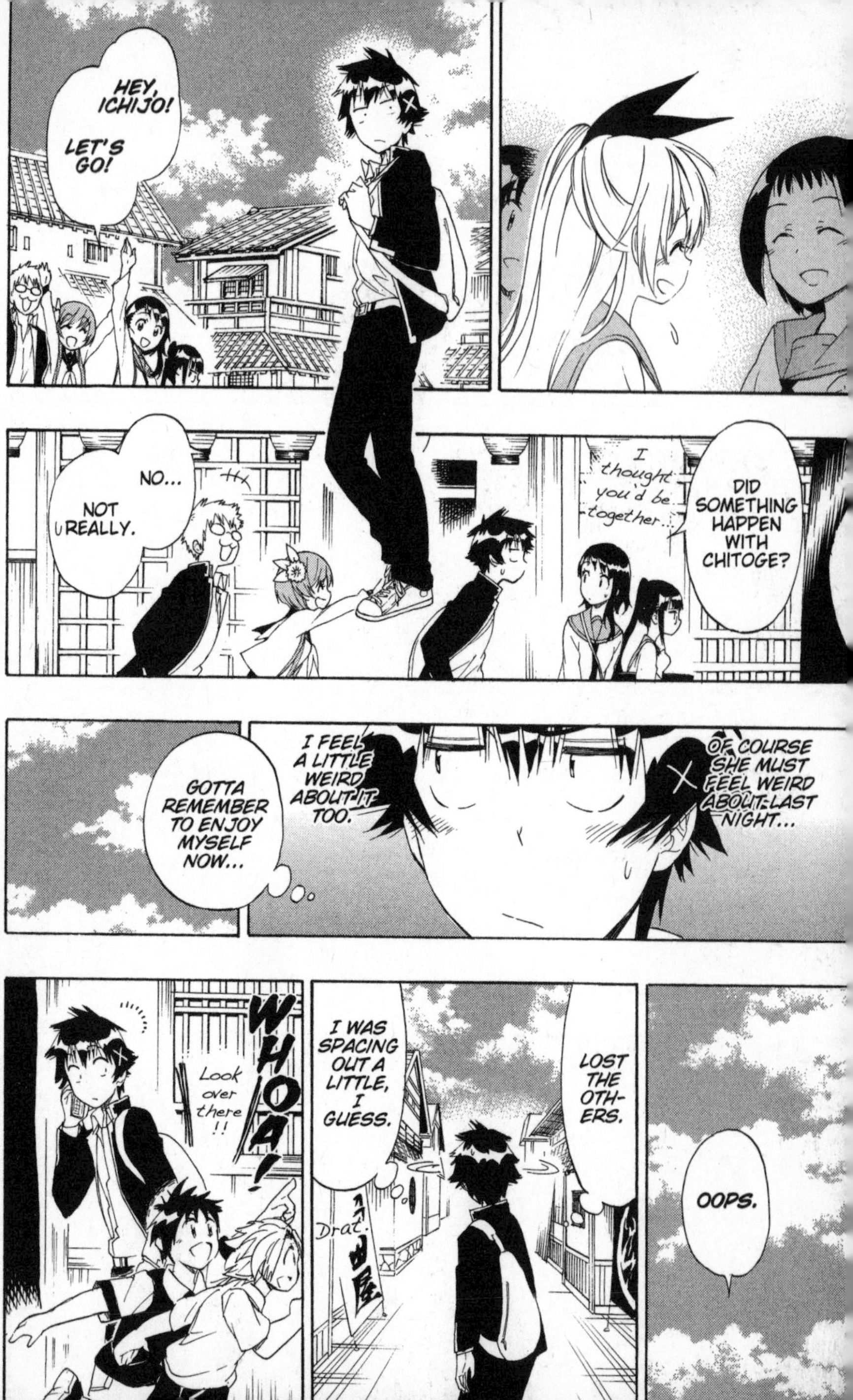
HEY, ICHIJO!
LET'S GO!
DID SOMETHING HAPPEN WITH CHITOGE?
I thought you'd be together...
NO...
NOT REALLY.
OF COURSE SHE MUST FEEL WEIRD ABOUT LAST NIGHT...
I FEEL A LITTLE WEIRD ABOUT IT TOO.
GOTTA REMEMBER TO ENJOY MYSELF NOW...
OOPS.
LOST THE OTH-ERS.
I WAS SPACING OUT A LITTLE, I GUESS.
Drat.
WHOA!
Look over there!!

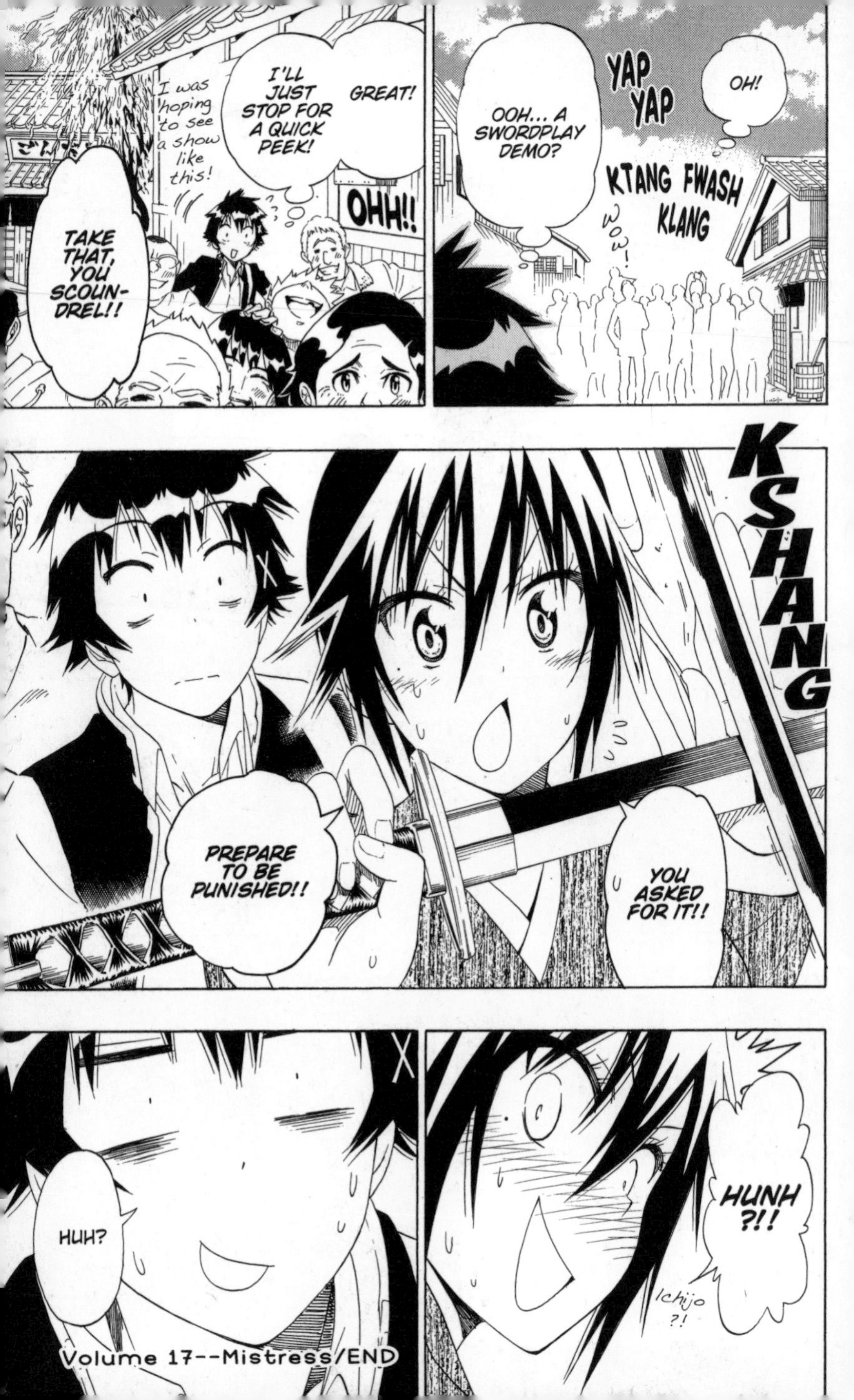
OH!
YAP YAP
OOH... A SWORDPLAY DEMO?
KTANG FWASH KLANG
WOW!
GREAT!
I'LL JUST STOP FOR A QUICK PEEK!
I was hoping to see a show like this!
OHH!!
TAKE THAT, YOU SCOUN-DREL!!
KSHANG
YOU ASKED FOR IT!!
PREPARE TO BE PUNISHED!!
HUNH ?!!
Ichijo ?!
HUH?
Volume 17--Mistress/END

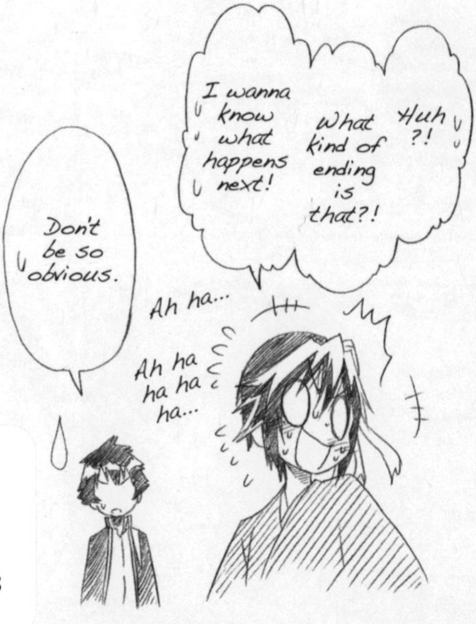
Huh ?!
What kind of ending is that?!
I wanna know what happens next!
Don't be so obvious.
Ah ha...
Ah ha ha ha ha...

☆Bonus☆

Deluxe 4-Panel Theater

You've Got It Wrong, Chitoge!

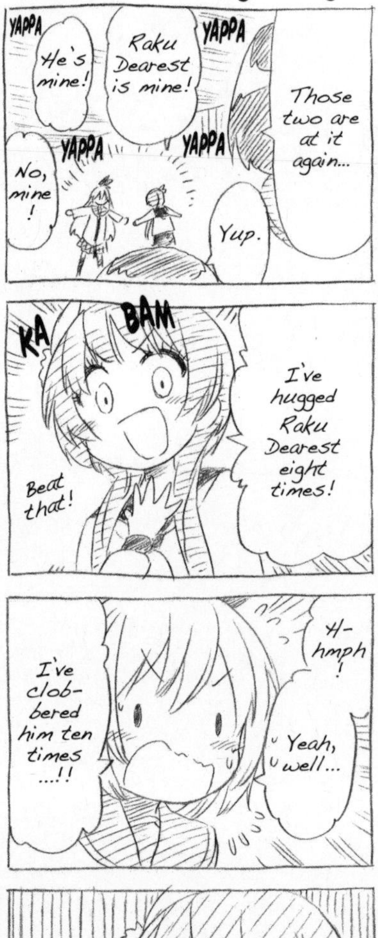
Those two are at it again...
Yup.
YAPPA
Raku Dearest is mine!
He's mine!
YAPPA
YAPPA
YAPPA
No, mine!
I've hugged Raku Dearest eight times!
BAM
KA
Beat that!
H-hmph!
Yeah, well...
I've clobbered him ten times ...!!

Fruitless

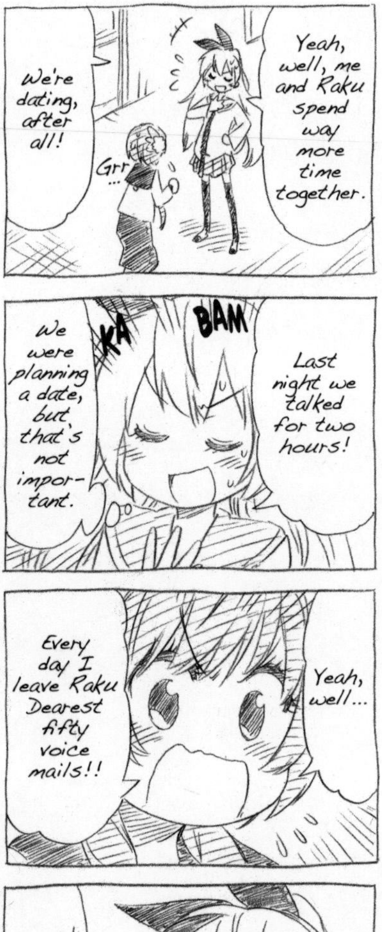
Yeah, well, me and Raku spend way more time together.
We're dating, after all!
Grr...
Last night we talked for two hours!
BAM
KA
We were planning a date, but that's not important.
Yeah, well...
Every day I leave Raku Dearest fifty voice mails!!
Ngghh...
How can I beat that?

The End

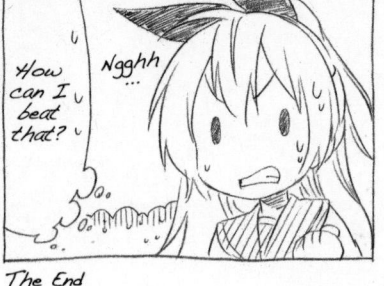

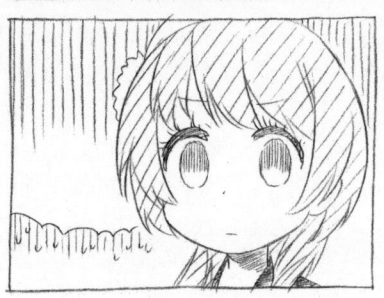

You're Reading the WRONG WAY!

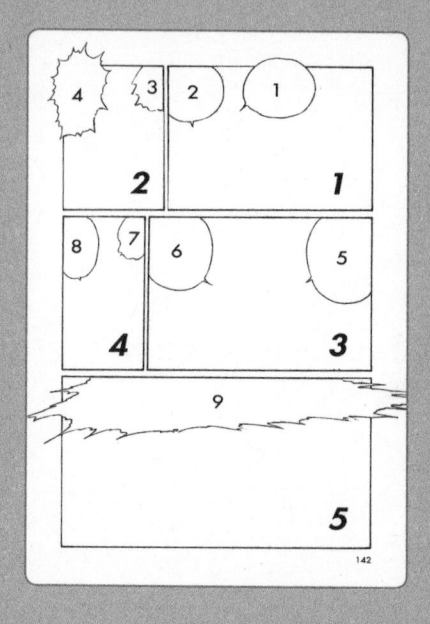

NISEKOI reads from right to left, starting in the upper-right corner. Japanese is read from right to left, meaning that action, sound effects, and word-balloon order are completely reversed from English order.